EXPLORATIONS IN SELF PSYCHOLOGY

Progress in Self Psychology
Volume 19

Progress in Self Psychology
Editor, Mark J. Gehrie, Ph.D.

Contributors: Please submit your original manuscript (double-spaced, including references, footnotes, quoted passages, and dialogue) via email as an attached file in MS Word format (Progress@psychologyoftheself.com). The manuscript style should conform to previous issues of *Progress* and must include all footnotes and complete references. All submissions are refereed and will not be returned. If an electronic version is not available, please mail the original manuscript and four copies to:

William J. Coburn, Ph.D., Psy.D.
12011 San Vicente Blvd., Suite 300,
Los Angeles, CA 90049

EXPLORATIONS IN SELF PSYCHOLOGY

Progress in Self Psychology
Volume 19

Mark J. Gehrie
editor

THE ANALYTIC PRESS

2003 Hillsdale, NJ London

101 West Street
Hillsdale, NJ 07642

www.analyticpress.com

ISBN 0-88163-373-9
ISSN 0893-5483

Printed in the United States of America
10 9 8 7 6 5 4 3 2 1

Contents

Contributors

Lewis Aron, Ph.D. ABPP is Director, New York University, Postdoctoral Program in Psychotherapy and Psychoanalysis; President, International Association of Relational Psychoanalysis and Psychotherapy (IARPP), New York City.

Richard M. Childs, M.D. is Clinical Professor of Psychiatry, University of Missouri at Kansas City; Distinguished Life Fellow, American Psychiatric Association.

Michael A. Cowan, Ph.D. is Professor, Loyola University, New Orleans.

Stan T. Dudley, Ph.D. is the Educational Director, Cincinnati Center for Self Psychology; Member, Cincinnati Association for Psychoanalytic Thought.

Miriam Elson, M.A. is Emerita Lecturer, Masters Degree Program of the School of Social Service Administration, University of Chicago.

Henry J. Friedman, M.D. is Associate Clinical Professor of Psychiatry, Harvard Medical School; Teaching and Supervising Psychoanalyst, Massachusetts Institute for Psychoanalysis (MIP).

Constance Goldberg, M.S. is Faculty, Institute for Clinical Social Work and Center for Religion and Psychotherapy, Chicago.

Lester Lenoff, M.S.W. is Faculty, Training and Research Institute for Self Psychology (TRISP) and Faculty, Group Department of the Postgraduate Center for Mental Health, New York City.

Diane Lawson Martinez, M.D. is Training and Supervising Analyst, Houston-Galveston Psychoanalytic Institute.

Marc L. Miller, Ph.D. is an Executive Committee Member, Faculty and Supervising Analyst, Suffolk Institute for Psychotherapy and Psychoanalysis, Smithtown, New York; Faculty and Supervisor,

Adelphi University, Derner Institute, Post-Doctoral Program in Psychotherapy and Psychoanalysis, Garden City, New York.

Anna Ornstein, M.D. is Professor Emerita, University of Cincinnati; Lecturer in Psychiatry, Harvard University, Cambridge, Massachusetts.

Eva Rass, Ed.D. is Director, Lecturer and Supervisor, Institute of Analytic Child and Adolescent Therapy; Lecturer, University of Pedagogy, both in Heidelberg, Germany.

Jan L. Rieveschl, Ph.D. is in private practice of clinical psychology, New Orleans.

Gordon A. Schulz, Psy.D. is Staff, Child Abuse Unit for Studies, Education and Services, Chicago.

Estelle Shane, Ph.D.is Training and Supervising Analyst, Institute of Contemporary Psychoanalysis and the Los Angeles Psychoanalytic Society and Institute; Clinical Faculty, UCLA Department of Psychiatry.

Batya Shoshani, D.S.W. is Senior Lecturer and Faculty Member, The Paul Baerwald School of Social Work, The Hebrew University of Jerusalem; and Member, Tel Aviv Institute for Contemporary Psychoanalysis.

Michael Shoshani, Psy.D. is Faculty, Postgraduate School of Psychoanalytic Psychotherapy; Senior Lecturer and Supervisor, Bar-Ilan and Tel Aviv Universities; Founding Chair, Tel Aviv Institute for Contemporary Psychoanalysis; and Founding Chair, *Israel Psychoanalytic Journal.*

Mark D. Smaller, Ph.D. is Faculty, Institute for Psychoanalysis; Faculty and Board of Trustees, Institute for Clinical Social Work, Chicago.

Jeffrey Stern, Ph.D. is Faculty, Institute for Psychoanalysis; Lecturer in Psychiatry, Pritzker School of Medicine; Lecturer in Humanities, University of Chicago; Lecturer in Psychiatry, Rush University, Chicago.

Robert D. Stolorow, Ph.D. is Founding Faculty Member and Training and Supervising Analyst, Institute of Contemporary Psychoanalysis, Los Angeles.

Hideki Wada, M.D. is Psychiatric Consultant, Kawasaki Saiwai General Hospital; Faculty of Medical Economics, Hitotsubushi University, Japan.

Todd F. Walker, Psy.D. is Adjunct Professor at the School of Professional Psychology, Wright State University, Cincinnati, Ohio.

Joye Weisel-Barth, Ph.D., Psy.D. is a member if the Institute of Contemporary Psychoanalysis (ICP) and the Los Angeles Psychological Association.

Preface

Mark J. Gehrie

Given the rapid proliferation of theory and techniques in self psychology, various examples of which are represented in this volume, I am inclined to offer a comment based on a long-term view of the implications of some of these ideas. I think it is useful to recall that when Heinz Kohut began his paradigm-shifting work on narcissism, he was operating from within the "one mind" perspective of ego psychology, an unabashedly modernist, objectivist position that viewed the psychological data at issue in psychoanalysis as "inside the head" of the analysand. As the complexities of the "widening scope" began to reveal themselves in the actual clinical psychoanalytic endeavor, however, it became increasingly difficult to maintain that position; even Kohut's emphasis on the "subjectivity" of the patient began to yield increasingly to the impact (and hence role) of the analyst's subjectivity, the implications of self-disclosure by the analyst, and the intersubjective context of analysis. Rapidly, as our selection of patients with more archaically organized developmental derailments began to increase (and our ability to recognize these issues also increased), there evolved a growing emphasis on the idea that manipulating the actuality of the dyadic relation in psychoanalysis could be mutative—in large part, I believe, because of the often overwhelming difficulties that occurred in attempting to access primitive, split-off states and subject them to "analysis" in the usual sense. It became, in other words, much more difficult to properly apply "analytic" principles to instances in which the pathology in question was often characterized by global archaic (and often negative) transferences, which were extremely difficult to interpret without major disruption of narcissistic equilibriium and that were also often embroiled with severe character pathology. The increasing emphasis of those theories that shift the focus of emphasis toward the relationship in the moment, often at the expense of the consideration of the unconscious, provided an apparent solution to this mounting technical problem by offering a shift in the focus of what was at issue: instead of what was "inside the patient's head," we are now singularly invited to address "the relationship between us," as if this shift could somehow do away with the underlying structural issues that the patient brings in; in other words, that which was more accessible in these difficult clinical encounters became defined as the locale for influence at the expense of the underlying configurations.

It is undoubtedly true that this dyadism has brought attention to heretofore underemphasized (if not ignored) aspects of the psychoanalytic interaction which are of great significance, including the proper contextualization of experience, and the impact and appropriate use of the analyst's subjectivity. These perspectives are essential for the analyst to understand and often require technical innovation to make the work productive but, in and of themselves, do not, in my view, require a shift away from the basic understanding of the psyche as structuralized. The use of actions (or enactments) in the analytic process, as vital as they are to helping gain access to states organized around presymbolic and even preverbal experiences, are not cures in and of themselves: the sequellae of these interventions must be subsequently "analyzed" (via interpretation) if we wish to have a lasting impact. The relationship, in other words, must be used and not confused with the treatment.

The psychology of the self revolutionized psychoanalysis by shifting the perspective of the analyst onto the various levels of the patient's self-experience (both conscious and unconscious), from a more externalized view from the "outside." But this did not, and in my opinion does not, demand a shift in our understanding that, when a patient walks into our office, she walks in with something inside her head and that, when she walks out, she will take something with her, something more than some "new relationship" with a person who, in one way or another, has created an environment in the treatment. Something must happen that engages derailed development, and indeed, this may include various types of other-than-verbal action on the part of the analyst, as well as basic empathy, but in the end our patient must be helped to engage herself such that her new relationships will reflect her new, emotionally integrated understandings of herself, rather than repeated efforts to engage archaic longings.

The upshot of all this is my concern that the extraordinary contributions of the psychology of the self may be lost, obscured, or overwhelmed by the push to simplify its application. When we struggle with patients whose pathology is rooted in archaic organizations, there is no less of a requirement to address the underlying structural conditions of the self, despite the formidable nature of the task. To relinquish this imperative is, in my view, tantamount to relinquishing our identity as psychoanalysts.

Introduction

Henry J. Friedman

The annual volume of *Progress in Self Psychology* serves the valuable function of providing an outlet for ongoing contributions to the expansion of self psychology in regard to both theory and clinical practice. It also offers the reader the opportunity to discern the current central issues among those who have been influenced in their practice of psychotherapy and psychoanalysis by Kohut's contributions. Identifying a central theme from this yearly collection of chapters has been a practice of many who have written this introduction. The subjectivity of the author of the introduction sometimes can be discerned, even without any effort on his or her part to explicitly identify it to the reader. Having myself found Kohut's papers essential in a process of liberating myself from the now obvious oppressive constraint of classical theory and technique, I have, in turn, found aspects of self psychology excessively restrictive in regard to how the analyst's participation in the process is conceived. This concern has been shared and expressed by many psychoanalysts from the relational schools, as well as those psychoanalysts like Renik and Hoffman who have attempted to modify classical psychoanalytic technique. The abstinent-anonymous self of the analyst as prescribed by the classical approach could at times seem to have been replaced by a selfless analyst of self psychology who participated in the process of analysis only in the service of repairing the injured narcissism of the patient. From my perspective, the appeal of such a version of the analyst's role has always been problematic. It could only be acceptable to the degree that remaining in this position of unconditional acceptance of the patient's subjectivity as essentially dominant was compatible with both therapeutic action and the safety of the patient's interpersonal relationships, both in his or her world and in the intimacy of the analytic relationship.

The relevance of my concerns regarding the degree of freedom permitted in the analyst's participation in the process is immediately apparent in considering a theme that emerges in several important chapters in this volume. Namely, how authentic and related can the self psychologically informed psychoanalyst be; is self-disclosure of the analyst's subjective difference in perspective regarding the meanings attributed by the patient to his personal experience either permissible, constructive, or essential? Dudley and Walker, in their paper, "'To Be or Not to Be? The Question of Authenticity, Therapist Subjectivity, and the Role of Interpretive Moments in Treatment," open this collection with a strong case against self-disclosure of either the therapist's separate subjectivity or personal experience. They align themselves with Teicholz in the position that empathically based interpretation of the patient's subjective state conveys enough of the therapist's subjectivity for the patient to perceive the therapist's authenticity; more than this is seen as detrimental to the patient's well-being. Like Teicholz, they believe that relational therapists who "believe that providing the patient an explicit expression of the therapist's subjective experience inherently facilitates psychological growth" are mistaken in this assertion. They believe that spontaneous reactivity prevents adequate reflection on the therapist's part. For them, the analyst's responding from within his or her subjectivity will inevitably deprive the patient of a needed empathic response, favoring the analyst's subjectivity over the patient. Clearly, those analysts who believe that it is essential for patients to achieve a new experience with the therapist as a functional individual and find self-disclosure an essential growth-promoting part of the therapeutic experience believe that patients need more than consistent empathic attunement and interpretation of their affective states. Ultimately, the reader will find some method of deciding where he or she stands in regard to the inclusion of the analyst's authentic responsiveness to his or her patients. To simply conclude that the analyst's ability to remain authentic within him- or herself while cleaving only to empathic interpretations misses the point made by those who see interaction between intersubjectivities as essential to the therapeutic action of psychoanalysis. The authors' concern about the increasing trend toward therapist self-expression is expressed in a list of cautionary notes about self-disclosure and the superiority of interpretations of the patient's "deeper pain and core psychopathology."

A near perfect contrast to Dudley and Walker's chapter can be found in Marc L. Miller's engagingly titled chapter, "Empathy and Self-

Expression: Confessions of a Sometimes Angry Self Psychologist," in which he questions the seemingly endless attempt by some self psychologists to "decenter" from "his or her frustration or anger to maintain a sustained empathic stance with the patient." Miller is clearly in favor of authentic self-expression by that therapist, particularly in response to persistent, angry, unwarranted attacks and demands by patients. It should be noted that he introduces the idea that some patients' attacks on the therapist are, indeed, unwarranted, a position often rejected by those with what I would call a narrow interpretation of self psychology. He questions whether patients judged as too vulnerable to bear the experience of the analyst's "dysjunctive subjectivity" actually are as fragile as they are seen to be; after all, as he illustrates with a clinical vignette from Teicholz's book, the disruption could also be seen as necessary for the treatment to begin. In his opinion, waiting even longer than 15 months wouldn't insure that the disruption wouldn't occur at some later date.

Miller is sympathetic to the concerns of many relational psychoanalysts that the exclusively empathic stance of strict self psychologists may deprive patients of the opportunity for growth inherent in encountering the very different authentic subjectivity of the analyst, a subjectivity that may be a necessary building block in achieving a reconstituted self even in individual patients who may be judged as too fragile to tolerate such an experience. Paraphrasing Aron, he raises the question of the patient's capacity to empathize with the analyst as an indication of having achieved true interpersonal relatedness. His discussion of spontaneously occurring emotional reactions from even the most self-psychologically dedicated analyst in response to difficult patients should be important to any clinician who has engaged in such treatments. Furthermore, he is willing to describe a case in which the breakthrough of his angry affect led to the patient's abruptly leaving therapy. This is, fortunately, countered with an example in another patient where remaining firm and real in the face of the patient's unfulfillable demands led to an improvement in the treatment relationship. Miller expresses awareness that his dedication to the empathic stance may have delayed his utilization of his own feeling state in responding strongly enough to the patient.

Questioning the utility of a constant insistence on the analyst's part of remaining in an empathic stance continues in the discussion. Joye Weisel-Barth's presentation of her patient's analysis stimulated Aron to risk an unpopular position by his indicating that he experienced the patient and the therapy as containing a great deal of sadomasochism; in particular, he questioned Weisel-Barth's persistent maternal (masochistic) acceptance of the patient's destructiveness (sadism) when directed at her. His discussion is aptly entitled, "A Ruthless Examination of an Empathic Clinical Presentation." Aron's position represents a rare recognition, at least as represented in the self psychology literature, of the degree to which patients who have been exposed to destructive parental figures may be less damaged and more damaging than is usually maintained by those drawn to a self psychological worldview; identification with the aggressor may be a primary operation that protects the patient from more devasting psychological injury but also leads to destructive interpersonal responses as an organizing principle that operates throughout the lifecycle of the individual.

Stolorow's equally incisive and critical discussion specifically delineates the transference interpretations that he would have made were he Weisel-Barth. On the other hand, he acknowledges that, despite her omission of such interpretations, the analysis did work well enough for the patient to improve in her functioning. He reminds us that there is no understanding or interpretation of the other that isn't influenced by the therapist's subjectivity and experience. The fact that the panel's content extends the thrust of the argument of both Walker and Dudley's and Miller's chapters is fortuitous because it enables readers to reflect upon the clinical reality of their theoretical positions.

By choosing to highlight the theme of the analyst's need to transcend the constraints of the insistently exclusive empathic stance, to, in essence, shift from a patient-centered perspective to one that is analyst-centered, I mean to raise questions in regard to both the timing and the inclusion of the analyst's empathic perception of primary destructiveness in the patient. Empathy, when correctly applied, remains an invaluable cornerstone of any therapeutic endeavor; we are left with the necessity of judging those instances where the correct application appears to be other than accepting the patient's view of what is unfolding in front of us as correct or reasonable. Of course, in selecting this conflictual theme in self psychology and attempting to trace it through a number of chapters in this volume, I am following my own subjectivity, unregrettably irreducible according to Renik. I believe, however, that, in this case, my subjectivity and interests have naturally aligned themselves with the essential and currently active core issues that these authors address. The emergence of this theme in many of the chapters in this volume certainly reflects current controversies and debates in the world of self psychology. I hope that this emphasis can draw the reader into the very real clinical and theoretical issues that are relevant to those of us who, while working with the advantages that Kohut and self psychology have brought us, continue to feel that any psychoanalytic theory must be open to revision based on the growing clinical experience of analysts dedicated to its application. Certainly, the attempt to include the real persona of the analyst even beyond the recognition of "irreducible subjectivity" is a worthwhile endeavor. While we need to be certain that such an inclusion won't traumatize our patients or, for that matter, truncate a true psychoanalytic exploration of their subjectivity, it is equally important that the exclusively empathic stance not deprive patients of an opportunity to discover the importance of mutual empathic relatedness through the medium of the psychoanalytic relationship.

Included in this volume are many other chapters that, while not lending themselves to the central theme I have chosen to emphasize, are important in their own right and advance the utilization of self psychology in any number of spheres. Diane Martinez and Jeffrey Stern address the treatment of patients with sexual orientation issues; both in their own way demonstrate the utilization of empathic understanding in helping their patients achieve a new and more robust self-state. Martinez deftly demonstrates the importance of developing a twinship transference–countertransference in order for a relationship of sufficient strength to develop and influence the emergence of a more feeling and functional patient. Stern reminds us that an approach free of preconceived notions and theories may actually result in a true resolution of sexual ambivalence. Anna Ornstein reexamines assertions about concentration camp survivors, dispelling the image of the survivor as permanently scarred and incapable of healthy functioning. She reminds us that the precamp self-experience is crucial in determining the different types of adjustment made by survivors of atrocities like the Holocaust. Her conclusion, once stated, that one size doesn't and cannot fit all seems axiomatic, but as she demonstrates was far from the case in the classical pre–self psychology literature. The section on applied psychoanalysis includes some five chapters ranging widely in subject matter but all stimulating thought well beyond the confines of the specificity of their subjects. Finally, the volume ends with a personal picture of Heinz Kohut by Constance Goldberg in which he emerges as an individual beyond the picture of him that emerges from reading his papers. While there are glimpses here of the private man, they serve to increase our appreciation of how dedicated he was to formulating a new theory that was capable of increasing our therapeutic impact on a broad range of patients.

As the reader of this volume attempts to grapple with the emerging and competing theoretical positions within self psychology, it is helpful to remember that, compelling as theory can be, it is the individual patient who determines the utility of any theory. Patients may respond differently to truly interactive experience with their analyst. It is important to remember that the application of any theory always involves the possible prevention of a true relationship based upon the authentic participation of the analyst, a participation that may suffer when the humanity of the analyst, including understandable negative affects, is subsumed by his or her dedication to theory over personal subjectivity. The increasing dialogue among self psychology, relational and intersubjective schools of thought, which is so well reflected in this current volume of *Progress,* serves to remind us that self psychology is a revolutionary theory that grew out of Kohut's clinical experience. As such, it remains, more than other theories that are not so experience-near based, open to revision and addition in a fashion that is both lively and welcome.

I

Theory

Chapter 1

"To Be or Not to Be?": The Question of Authenticity, Therapist Subjectivity, and the Role of Interpretive Moments in Treatment

Stan T. Dudley
Todd F. Walker

Psychoanalysis has evolved well beyond the concept of the selfless analyst, who on theoretical grounds had to remain neutral, authoritarian, and withholding. This neutrality required the therapist to attempt to be emotionally uninvolved, thereby offering the patient a blank screen on which to project his or her inner world. In practice, this often led to the emotional unavailability of the analyst.

In sharp contrast, the current literature is replete with emphasis on the paramount importance of the analyst's human presence and participation in the interpretative process and nonverbal therapeutic engagement. The term authentic has been used to describe the overt expression of the therapist's distinct subjective experience. This type of sharing has been contrasted with working in the interpretive mode, where a primary emphasis is placed on achieving an in-depth, empathic

The authors are grateful to Paul Ornstein, M.D., Ben Blom, Ph.D., and Sr. Joan Williams, O.C.D. for their careful reading and critique of this chapter and to Gianni Nebbiosi, Ph.D. for his helpful suggestions. We thank Jeannie Busemeyer for providing invaluable assistance in editing.

understanding and explaining of the patient's experience; however, there is a glaring lack of consensus regarding authenticity and its role in the treatment process.

The current metapsychological emphasis on promoting the open expression of the therapist's feelings and viewpoints suggests that such self-expressions have primary curative power in their own right, which is independent of empathic understanding and interpretation. Teicholz (1999) differentiates empathy, subjectivity, and authenticity yet notes that affect is the common thread linking these essential factors in the therapeutic process. While Teicholz clarifies the need for integration of these therapeutic components, there has been relatively little detailed exploration and discussion of how this actually occurs in treatment.

In this chapter we first review models that focus on the concept of authenticity. We explore the potential dangers of the fundamental assumption that "genuine" therapist self-expression inherently provides missing selfobject experiences and transformative moments in the absence of empathic understanding and interpretation of the patient's subjectivity. We question the therapeutic significance of the current emphasis on therapist sharing of subjective experience as the primary means of providing the patient with experiences of closeness and support. Aren't empathic interpretations of both the understanding and explaining kind that are tailored according to the patient's chronic and current experiences rooted in and saturated with therapist subjectivity? What exclusive mutative power does spontaneous therapist self-expression—often offered without analytic self-reflection—have over empathic interpretations that contain the therapist's perceptual and subjective experiences? What dangers are present and need to be better understood before encouraging such a "technique" in the training of future psychotherapists?

Second, we present a frame through which to look at the transformation of the therapist's subjectivity into empathic interpretations that facilitate ever-deepening moments of understanding and connection with the patient. Finally, a case presentation illustrates how therapist understanding of self and patient facilitates an interpretive mode that promotes an empathic and experience-near therapeutic encounter.

REVIEW OF SELECT CONTEMPORARY MODELS OF THERAPIST AUTHENTICITY AND EXPRESSIVE RELATING

An increasing number of analysts and psychotherapists are writing about the explicit sharing of the therapist's subjectivity as the primary or exclusive way in which a patient can experience them as authentic (Ehrenberg, 1996; Preston, 1998; Renik, 1998; Stern et al., 1998; Davies, 1999). These and many other clinicians seem to be equating the patient's experience of genuine interest and caring as synonymous with the therapist sharing his feelings and perceptions. There is a corresponding emphasis in the literature on "moving the patient to a better place" (Shane and Weisel-Barth, 2000) and providing "shared tender moments" (Bacal, Lenoff, and Munschauer, 1999). These authors provide case presentations to show that patients often need explicit reassurance that they are acceptable and that the therapist can tolerate their feelings of horribleness. There is a strong implication that, when a therapist primarily works in the interpretive mode of understanding and explanation, the patient does not experience the therapist as fully present and engaged. Teicholz (1999) notes how many relational theorists believe that providing the patient an explicit expression of the therapist's subjective experience inherently facilitates psychological growth. She underscores that these authors do not fully appreciate that the therapist can recognize and effectively utilize their subjective experience and not necessarily explicitly express this to the patient.

At the heart of this issue is the question of how a caring and emotional presence can be expressed and whether it has to be stated to be felt by the patient. We believe that, when the patient's self-experience is grasped by the therapist and the patient feels deeply understood, explicit self-expression by the therapist may not be necessary for the patient to experience the therapist's genuine presence (P. Ornstein, 2000, personal communication). There also appears to be a relative lack of exploration and emphasis on how interpretive moments are often experienced as very affect-laden, personal, and experience-near by patient and therapist, which was identified by Tolpin (1988) as "optimal affective engagement." Providing the patient with direct expression of the therapist's experiences in a noninterpretive and supportive mode seems to run the risk of missing core aspects of the repetitive dimension or trailing edge of the transference. Stolorow (1999) explains that, when the therapist attempts to provide closeness and support in an effort to avoid painful repetition of past childhood trauma, the primary goal of working through of the patient's inner experience may be neglected. Thus, clinical models and techniques primarily oriented toward rescue and relief from enduring pain seem to lack the requisite empathic focus on the more shameful and agonizing self-states, which if left unresolved, will remain pathogenic.

Within self psychology, the model of optimal responsiveness proposed by Bacal and numerous contributors (1985, 1997; Bacal et al., 1999) promotes the explicit sharing of the therapist's experience as a distinct selfobject experience. Herzog (1998) notes that, when the therapist communicates that he or she shares the patient's experience and its associated affect state, it may provide an optimal response in psychoanalytic treatment. He emphasizes, "I believe that the need to engage in the sharing of affect with a significant other is one of the specific components involved in the establishment of an empathic connection in therapy" (p. 176). "The empathically attuned therapist may now consider that, in order to be optimally responsive to the patient, he might indicate in one way or another that he cannot only understand the patient's experience, but that he is actually sharing in that experience" (p. 189).

Similarly, L. Jacobs (1998) states, "But at crucial points in therapy, for instance, in efforts to address serious disruptions in the therapy relationship, or at certain developmental thresholds, the patient may be intensely interested in, and require, access to the therapist's experiencing" (p. 199). "There often comes a time when the empathic inquiry into the patient's experience leads to an apprehension that the patient seeks to meet the analyst's otherness" (p. 202). Preston (1998) describes "expressive relating" as "the authentic expression of feelings and perceptions on the part of the analyst, arising out of the immediacy of the interaction and conveyed in a conscious and responsive way" (p. 204). She adds, "Mutuality requires that the analyst cultivate an attitude of openness and personal sharing" (p. 211).

Many relational analysts propose that therapist self-disclosure validates the patient's emotional responses and promotes the feeling and recognition of hidden affects. Maroda (2002) refers to therapist self-disclosure of affect as the essential therapeutic action. She states "There are many times when neither interpretation nor empathy succeed in the difficult task of communicating with a patient who is in the throes of deep, primitive feelings. They (patients) want, and need, an emotional response and will typically keep stimulating the analyst until they get one" (p. 114). Safran (2002) notes that the therapist's ability to understand and disembed from unconscious enactments often involves countertransference disclosure. He states, "For example, by acknowledging to the patient one's feelings of being stuck or hopeless, one can reopen for oneself an analytic space that had previously been collapsed" (p. 183).

We believe that patients and therapists can experience intense emotional resonance during deeply moving interpretive moments that contain and convey a sense of the therapist's subjective experience. We do not dismiss the possible therapeutic benefit of the therapist responding to questions about how he or she experiences the patient or a particular event in or out of the treatment setting.

Spontaneous, improvisational and emotionally expressive responses by the therapist have an important role in promoting and deepening the treatment process (Stern et al., 1998; Ringstrom, 2001). Shared feelings, perceptions, or activities by the therapist are not a substitute for the interpretive process; they are different ways of responding and relating. As Siegel (1999) notes, there is a danger of diminishing, if not losing, the central role of the interpretive process because there is an increasing emphasis on providing missing psychological experiences (p. 77). This loss becomes particularly problematic in that the subtleties associated with explicit self-disclosure remain very unclear and may represent a number of attitudes toward the patient, some of which may not be therapeutically beneficial (Busch, 1998). It is important to clarify how intensely experienced emotions in the therapist can be conveyed through empathic interpretations and silent moments of emotional resonance. Such elucidation further assists us in identifying the connection-promoting and transformative aspects of working in the interpretive mode.

The Ornsteins (1996, 1998) have emphasized that "speaking in the interpretive mode" is the articulation of the therapist's perceptions of the patient's subjective experiences. They provide clinical illustrations of how articulating empathic understanding of the client's experience conveys the therapist's genuine involvement through his persistent effort at making contact with the patient's subjective world. Experiencing the therapist as making an effort to more deeply understand the patient also facilitates the use of the therapist as a needed selfobject. It is imperative to note that such empathic contact is usually experienced by patients and therapists as very connecting and genuine because it is based on a mutually constructed sense of meaning. As Kohut (1984) stated, the analyst's "on the whole adequately maintained understanding leads to the patient's increasing realization that, contrary to his experiences in childhood, the sustaining echo of empathic resonance is indeed available in this world" (p. 78). His reference to empathic responsiveness includes aspects of warmth and emotional presence that result from the therapist's deep involvement and concern. It is important to note that emotional responsiveness is not a technique, as has been suggested in the term *countertransference technique*. A sense of affective realness involves an empathic resonance with the patient's feelings and needs, which is dependent upon the therapist's capacity to recognize and connect with his or her own subjective experience as well as the patient's. The notion that this experience must be articulated by the therapist to be deeply felt by the patient is simplistic and does utilize more recent intersubjective and developmental theory. These models suggest that "understanding of the other and being understood by the other is an indivisible process that is mutually regulated on a moment-to-moment basis" (Sucharov, 2000, p. 275).

Stolorow (1994) defines interpretation as "an act of illuminating personal meaning" (p. 43). He underscores the importance of showing the analyst's attunement to the patient's affective states and developmental longings through interpretations that provide the patient with a new experience of being deeply understood. We are in agreement with Cooper (1998), who writes that analytic authenticity is the precondition of interpretation. He states, "To some extent the analyst's personal participation and subjectivity are involved in every interpretive effort. The subjectivity of the analyst is embedded in other functions besides self-disclosure" (p. 383). As such, a feeling of genuine connection is not necessarily more experientially present in self-disclosure than it is in interpretive moments. Mitchell (1998) echoes this sentiment in stating, "Authenticity in the analyst has less to do with saying everything than in the genuineness of what is said" (p. 86). Gill (1982) cautioned that "the analyst must recognize that his subjective experience may be as defensive on his own part as he believes the patient's conscious attitudes are. Therefore he cannot assume that if he reports his own experience that is the end of the story" (p. 228). Aron (1996) has cautioned that "for analysts simply and directly to say what they are experiencing may encourage the assumption that they are fully aware of their motivations and meanings" (p. 84). These cautions appear to be sorely needed at a time when many clinicians are promoting the therapist's explicit articulation of their own feelings, perceptions, and needs as an optimal response. These models suggest that this type of therapeutic interaction provide the patient with an experience of authentic and truthful "contact." We believe that this current emphasis fails to acknowledge that empathic interpretations are made up of the analyst's cognitive and emotional understanding, including the expressive use of the therapist's subjectivity, and that an interpretive process facilitates the patient's increased depth of insight and emotional connection with the psychotherapist.

THE TRANSFORMATIVE FUNCTIONS OF THE INTERPRETIVE PROCESS

Recent writings on the selfobject function of interpretation further highlight how patients are able to use interpretations to increase self-understanding "and promote self-cohesion and the integration of affect into experience" (Buirski and Haglund, 1999, p. 35). Self psychology continues to explicate the therapeutic effects of interpretation in the areas of increased cognitive understanding, an experience of feeling deeply understood, and the selfobject experience of understanding, continuity, and cohesion. Siegel (1999) refers to the interpretive process as structure building by "the effect the explanation has in linking the analysand with his or her own history" (p. 75). Stolorow (1994) identified the therapeutic benefit of new selfobject experiences supplied by the analyst's communication of empathic understanding through interpretations. These authors underscore the importance of interpreting disruptions in the therapeutic process from the patient's perspective and therapist self-reflection regarding his or her contribution to the impasse. It is essential to listen to the patient's unique experience of the therapist's nonverbal and interpretive actions as disruptive before providing a personal explanation, which may interfere with a deeper understanding of these crucial moments. Self-disclosure at these times may limit the patient's opportunity to elaborate on his experience, which A. Ornstein (1998) has described as "missed now moments of disruption" that may prevent repair (p. 2). As the patient feels that distressing and painful emotions received from and directed toward the therapist are understood and contained through interpretive responses, hoped for selfobject experiences occur and "the selfobject dimension of the transference is strengthened and expanded" (p. 5). Similarly, Wolf (1993) stated, "Now we can dynamically explain how the experience evoked by interpretations and explanations strengthens the very fabric of the self via the strengthening of the selfobject tie" (p. 30). He emphasized the role of interpretation in the cycle of disruption and repair of the self–selfobject bond, which provides the patient with an experience that is very different from their expectations of a repetition of selfobject failure (A. Ornstein, 1974). Schwaber (1990) states "Treatment helps by sustaining that hope, however tentative and defended it may have been, that had led the patient to seek help in the first place; for it is ultimately a hope for recognition—of one's feelings, wishes, defenses, perceptions—linked from past to present, articulated by another and by oneself. This is the interpretive art" (p. 238). Similarly, Sander (2002) notes "How the experience of specificity of being known or recognized is conveyed obviously is at the heart of what the effective interpretation accomplishes—bringing the patient and therapist into new 'moments of meeting'—the inclusiveness of new, expanded states of conscious connection" (p. 39).

Empathic interpretation and authentic self-expression by the therapist are distinct, yet inseparable, elements in a successful therapeutic process. Orange (2001) states "There is no need for a choice between empathy and authenticity. Empathy (a mode of understanding by participation) and attunement (mutual regulation), as construed here, require no abandonment of my ongoing organizing of experience, no loss of personal authenticity or genuineness" (p. 21). However, overemphasizing therapist self-revelation is often at the expense of losing sight of the mutative powers of depth psychological interpretation. Siegel (1999) has clarified that, when therapists attempt to provide missing psychological experiences, the primary aim of self-disclosure is then the creation of an experience of closeness or intimacy for the patient. When this occurs, there is an inherent danger of underemphasizing the transformative potential of interpretive moments. Gehrie (1996) identifies the potential boundary violations that may occur when we "attempt via relational intimacy to overcome (usually unrecognized) failures in understanding in the attempt to heal a breach that is painfully experienced by both analyst and analysand" (p. 88). As such, he believes that the therapist may attempt to emphasize intimacy over understanding in order to avoid painful disruptions in the treatment. Such disruptions may occur when the therapist has been unable to maintain an empathic connection with the patient's subjective experiences, possibly because of the therapist's attempt to rescue both from such intolerable and often unrecognized pain. While the therapist's sharing of feelings and perceptions is not necessarily indicative of disruptions in the treatment, the therapist must remain alert to the potential pathogenesis of pressure to provide new and positive experiences that might obfuscate the needed psychoanalytic process of exploration–understanding–explanation. Additionally, Davis (2002) highlights how therapists in training are more often tempted to use or withhold self-disclosure to avoid or avert feelings of love, hate, anger, dependence, idealization, and sexual excitement that appear in the treatment. Writing from a relational perspective, Maroda (2002) highlights the need to address the issue of self-disclosure more comprehensively and provide guidelines, especially for inexperienced therapists.

THE TRANSFORMATION OF THERAPIST SELF-EXPERIENCE INTO INTERPRETIVE MOMENTS IN THE THERAPEUTIC PROCESS

A model we support for therapist transformation of self-reflection into interpretive moments is embedded in the following theoretical–clinical beliefs:

(1) Uncensored therapist self-expression that does not resonate with the patient may interfere with an analytic process that requires deeper exploration, understanding, and explaining.

(2) The promotion of such raw and unanalyzed therapist self-expression may be related to the trend in psychoanalysis toward facilitating increased therapist emotional participation with the patient. However, self psychology and models of intersubjectivity have already proposed the mutative powers of interpretation that is experienced by the patient as open-minded, creative, genuinely human, and filled with vitality and empathy.

(3) Explicit self-expression may have other conscious or unconscious functions for the therapist and patient, including protection against intolerable psychological pain and "killer organizing principles" (Stolorow, 1999, p. 232). These defensive maneuvers by the therapist must be identified and understood so that the therapeutic action can be redirected toward the patient's deeper pain and core psychopathology.

(4) Empathic interpretations are made up of the therapist's understanding on both cognitive and affective levels. Thus, the therapist's interpretive comments contain the therapist's personal, emotional reaction to the patient.

(5) Therapist empathic self-reflection and understanding facilitates the utilization of therapist-with-patient subjectivity in the formulation of empathic interpretations. We believe that interpretations designed in accordance with the patient's self-experiences are often the most crucial transformative moments in the therapeutic process.

(6) Postsession retrospective analysis of the therapeutic process include therapist self-reflection, review of relevant research and literature, and consultation when possible.

The following steps summarize the process of how therapist subjectivity can be transformed into interpretations that promote deeper therapist–patient connection and therapeutic dialogue. This deepening of the therapeutic process allows for the emergence of new selfobject experiences with resulting transformation in self-organization:

(1) There is an emergence of new and unidentified self-with-patient experience in the therapist.

(2) Therapist self-reflection into the phenomenology and meaning of this unique personal experience triggered during encounters with the patient begins.

(3) The therapist reflects on what aspects of this self-experience should be kept private in that they are more relevant to his or

her vulnerabilities and idiosyncrasies rather than empathically resonant with the patient's self-experiences.

(4) Now with increased self-awareness, the therapist postulates what his or her self-experiences may illuminate about the inner world of the patient with consideration of repetitive and newly activated transference phenomenon.

(5) The therapist formulates an interpretation that is empathically tailored to grasp the patient's current constellation of self-experiences at this unique moment in the therapeutic process. The therapeutic value of an interpretation depends upon the patient's experience of it as experience-near, emotionally rich, and self-integrating.

(6) Post-session retrospective reflection upon moments of disruptions and repair in the treatment process educates the therapist about how to interact and interpret more therapeutically with the patient in future sessions.

THE CASE OF DR. DILLON

The following case illustrates a short-term psychotherapy in which Dr. Walker experienced a strong personal reaction to the story of the patient's significant pain and loss surrounding diabetes. However, rather than spontaneous, explicit self-disclosure, the therapist attempted to use his reactions to better connect with the patient's experience of her progressively increasing disabilities.

Dr. Dillon was referred for psychotherapy after she requested a psychotherapist who could understand what it was like to live with diabetes. She had met with three other mental health professionals, all of whom she felt could not grasp her painful story of living with the disease. She was referred to me after hearing from a fellow physician that I also had diabetes. The only information known before the interview was that Dr. Dillon had recently suffered some debilitating complications and that she was experiencing a severe depression.

I greeted Dr. Dillon, and she walked up the staircase to the second floor office with a significant limp and her hands alternatively gripping the banister to steady herself. She first thanked me for seeing her so quickly after her initial telephone call two days earlier. She then proceeded with, "Diabetes has ruined my life, and I'm not sure if I can pull out of the tailspin that I'm in. I'm not even sure that I want to—I feel like I've lost my world. I'm ashamed to say this to you, but I feel as if you are my last hope in life. I can't find a reason to go on."

She stated, "It helps a lot to know that you have diabetes too" and began to tell her narrative about her life with diabetes. She was diagnosed with the disease when she was 12 years old, which was the same age that I was diagnosed.

Her pediatric endocrinologist had told her that she was "his best diabetic patient," and he assured her that she could avoid secondary complications if she maintained her normal blood sugar levels. It evoked a memory in me of my endocrinologists affirming that I could live a rich and full life without complications if I learned to effectively manage my blood sugars. Dr. Dillon described how she diligently managed her diabetes by "exercising at least six days per week, never, ever eating something that I wasn't supposed to, and testing my blood sugars at least four times per day with insulin injections whenever my blood sugars got into the potentially dangerous zone of 240 mg or above. I always felt like I could control the disease rather than letting it get the best of me. I lived with the belief that my destiny was in my hands and that I could prevent any of the horrible complications that ruin the lives of so many diabetics." I could relate! I felt a strong resonance with her passion to keep diabetes at the level of a manageable medical difficulty that wouldn't interfere with her life pursuits; however, I felt myself becoming increasingly curious about what had happened in her life to send her into such a downward trajectory. I felt my shoulders and neck tighten as my anxious curiosity about her debilitating complications intensified.

"How long have you had diabetes?" she asked. This question caught me off guard as it broke my train of speculations regarding the causes, timing, and nature of her complications. While I still felt like I was primarily focused on her subjectivity and the content of her story, I became aware that it was becoming harder for me not to think about my own diabetes. Her question caught me in the midst of a fantasy that the causes of her secondary complications were not something to which I felt vulnerable, that is, that we were inherently different. After realizing my avoidance of this diabetic intersubjectivity, I could better understand how much she needed me to share with her. I felt comfortable in replying, "Like you, I have lived with diabetes since I was 12 years old." I felt as if revealing this fact to this woman might facilitate a therapeutic engagement and that withholding this fact would likely be experienced as a nonempathic, impersonal "bedside manner" that would increase her aloneness and despair.

She smiled and said, "That's neat; I've never met anyone else who got it at the same time in their life. I'm glad. Well, I'm sorry you got it too, but I'm glad for me that you did. Maybe somebody can understand and maybe even help." She went on to discuss the medical school era of her life and discussed her vivid memory of having a hypoglycemic seizure while studying late at night with three of her classmates. "It was the first time I really ran out of sugar this bad. My parents, usually my dad, used to give me juice when I would get a little spacey or sweaty, but this was something different. To this day, I can still see me trying to explain to Peter [classmate] how to remember all the bones in the hand and not being able to pronounce things correctly. Then I remember my head starting to convulse and gyrate, and I banged my head on the library table. Then, everything gets a little hazy, but I remember that my body was totally out of my control and I felt like I was going to fly apart or knock myself out. Then I woke up with my friends and some of the third-year students looking down at me in the emergency room. You probably know about that miserable feeling!"

"Yep, I sure do. It's something you really have to go through to really know the feeling. Like your body is going to fly apart into pieces and you can't stop it!" I knew this feeling all too well because I had been taken to the emergency room only two weeks earlier for hypoglycemic seizures with the accompanying total loss of control over my fragmenting bodily experiences like she was describing.

She took off her sunglasses to wipe a tear that was running down her cheek. "I almost didn't come today 'cause I really don't see how anybody can bring back any kinda life for me. I almost hate to admit it, but I can feel that you understand and it feels good. I'm just scared to hope again and then get burned." She held her head in her hands as her tears turned into quiet sobbing. "I do understand how diabetes can wear you out, beat you down, and make you hopeless. Sometimes it's hard to imagine that anybody else can know what it feels like. It feels good, but it doesn't cure the disease!" She smiled and chuckled. She went on to tell me about graduating from medical school and doing her residency in neurosurgery and how she had never run out of sugar during surgery—something of which she was very proud and which gave her the feeling that diabetes was "nothing more than a constant pain in the butt, and fingers, and arms."

"I remember thinking that I was okay and on top of it [diabetes] when I celebrated my 25th anniversary of getting diagnosed." I felt an uneasiness creep into me because this session was only two days after my 25th anniversary. I started to get hot and fidgety as I could feel that we were getting very close to her twist of fate. I could never remember any diabetic patient narrative hitting so emotionally close to me. It was like she had knocked the wind out of me!

Dr. Dillon went on to describe how her right eye began to get blurry a few days after her anniversary, but she didn't pay any attention to it because she had just had her eyes checked two months earlier. Then she told me how she noticed that she had an ulcer on her right foot. As she became increasingly tearful, she described the progression of her foot infections and ulceration through the removal of three toes on her right foot—the reason for her limp. With the microscopic detail of a surgeon, she elaborated on the surgical process of amputating her three toes, the phantom pain, and the imbalance and instability that it caused her. I noticed that I was wiggling my toes in order to prove that I could move them and that I could feel the sensation of them rubbing against my shoe. This self-affirming process then allowed me to focus more empathically on her story of loss. She proceeded to talk about the postoperative infection and how her vision in her right eye continued to diminish such that it was hard for her to drive. At this point, I resorted to an old habit that I used to use to prove that my vision was fine—I would try and focus on something to test my visual acuity. The books on my shelf provided the needed validation of my visual acuity.

She went on to describe losing two toes on her left foot and becoming increasingly visually impaired such that she had to cease her surgical practice and take a job as a medical consultant in a managed care company. "Can you imagine what it felt like to go from being a respected surgeon and helping save people's lives to not being able to drive, read, and [begins to sob]. . . . How can I go on? Everything is so humiliating and embarrassing—my daughter had to drive me down here today for my appointment. I can't stand being such a burden to her! How would you feel?"

I was trying to fathom how or if I could have survived such losses. I couldn't play tennis and that would kill me. But I could continue my practice, and she didn't have that raison d'être. Then I began to imagine what it would be like to be visually impaired. Could she read her blood sugar machine, or did her daughter have to do it for her? Did she listen to books on tape? How would I spend my time and try to cope with the sudden changes? How hard it must be to depend on significant others to do things for you every day; I'm not sure I could reconcile myself with such an existential plight! What should I say? What shouldn't I say?

I responded, "While I don't pretend to know all the pain that you have suffered, I think I can imagine how agonizing it is for you to go from being on top of your diabetes and your career, and then 'wham!' all of a sudden you lose toes, your vision, and your career. It's hard to imagine all of those things happening to you all at once. Life was hard enough before, but now the shame and sadness about what you've lost and your dependency on others is intolerable!"

She said, "I don't deal well with things that can't improve." She cried, and we sat in silence for several minutes. I needed the time to review the session in my mind and hoped that she was feeling the silent merger with me that I felt with her. I hoped this silence might convey to her that I could sit with her pain about diabetes and that we might get used to her new immutable reality together. "I'm glad I came; I feel like you can understand me! Do you think you can help me find my way to a new life?"

I replied, "If you don't mind, let me ask you for your opinion first before I answer."

"Well, I didn't have to say much before I started to feel that you understood me today. So, I guess I can count on you to understand my feelings, I'm just not sure if you can help me find a new life where I won't be such a pain to others, especially Michelle [daughter]. I also don't want people to feel sorry for me—I'm sure you're the same way, aren't you?"

"Yes, you're right—we are the same in that way! To answer your question, it is relatively easy to understand what it feels like to walk in your shoes because you are quite eloquent in telling your story. From one diabetic to another, I promise I'll try my hardest to help you accept the things that we can't change but, more importantly understand how we can create a new beginning for you in your life where you don't have to feel so ashamed of who you are."

DISCUSSION

Much of the current debate in psychoanalysis seems rooted in the specifics of the purpose, content, and subjectivity of what is being explicitly disclosed by the therapist. This case highlights the ways in which a therapist is able to connect with how he experiences the patient's traumas and losses and is then able to use this experiential insight to convey a sense of genuine understanding. He first resonated with the similarities in their way of attempting to manage diabetes and was then able to be aware of his physical sensations, which signaled concerns about his own health and their lack of control over the disease. This allowed him to remain available to the patient by refocusing on her core experiences and acknowledging her difficulty in imagining that anyone could understand her diabetic experiences. This recognition also expressed the shared and sad realization that empathy alone does not cure the disease.

Dr. Walker responded directly to a question from the patient by revealing specific facts from his history with diabetes. It should be noted that the therapist's factual disclosure of when he was diagnosed with diabetes in response to the patient's inquiry appears to have facilitated a deeper exploration and sharing of her agonizing physical losses and emotional pain and her new debilitated, loathsome self-image. Retrospective analysis of this first session and the overall process of treatment seems to indicate that this historical, factual self-disclosure promoted a therapeutic ambience in which understanding and explaining interpretations were facilitative. She also explicitly expressed her simultaneous hope to create a new life and her dread of being "burned" again. After experiencing the subjective imbalance that her story generated in him, he briefly reaffirmed his own physical integrity and continued to be emotionally available. Then, with this self-reflection and regulation, he decentered from his temporary and necessary self-immersion and remained focused on her experience, especially in response to her direct questions about how he felt and whether he could help her. He stated, "I think I can imagine how agonizing it is for you. . . . If you don't mind, let me ask you for your opinion first before I answer." He was then able to agree with her that some things can't be changed, but he also acknowledged the importance of mutually understanding how they could create a context in which she could "find a new life." Spontaneous self-disclosure by Dr. Walker would have likely disrupted a primary focus on Dr. Dillon's experiences. Awareness of self-with-Dr. Dillon experiences permitted the appropriate analytic self-reflection and transformation of therapist subjectivity into facilitative interpretative comments. Thus, therapist self-experience, through self-reflection, was transformed into moments of factual sharing and interpretations that contained transformations of his real self-with-patient subjectivity that were oriented toward the patient's self-experiences.

SUMMARY

In summary, we believe that empathic interpretations and authentic self-expression seem to be intrinsically linked, can be integrated in treatment, and contain aspects of the therapist's subjectivity. A process of self-reflection and empathic responsiveness is the sine qua non of growth—promoting emotional dialogue that occurs in healthy and mature relationships. However, such integration needs further critical examination in our clinical theory and case presentations, particularly given the central place that is being given to authentic therapist expression. Pivotal moments in the therapy represent the opportunity for "new beginnings" (Ornstein, 1974) for the patient, yet they require the therapist to regulate, recognize, and transform his extraordinary self-experiences into mutative empathic interpretations. Authenticity is to be judged by the goodness of fit between the therapist's interpretative and nonverbal behavior and the patient's experience of feeling understood and connected with the therapist in a deep and a forward-moving therapeutic–developmental process. This deep exploration of emergent moments in our consulting rooms and in clinical outcome research will advance our scientific–clinical understanding of the multidimensionality of the intersubjective context of treatment and further illuminate the multifaceted nature of cure.

REFERENCES

Aron, L. (1996), *A Meeting of Minds: Mutuality in Psychoanalysis,* Hillsdale, NJ: The Analytic Press.

Bacal, H. A. (1985), Optimal responsiveness and the therapeutic process. In: *Progress in Self Psychology, Vol. 1,* ed. A. Goldberg. Hillsdale, NJ: The Analytic Press, pp. 202–227.

——— (1997), The analyst's subjectivity: How it can illuminate the analysand's experience. *Psychoanal. Dial.,* 7:669–681.

——— Lenoff, L. & Munschauer, C. A. (1999), Optimal responsiveness: The application of specificity theory in relational self psychology. Presented at the 22nd Annual Conference on the Psychology of the Self, October 28, Toronto, Canada.

Buirski, P. & Haglund, P. (1999), The selfobject function of interpretation. In: *Pluralism in Self Psychology: Progress in Self Psychology, Vol. 15,* ed. A. Goldberg. Hillsdale, NJ: The Analytic Press, pp. 31–50.

Busch, F. (1998), Self-disclosure ain't what it's cracked up to be, at least not yet. *Psychoanal. Inq.,* 18:518–529.

Cooper, S. H. (1998), Analyst subjectivity, analyst disclosure and the aims of psychoanalysis. *Psychoanal. Quart.,* 67:379–406.

Davies, J. M. (1999), Getting cold enough feet, defining "safe enough" borders: Dissociation, multiplicity, and integration in the analyst's experience. *Psychoanal. Quart.,* 68:184–208.

Davis, J. T. (2002), Countertransference temptation and the use of self-disclosure by psychotherapists in training. *Psychoanal. Psychol.,* 19:435–454.

Ehrenberg, D. B. (1996), On the analyst's emotional availability and vulnerability. *Contemp. Psychoanal.,* 32:275–286.

Gehrie, M. (1996), Empathy in broader perspective: A technical approach to the consequences of the negative selfobject in early character formation. In: *Basic Ideas Reconsidered: Progress in Self Psychology, Vol. 12,* ed. A. Goldberg. Hillsdale, NJ: The Analytic Press, pp. 159–179.

Gill, M. M. (1982), The interpersonal paradigm and the degree of the therapist's involvement. *Contemp. Psychoanal.*, 19:200–237.

Herzog, B. (1998), Optimal responsiveness and the experience of sharing. In: *Optimal Responsiveness: How Therapists Heal Their Patients,* ed. H. A. Bacal. Northvale, NJ: Aronson, pp. 175–190.

Jacobs, L. (1998), Optimal responsiveness and intersubjective relating. In: *Optimal Responsiveness: How Therapists Heal Their Patients,* ed. H. A. Bacal. Northvale, NJ: Aronson, pp. 191–212.

Kohut, H. (1984), *How Does Analysis Cure?* ed. A. Goldberg & P. Stepansky. Chicago: University of Chicago Press.

Maroda, K. (2002), No place to hide. *Psychoanal. Inq.*, 36:101–120.

Mitchell, S. A. (1998), The analyst's knowledge and authority. *Psychoanal. Quart.*, 67:1–31.

Orange, D. (2001), There is no outside: Empathy and authenticity in psychoanalytic process. Presented at the 24th Annual International Conference on the Psychology of the Self, November, San Francisco, CA.

Ornstein, A. (1974), The dread to repeat and the new beginning. *The Annual of Psychoanalysis,* 2:231–248. Madison, CT: International Universities Press.

——— (1998), Transitional phases and "now moments": Tracing structural changes in psychoanalysis and psychotherapy. Presented at the 21st Annual Conference on the Psychology of the Self, October 24, San Diego, CA.

——— & Ornstein, P. H. (1996), Speaking in the interpretive mode and feeling understood: Crucial aspects of the therapeutic action in psychotherapy. In: *Understanding Therapeutic Action: Psychodynamic Concepts of Cure,* ed. L. E. Lifson. Hillsdale, NJ: The Analytic Press, pp. 103–125.

Preston, L. (1998), Expressive relating: The intentional use of the analyst's subjectivity. In: *The World of Self Psychology: Progress in Self Psychology, Vol. 14,* ed. A. Goldberg. Hillsdale, NJ: The Analytic Press, pp. 203–218.

Renik, O. (1998), Getting real in analysis. *Psychoanal. Quart.*, 67:566–593.

Ringstrom, P. A. (2001), Cultivating the improvisational in psychoanalytic treatment. *Psychoanal. Dial.*, 11:727–754.

Safran, J. D. (2002), Brief relational psychoanalytic treatment. *Psychoanal. Dial.*, 12:171–195.

Sander, L. W. (2002), Thinking differently: Principles of process in living systems and the specificity of being known. *Psychoanal. Dial.*, 12:11–42.

Schwaber, E. A. (1990), Interpretation and the therapeutic action of psychoanalysis. *Internat. J. Psycho-Anal.*, 71:229–240.

Seigel, A. M. (1999), The optimal conversation: A concern about the current trends within self psychology. In: *Pluralism in Self Psychology: Progress in Self Psychology, Vol. 15,* ed., A. Goldberg. Hillsdale, NJ: The Analytic Press.

Shane, E. & Weisel-Barth, J. E. (2000), The role of the relationship in the therapeutic process. Presented at the 23rd Annual Conference on the Psychology of the Self, November 11, Chicago.

Stern, D. N., Sander, L. W., Nahum, J. P., Harrison, A. M., Lyons-Ruth, K., Morgan, A. C., Bruschweiler-Stern, N. & Tronick, E. Z. (1998), Non-interpretive mechanisms in psychoanalytic therapy. *Internat. J. Psycho-Anal.*, 79:903–921.

Stolorow, R. D. (1994), The nature and therapeutic action of psychoanalytic interpretation. In: *The Intersubjective Perspective*, ed. R. Stolorow, G. Atwood & B. Brandchaft. Northvale, NJ: Aronson, pp. 43–55.

——— (1999), Antidotes, enactments, rituals, and the dance of reassurance: Comments on the case of Joanna Churchill and Alan Kindler. In: *Pluralism in Self Psychology: Progress in Self Psychology, Vol. 15*, ed. A. Goldberg. Hillsdale, NJ: The Analytic Press, pp. 229–232.

Sucharov, M. S. (2000), Secret conversations with my father: The psychological dimension of theoretical discourse. In: *How Responsive Should We Be? Progress in Self Psychology, Vol. 16*, ed. A. Goldberg. Hillsdale, NJ: The Analytic Press, pp. 339–358.

Teicholz, J. G. (1999), *Kohut, Loewald, and the Postmoderns*. Hillsdale, NJ: The Analytic Press.

Tolpin, P. (1988), Optimal affective engagement: The analyst's role in therapy. *Learning From Kohut: Progress in Self Psychology, Vol. 4*, ed. A. Goldberg. Hillsdale, NJ: The Analytic Press, pp. 160–168.

Wolf, E. S. (1993), The role of interpretation in therapeutic change. In: *The Widening Scope of Self Psychology: Progress in Self Psychology, Vol. 9*, ed. A. Goldberg. Hillsdale, NJ: The Analytic Press, pp. 15–30.

Chapter 2

Consequences of "Empathy": Rereading Kohut's (1959) "Examination of the Relationship Between Mode of Observation and Theory"

Lester Lenoff

The 50 years since Kohut's classic 1959 paper "Introspection, Empathy, and Psychoanalysis" have witnessed widespread changes in psychoanalytic theory and practice. In particular, the emergence of what has become known as "Relational Psychoanalysis" has attracted the attention of many "second-generation" self psychologists. In my own city, a leading local self psychological professional organization devoted their 2000 annual conference, at members' request, to a day with a prominent Relational theorist. And this organization is devoting much of the 2002–2003 programming year to the issue of clarifying the distinction between relational psychoanalysis and a "relational" self psychology. This distinction has become increasingly relevant to self psychologists seeking to move from a "one-body" approach to treatment toward a

---

Encouragement for my thinking and support for my writing has been consistently provided by Howard Bacal, William Coburn, Bruce Herzog, and Martin Livingston.

"two-body," "relational," theory of reciprocal engagement, but one that retains Kohut's innovations in regard to such issues as consistent vicarious introspection, the paradigm of "repeated relationships" (Stern, 1994, p. 318), and the nature of aggression. A reconsideration of Kohut's seminal paper provides both a starting point for thinking about clinical process and a touchstone for self psychologists seeking to locate themselves in the contemporary landscape of psychoanalytic thinking.

The richness and depth of Kohut's presentation preclude addressing its entire substance in the space of a single paper. I will focus here on explicating Kohut's first section, "An Examination of the Relationship Between Mode of Observation and Theory" (pp. 205–212). This section embodies: (1) Kohut's crucial assertion that "we designate phenomena . . . as psychological if our mode of observation includes . . . [vicarious introspection[1]] *as an essential constituent* (p. 209) and (2) his operational description of "vicarious introspection" as the means by which we come to an understanding and explanation of the patient's introspective reports and external behavior. In its time, it was a radical step away from the conventions of Kohut's own analytic milieu. In addition, the implications of Kohut's operational framework for practice, some of which I will illustrate below, bear restatement and elaboration as a means of delineating a distinctively self psychological sensibility toward thinking about and working with patients.

THE RELATIONSHIP BETWEEN MODE OF OBSERVATION AND THEORY

Kohut begins by delimiting the *psychological field* as the domain of a person's "thoughts, wishes, feelings, and fantasies."

> The *inner world* [of another person] cannot be observed with the aid of our sensory organs. Our thoughts, wishes, feelings, and fantasies cannot be seen, smelled, heard, or touched. They have no existence in physical space, and yet they are real, and *we can observe them as they occur in time: through introspection on ourselves, and through empathy (i.e., vicarious introspection) in others* [pp. 205–206].

[1] I have chosen, for purposes of clarity, to replace *empathy*, even in direct quotes, with *vicarious introspection* to emphasize that, in the 1959 paper, Kohut is referring to empathy as a mode of observation rather than as a form of relating or a source of therapeutic action.

Kohut asserts that "the only fruitful definition [of such *psychological* phenomena] is operational"—that is, the nature of *psychological phenomena* is delimited through the *means by which we apprehend it*.

> We speak of physical phenomena when the essential ingredient of our observational methods include our senses, we speak of psychological *phenomena* when the essential ingredient of our observation is *introspection* [by the patient] and *[vicarious] empathy* [by the analyst] [p. 206; emphasis added].

Kohut then describes the crucial aspects of the operation of gathering *psychoanalytic* data. He tells us what we are to observe: that is, what the patient can report, through acts of introspection, about his or her "thoughts, wishes, feelings, and fantasies." Yet, even by the article's second paragraph, the terms of observation Kohut sets out, *as regards the observing analyst*, are more restrictive than they seem at first glance. In particular, the analyst's inner world also includes "thoughts, wishes, feelings, and fantasies." But for psychoanalysis, as Kohut "operationally" defines it, *only* those of the analyst's thoughts, wishes, feelings, and fantasies arrived at through vicarious introspection fall within the psychoanalytic domain.

Over the next four pages (pp. 206–209), Kohut delimits which aspects of the analyst's inner world are included within and which are excluded from "vicarious introspection." He speaks of vicarious introspection, not "in the narrow sense of an *actual operation* that is taking place at a particular time," but "in the widest sense of *an attitude of the observer* [the analyst] toward the phenomena under investigation" [i.e. the patient's inner world] (p. 206; emphasis added). Kohut's example involves our reaction to a person who is unusually tall.[2] It is instructive first to consider two renditions of an example offered by Theodore Jacobs (1986), who, in asserting the inevitability of an analyst having subjective reactions to a patient, also describes the impact of a patient's size on the analyst.

> A colleague of some renown who . . . was extremely small in stature received a call [for] a consultation. . . . [At] the arranged time the new patient arrived. . . . About to enter the waiting room to greet him, the analyst suddenly stopped at the threshold and, momentarily, stood transfixed. There in front of him was a Paul Bunyan of a figure, fully six feet, eight inches in height, weighing perhaps 260 pounds, and wearing cowboy boots and a ten gallon hat. For several more seconds

[2] Mark Gehrie provided the second rendition of the "Paul Bunyan" anecdote.

> the analyst looked at him in silence. Then, with a shrug of his shoulders and a resigned gesture, he motioned toward his office. "Come on in, anyway," he said [p. 289].

Jacobs goes on to comment, "This opening phrase . . . highlights the well-known yet sometimes overlooked fact that from the very outset of treatment, *transferences are activated in the analyst as well as the patient*" (pp. 289–290; emphasis added). Thus far, Jacobs presents what we can imagine to be the analyst's instantaneous introspection of his own "thoughts, wishes, feelings, and fantasies." Kohut explicitly asks us to go further; the analyst's introspection must be *vicarious*, that is:

> Only when we think ourselves *into his place* . . . by vicarious introspection, begin to feel his unusual size *as if it were our own* and thus *revive [our own] inner experiences* in which we had been unusual or conspicuous, only then do we begun to *appreciate the meaning* of that the unusual size may have *for this person* and *only then have we observed a psychological fact* [pp. 207–208; emphasis added].

The point here is that Kohut's notion of "the total attitude of the observer" (p. 206) places the *priority of observation on the patient's experience*. We consult our own inner experiences in an attempt to evoke, within ourselves, in Evelyn Schwaber's (1979) classic phrase, "how it feels *to be the subject*, rather than the target" (p. 472; emphasis added) of the patient's subjectivity (i.e., of the patient's ideation, affect, and impulses). The second rendition of this anecdote makes just that point. Mark Gehrie (2001) insists:

> It was *not* a story about the impact in the analyst! The point was precisely about "the priority of orientation on the patient's experience," and in this instance the analyst's ability to use that in the construction of an empathic response: i.e., I see you are disappointed in how small I am, how could I possibly be of help to you, but despite it all, "Come in anyway." [The analyst's] response demonstrated his empathically-derived understanding of the patient's disappointment in the analyst's appearance, as if his small stature would limit his ability to help such a large and imposing person [pp. 2–3].

"SCRUTINY" AS AN ALTERNATIVE TO VICARIOUS INTROSPECTION

Continuing Kohut's (1959) delimitation of what is "psychoanalytic," we note that the analyst's "thoughts" may well include the process of *scrutiny* as "the *major tool* of psychoanalytic observation"

(p. 209; emphasis added), which Kohut rejects in favor of "vicarious introspection."

> Here we must consider the objection which may be raised by some that the *major tool of psychoanalytic observation* is not introspection but *scrutiny by the analyst* of a certain kind of behavior of the patient: free association [p. 209; emphasis added].

In both cases, scrutiny and vicarious introspection, the patient is providing the same material: "introspective self-observation . . . to which the analyst is witness" (p. 209). Kohut suggests that the "analyst's ability to maintain a level scrutiny" (Friedman, 1997, p. 35) is seen as the major component of analytic work by traditional analysts. The contemporary vitality of this stance—suspicious anticipation of irregularities—is borne out by Michael Franz Basch (1995): "I asked the candidate, 'What were you thinking during the patient's silence?' 'I wondered what he was trying to get away with,' my student replied" (p. 367). In contrast, Kohut implies that analysts should avoid such scrutiny. But he does not explicitly define *scrutiny*.

The etymological derivation of the word *scrutiny* itself provides unexpected help to our understanding. The *Concise Oxford Dictionary* (1960, p. 1116) begins a list of related entries with the term *scrutin* (italicized to indicate that it is a French word), referring to a method by which a citizen votes for representatives of a smaller or larger electoral district. "Scrutineer" is then "a person *examining* ballot papers *for irregularities*" (emphasis added). "Scrutiny" is a "*critical gaze*, close investigation, examination into details . . . when *suspicion of irregularity* makes it desirable" (emphasis added). The analyst's "scrutiny" then goes beyond close examination of the patient's presentation and extends to anticipation and *suspicion of irregularities*. Lawrence Friedman (1997) comments that analysts

> welcome what the patient is saying, but *we think he's revealing it in order to conceal something more important*. . . . Justified or not, the profession's response to . . . Kohut was surely influenced by the fear that [he was] diluting *a fundamental, adversarial attitude* [p. 30; emphasis added].

This critique of Kohut's influence persists because, in contrast to "a fundamental, adversarial attitude," vicarious introspection demands that we suspend such suspicions and "*think ourselves into [the patient's] place*" (pp. 207–208; emphasis added).

Contrary to a popular stereotype, this does not mean that Kohut calls upon the analyst to think only the same thoughts as the patient.

In both cases, scrutiny and vicarious introspection, "the psychological insights of the analyst are frequently ahead of the analysand's comprehension of himself" (p. 209). Yet, for Kohut, the analyst reaches this position, ahead of the patient, by a process, not of scrutiny, but as "the result of the *trained introspective skill [of] the analyst* used in the *extension of introspection* (vicarious introspection)" (p. 209; emphasis added). Vicarious introspection, as an attitude of the observer, reflects an attempt to establish a resonance with, rather than to get at what is behind, the patient's material.

TAKING ANALYTIC MATERIAL IN A "STRAIGHT" MANNER

Jule Miller's (1985) description of supervision with Kohut between 1978 and 1981 highlights this contrast between scrutiny and vicarious introspection. (Kohut may or may not have given the same supervision in the late 1950s, but what Miller describes is clearly implicit in the 1959 paper.) Miller's rendition is valuable in that it highlights Kohut's concept of the analytic space and task.

Miller's patient had mistakenly arrived an hour early for his session and seen someone else in the waiting room, leading to a state of anxiety and dislocation. In reaction, the patient felt, and acted on, an impulse to visit a nearby bookstore to look at homoerotic material. Miller interpreted to the patient that the sense of dislocation had led to the seeking out of the homosexual stimulation in an attempt to restore self-cohesion. But Miller, coming from what he himself describes as "a more traditional analytic climate" (1985, p. 16) also *scrutinized* the patient's report and found a disavowed "irregularity" with which he confronted the patient. "I added, however, he had set up the situation by coming an hour early (he was well aware of the time) and then had reacted, in part, blaming me as if I had deserted him and been involved in causing his dislocation" (p. 15). Kohut's supervision and Miller's response is worth quoting at length, including interpolated references to Kohut's ideas on vicarious introspection versus scrutiny.

> Kohut disagreed with my interpretation that the patient had arranged the incident. He said that although it might be correct, he felt it was an unnecessarily complicated initial formulation. He enunciated a basic principle: *one should take analytic material first in a "straight" manner, as if it means what it seems to mean.* . . . Kohut felt the tendency of analysts to look first for a hidden meaning *[to scrutinize—to anticipate irregularities]* was a mistake. In this specific instance he added that he

> would have been inclined *[vicarious introspection as an attitude]* to believe that the patient was eager to see me. *[This might reflect a way in which Kohut, through vicarious introspection, connected with his own memories and feelings of being a child eager to see his father.]* Like a young child, eager to see his father, he had come early to the session. Once he opened the door and found the other patient sitting there, the sequence was much as I had described it, but *the patient's motivation should be regarded first as one of an intense, childlike wish rather than an attempt to "set up" a situation of disappointment.* Interpretation should be directed primarily along those lines [pp. 15–16; emphasis added].

Miller notes, "This was a strange conception to me, since I came from a more traditional analytic climate" (p. 16). In this instance, Miller apparently saw the patient as having "set up" the situation in order to reenact a theme of early disappointment[3] and fulfill a forbidden aggressive wish by "blaming" the analyst in the present, while disavowing the roots in the past of the disappointment and anger. Miller (1985) continues:

> Following my consultation with Kohut, the patient again brought up the incident, which he considered of "extraordinary importance." This time I was able to modify my interpretive understanding. *I emphasized his strong wish to see me and his coming early as an expression of that wish, rather than as an attempt to "set up" a frustration.*[4] He was visibly relieved at this second formulation, and it was followed by a flood of material, including the comment that it felt much more right to him than what I had said previously, which he had acknowledged made intellectual sense but which he could not feel. Kohut was correct in stating that *I had underestimated the importance and the intensity of the patient's wish to see me at this particular time in the analysis* [pp. 15–16; emphasis added].

Miller's realization involves an explicit reconfiguration away from the scrutiny of hidden, forbidden wishes and toward the vicarious introspection of "analytic material first in a 'straight' manner, as if it means what it seems to mean" (p. 5). Further, this shift does not demand the assertion of "empathy" as a mode of interaction or as a source of therapeutic action, although these issues demand their own study. Instead, it flows directly from Kohut's (1959) substitution of consistent vicarious introspection for the various forms of scrutiny.

---

[3] See the discussion of the paradigm of "repeated relationships" in Stern (1994, p. 318).

[4] Compare to Tansey (1992), a contemporary relational analyst, who writes that the patient's motivation comprises "not only a desire for positive change but also *powerful unconscious elements of self-sabotage and self-fulfilling prophecy*" (p. 311; emphasis added).

THE ANALYST'S SUBJECTIVITY AND THE "DECISIVE OBSERVATION"

Returning to the 1959 text, in a passage that seems to have been overlooked by both sympathetic and critical commentators, Kohut addresses the question of that part of the analyst's own subjectivity that reflects him- or herself, rather than the patient. He writes that "introspection and [vicarious introspection]," despite being "essential constituents of observation, are often . . . amalgamated with other methods of observation" (p. 209). These "other methods" presumably reflect the analyst's thoughts, wishes, feelings, and fantasies that make up the *analyst's subjectivity*. Not only this, but the *analyst's subjectivity* frequently *contradicts* that of the patient. This is especially the case when the patient asserts that he has sustained unprovoked injury at the hands of some third party or of the analyst him- or herself. Kohut's comment recognizes that it is untenable to picture that analyst as being in such synchronization with the patient that such contradictions between the two subjectivities fail to arise.

Nor do Kohut's comments demand that all divergences of view between analyst and patient are the result of countertransference interference.[5] The *operational* issue that arises is the *clinical handling* of such contradictions. That is, whatever these other methods may inform the analyst, the "decisive observational act, however, is [vicariously introspective]" (pp. 209–210). That is, the *decisive observation*, which determines whether the analyst stays silent or if he or she comments on what is said, comes from the viewpoint of "how it feels to be the subject rather than the target of the patient's needs and demands" (Schwaber, 1979, p. 472). In this context, the issue of countertransference interference arises when the analyst stops short of a stance of vicarious introspection and interprets the contradiction of his or her own renditions of the situation as the patient's "distortion" or "resistance" (see Bacal and Thomson, 1998; Ornstein, 1998).

Paul Ornstein (1998) has recently offered an example that will help to illustrate how a clinician operationalizes Kohut's theoretical approach. I chose Ornstein's example because (1) his historical and theoretical proximity to Kohut identifies him as a leading exponent of the central tenets of self psychology and (2) his examples provide clarity and accessibility. Ornstein describes a situation, common in both

[5] For a discussion of instances in which such divergences *do* represent a countertransference interference, see Bacal and Thomson (1998).

contemporary literature and clinical discussions, of the analyst being devalued for a perceived inability to recognize and tolerate the depths of the patient's affect. The patient, Mr. T,

> complained during one of his Friday sessions that he experienced his childhood as if he had lived in a dungeon. . . . He expressed these thoughts at a time when he was already beginning to free himself from the consequences of those experiences. *I was therefore surprised* that he compared his childhood to living in a dungeon. In his Monday session, Mr. T complained bitterly and accused me of having disrupted his efforts at experiencing himself once again in his childhood dungeon. He believed that I could not tolerate his experiences and . . . [that I] asked him for his reflections, instead of remaining with his experiences and accompanying him in his descent into his dungeon [Part II].

Ornstein's (1998) own experience, drawn on direct, rather than vicarious, introspection differed in essentials from the one ascribed to him by the patient: "Although I was astonished at this new image of his childhood on Friday, I thought I was able to . . . accompany him and resonate with his affects. *I did not experience the task [as] painful or repulsive*" (Part II, emphasis added). Ornstein's response to this discrepancy is distinctively self psychological. His own direct introspection contradicts the patient's rendition of his analytic behavior and of his underlying intentions. But Ornstein's "decisive observational act, however, is [from the viewpoint of vicarious introspection]" (Kohut, 1959, pp. 209–210).

> Nevertheless, this is how *he* pictured the reasons for my interference with his efforts. I then responded by saying that, *I could well understand his embittered complaints, if he experienced me as not accompanying him* on his descent into his dungeon and *actually obstructing* his descent [Ornstein, 1998, Part II; emphasis added].

The patient paused and then became self-reflective. He noted that it seemed to him that Ornstein had failed to accompany him on the descent. Then he added: "Perhaps it was my anxiety that you would not accompany me that created in me the feeling that you did not remain with me. I know, I am very sensitive on this score" (Part II).

Ornstein explains his clinical stance in a manner directly reminiscent of Miller's (1985) report of Kohut as a supervisor, insisting, "one should take analytic material first in a 'straight' manner, as if it means what it seems to mean" (p. 15). In Ornstein's (1998) words: "Even if this image [i.e., the patient's rendition that is at odds with the analyst's experience] is over drawn *it is important to accept it*, to understand it, . . . *rather than view it and interpret it as a distorted perception*, by insisting that I had, indeed, accompanied him" (Part II; emphasis added). Ornstein responds to the difference between the patient's perceptions and his own by consistently focusing "on the patient's inner reality (on his subjective experience)" (Part I), a stance directly derived from Kohut's insistence that the "decisive observational act" (1959, p, 209) is obtained through *vicarious* introspection.

SELF PSYCHOLOGY AND "RELATIONAL PSYCHOANALYSIS"

Ornstein's stance and response represent a Kohutian sensibility, derived directly from the "Empathy" paper. The value of reconsidering "empathy" arises in juxtaposing this stance with the ways an analyst representing other traditional and contemporary orientations might view this clinical passage. The present purpose is not to demonstrate the superiority of self psychological theory or practice over those other orientations. Instead, it is to delineate differences in approach, but with the caveats inherent in all such comparisons. That is, any attempt to generalize about the approach of any given "school" in psychoanalysis is bound to provoke the protest that the ideas of some writer or writers within that school are being overlooked. What is more, the specific clinical choices of any particular practitioner, made on a pragmatic or theoretical basis, defy any such generalization. As a result, the comparisons that follow are inevitably "illustrative . . . rather than evidentiary in their nature" (Cooper, 1996, p. 897). And, like any such comparisons, they should be measured against the reader's experience in reading the literature, in working with patients, and in his or her own discussions about theory and practice.

These comparisons usually begin by noting Stephen Mitchell's (1988) three-part division of psychoanalytic frameworks, which has been widely cited and followed in contemporary literature. The first division, the traditional analytic orientation, is described as a "drive-conflict" model. This model portrays the patient as a closed system, and the analyst as an objective, external observer, for whom "nothing is more characteristic . . . than [an] inclination to *see through* everything" (Friedman, 1997, p. 30). For many of these analysts, the disparity of the patient's and the analyst's renditions of Mr. T's Friday session would be taken as the starting point for an approach that *presumes* the patient's *transferentially derived distortion* of the analyst's behavior and intentions. It is this "fundamental, adversarial attitude" (Friedman, 1997, p. 30) that was likely in Kohut's mind when he "enunciated a basic principle: one should take analytic material first in a 'straight' manner, as if it means what it seems to mean" (Miller, 1985. p. 15). The specific technical response based on the drive-conflict model could include, on a *pragmatic* basis, a *temporary restraint* from confronting the patient with this disparity. But the ultimate goal would remain the resolution, through consistent interpretation, of what was presumed to be the patient's distortion.

For contemporary self psychologists the most relevant comparison of Kohut's stance is with Mitchell's (1988) second division, the "relational conflict" models. In this context, no survey could do justice to the variety of theory and practice that has emerged as "Relational Psychoanalysis." But Relationally oriented writers seeking a synthesis of ideas note two common features that would suggest a clinical direction diverging from Ornstein's self psychological approach. The first of these addresses the role of repetition in clinical process. Irwin Hirsch (1994) describes the "model of clinical action," preferred by Mitchell, the preeminent relational theorist:

> Problems in living are a function of adhesion to the loved ones of the past, an inability to separate from the familiar and the familial. . . . It reflects *an active striving to maintain old attachments*. . . . In this context, patients in analysis are viewed as both striving for new and richer experience while also *looking to repeat internalized old patterns*, which most define one's sense of self [p. 181; emphasis added].

From this paradigm of "repeated relationships" (Stern, 1994, p. 318), which has been widely adopted in contemporary relational approaches, Ornstein's response would be portrayed as having missed an important aspect of the interchange, that is, the patient's looking to *"repeat the old and bad experience"* of a "familiar" interchange with a "depriving or harmful internalized figure" (Hirsch, 1994, pp. 181–182; emphasis added).

The second feature that appears common to relational conflict models—interpretation of the countertransference—is a technical corollary to this paradigm of "repeated relationships." This paradigm (Stern, 1994)

> focuses on the patient's tendency to organize his or her current experience of the analyst (and analytic relationship) in terms of familiar pathogenic relationship patterns from the past and (via projective identification) unconsciously to elicit the analyst's unwitting participation in these old interactional scenarios. . . . Theorists who emphasize the repeated relationship tend also to emphasize the role of interpretation . . . particularly interpretation of the transference-countertransference enactments [p. 318].

Elaborating the technical implications of this model, Michael Tansey (1992) writes:

> Although the relational-conflict analyst remains deeply interested in the patient's views and makes every effort to understand how they may be "plausible,"[6] he is *not reflexively called on to subjugate what may be his own dissonant experience* in an effort to see things from "within" the patient's perspective; quite the contrary, it is often *by paying closer attention to his own, at times highly discordant, responses to the patient* that the analyst may eventually *come to gain a clearer and deeper appreciation of what is happening* in the patient's shoes [p. 312, emphasis added].

And the thrust of the relational model of therapeutic action suggests that confrontation of the patient, whose motivation comprises "not only a desire for positive change but also powerful unconscious elements of *self-sabotage and self-fulfilling prophecy*" (Tansey, 1992, p. 311; emphasis added), would be an inevitable and crucial aspect of the treatment. While allowing for individual differences among relationally oriented analysts, this viewpoint stands in clear contrast to Kohut's supervision of Miller (1985): "The patient's motivation should be regarded first as one of an intense, childlike wish rather than an attempt to set up a situation of disappointment." (p. 6), as well as to Ornstein's (1998) proviso: "Even if this image [of the patient's rendition that is at odds with the analyst's experience] is overdrawn *it is important to accept it*, understand it" (Part II; emphasis added).

SELF PSYCHOLOGY AND THE "DEVELOPMENTAL TILT"

In considering the continuing value of "empathy" to contemporary self psychology, Mitchell's (1988) third division, that of "developmental arrest" or "developmental tilt" models, seems less instructive. These terms have gained currency in the literature as shorthand for references to aspects of Kohut's or Winnicott's ideas that focus on maintaining relatedness, rather than recognizing

---

[6] While the patient's experience is seen as "plausible" (see Gill, 1983), rather than inherently distorted, in this model, which remains within Stern's (1994) relational paradigm of repeated relationships (p. 318), the patient remains rendered as the *initiator* of the analyst's response. Irwin Hoffman (1983) writes: "Because the analyst is human, he is likely to have in his repertoire a blueprint for approximately the emotional *response that the patient's transference dictates* and that response is likely *to be elicited*, whether consciously or unconsciously. Ideally this response serves as a key—perhaps the best key the analyst has—to the nature of the interpersonal scene that *the patient is driven by transference to create*" (p. 413; emphasis added).

"relational conflict" (Hirsch, 1994, p. 181). For example, Steven Cooper and David Levit (1998) write, "Each of these [British Kleinian and American Interpersonal] models actually differs in some ways from the *'developmental tilt' (Mitchell, 1988) models of Kohut and Winnicott*, which emphasize more the need of the analyst to meet certain aspects of the patient's experience of impingement and deprivation" (pp. 606–697; emphasis added). Yet their article includes no explication of the phrase "to meet certain aspects of the patient's experience," apparently a reference to what Barry Protter (1988) describes as "a *developmental tilt* . . . which insists on seeing the analyst as playing a *remediating or restorative* role" (p. 512; emphasis added). Nor do Cooper and Levit (1998) refer to the ongoing controversy in self psychology over this exact issue.[7] Such references to "developmental arrest" and "developmental tilt" models function as proxies for references to Kohut and/or Winnicott, whose approaches are associated with "corrective emotional experience" (Frank, 1992, p. 74); "treatment [consisting] more of caretaking than what many of us know as psychoanalysis" (Hirsch, 1994, p. 180); "the tendency to portray the patient as passive, detached and victimized . . . which I have characterized as the 'Sleeping Beauty' model" (Mitchell, 1984, p. 492); and "models [that] allow the analyst to gratify the patient in the context of addressing early deprivations and tend to play out patient's and analyst's fantasies of a magical cure"[8] (Slochower, 1991, p. 710).

One value of reconsidering "Empathy" is to begin to disentangle Kohut's ideas from this condensed amalgam of Kohut and Winnicott, which obscures the specific distinctions of the theory and practice that each developed. Ornstein (1991) reminds us that Kohut began with: "the psychoanalytic exploration of patients with narcissistic personality disturbances and . . . the study of the working through of these (then called narcissistic) transferences" (p. 188). The fruits of this study (Ornstein, 1991) was Kohut's recognition that these patients'

> expectations, needs, demands, and fantasies centered around two main issues. . . . First, the patients expressed their need for someone to serve as an echo, and for affirmation, approval, admiration, and the bolstering of their self-esteem. . . . This "mirror transference," once

---

[7] See also footnote 12. Cooper and Levit (1998) include Winnicott, but not Kohut, among their references; Protter (1988) includes Kohut, but not Winnicott, among his.

[8] While Slochower (1994) goes on to critique Mitchell's portrayal of this aspect of Winnicott, she describes a characterization of "developmental tilt" or "developmental arrest" models (that is, Kohut and Winnicott) that has gained widespread acceptance, especially in formal and informal case discussions.

> established . . . served as the necessary "psychic glue." . . . The second cluster of experiences, which Kohut called an "idealizing transference" is expressed by the need of some patients to attach themselves to the analyst by putting him on a pedestal. . . . These expectations and needs, when experienced as having been met, also lend the patient a modicum of cohesiveness and vitality as well as inner calm [pp. 188–189].

Kohut explicitly legitimized the patient's need for "psychic glue" in life and in treatment. And many writers have noted that "because the self psychologist is 'tuned more sharply to how it feels to be the subject rather than the target of the patient's needs and demands' (Schwaber, 1979, p. 472), there is a more collaborative and less adversarial quality to the therapeutic process than that which is informed by the more traditional analytic perspectives" (Bacal, 1995, p. 355). Yet this is not the result of seeking to offer "a new atmosphere for conducting analysis, [nor] a special sort of humanity or kindness, but simply (and profoundly) a new theory" (Goldberg, 1985, p. 63). Rereading "Empathy" as "the actual beginning . . . of Kohut's [theory] of the self and its disorders" (Ornstein, 1993, p. 5) then helps self psychologists to locate ourselves in contemporary theory and practice, not by external characterizations (and sometimes misattributed stereotypes), but *on self psychological terms*.

VICARIOUS INTROSPECTION WITHIN THE "WIDENING SCOPE" OF TREATMENT

The relevance of "empathy" to contemporary self psychology does not end at that point. We usually envision the content of vicarious introspection as the patient's subjectivity—the combination of ideation, impulse and affect the patient brings to us. But there is another level of the patient's experience, that is, the state—cohesive or fragmented; vital or depleted; realistically confident, grandiose, or mortified—of the patient's underlying self system. This self-stabilization[9] determines and supports the patient's capacity for the psychological functions required to participate in an analytic process. In many instances, we can count on a degree of underlying self-stabilization sufficient to allow us to focus, for the most part, on vicarious introspection of the patient's subjectivity. But with some patients (perhaps with all patients, some of the time), it seems that

[9] "The subjective perception of the self as 'stabilized' is the opposite of feeling prone to [disintegration, depletion, and grandiosity or mortification] and the term I will use for that combination of support, enhancement, and comfort of the self that describes a self–selfobject experience" (Lenoff, 1998, p. 148).

the two levels do not move concurrently. Vicarious introspection and interpretation of the patient's ideation, impulse, and affect does not seem to provide the consistent self-stabilization required for self-reflective inquiry and exploration.

For example, Gehrie (1993) writes of Ms. B, a patient

> with a traumatic history of abandonments by mother and sexual abuse by father and brothers. . . . The empathic grasp of this patient's subjective world . . . precipitates anxiety that is characteristic of her continual state of partial fragmentation—a chronic traumatic state—which is mitigated only by the fantasy that the analyst will become her lover, and she will not experience this as intrusive and damaging, as with sexuality in real life . . . [and] has led to a mixed result, in which she experiences the available mirroring and understanding as always inadequate because they do not lead to the act of sexual intimacy, and therefore, for her, are essentially rejecting in quality [pp. 1086–1087].

Even in clinical situations less dramatic than that of Ms. B, we encounter patients for whom "the available mirroring and understanding," because they do not fulfill the equivalent of Ms. B's fantasy of intimacy with the analyst,[10] are "always inadequate" (p. 1086).

In these situations in which patients seem stalled in treatment or even deteriorating, clinicians are called upon to push at or go beyond the conventional practice of the orientation in which they were trained. Some writers have suggested that a form of pragmatic clinical eclecticism (as opposed to theory-building) is inevitable and itself the "normal science"[11] of psychoanalytic practice. Charles Spezzano notes Mitchell's claim "that mixing models of mind and development produces unstable hybrids" (Spezzano, 1998, p. 384), yet quotes Mitchell as going on to write that:

---

[10] Bacal (1995) describes these fantasies, which are frequently difficult or impossible to fulfill in clinical work, as "phantasy selfobjects." "Selfobject experiences may be substantively fueled by the patient's creative imagination, that is, by the elaboration of conscious or unconscious phantasy. This is often a significant component of the patient's hope that the therapist will respond in ways that will meet his or her basic psychological needs, perhaps for the first time. When phantasy plays a predominant part in the patient's sense of the selfobject, we may speak of a phantasy selfobject. In this situation, the therapeutic relationship is particularly vulnerable to the therapist's potentially disruptive responses" (p. 362; see also Lenoff, 1998).

[11] This approach, in Mayer's (1996) view, provokes "echoes of what Kuhn and others have described as the pursuit of *normal science*. Inconsistent or contradictory observations are assimilated by making plenty of room for anomalies, such that an original and overarching paradigm can be retained, while it stretches to incorporate as many new observations as possible" (pp. 173–174; emphasis added).

> To claim that model mixing is conceptually unstable and costly says nothing about how analysts use psychoanalytic theory in the consulting room [where] an analyst may use concepts from many different authors, but reset those concepts within an implicit, unarticulated, but generally consistent metapsychological framework of his own design. Similarly, the fact that some clinicians draw on different models for understanding and treating different kinds of patients, or the same patient at different times, says nothing about whether these various models fit meaningfully together in any logical sense [Mitchell, 1988, p. 60].

Similarly, Joseph Sandler (1983) proposes that analysts develop "private theories":

> With increasing clinical experience the analyst, as he grows more competent, will preconsciously (descriptively speaking, unconsciously) construct a whole variety of theoretical segments . . . which have the quality of being available in reserve, so to speak, to be called upon whenever necessary. That they may contradict one another is no problem [p. 38].

Elizabeth Lloyd Mayer (1996) writes that Sandler regards such private theories

> as an adaptive response to the useful but constraining nature of our public theory; thus he is able to argue that contradictions between private and public theory can and do "coexist happily" in the minds of analysts, as long as they remain unconscious (or preconscious) [p. 172].

Some clinicians are comfortable to work within this pragmatic eclecticism and practice effectively and ethically. Other clinicians feel more of a need for a theoretical and clinical anchor, even as they conduct treatment with patients for whom therapeutic engagement "rests on [access to and] alteration of emotional patterns of experience which may not be accessible by ordinary analytic means" (Gehrie, 1993, p. 1092). Mayer (1996), however, asserts that the problem goes beyond this individual need:

> Contradictions between private and public theories [do not] coexist as happily as Sandler suggests. . . . As time goes on, many analysts start to feel less and less like "real" analysts doing "real" analysis. . . . Those analysts develop an increasing and often uncomfortable sense that much of how they think they help their patients doesn't fit with the model of analytic technique to which they in principle adhere. . . . A variety of consequences can follow—ranging from an insistent muddiness of thinking which is required to prevent contradictory ideas from encountering each other, to severe and disturbing lapses in conscience [pp. 172–173].

Mayer (1996) documents her concern with an uncommon case example in which a colleague's disjunction between his public and private theories led to a lapse in professional discipline sufficient to allow a sexual involvement with his patient (pp. 175–180). What is much more common is concern about "muddiness of thinking which is required to prevent contradictory ideas from encountering each other," and what it means to be a "real" self psychologist doing "real" self psychological treatment.

Gehrie (1993) frames the problem well:

> While our initial diagnostic impressions and treatment recommendations are often incorrect, our treatment goals are adjustable with changes in understanding. *Adjustments in our goals should be reflected in adjustments in technique*, and eventually a picture of our justifiable expectations are likely to emerge [p. 1085; emphasis added].

While Gehrie (1993) himself differentiates sharply between psychoanalysis and psychotherapy (pp. 1084–1085), he addresses the issue of technical flexibility within a self psychological perspective in a manner that transcends the analysis/therapy controversy. And prominent among the sources he cites to support the call for flexibility in goals and technique is empathy:

> Particularly in the case of patients with traumata at early, presymbolic and/or preverbal levels, interpretations couched in symbolic, verbal terms will be less likely to be affectively understood and used by the patient. . . . Under these conditions, interpretations often rely on alternative modes of communication, which are created by the analyst out of his own personal repertoire,[12] and subject only to his own

---

[12] Gehrie (2001) also differentiates sharply "as central to how we understand our work," between "empathy as a mode of observation [as opposed to] its definition as a form of response or a mode of relating. . . . [It] is one thing to use empathy to understand, and therefore be able to help the patient to understand what he or she may be experiencing, and another thing altogether to use empathy as a basis for then providing for the patient what they believe they require or desire from you" (pp. 1–2). In fairness, my own use of the quote may well be read as implying a wider continuum of "alternative modes of communication" than Gehrie himself had in mind. But I believe that Gehrie's description remains relevant to this discussion because of the centrality with which he places empathy in the consideration of this highly controversial issue. The wider recognition of such centrality of empathy as the "the actual beginning . . . of Kohut's later systematic study of the self and its disorders" (Ornstein, 1993, p. 5) might help focus the exploration of this issue among self psychologists. The authors included in Bacal's 1998 edited volume and Lenoff (1998), among others, make a case for the validity and self psychological provenance of a continuum of clinical responses embodying "optimal responsiveness" or "optimal provision" (Lindon, 1994).

> personal and ethical limits. *Kohut's (1959) definition of psychoanalysis as that field defined by the acquisition of empathic and introspective data* also suggests that *"whither the analysand goeth, so must the analyst go,"* if contact based on empathy is to be maintained [p. 1097; emphasis added].

"Empathy" reminds us that it is by *consistent vicarious introspection with the patient's underlying self-state* that we can frame our clinical responses. Our evaluation of those responses will remain the same self-psychological criteria that Ornstein (1990) has outlined: "how well the analyst will be able to understand the patient's communications, how well he/she will be able to get this understanding across (verbally and nonverbally), and finally how well this will enhance the patient's deepening self-explorations by making him/her feel understood" (p. 479).

In this way, empathy rewards our rereading and reconsideration by serving as a touchstone, allowing clinicians to adapt Kohut's innovations to the specific needs of their own work and patients, while remaining within distinctively self-psychological sensibility.

REFERENCES

Bacal, H. A. (1995), The essence of Kohut's work and the progress of self psychology. *Psychoanal. Dial.*, 5:353–366.

——— ed. (1998), *Optimal Responsiveness: How Therapist's Heal Their Patients.* Northvale, NJ: Aronson.

——— & Thomson, P. (1998), Optimal responsiveness and the therapist's reaction to the patient's unresponsiveness. In: *Optimal Responsiveness: How Therapist's Heal Their Patients,* ed. H. A. Bacal. Northvale, NJ: Aronson, pp. 249–270.

Basch, M. (1995), Kohut's contribution. *Psychoanal. Dial.*, 5:367–373.

Concise Oxford Dictionary. (1960), London: Oxford University Press.

Cooper, S. (1996), Further remarks on papers by Spezzano and Gerson. *Psychoanal. Dial.*, 6:895–901.

——— & Levit, D. (1998), Old and new objects in Fairbairnian and American relational theory. *Psychoanal. Dial.*, 8:603–624.

Frank, K. (1992), Combining action techniques with psychoanalytic therapy. *Int. R. Psycho-Anal.*, 19:57–79.

Friedman, L. (1997), Ferrum, ignis, and medicina: Return to the crucible. *J. Amer. Psychoanal. Assn.*, 45:20–36.

Gehrie, M. (1993), Psychoanalytic technique and the development of the capacity to reflect. *J. Amer. Psychoanal. Assn.*, 41:1083–1111.

——— (2001), Discussion of Lenoff's "Consequences of 'Empathy': Re-reading Kohut's (1959) 'Examination of the relationship between mode of observation and theory.'" Presented at the 24th Annual Conference on the Psychology of the Self, November, San Francisco.

Gill, M. (1983), The interpersonal paradigm and the degree of the therapist's involvement. *Contemp. Psychoanal.*, 19:202–237.

Goldberg, A. (1985), The definition and role of interpretation. In: *Progress in Self Psychology, Vol. 1*, ed. A. Goldberg. Hillsdale, NJ: The Analytic Press, pp. 62–65.

Hirsch, I. (1994), Countertransference love and theoretical model. *Psychoanal. Dial.*, 4:171–192.

Hoffman, I. (1983), The patient as interpreter of the analyst's experience. *Contemp. Psychoanal.*, 19:389–422.

Jacobs, T. (1986), On countertransference enactments. *J. Amer. Psychoanal. Assn.*, 34:289–307.

Kohut, H. (1959), Introspection, empathy, and psychoanalysis: An examination of the relation between mode of observation and theory. In: *The Search for the Self, Vol. 1*, ed. P. H. Ornstein. New York: International Universities Press, pp. 205–232.

Lenoff, L. (1998), Phantasy selfobjects and the conditions of therapeutic change. In: *The World of Self Psychology: Progress in Self Psychology, Vol. 14*, ed. A. Goldberg. Hillsdale, NJ: The Analytic Press, pp. 147–167.

Lindon, J. (1994), Gratification and provision in psychoanalysis: Should we get rid of "The rule of abstinence"? *Psychoanal. Dial.*, 4:549–582.

Mayer, E. (1996), Changes in science and changing ideas about knowledge and authority in psychoanalysis. *Psychoanal. Quart.*, 65:158–200.

Miller, J. P. (1985), How Kohut actually worked. In: *Progress in Self Psychology, Vol. 1*, ed. A. Goldberg. Hillsdale, NJ: The Analytic Press, pp. 13–30.

Mitchell, S. (1984), Object relations theories and the developmental tilt. *Contemp. Psychoanal.*, 20:473–499.

——— (1988), *Relational Concepts in Psychoanalysis.* Cambridge, MA: Harvard University Press.

Ornstein, P. (1990), How to "enter" a psychoanalytic process conducted by another analyst: A self psychology view. *Psychoanal. Inq.*, 10:478–497.

——— (1991), From narcissism to ego psychology to self psychology. In: *Freud's "On Narcissism: An Introduction,"* ed. J. Sandler, E. Person & P. Fonagy. New Haven, CT: Yale University Press, pp. 175–194.

——— (1993), Is self psychology on a promising trajectory? In: *The Widening Scope of Self Psychology: Progress in Self Psychology, Vol. 9*, ed. A. Goldberg. Hillsdale, NJ: The Analytic Press, pp. 1–11.

——— (1998), My current view of the psychoanalytic process. *Self Psychology Page* [on-line]. Available: http://www.selfpsychology.org/1998conf/preConferenceOrnstein.htm.

Protter, B. (1988), Ways of knowing in psychoanalysis: Some epistemic considerations for an autonomous theory of psychoanalytic praxis. *Contemp. Psychoanal.*, 24:498–526.

Sandler, J. (1983), Reflections on some relations between psychoanalytic concepts and psychoanalytic practice. *Internat. J. Psycho-Anal.*, 64:35–45.

Schwaber, E. (1979), On the "self" within the matrix of analytic theory: Some clinical reflections and reconsiderations. *Internat. J. Psycho-Anal.*, 60:467–479.

Slochower, J. (1991), Variations in the analytic holding environment. *Internat. J. Psycho-Anal.*, 72:709–717.

——— (1994), The evolution of object usage and the holding environment. *Contemp. Psychoanal.*, 30:135–151.

Spezzano, C. (1998), The triangle of clinical judgment. *J. Amer. Psychoanal. Assn.*, 46:365–388.

Stern, S. (1994), Needed relationships and repeated relationships: An integrated relational perspective. *Psychoanal. Dial.*, 4:317–346.

Tansey, M. (1992), Psychoanalytic expertise. *Psychoanal. Dial.*, 2:305–316.

Chapter 3

Twinship Selfobject Experience and Homosexuality

Diane Lawson Martinez

The ubiquity of themes of differentness and alienation in the life stories of our gay patients suggests a consideration of the vicissitudes of the twinship selfobject experience in the psychological development and psychoanalytic treatment of people who are homosexual. In this chapter, I attempt to begin such an exploration and, in doing so, hope to make some contribution to an understanding of normal homosexual development and experience.

Kohut did not elaborate on the twinship selfobject need as thoroughly as he did that of the mirroring and idealizing self experiences. He did, however, emphasize two aspects of the twinship selfobject experience: (1) the feeling of alikeness and (2) the role of twinship in the acquisition of talents and skills (Kohut, 1971, 1984). Alikeness, he proposed, was the foundation of a healthy sense of belonging. With regard to the latter aspect, Kohut felt that an adequate twinship selfobject experience is the basis for a full actualization of the self, in that the development of talents, skills, and efficacy occurs in the context of shared human experience. The twinship selfobject experience, like the mirroring and idealizing selfobject experiences, has its own developmental trajectory. This begins as one comes to feel oneself a member of the human species in the most basic way, proceeds through gender identification, and extends to differentiated experiences of alikeness derived from uniquely determined aspects of the mature self. Kohut (1984) regarded twinship as especially critical during the oedipal phase, when gendered identifications are becoming solidified. I expanded on this point with regard to female oedipal development in a 1993 paper. For a thoughtful review of the work of Kohut and others on the general topic of twinship, one would do well to read Rector (2000).

When, during the course of development, a significant failure has occurred in the realm of the twinship selfobject, the self disturbance reveals itself clinically in feelings of aloneness, isolation, and lack of relatedness to others. Rector (2000) outlines the characteristic vulnerabilities that can be expected when twinship experiences are not adequately provided early on. Detrick (1985, 1986) has described how this particular self-disturbance can be sexualized. He notes, as does Rector, that the more archaic the deficit, the more important it may be that the partner not give evidence of a separate individual personality. As one of my gay patients put it, "I always hope he won't say anything and ruin my fantasy."

Basch (1988, 1992) used the term *kinship* in his elaboration of Kohut's twinship concept. Basch felt that the kinship selfobject experience was the most basic in what he considered a hierarchy of the three selfobject functions. He asserted that a fundamental intactness in this part of the self is a prerequisite for engagement in a therapeutic process. In the same vein, Gorney (1998) has suggested that immersion in the twinship selfobject experience is a precondition for the generation of vitality in therapy. In sum, self psychological theory holds that an adequate twinship selfobject experience is the basis for feeling genuinely a part of the human race and one's gender and for the development of competence and vitality. It may even be a requirement for making use of psychotherapy.

In the life narratives of people who are gay, the feeling of alienation may first be manifest as a sense of being essentially different and may long precede any conscious awareness of homosexual orientation. This experience of differentness is confusing and painful. Vaughan (1998) poignantly describes this situation and how it can compromise the development of the self:

> The sense that one is different is generally not neutral; many lesbians have an idea from early childhood that they are not only different but that such difference is problematic and bad. They conclude that they should keep whatever is different hidden—that they should sequester a part of themselves from others, sometimes even before quite knowing what that part actually is [p. 162].

Gardner (1987) has proposed that self-esteem goals and values take different forms in the two genders because cultural attitudes about women affect child rearing. She wonders that if this is the case for male and female heterosexuals, how much more might it be an issue for people with homosexual, bisexual, or transgendered orientations.

Galatzer-Levy (2001) has thoughtfully questioned how much the life stories of homosexual people are retrospectively reframed around the issue of sexual orientation to create a coherent narrative. Although this point is well taken, it does not seem to me to detract fundamentally from the particular importance of the twinship experience in such circumstances. I suggest that the internalized feelings of differentness and the experience of alienation that are usual and expectable parts of being gay in this culture will of necessity intensify twinship selfobject needs. Traumas in the realm of twinship experience arise out of two distinct types of empathic failure: (1) the absence of a needed twinship response and (2) a toxic, rejecting response to a normal twinship yearning. In our culture, people who are homosexual are at particular risk for both types of injury throughout their development.

CLINICAL EXAMPLE

The following material[1] is organized around three interventions that, during the course of treatment, had special meaning for my analysand. They qualify as "moments of meeting" as defined by Stern et al. (1998), in that they were nodal events that altered the intersubjective context and proved mutative. Specifically, following each intervention, the analysand demonstrated an increased capacity to tolerate painful affects and seemed to relate from a more integrated self. The relevance of these moments to the twinship selfobject experience will be addressed in my discussion.

Larry, a 30-something lawyer, came to see me requesting an analysis. He had heard about analysis from a friend of a friend. His stated reason for wanting an analysis was fairly unusual. He wanted to be able to sing and dance in public without anxiety. As an afterthought, he added that an analysis might lead to an improvement in his love relationships. Larry is gay and was in his first long-term relationship. He and his lover Tom had been commuting to see each other since they had met about a year and a half before. Larry was ambivalent about Tom. Although he felt genuinely fond of him and valued their history, Tom was not as handsome, bright, or sensitive as he might be. Nonetheless, Larry thought Tom might be the best he could expect. Larry wanted him to relocate so that they could live

---

[1] Names and other details have been altered in this clinical example to protect confidentiality. The patient has reviewed the paper and agreed to its publication. The clinical process is as exact a replication as memory and notes allow.

together. Tom, however, could not find a job to equal the one he had and was conflicted about fully embracing a homosexual lifestyle. On the professional front, Larry seemed to be well regarded at his firm, despite his tendency to deliberately make the more conservative members there uneasy with his homosexuality.

Larry was the fourth child in a large family. His parents were farmers who were not very expressive. Larry always felt himself to be "odd man out." Unlike his siblings, he was interested in music and academics. His parents seemed to have recognized his differentness, and he thought they were more puzzled by him than overtly rejecting. His father seemed progressively at a loss for how to connect with Larry as he grew into latency and adolescence. Larry felt most acutely out of place in high school, where he was ridiculed by peers and called "fag." While he earned respect for academic success, he was cruelly teased and rejected by the "jocks."

Larry had had sexual fantasies about boys from earliest memory. He did have a girlfriend in high school with whom he had intercourse. It was pleasurable enough, but Larry hated the kissing and avoided her breasts, which he found distasteful. He became openly homosexual during his college years and engaged in brief, emotionally uninvolved sexual encounters through law school and beyond. He prided himself on his sexual prowess and versatility, yet carried a deep feeling of inadequacy about himself "as a man." While he longed for a life partner, he was unable to make this kind of connection.

Although Larry professed to be no longer grieving, I was moved by his description during our first session of the death of both his parents and an older brother during the preceding few years. His mother's death, about a year before he came to see me, had been particularly painful for him. Larry had assumed a caretaking role with her after his father had died, and they were "like girlfriends." Without her, he felt very alone. He was moved to tears by my simple comment that he had had a lot of losses. Larry reported the following dream in his first session on the couch: "My mother's voice was on my answering machine. She said a storm was coming." Larry dismissed the dream as "meaningless." This corresponded with my impression that Larry was out of touch with his affective self and unconsciously fearful of it.

"I Know You Do, Larry"

In the early months of the analysis, Larry tended to talk nonstop, articulately but with detachment, detailing daily occurrences. There was little space (and no demand) for me to respond. In keeping with the expected countertransference to a primitive, mirroring selfobject transference, I would at times feel near anesthetized. He wanted me to listen and remember, but none of my attempts at interpretive intervention had a deepening effect on the process. Where was that storm, I wondered? The content of the sessions was about Tom and encounters with other homosexual men. He discussed which men he found attractive, which men found him so, and whether he could have sex with them if he desired. He lusted after very handsome, muscular men with "perfect bodies." Their finding him attractive would send his self-regard rocketing. He would "lick boots" for compliments from such a man. He said, "Whenever someone consents to have sex with me, it is like I get possession of their admired attributes. The parts of them I'm jealous I don't have. I want some guy to *want* to be with me, to hold me, to make me more confident. To make up for my weaknesses." He most dreaded being considered a "queen" by a masculine man. What he felt he was missing were not physical attributes, but some hard-to-define sense of manliness that came from being a man connected to another man. If, instead, he felt ignored or insulted by someone, he always had a ready angle from which to devalue that person. He had similar but nonsexualized concerns in his interactions with others he encountered during his day. In short, Larry was involved in a constant effort to regulate his self-esteem in this fashion.

After a few weeks, it became apparent that his long-distance relationship with Tom, even with nightly calls and phone sex, was not enough to provide what Larry needed if he was to avoid sexual involvements with other men, as he aspired. These "slip-ups" seemed to me a response to disappointments. For example, one evening when he could not reach Tom, Larry placed himself where he was sure to be picked up. He declined my suggestion, however, of any link between the behavior and his disappointment. Rather, he insisted that the episode and his lack of discrimination about his partner that night were caused only by his healthy, though near-insatiable, sexual appetite.

About five months into the analysis, Tom precipitously ended the relationship. Larry launched into a frantic search for a replacement. With me, he alternated between brief moments of deep sadness and prolonged stretches in which he defended himself from painful affect by devaluing Tom. It was important to him that I appreciated his sadness even though he found it hard to bear for more than a few seconds at a time. At termination, he still considered one of the three most memorable moments of the analysis to have been my response to his tearful, "I want Tom back." I had said, matter-of-factly, "I know you do, Larry." In the wake of this comment, Larry came to acknowledge for the first time that the nature of his search was perhaps not as discriminating as seeking a boyfriend. He ultimately labeled it his "any willing provider" state, and the dilemma as Mr. Right versus Mr. Right Now.

"Chinese Food"

Once, after I had announced I would be away, Larry took what he characterized as a "simple walk" to a park well known for homosexual cruising. He protested the connection I saw between the two events: "I wasn't horny last Wednesday because you canceled." I took this disruption as the first clear indication that a sustaining, selfobject transference had been established. Larry began to speak openly, though cynically, about wanting me to admire him. He would blatantly fish for compliments but would brush off the significance of these feelings whenever I tried to address his apparent yearning. He was even more uneasy around fantasies and thoughts that reflected his idealized experience of me. For example, he sheepishly reported a dream that consisted only of seeing me. I looked "radiant" and was "beautifully dressed." The best part, he said, was that he could look at me as long as he wanted. I said it sounded as if he was yearning to take in something from me. His response was that if my life was wonderful, then his would be too. He went on to say that he had been told recently by friends that he was calmer. He had even begun to wonder if he might be able to have a relationship with a woman but just could not imagine any sexual feelings, especially with me. He thought it would be very different if I were a man. He had a fantasy of falling as he left a session and of my picking him up without effort. It was in this context that he reported a dream:

> My cat was acting strange. There was some noise in the house. She sees a strange cat. I throw it outside gently. Before I can get the door closed, the cat comes back in as a person: a young, bare-chested guy. Someone had been messing around with my stereo. Then we were transported to a rocky cliff. I invited him to join our group. The others came and we were all dressed similarly in white jockey shorts. We crossed the river easily, like in a herd. Everyone was nice to me. A strong person barges into the house. I deal with him and they develop respect for me. I was no longer a sissy.

Larry thought the dream reflected a better feeling about himself that just perhaps had to do with his analysis: the feeling that he was no longer a sissy (or a "pussy," in keeping with the dream imagery). Being part of the herd of men was absolutely exquisite, he said, the very experience for which he had always longed. My understanding of the analytic process was that an idealized selfobject transference had been established and that he could experience being twinned with me as an idealized male.

About a year into the analysis, the following session took place:

Larry: I think I'm running out of things to talk about.

DM: (I associate to the last line of Roth's *Portnoy's Complaint*: "So. Now vee may perhaps to begin. Yes?")

Larry: (Proceeds immediately to recount the previous evening's events, which included a blatant sexual flirtation with Ruben, a man he had met.)

DM: (To my mind, this was a rather predictable response to a disappointment in a relationship. In this case, it was Roger, another man he had just started dating, whom Larry had described in the previous session as having been cool to him.) I wonder if the shape of your encounter with Ruben doesn't have to do with your being shaken up by Roger's coolness.

Larry: So, I need *someone's* interest, some positive response to my appearance. After all, *you* never tell me what you think about my body. That I have a nice chest or a nice butt. But I do. I see myself in the mirror when I'm jacking off. My chest all pumped up. I look like a burly man.

DM: [As Stern et al. (1998) describe as typical for "now moments," I was feeling unbalanced by this uncharacteristic and intense focus on my response.] You know, at times when you're unsure of your appeal, you so much yearn for those compliments—feel you need them, as if they'll provide something essential for you. Yet I've noticed that the positive effect is gone in 30 minutes—like that saying about eating Chinese food. (Even at the time, I wondered to myself why I was using this tired analogy.)

Larry: (uncharacteristically reflective) It *is* about an old feeling—like feeling excluded from the company of jocks in high school. They didn't want me on their teams. (Tears) Why didn't they find me okay? (quickly distancing himself from the affect) I think I'm just not happy with how my house looks these days.

DM: It's about your self, Larry, not your house.

Larry: (testily) About what then! My gayness? Okay. So I'd rather not be gay. But that's the way it is. I could have lived without being gay. I wanted to fit in with those guys more than anything. So what? So it will be a short-lived pleasantry with Ruben. He'd look okay with his clothes off.

DM: A fix for your self-esteem.

Larry: I *know* that. Okay? Life just dealt a different hand to me. If I had a boy, he would be on team sports. I'd not have him go through what I went through.

This session was notable on two counts, which, as I'll discuss later, I now think are related. It was the first time I felt I'd "lost it" and let my frustration show. And, surprising to me, Larry's response was a profound and genuine acknowledgment of his sense of deficiency. The next day, we continued:

Larry: I had a dream last night: There was a sharp edge on some playground material—like a metal slide or something. I'm on some sort of flying machine. I cut my knee on the edge. There was a huge gash. About five inches long. Very bloody. My mother was there. I wasn't crying. I have *no* idea what that dream was about. I really don't cry when I'm hurt. Didn't when I was a kid either, for that matter.

DM: I wonder if you felt I had a sharp edge yesterday.

Larry: Yeah. The thing about Chinese food. I don't need compliments *all* the time. Well, maybe from heterosexual white guys I do. From them I want to feel truly accepted. Not because I am a rich lawyer and could get them out of trouble someday. I want approval from those least likely to give it. They'd say, "This little fag. Who does he think he is?" Dismiss me as an idiot. I want to be accepted by straight guys. That's why I was rude to that client the other day. He wants to avoid paying child support. *He* doesn't feel like a grown man. He has a kid and doesn't feel like a man! I *never* feel like a man. To be grown up you need to be married to a woman and have two kids. I'll never have that. I should get married. But my wife would have to let me have a gay man around. I wonder what it would be like to have sex with a woman. That's a stupid thing to say. I *know*. I did it when I was a teenager. It wasn't *too* bad. Wonder whatever happened to that woman lawyer from the other firm who seemed interested in me. She never called like she said she would. I can be a top. What's the difference? I don't think I'm *afraid* of women. How could it *not* be fun to play kissy-kissy with her? Especially if she kissed my neck the right way. What do you think?

DM: I think there is a lot of pain around these longings to be accepted – and that you felt cut down by my comments yesterday rather than understood.

Larry: I suppose I did. But there is no good resolution to this longing for acceptance. I'm not going to have a kid. I can go to Bali, but no baby. I can buy a beach house, but no baby. (Very sad) But don't worry, I'll be okay. I don't *always* think about it. Straight guys have it easy. They can walk around proud, head up. Showing pictures of their baby in a sailor suit like my mom had me wear. I'll never *really* be a man. *Never*. Never father a child. I'll just be an old gay guy. And I would be a good father.

"Armani Suit"

Following this, affects of rejection, loss, inadequacy as a man, and yearning for acceptance continued to be more accessible. In parallel, Larry's urgent sexual behavior diminished. Then, over a weekend, Larry had sex with several different partners, including one from a cruise in the park. He recounted each in dispassionate detail, as if it were all great, deliberate fun. He then related a dream about a plant he watered that "overflowed—really overflowed." He insisted he had no associations to this dream. I suggested it might have to do with the intense feelings he had been getting in touch with threatening to overflow.

Larry: (with a bored dismissive tone) Oh I don't think so. I *am* surprised that *you* aren't more upset about my going to the park. You think it's more dangerous than I do. But I did say I'd never go again and then I did. Now you won't believe what I say. Credibility is essential for an attorney.

DM: (in fact, very much concerned about the risks of his behavior and the strength of his disavowal) You don't have as much control over that behavior as you try to tell yourself you do. I know that the resolve you can feel at one moment disappears when you're in another state of mind.

Larry: I wasn't dissociated. I knew what I was *doing*. I can't use that for a defense strategy. I'm just looking for a boyfriend. I don't want to spend my life alone. You don't understand what it is like for a gay man. Where else am I going to find someone?

DM: (my frustrated response out of my mouth before I could think) Larry, looking for a life partner in that park is like shopping at Kmart for an Armani suit.

Larry: (uncharacteristic moment of silence, punctuated by sighs) So . . . okay, Dr. Martinez. Where is the Armani store?

DM: I know it's not easy.

Larry: My hands are getting numb.

DM: That usually tells us that you're anxious.

Larry: (starts recounting in graphic detail his most prized sexual encounter of the weekend.)

DM: You're focusing on sex to try to manage your anxiety.

Larry: Oh, God, you're making too much of this. I went to the park because I'm a horn dog. (More reflectively) But, you are right, I don't know why I was *so* horny. Last weekend, I did feel compelled to rent those dirty videos when it became clear it wasn't going to work out with Roger. Tomorrow is Valentine's Day. I have *no one* to send roses to. (genuinely sad) Now the thought comes that I could send them to you. I wouldn't! Don't worry. But what would that thought mean? Richard says I'm getting snooty about my analysis. I don't know why I'd be anxious now. It must be that I just don't like the idea of not being in control of myself.

DM: I think it is very difficult to have me become so important to you.

Over the next several weeks, Larry would more often share his longings to see himself as being special to me and to look up to me as someone who could take care of him. However, these thoughts continued to be expressed in his self-mocking "hit-and-run" fashion that allowed for little discussion. He struggled with the impulse to find out from others in the community more about my personal life. He wanted to know but feared he might learn something that would disappoint him. Then in one of his ambivalent forays, he learned that I was divorced. His first response was to see me as a victim and my "ex" as a scoundrel. He felt depressed and hopeless about his own future. I said that learning that my life was not ideal had shaken his sense of security. He dreamed that a building was "shattered" by a huge earthquake. Within a week or so, he had reconstituted himself and the idealizing aspect of the transference by focusing on how remarkably well I had weathered the divorce. With regard to his twinship yearnings, it made him feel more of a bond to me that I'd survived a loss like the one he had experienced with Tom. He went out of town for a weekend alone and did not seek any sexual encounters. He felt pleased with himself that he could do this; in his mind, not hopping "willy-nilly" into another relationship made him resemble me.

A session several months later, two days before I was to leave for a vacation, demonstrates Larry's increased tolerance of affect and self-cohesion:

Larry: Last night I had a dream that I was punched in the face. (somewhat playfully) What could that have to do with?
DM: Any chance it might have to do with my vacation?
Larry: Hmm. Maybe. You will be out of a three-week vignette of my life. If there were a sad feeling about that, it would be about the things you won't know. (sarcastically) You won't know about all the people who "ooh and aah" over me.
DM: It's a lost opportunity to feel appreciated?
Larry: This analytic exercise can be drudgery. But, basically, I'm so narcissistic I like to hear myself talk.
DM: There seems to be a sustaining quality to knowing that I know.
Larry: Better put, there is a bleakness to no one knowing.
DM: Was there anyone who you felt knew you in this way when you were young?
Larry: Nobody. My mother was too busy putting out fires with my siblings. I have a soothing part of me that is from my mother, but an interested part? It's just not there. There is an antagonistic, critical part that's from her too. "Your problems with others may be your own fault." But my prissy, narcissistic character traits do bring on some things. I'm more like my mom than my dad. That was a tender, empathic question you asked, by the way. My mother would *forget* my birthday. I could never understand that. That's why I don't care about my birthday. You know, there was a teacher in high school who asked me who I could tell my problems to. I said I didn't have anyone. She said, "Everyone needs *someone* to talk to who will give them milk and cookies when they need it." She said, "I'll be your cookie lady, Larry." I guess that's what you have become, and I'll miss having that for three weeks.

DISCUSSION

Throughout the analysis, Larry referred to the "I know you do, Larry," "Chinese food," and "Armani suit" interventions as turning points in our work. When I would ask Larry what it was about these particular interventions, he would say things like they were not the usual analyst sort of comments and must therefore have really come from me or that the affect accompanying these interactions made him feel that I cared about him. The depiction of a "moment of meeting" (Stern et al., 1998) resonates with Larry's explanation. I have come to believe that the importance of the three comments—what made them "moments of meeting," in that something occurred that resulted in a progressive shift in Larry's self-organization—had very much to do with the twinship selfobject transference. This idea did not come at once. First, I had to realize that Larry did not take for granted, as I was inclined to assume, that he and I had an essential alikeness.

Another part of this process was the realization that, despite Larry's enthusiasm, I felt some discomfort about these interventions. The first comment felt lame, and the other two actually felt slightly foreign to me. In retrospect, the first comment was a blatant declaration of twinship: "I know you do, Larry." That is, we humans feel that way. As for the latter two interventions, I considered how Larry greatly appreciates fine objects and food, particularly when obtained at a good price. Most of the time, he saw his analysis as meeting these criteria. He also often made use of metaphor in a way that includes humor and some distancing. So these latter two interventions, in their content and form, were in a sense my version of *his* style. These three episodes might even be considered enactments, in that I responded to the intense pull from him for us to "speak the same language" or be alike. Thus, the twinship aspect of the experience of these moments seemed to be an active therapeutic factor.

These three spontaneous comments emerged at times when I was frustrated with the process. To the extent that they were premeditated, they were directed at undermining Larry's disavowal of painful affects of loss, inadequacy, and desperate aloneness. Unconsciously framed in ways that emphasized our alikeness, the interventions forged a connection between us and, in doing so, seemingly fostered integration of disavowed affects and the behaviors they fueled. In other words, my best understanding of these moments is that, for Larry, they consolidated a feeling that we were enough alike that he could bear to embrace the urgent experience of his self-deficits. Later in the analysis, his experience of our alikeness in our both being professionals and in the vicissitudes of a monogamous relationship (he with a man about his age—named, of course, Larry) were more mature expressions of the twinship experience with me. Consistent with Gorney's (1998) suggestion, the vitality of Larry's life experiences increased in conjunction with the experience and understanding of our twinship bond.

In a previous discussion of this case, Fisch (1996) speculated that, for Larry, the twinship route was the most viable path for consolidation of the self. He wondered if Larry may have chosen a female analyst in hopes that he could reestablish the twinship selfobject experience he had had with his mother. This time, however, the experience was with a selfobject who could connect with and appreciate his particular form of manliness, as opposed to his capacity to be a "girlfriend." Fisch made the point that a mother who enjoys and accepts her son's maleness is a factor as powerful as the bond to his father in the consolidation of a male-gendered self. Although his mother's acceptance of him as her "girlfriend" may have served to keep alive Larry's sense of being part of the human race, it may also have undermined his sense of what optimally might have been a proud sense of gay manliness. In other words, his mother offered a twinship experience at the expense of his masculinity.

Considering now the acquisition of talents and skills and twinship, it has seemed to me that the inability of Larry and other gay male patients of mine to feel a twinship bond to their fathers served to undermine their experience of being effective and successful in ways that have nothing to do with sexuality. This would support Kohut's contention that alikeness and acquisition of skills and talents are tied together. I have seen this again recently in my treatment of a 40-year-old gay man who has felt inadequate and unqualified in his profession despite being highly regarded in his field and quite financially successful. A belated capacity, acquired in his work in therapy, to feel that he is in some essential ways very like his father, despite the difference in their sexual object choice, seemingly allowed him to experience himself as competent and accomplished. This occurred in a parallel way in the transference, as revealed around his giving me a CD for the holidays: "It is Ella Fitzgerald in her forties; like you and me: in her prime, effortlessly doing her work."

One implication of all this for treatment would seem to be that the therapist or analyst need be particularly sensitive to twinship/kinship issues in work with gay patients. Does this mean that a gay person should see only a gay therapist, as some would have it? Obviously, I do not think this is true. One of my gay male patients had in fact worked with a gay male therapist prior to seeing me. This therapist had very clear and fixed ideas about what a gay man should be about. This patient, although the treatment had been of some benefit to him, had come from it with the idea that he was no better at being a *gay* man, as defined by his therapist, than at being a heterosexual man. Like the other selfobject transferences, a twinship transference may go entirely unnoticed until something disrupts the bond. Also, as demonstrated in Larry's case, a twinship selfobject transference may be somewhat obscured by manifestations of mirroring and idealizing selfobject transferences, which are generally more noticeable to us.

It is worth mentioning in this context how the therapist's grounding in heterosexist cultural norms may interfere with the kind of empathic knowing that provides the basis for twinship experience. In recent papers, Friedman (1998), Galatzer-Levy (2001), and Roughton (2001) emphasize the risk of such misattunements. Specifically, Friedman makes the point that heterosexual analysts or therapists are, at times, unempathic toward gay male patients around the issue of anonymous or promiscuous sex, which he feels is not necessarily a manifestation of pathology: "If the analyst is unable to resonate with bisexual activity with multiple partners then a vital part of many gay patients will be perceived as unappreciated" (p. 3). In retrospect, I think I may have been too quick to pathologize some of Larry's sexual involvements. Although there clearly were times when his sexual activity served to ward off fragmentation experiences or bolster a shaky sense of self, there were also times when it was consensual, fun sport—a belated jock experience, perhaps.

Finally, my point is that people who are gay are particularly vulnerable to experiencing failures in the environment's capacity to provide the twinship selfobject experience necessary for healthy self-development. This happens, in part, because images of the self are *so* dependent initially on gendered images of self and other held by primary caretakers. Later experiences with siblings and peers are also crucial. The gay child often has difficulty experiencing twinship with same-sex others, whether parents, siblings, or peers. This may be because of the child's ability to find the self in the other, but may well have to do with the withdrawal of the other in the face of finding differentness, as we so often see with fathers of gay sons. Such a withdrawal of engagement and availability for selfobject experience affects not only the formation of the child's gendered self. Also potentially at risk are a more global sense of membership in the human race, the opportunity to cultivate skills and talents, and the experience of the self as vital and effective. The analyst or therapist must be sensitive to the development and importance of the twinship selfobject transference, particularly to reactions and biases in him- or herself that may interfere with the gay patient's opportunity to make use of this avenue of renewed self-development and healing.

REFERENCES

Basch, M. (1988), *Understanding Psychotherapy: The Science Behind the Art.* New York: Basic Books.

——— (1992), *Practicing Psychotherapy: A Casebook.* New York: Basic Books.

Detrick, D. (1985), Alterego phenomena the alterego transferences. In: *Progress in Self Psychology, Vol. 1,* ed. A. Goldberg. New York: Guilford, pp. 240–256.

——— (1986), Alterego phenomena and the alterego transferences: Some further considerations. In: *Progress in Self Psychology, Vol. 2,* ed. A. Goldberg. New York: Guilford, pp. 299–304.

Fisch, J. (1996), Discussion of case presentation by Diane Martinez. Panel I: From the standpoint of the self–selfobject matrix. Presented at the 19th Annual Conference on the Psychology of the Self, Washington, DC.

Friedman, H. (1998), Self psychology and homosexuality: Potentials and liabilities in the psychoanalysis of gay men utilizing self psychology. Unpublished manuscript.

Galatzer-Levy, R. (2001), Finding our way in perplexity: The meanings of sex in the analysis of a gay man. *J. Amer. Psychoanal. Assn.,* 49:1219–1234.

Gardner, J. (1987), Self psychology as feminist theory. *Signs,* 12:761–780.

Gorney, J. (1998), Twinship, vitality and pleasure. In: *The World of Self Psychology: Progress in Self Psychology, Vol. 14,* ed. A. Goldberg. Hillsdale, NJ: The Analytic Press, pp. 85–106.

Kohut, H. (1971), *The Analysis of the Self: A Systematic Approach in the Psychoanalytic Treatment of Narcissistic Personality Disorders.* New York: International Universities Press.

——— (1984), *How Does Analysis Cure?* ed. A. Goldberg & P. Stepansky. Chicago: University of Chicago Press.

Martinez, D. (1993), The good girl, the bad girl, their mothers, and the analyst: The role of the twinship selfobject in female oedipal development. In: *The Widening Scope of Self Psychology: Progress in Self Psychology, Vol. 9,* ed. A. Goldberg. Hillsdale, NJ: The Analytic Press, pp. 87–107.

Rector, L. (2000), Developmental aspects of the twinship selfobject need in religious experience. In: *How Responsive Should We Be? Progress in Self Psychology, Vol. 16,* ed. A. Goldberg. Hillsdale, NJ: The Analytic Press, pp. 257–275.

Roughton, R. (2001), Four men in treatment: An evolving perspective on homosexuality and bisexuality, 1965 to 2000. *J. Amer. Psychoanal. Assn.,* 49:1188–1217.

Stern, D. N., Sander, L. W., Nahum, J. P., Harrison, A. M., Lyons-Ruth, K., Morgan, A. C., Bruschweiler-Stern, N. & Tronick, E. Z. (1998), Noninterpretive mechanisms in psychoanalytic therapy: The something more than interpretation. *Internat. J. Psycho-Anal.,* 79:903–921.

Vaughan, S. (1998), Psychoanalytic and biological perspectives on lesbian patients: Why developmental themes are more important in psychotherapy. *Harvard Rev. Psychiat.,* 6:160–164.

Chapter 4

Empathy and Self-Expression: Confessions of a Sometimes Angry Self Psychologist

Marc L. Miller

Self psychologically oriented analysts[1] (in contrast to analysts of other analytic schools) tend to be particularly attuned to the developmentally based fragility of their patients' self-organization. These analysts tend to see their patients as requiring them to provide certain needed selfobject functions (including mirroring and idealizing) for prolonged periods of time, during which the patients are assumed to be unable to tolerate the direct (i.e., verbal) expression of the analyst's experience as a separate subjective "other." While interpersonal, relational and other analysts have criticized self psychologists for underestimating their patients' resiliency in the face of nonempathic (let alone confrontational and aggressive) interventions, self psychologists as a group seem much more comfortable taking the risk of erring on the side of being "too empathic," rather than risking doing harm to potentially vulnerable patients by imposing their own nonempathic subjectivity on the patient. The self psychology literature has numerous examples (see Trop and Stolorow, 1992; Teicholz, 1999) of analyses that lasted for long periods (sometimes

[1] I am including the "intersubjective" writers, namely Robert Stolorow and his collaborators, in this category.

many years) during which the analyst valiantly strove to "decenter" from his or her frustration and/or anger to maintain a sustained empathic stance with the patient. For prolonged periods, these analysts deemed their patients too narcissistically vulnerable and fragile to tolerate any shift from such a stance.

Judith Teicholz (1999), a self-psychological author who has written extensively about the interface between self psychology and postmodern, relational theory, exemplifies this perspective. She wrote, "on the few occasions when I seem to have 'broken down,' when intense countertransference pressures and failure of self-containment have led me to *impose* my subjectivity on a patient who was not ready to handle it, I have felt that our relationship and the treatment process suffered a major setback that sometimes took months or even years to make up" (p. 149; emphasis added). She presents case material that I find very interesting, and somewhat troubling. She reports:

> With one such patient—after my professional guilt had been building for 15 months for offering him none of what I then thought of as my psychoanalytic repertoire—I "broke down" and tried to "test the waters" of his tolerance by making a simple observation that went slightly beyond what he was presenting of himself. He reddened, stopped speaking for five minutes, and then fled the session. Until then a patient with "perfect attendance," he missed the following session without even calling to cancel or explain. When he returned he was able to speak only haltingly of the mortification I had caused him by my observation in the previous session. He said, "Until last session, coming to my meetings with you had been like taking a long warm shower, playfully lathering myself with soap, singing off-key at the top of my lungs—reveling in the good feeling and feeling safe and accepted by you. But when I realized you were observing me from the outside, I suddenly felt that I hadn't been alone and private all that time at all. I suddenly felt as if the whole time I thought I'd been enjoying a private shower, everyone I knew and strangers, too, had been standing outside of the shower, watching me through a huge picture window that I'd believed had been an opaque wall or mirror" [pp. 149–150].

This patient eloquently articulated his subjective experience of solipsistic self-involvement in the presence of the invisible, unrecognized archaic selfobject/analyst and also the experience of having that fantasy shattered by what he experienced as the analyst's unempathic intrusion.

Teicholz (1999), reflecting on what happened between her and her patient, states the following:

> Feeling that we were not getting any analytic work done, concerned that I was "allowing" the patient to have too good a time at the expense of his treatment and potential for change, worrying that he did not recognize me as a separate individual, I had made an interpersonal observation of my patient that turned out nearly to destroy the analytic relationship. After these feelings and judgments had persisted in me for several months, I had impinged on my patient with an observation that brought my separateness too much into his awareness. I believe that I disrupted something very important that was going on beneath the surface of our interactions, which had to do with the patient's using our sessions to feel my recognition and affirmation. On the basis of my later experience with other patients who showed similar degrees of vulnerability but with whom I tolerated my feelings of psychoanalytic uselessness longer than with the patient I just described, I believe that, had I been able to hold on to my interpersonal observations a little bit longer, my patient would have begun to develop the "observing ego" and self-cohesion to begin making useful and growth-promoting observations of himself; and I could have saved the treatment from the unnecessary setback caused by my having exposed him to feelings of mortification [p. 150].

While Teicholz acknowledged that "with the majority of the patients [she has] worked with, the analyst's self-expressiveness has not been an issue at all" (p. 150), with certain patients the analytic relationship is seen, potentially, as an encounter between the patient's fragility and the analyst's power to inflict injury.

In the case presented by Teicholz, she felt frustrated because, for 15 long months, she had been unable to provide anything to the patient except "verbalizations of recognition and affirmation," reflecting exactly what he told her, or else remaining silent. She does not tell us about her earlier attempts to do otherwise with this particular patient but does suggest that her empathic attunement to similar patients' "body language or through cues from their autonomic nervous system" let her know that they were "extraordinarily fragile," and therefore, it was not "safe" for her to intervene in any other way. Being with the patient under such self-negating conditions apparently proved too difficult for her to contain and decenter from her own subjective experience. When she did "break down" and "test the waters" by "making a simple observation that went slightly beyond what he was presenting himself," he "fled the session" and missed the next session. When he returned (and he *did* return), he was quite eloquent in his ability to talk about the experience. Based on Teicholz's report, I remain unconvinced about her inference that this episode was particularly catastrophic to either the patient or to the treatment process. If she had been even more patient and withheld her "disjunctive subjectivity" for "a little bit longer," I'm not so sure things would have been any different at that point.

It seems to me that her intervention marked an important turning point in the treatment. From that point on, her patient could no longer maintain the solipsistic fantasy that he was alone in the room, could survive the dissolution of that fantasy, and could begin to work collaboratively with his analyst to address issues that both of them had previously been avoiding. The fact that this patient was able to return after missing only one visit and to discuss his experience so articulately upon returning speaks to his having more "observing ego" than his analyst had realized. This also speaks to the solidity of the selfobject bond, the interpersonal connection between patient and analyst, that had been developing and had been operating silently "in the background" during the previous months of treatment. Whether this particular patient needed all of those 15 months to establish a strong-enough selfobject bond to withstand the so-called "empathic failure" described in this anecdote, or whether less time would have sufficed, is a difficult and probably impossible question to answer. I assume that the treatment process that ensued was often a difficult one, for both patient and analyst, and that it took a while to reestablish anything close to the sense of safety and security that the patient had experienced during the previous period of treatment. I am not so sure that the analyst's appraisal that their "relationship and the treatment process suffered a major setback" takes into account the positive, growth-promoting aspects also derived from this experience.

I think it is safe to generalize that self psychologists as a group tend to avoid expressing their own subjectivity if they sense that such self-expression might be experienced as threatening to the patient's vulnerable self-organization. In so doing, the analyst may underestimate the patient's ability to tolerate such a disjunctive experience. I think this is especially true about the expression of the analyst's anger, a point to which I will return later.

In contrast, I think that many analysts who are not self-psychologically oriented tend to underestimate the vulnerability and fragility of their patients, especially in the context of a regressive transference. They tend to be more likely to intervene more quickly and with less empathic sensitivity vis-à-vis their patients. At times, this will not be harmful because the patient may indeed have the strength and resiliency to tolerate and even benefit from the analyst's input. At other times, however, with those patients whose self-structure or ego strength is truly fragile, such interventions might be experienced by the patient as assaultive and may be experienced as retraumatizations (i.e., repetitions of earlier selfobject failures against which the patient had been powerless to protect himself or herself in childhood). It is in response to such early traumas that "structures of pathological accommodation" (Brandchaft, 1994), namely defensive, self-protective personality patterns, develop. The reexperiencing of such traumas in the therapy context can, potentially, be extremely useful; however, if such experiences flood the patient with anxiety or recreate an intersubjective atmosphere of danger, the therapeutic benefit can be replaced by the patient's self-protective (defensive) need to "simply" survive the trauma.

Within the world of contemporary psychoanalysis, for those analysts who identify themselves as "relational," "interpersonal," and "neo-Kleinian," for example, the self psychological approach (as exemplified in Teicholz's case), with its clear emphasis on the analyst's empathic attunement to the patient's fragility and vulnerability, would likely be seen as too gentle, too infantilizing of the patient, avoidant or in denial of the patient's anger and aggression, and even "inauthentic." Postmodern–relational analytic writers, including Irwin Hoffman, Owen Renik, Lewis Aron, and Stephen Mitchell, have written about possible limitations and pitfalls inherent in the analyst's overcommitment to the maintenance of an empathic stance. These authors have focused on the potential for the analyst's "ritualization" of empathy to undermine the patient's sense of trust in the analytic relationship, the potential of the analyst's empathy to infantilize the patient and weaken the patient's sense of autonomy, and the possible incompatibility between the analyst's maintaining an empathic stance and being authentically present in the analytic relationship.

In his book *A Meeting of Minds,* Aron (1996) wrote:

> It seems obvious that analysts need to empathize with patients. One of the earliest and most consistent findings in the psychotherapy research literature is the importance of the therapist's empathy for the patient. What may be less immediately apparent is that the patient must mutually empathize with the therapist if the therapy is to move forward [p. 129].

In agreement with Aron, I want to emphasize how essential the analyst's empathy is in the psychoanalytic process. Aron's assertion "that the patient must mutually empathize with the therapist" (p. 129) presents much more of a problem, however, as there can be (and is) considerable disagreement about when we can expect our patients to be capable of such "mutual empathy." As a self psychologically oriented analyst, I remain committed to the "stance of sustained empathic inquiry" (Stolorow, Brandchaft, and Atwood, 1987) as the fundamental approach I take in engaging and relating with my patients in the analytic relationship, and I believe that there is nothing inherently "inauthentic" about doing so. However, I frankly believe that some of the concerns expressed by the relational authors do have some justification. I think that self-psychologically oriented analysts, in our commitment to maintaining an empathic stance and our sensitivity to our patients' vulnerabilities, may tend to underestimate their ability to tolerate expressions of our disjunctive subjectivity and to grow from such encounters. I think we should be open to self-scrutiny about becoming too locked into being empathic in a too standardized or "ritualized" way or about feeling compelled to always maintain the empathic stance, even in the face of our own subjective reactions, which are dissonant with being empathic.

These are very complex issues, and I fear that, in reaction to the relational critiques, too many analysts may think they have to abandon empathy altogether (which is clinically impossible) and may adapt a stance of self-disclosure and confrontation that disregards the limitations and vulnerabilities some of our patients might realistically have. While our use of empathy is far from infallible, based as it is on the multifaceted interactions between our patients' subjectivities and our own, I believe it is our efforts at being empathically attuned with our patients' subjective experiences that help inform us about what they can and cannot therapeutically bear. Our theoretical perspectives as analysts undoubtedly influence our empathic assessments.

The self-psychological and intersubjective approaches propose that the analyst's relatively "accurate" empathic attunement to the patient's conscious subjective experience creates an intersubjective connection (or selfobject bond) between patient and analyst that the patient experiences as relatively safe and secure. This sense of safety and security is seen as fostering the gradual integration of dissociated, unconscious experiences, that is, those experiences from childhood that were originally so anxiety-provoking (because they were so threatening to the child's sense of connection with the needed parental figures) that they had to be dissociated or split off into the realm of unconsciousness (i.e., "the dynamic unconscious," as described by Stolorow and Atwood, 1992) to maintain the needed selfobject ties. It is hoped that, in the context of the empathy-based selfobject relationship of the therapy situation, the patient will be able to feel safe enough to permit the uncovering of his or her unconscious, dissociated experiences (including those involving shame, fear and rage), which can then become integrated into the patient's expanded syntonic sense of self.

One complication is that some patients' earlier experiences may have taught them that it is too dangerous to trust "even the most authentic expressions of empathy" and that they "are terrified of the hopes and longings that genuine empathy may stir up" (Teicholz, 1999, pp. 138–139), because of "the dread to repeat" the trauma of empathic failure (Ornstein, 1974, 1990). In such cases, the empathic interpretation of this self-protective dynamic, often repeatedly over time, will foster the patient's taking the risk of engaging with the analyst in the therapeutic process.

Another complication involves the collusion of analyst and patient in avoiding issues that are at all experienced as potentially anxiety-provoking. In striving to maintain the process of sustained empathic inquiry, which is sensitive to their patients' vulnerability, self psychologically oriented analysts may tend to avoid issues that they assume will be experienced as dystonic and threatening for their patients. They may also avoid these issues to maintain their own sense of safety. In addressing such issues with their patients, they may be likely to provoke a rupture in the selfobject bond, which may result in a reaction of intensified anxiety and withdrawal in some patients and overt expressions of anger (including rage) in other patients. Accordingly, both analyst and patient may collude in the avoidance of attending to dystonic issues, often for long periods and sometimes indefinitely (Miller, 1997). Optimally, the analytic relationship can provide a context of connection, a selfobject bond between the two co-participants that can allow the exploration of even dystonic experiences, without threatening the patient's fragile sense of safety and integrity too severely. The relative success that any of us has in approaching this ideal constitutes the greatest challenge to us as analysts and represents the art of the analytic work.

Self psychological authors consistently have recognized that the analyst, as well as the patient, has selfobject needs that are active, and often intensified, in the analytic relationship. Stolorow and Atwood (1992), for example, note: "Not only does the patient turn to the analyst for selfobject experiences, but the analyst also turns to the patient for such experiences" (p. 3). These experiences include our own need for empathic attunement, the need to be recognized as a separate and distinct person, the need to be mirrored and appreciated by our patients, and the need for a sense of emotional safety. As Donna Orange (1995) points out, "Self psychologists at times can be so involved in and devoted to getting and staying close to the patient's experience that we may forget that we are there too" (p. 66). Whether we are always consciously aware of them or not, our selfobject needs are inevitably operating as part of the intersubjective mix. Many of our patients meet our selfobject needs exceedingly well, and some are especially attuned to doing so (Livingston, 1996; Miller, 1997). These tend to be the "nondifficult" patients we enjoy working with most. Much more challenging are those other patients with limited or nonexistent ability to empathize with us and to meet even minimally our own selfobject needs. Whether patients spontaneously develop greater empathic awareness and sensitivity vis-à-vis the analyst is not necessarily a "given." For some patients, empathic awareness of the analyst as a separate subjectivity may be a developmental achievement they have not yet acquired, despite prolonged periods of experiencing the analyst's empathic attunement to them.

Especially challenging are those patients who have a propensity for directing a great deal of hostility at us. While self psychological theory explains that a patient's rage is a reactive response to selfobject failure (with the analyst usually recreating earlier selfobject failures in the current context of the therapy relationship), this theoretical understanding does not always suffice in protecting the analyst from the experience of feeling assaulted and abused. The hostile interpersonal behavior of these patients is very self-defeating because, when the analyst's own sense of safety, security, or self-esteem feels threatened in the context of working with a particular patient, the analyst's ability to provide an empathic milieu for that patient is inevitably diminished. It would ultimately be beneficial for this intersubjective aspect of the relationship to be collaboratively explored in the treatment, but it is precisely this aspect of the relationship that is usually most difficult *to* explore. Such hostile patients, by whom we feel attacked and toward whom we often feel our own considerable anger, are undoubtedly our most "difficult" cases, regardless of our theoretical orientations. These are also the patients who, optimally, force us to stretch ourselves most, as analysts and as people.

While self psychological and intersubjective theorists clearly recognize the inevitable presence of the analyst's subjectivity, they seem to consistently assert that it is the analyst's responsibility to introspectively monitor his or her own subjectivity as much as possible and decenter from it. The therapeutic emphasis is always on attunement with the patient's subjective experience, so the analyst is expected to continually monitor his or her countertransference introspectively in order to return to the stance of empathic inquiry as consistently as possible.

Stolorow and his collaborators (Orange, Atwood, and Stolorow, 1997) clearly recognize "that the analyst is constantly unwittingly revealing his or her psychological organization to the patient," but they do "not prescribe deliberate self-disclosure by the analyst" (p. 44). They recommend that treatment interventions should be made by the analyst "on the basis of his or her best understanding of the likely meanings of such disclosures for the patient and analyst, and on his or her assessment, arrived at with varying degrees of collaborative input from the patient, of whether such interacting meanings are likely to facilitate or obstruct the analytic process" (p. 44). In this last statement, they seem to have the expectation that the analyst should be able to decenter relatively quickly and efficiently from his or her own subjective experience, while they seem to minimize the possibility that the analyst may become so entangled in the throes of *his or her own* powerful countertransference reactions as to be unable, at least for a time, to engage the patient in a "collaborative" discourse and then to make wise assessments of what will "facilitate or obstruct the analytic process." In other words, they see it as the analyst's responsibility to assess what interventions (including the possibility of deliberate self-disclosures) are needed to be "optimally responsive" (Bacal, 1985) to the patient's therapeutic needs and to exercise "optimal restraint" (Shane and Shane, 1996).

Postmodern thinking presents a serious challenge to concepts of "optimal" behavior by the analyst. Is it helpful to maintain therapeutic ideals that are impossible to achieve? Is the ideal of "optimal responsiveness" (Bacal, 1985) helpful in "light of the analyst's irreducible subjectivity" (Renik, 1993), the presence of which inevitably interferes with the analyst's ability to set aside his or her own subjectivity to "optimally" assess the patient's needs? As long as we are aware enough to recognize the inevitable relativity of all of our concepts, including those held as "ideals" for the treatment process, perhaps there is no harm in continuing to employ them. However, I believe that much of the self psychological literature continues to reflect the assumption that we can and should be able to exercise "optimal responsiveness" by consistently maintaining control over our subjective reactions to our patients and that those analysts who fail to do so are guilty of inappropriate and unprofessional behavior.

When I am not in the throes of strong countertransferential feelings and involved in intense intersubjective enactments with my patients, I believe that I am as adept as anyone at decentering from my own subjective experience, readily returning to a stance of sustained empathic inquiry and being relatively successful at evaluating what interventions will "facilitate or obstruct the analytic process." In contrast, when I am in the throes of the intense emotional *Sturm und Drang* of certain "difficult" analytic relationships, I know that my capacity to decenter from my own subjectivity tends to fall far short of the ideal. There have even been times when I have found myself expressing my anger in ways that I knew, even at the moment, were coming from my "gut," not from my "head." It is my contention (whether we wish to acknowledge it or not) that such subjectively driven behavior is inevitable for all analysts at times, if we allow ourselves to engage in the intense, regressive intersubjective relationships that our "difficult" patients elicit and require. Whether such authentic self-expression "facilitates or obstructs the analytic process" is a question I will discuss later. First, I would like to present two case examples.

I knew from the beginning that working with Marilyn would be a challenge. Her therapist for the previous eight years, Dr. R, had to terminate with all his patients in order to undergo treatment for cancer, and Marilyn let me know that she was devastated by the loss of "the only person who has ever understood" her. When she first saw me, she let me know that she "could never open up to anyone" the way she had with Dr. R. She was holding onto the hope that he would recover soon, so they could resume her therapy. But he had urged her to find a new therapist, and this suggested (even to her) that he might not be planning to return to his practice. While she needed to minimize the severity of his illness and maintain an optimistic attitude, it was apparent that Dr. R was a very ill man. Clearly, Marilyn needed help in mourning Dr. R, and I felt empathically attuned to her painful sense of loss. I realized that it would be difficult for Marilyn to accept me as a replacement for Dr. R, but I was cautiously optimistic that I could engage her in treatment.

She presented herself to me as a chronically unhappy woman. At 43 years old, Marilyn was married to a man who "never earned a good-enough living" and whom she experienced as often angry and distant with her. She deeply regretted and resented never having had children, a reality necessitated by her life-long history of poor health. She was frustrated and unfulfilled by her career as an elementary school teacher. Her parents, who had divorced when she was 10, were "never there" for her emotionally: her father was described as cold and detached, while her mother was "selfish" and "guilt-provoking." She was an only child and had no close friends.

Over the next five months, usually on a twice-a-week basis, Marilyn would invariably come into my office looking annoyed and would proceed to complain about her life: her miserable, insensitive husband; her miserable, insensitive parents; her miserable, frustrating job; her miserable physical health; her miserable childhood. The only bright spot in her life, it seemed, had been her relationship with Dr. R, but now even thinking about him left her feeling terribly sad. Most of the time, I listened empathically and tried to communicate that I could hear how disappointed she felt with her life and how much she missed Dr. R. Unfortunately, whatever I said did not help her feel any better, as she told me repeatedly, usually with a tone of sarcasm and derision. However empathic and supportive I thought I was being, I simply could never understand her as perfectly and instantaneously as Dr. R always had, and I certainly could not help her feel better, as he always had. At least once a week, she would tell me, "This is just not working," as she just could not feel comfortable and connected with me. We talked about how hard it was for her to accept any therapist other than Dr. R and how she inevitably always compared me with him, to my detriment. One time I suggested that it was particularly difficult for me to measure up to someone whom she held in such high esteem that he seemed almost perfect to her. At first she agreed, but then she thought I was assuming that her view of Dr. R was an exaggerated distortion, and she became very angry and verbally contemptuous of me. I felt unfairly attacked, but decentered enough to realize that she probably was picking up on my real feelings: I was aware that I had inadvertently disclosed my competitive and annoyed feelings about her idealization of Dr. R. I wanted us to be able to talk about what was happening between us, but she was so angry with me that she refused to discuss the matter further. Being met with such a negative reaction from her, I retreated back into the safer posture of silent listening. I knew that we should get back to what happened in the next session, and I tried, but she dismissed me as "making a big deal out of it" and changed the subject. I did not want to fight with her, so I backed off again.

There were occasional periods of relative calm in the therapy, even a few sessions when I thought we were beginning to work more comfortably together. These periods never lasted long. Before long, she would let me know that whatever I did or said, whenever I was silent, or whenever I spoke, however I looked at her or glanced away, it was just not right and was certainly not what Dr. R would have done, said, or looked like at a similar moment in therapy. She explained that Dr. R was the most empathically attuned person she had ever met. He always seemed to know exactly what she needed. In contrast, it seemed, I never did. I often felt attacked, frustrated, and angry, in spite of my ongoing efforts at decentering from these feelings. On a few occasions, I tried to address what was going on between us again, sometimes even self-disclosing, by letting her know that I was having trouble not reacting defensively and angrily to her constant barrage of negativity, but I was already pretty angry when I brought these things up, and she knew it. She would respond either by angrily refusing to talk about our interaction (which had "nothing to do with" why she was seeing me) or by sarcastically commenting on my being "overly sensitive" and prone to taking things "too personally." As she repeatedly reminded me, Dr. R could always "handle" her moods, even when she was "irritable and cranky," "never took it personally," and always knew the right thing to say. Despite repeated efforts, I could not get her to recognize that what was going on between us was very important for us to talk about.

In contrast, when I empathically tried to address her feelings about Dr. R's illness and her feelings about having to end her treatment with him, she was sometimes somewhat more amenable. At times she actually was able to talk about her profound sadness about Dr. R being so ill and about her intensely painful sense of loss in not being able to see him. A couple of times she was able to cry, briefly, about him. Occasionally, she was even able to acknowledge that she really was not giving me a chance, simply because I was not Dr. R, and seeing me reminded her of her sense of loss. She told me that she had been thinking of contacting Dr. R, to find out how he was doing, and after discussing her conflict about calling him, she decided to try to reach him. I encouraged her to do so, and when she did, the conversation, though very sad, meant a lot to her. At these times, when she was able to express her sadness and pain and not her denigrating anger toward me, I was able to feel much more empathically attuned to her. Soon after, however, her anger would return, as unrelenting as ever, together with her self-pitying complaints about her life. Feeling frustrated and ineffectual maintaining my usual empathic stance and undoubtedly acting on my anger, I tried to get her to look at how she might be contributing to the pattern of misery in her life. Not surprisingly, she experienced this approach, however gentle I thought I was being, as blaming her, and she responded with even more intense anger and expressions of contempt for me. I was able to engage her by empathically focusing on her experience of me as being unempathic and critical, but she could not be empathic with my experience of her as unempathic and critical toward me.

Around the fifth month of seeing me, she found out that Dr. R had died. She was able to cry in my presence, and I was able to feel an empathic connection with her in her pain. For a short while,

Marilyn seemed to be accepting Dr. R's death and also accepting that seeing me was not so bad. After a few weeks, though, things took a negative turn, with Marilyn becoming increasingly critical and hostile toward me again. She started questioning the value of coming twice a week and decided, unilaterally, that she would "have to cut down to once a week." Even then she cancelled a few sessions. I was feeling increasingly annoyed. When she returned, she seemed quite nonchalant about having missed her session and quite dismissive of my concern about what was happening. I attempted to talk with her about what was going on. She looked at me with a contemptuous sneer and stated that she had decided to tell me exactly what she thought of me, which she then proceeded to do: she "just never liked" me; something about me "just bothered" her, in spite of her efforts to feel differently; she was often annoyed about "little things" about me, even hating "the stupid ties" I wore. She was just warming up. She proceeded, in her very sarcastic and demeaning way, to criticize me for the multitude of ways I had been unable to "get anything right" during the preceding six months. I started out thinking that I could withstand her verbal assault, knowing that it was not "really" about me and was "really" about my not being Dr. R. I tried to address what her anger was "really" all about and how it was impacting on our ability to work together. I reminded her of our previously agreed-upon understanding that her loss of Dr. R prevented her from being able to accept me, but she insisted that it was more than that: it was me, my inadequacies, my insensitivity, my incompetence. After absorbing what felt like verbal abuse from her for quite some time and in spite of my best conscious effort at maintaining my decentered, empathic stance, I felt increasingly beaten up. I realized my anger was getting expressed, in spite of my conscious intent, in my tone of voice and in how I was saying things to her, and I realized that the more she "got" to me, the more she attacked me. I finally "lost it" and blurted out, "If I'm such a lousy therapist, then why don't you just leave?" At that, she glared at me, stood up, and left, slamming the door behind her. Not a pretty scene. Certainly not the way I wanted things to happen. As my anger dissipated, I felt an intense mixture of feelings, including shame, disappointment, and relief.

I waited a day and then called her to urge her to return so we could talk about what had happened between us. She seemed surprised to hear from me, but not angry, and listened politely as I told her that I thought what we had enacted together was important and worthy of our meeting again to review and discuss. She sounded almost pleasant as she told me that she would think about it and would get back to me. As it turned out, she never did get back to me. At the end of the month, I mailed her bill to her, with a brief note urging her to contact me. She mailed back her payment but did not send a reply or call, and I decided not to pursue her any further.

In dramatic contrast to Marilyn, Helen's transference was very positive from the earliest phase of treatment. She came for therapy because she had been feeling increasingly depressed, despite taking Prozac for a few months. She had no clear sense of what she was depressed about, but she thought it might be related to her grandmother's recent death. She was 47 years old and felt "content" with her life. She was married to a "very good man" who worked hard and was a good provider, and had three children who were "leaving the nest," but seemed to be doing well. Helen was the oldest of three children and the only member of her family who had emigrated to the United States from Scotland. Her parents had divorced after a stormy marriage when she was 14, and she had felt obligated to have no contact with her father after that, since she did not want to suffer her mother's wrath, if she could avoid it. Her mother had always been a very moody woman who "could fly into a rage and then not talk to you" for days, or even weeks, usually without any obvious cause for her upset. After many years of trying to placate her, Helen finally discontinued contact with her following a visit from her mother during which the older woman unleashed her anger on Helen's children. Her father had died a couple of years earlier, but fortunately, Helen and he had resumed contact several years before that. He had always been a rather detached father, who preferred spending after-work time at the local pub rather than at home, and this sense of detachment did not diminish much after their reconciliation. The adults Helen felt closest to throughout her childhood and thereafter were her maternal grandparents, who would provide her with a safe haven when her parents fought or when her mother was not talking to her, but her mother resented Helen's closeness to her grandparents and did whatever she could to limit their contact. Her grandfather had died about five years earlier, and her grandmother had died six months prior to her beginning therapy. She was troubled by the fact that she "could not cry" after her grandmother's death but knew that she missed her grandmother "terribly."

In her therapy sessions, Helen expressed appreciation for having someone she could talk to and who would actually listen to her without making any demands. She reported that she was feeling much better and looked forward to our sessions. She had several good friends, but it was she who was always in the role of "the listener" because she was good at it and also because she was usually not comfortable burdening others with her problems. Therapy was different: although she often checked with me about whether she was overburdening me, she felt grateful to have found such "a good soul" who was so patient, understanding and supportive.

It soon became clear that, although her husband was "a very good man," he was not a good listener or a good communicator, and she became increasingly aware of the disparity between the two of us. With this awareness came an increasing idealization of me, and although she was too inhibited and "proper" to verbalize such feelings even to herself, she obliquely let me know that she felt loving and erotic feelings for me. As time went on, her feelings for me became increasingly intense and increasingly burdensome for her because she felt guilty for having them, for she had never felt such feelings before, and she was feeling more and more distant from her husband. I tried to address these feelings with her, empathically reflecting their conflicted quality to her, and I tried to help her understand their intensity in the light of her history.

Sometime during this period she became aware, first through dreams, of dissociated memories from her early school years: there was a male custodian in her school who was very friendly and nice, who showed her a lot of attention, and who she would visit after school. When Helen started realizing that these memories involved some kind of sexual contact, she became frightened and was not willing to find out any more. I was supportive and did not pressure her but stated that these memories were very important and expressed the hope that at some point she would be ready to return to them.

As time went on, Helen let me know that she was again falling into a deepening state of depression. She felt that the only reason she was depressed was that she knew that she and I could not have the kind of relationship she wanted. She still looked forward to seeing me, but also dreaded seeing me, because doing so only heightened her love for me. She understood that I was her therapist, and the limits and boundaries of that reality were increasingly painful to her. Maintaining my empathic stance, I tried to help her express and understand her feelings, but nothing I said relieved her deep sadness. At times, in the evenings, she would drink too much, and on a few occasions she called me, clearly under the influence of alcohol, and verbalized more directly how much she loved me and how rejected she felt. The next day she would always express embarrassment for her behavior the night before. I expressed concern about her abusing alcohol and suggested that she could develop into an alcoholic (there is a family history), but she reacted with hurt and annoyance and refused to consider AA. Her drinking continued intermittently, and she became increasingly depressed. When I suggested that she schedule a medication consult with a psychiatrist, she reacted with tremendous upset and anger because she interpreted my suggestion as my way of "getting rid of" her or "giving up on" her. I tried to assure her that this was not my intent at all, that I was definitely not suggesting that we stop her therapy, but she remained hurt and refused to see the psychiatrist. I was feeling increasingly concerned about her deteriorating condition and was feeling increasingly out of control of what was happening in her treatment.

It was during this period that she announced that she had to "take a break" from therapy. I told her that I was not comfortable with that option, but she insisted that it was the only way she could deal with her feelings. She needed to take some time off because seeing me was just too painful for her. I could not change her mind, and I was very uncomfortable with this arrangement because I feared that she was potentially suicidal. After much discussion I felt that I was powerless in insisting that she stay, but she agreed to have phone contact, with me calling her in a week. In the interim, I had several silent messages on my answering machine, suspected they were left by her, but decided to wait until the week was up to call her back. Then, one evening while I was in session with another patient, my phone rang repeatedly, without a message being left. I do not answer calls during sessions, but after the sixth call in 10 minutes, I told the patient I was with that perhaps it was an emergency and I had better pick up the receiver. By the time I did, the caller had hung up. Next, instead of another call, my beeper went off, with Helen's number on it. At this point, it was the end of the session of the patient I was with, and before calling Helen back, I went out to the waiting room and told my next patient that I had an emergency call and would be a little late.

When I called and Helen answered, it was obvious from the way she spoke that she had been drinking. She told me that she was miserable, that she loved me so much it hurt her unbearably, and that she needed to know that I loved her, too. I answered that I cared very much about her, but this answer was not what she wanted to hear. I let her know that I could tell how hurt and upset she was about my not feeling the same way she felt, but my understanding words did not help her feel any better. After several minutes of "getting nowhere" with her, I told her that I had a patient waiting and that I could call her back after that session. At that point, she angrily told me that, if I got off the phone, she would swallow pills and kill herself. Usually very cooperative and agreeable, that night Helen was demanding and unwilling to compromise. I told her I would at least have to go to the waiting room and tell the patient that we would have to reschedule the appointment. This she "allowed" me to do. When I got back on the phone with her, she was not calming down, and she became ever-increasingly more demanding and more unreasonable in her demands. I found myself feeling increasingly powerless and angry but tried to stay calm, decenter from my own feelings, and address myself to helping her calm down. Nothing I said was helping, and my frustration and anger were mounting. Eventually, without a conscious decision, I found myself shifting my stance: without disguising the angry tone of my voice, I told her that I was feeling manipulated and blackmailed by her and that I was very angry at the way she was treating me. This clearly caught her by surprise, and she fell silent. I then told her that if she could not calm down and assure me that she would not harm herself, I would have to call 911. She let me know that she felt hurt that I would even think of calling 911, but I reminded her that it was she who had threatened suicide. By this time she already seemed to have calmed down considerably and, indeed, seemed quite sober. She told me that she felt upset that I was angry with her, and she sincerely apologized for emotionally blackmailing me. After a few more minutes of our talking together, she sounded much calmer and even "back to normal," and she promised that she would not harm herself. She agreed to come in for a session the next day, and by that point I felt that I could trust her to keep her promises. While Helen and I have lived through several other serious crises in her treatment since then, that phone conversation definitely marked a most important turning point in the therapy relationship.

In reflecting on both of the cases I just presented, it is clear to me that by the time I finally expressed my anger, I was no longer able to "decenter" from my subjective experience and rationally "decide" on an optimal therapeutic intervention. In both situations, with both patients, I was feeling very angry, and I reached the point with each of having to express my anger verbally. Was I "wrong" to have allowed myself to reach that point? Did I wait too long? I have no doubt that my theoretical commitment to decentering from my subjectivity and striving to return to an empathic stance played an important role in my waiting as long as I did, and I have no doubt that some other analysts who are not invested in such a stance, but are more comfortable with confrontation or self-disclosure, would have expressed their anger sooner. Regardless of the analyst's theoretical viewpoint, the process we are looking at is very complex because it inevitably involves the analyst's subjective reactions in the context of an intense interpersonal relationship.

Irwin Hoffman (1998) speaks to the complexity of such situations in a way I find quite helpful and reassuring. He writes:

> Whether the therapist is empathic or confrontational at a certain moment, for example, has much to do with what inner response the therapist has available, not merely with the needs of the patient construed in isolation from the analyst's experience. Given a combination of what the patient is eliciting, the analyst's affective dispositions, the analyst's resistance, and the analyst's understanding of the process at the moment, the analyst "decides" to act in some way, to speak or not speak, or to say one thing rather than another. We know how long even certain recognized patterns may continue without being spoken of and how common it is for therapists to kick themselves (or each other) for failing to do or say the "obvious." What this kind of reproachful attitude does not consider and respect enough (depreciating it usually as merely unfortunate countertransference) is the possible element of wisdom in the analyst's behavior, given the nature of the experience that it reflects. I said the analyst "decides" to do or say something, but usually there is no linear, temporal relationship between thought and action. The action occurs largely as an immediate expression of myriad considerations within the analyst's "unformulated experience" (Stern, 1997). Although the analyst may feel a good deal of conviction on the basis of that experience, the very fact that the analyst's subjectivity is implicated on multiple levels brings with it a measure of uncertainty about the meaning and wisdom of whatever he or she may choose to say or do. For example, if the analyst feels that he or she has been repeatedly depreciated by the patient and that, despite various attempts at interpretation and understanding, the depreciation has continued relentlessly, the analyst may feel a surge of anger and a conviction that it is justified and that it warrants expression [p. 170].

Hoffman's (1998) discussion of Frederickson's 1990 paper, "Hate in the Countertransference as an Empathic Position," is particularly relevant to the present discussion. In that paper, Frederickson reports eventually responding to a very provocative, hostile patient who was standing over him screaming at him, by standing up and face to face with the patient, yelling "Shut up!" The patient is reported as first responding, "Good. . . . The first human response I've gotten from you" (p. 483), but then the patient questioned whether the therapist's outburst had been "staged." Based on Frederickson's report, his outburst was clearly spontaneous and most assuredly "not staged." At first the patient felt he could no longer feel "free to do anything here," in his sessions, and his analyst replied, "You are free to say anything here, but not to do anything" (p. 483). In the aftermath of this interaction, Frederickson reports that the quality of the therapy improved dramatically.

It is in hindsight that Frederickson offers his explanation of what happened between him and his patient: Frederickson's explanation is that in his angry response to the patient's hostile and provocative behavior, the analyst was identifying with the patient's "abused child," while the patient's abusive behavior reflected the patient's identification with the aggressor, his abusive father; in angrily reacting to the patient's abuse, Frederickson sees himself as being empathic to the bullied little boy within the patient.

Hoffman challenges this "formulation [as] amount[ing] to a post hoc explanation for what seems to have been a more spontaneous personal reaction" (p. 172) and goes on to say:

> Such personal reactions may include inklings of where they fit in relation to the patient's history and intrapsychic world, but those inklings may be rather faint at the moment of action. At that moment, the analyst feels impelled to speak up for himself or herself, knowing that the action may turn out to mean any number of things and also that what follows is not fully predictable [p. 172].

I would amend Hoffman's last statement by suggesting that at the moment of feeling "impelled to speak up" in such a spontaneously angry way, the analyst is *reacting* and probably not *thinking* at all about the therapeutic implications of doing so. At such moments in which the analyst feels emotionally battered by a patient experienced as relentlessly obnoxious, provocative, controlling, condescending, argumentative, and totally lacking in empathy toward others (especially the analyst), it is most strikingly impossible for the analyst to "make a judgment about what to do . . . simply on the basis of some dispassionate understanding of the patient," because "the strength of the analyst's affect has to be taken into account" (Hoffman, 1998, pp. 170–171). Hoffman suggests that, "for the sake of the health of the relationship, which certainly includes the analyst's well-being, it may be important that the analyst react emotionally" (p. 171). While it is comforting to believe that we have at least some degree of conscious control over how we react, I believe that, at such moments of authentic upset and anger, our "post hoc" explanations mainly serve to reassure ourselves that there was method to our temporary madness or, as Frederickson (1990) suggests, that the anger felt and expressed by us was not "really" our own, but was an "empathic" response to the patient's projective identification. In contrast, I am willing to acknowledge that the anger I felt and expressed with both Marilyn and Helen was my own anger, not theirs, although I believe that both of them acted in ways that evoked my anger. But my responses were the products of my own unique subjectivity, for better or for worse.

As Hoffman (1998) points out, "Frederickson's example turned out extremely well, not surprising in a published vignette. . . . But how many published accounts are we likely to have of instances in which, following such an expression of anger on the therapist's part, the patient walks out and never returns?" (p. 172). In view of what happened for me with Marilyn, although not with Helen, I find Hoffman's continuing thoughts particularly reassuring:

> Reticence to publish such accounts is understandable, I think. How quick would many of us be then to point the finger at the analyst for his or her "unprofessional" behavior? It is misleading, however, to judge an action in an absolute way on the basis of what happens after it. The fact is that at the moment of action there is always more than one kind of handwriting on the wall. At that moment the emotional authenticity of the analyst has to count for something in its own right. What that authenticity banks on, as a general rationale within the context of the analysis, is the hope that there will be enough common emotional ground between the patient and the analyst so that when the dust settles, the participants will be able to locate some aspect of the analyst's response somewhere within the patient's patterns of interpersonal relationships and somewhere in the patient's intrapsychic world [p. 172].

The "common emotional ground" that Hoffman is "banking on" is, I believe, predicated upon the prior establishment of a strong intersubjective connection between patient and analyst, which can subsequently be reestablished in the aftermath of what has probably been experienced by the patient as a serious emotional disruption. It seems to me that the reestablishing of the selfobject connection after a disruptive intersubjective interaction is the process that self psychology has emphasized par excellence since its inception, and which is achieved via the analyst's empathic attunement with the patient's subjective experience of the disjunction (Kohut, 1971, 1977, 1984; Atwood and Stolorow, 1984).

Unfortunately, with Marilyn, there had not been enough of a previously established selfobject bond between us, and therefore, there was not "enough common emotional ground" between us upon which we could both stand, after "the dust settled," to process what had happened between us in a therapeutically meaningful way. In contrast, with Helen, there had been, and there was.

Throughout the time she saw me, Marilyn always had one foot out the door, not surprising in view of the circumstances under which she had to stop seeing Dr. R and in view of the idealized transference she had with him. In retrospect, I think that one of the problems from the start was that I was trying too hard to engage her in treatment with me. I denied it to myself at the time, but I now realize that I felt a definite sense of competition with Dr. R and actually harbored the grandiose fantasy that I would be able to "replace" him, in spite of my conscious awareness that competing with an idealized ghost was unrealistic and destined for disappointment and failure. For Marilyn to accept me as a substitute for Dr. R meant her being disloyal to him, and therefore, she could not accept me. When Marilyn would tell me the therapy with me "was not working," I thought I was responding empathically by addressing her feelings about losing Dr. R and having trouble accepting me. I believe that I was being empathic to those feelings, but at the same time I was being unempathic to her sense of hopelessness about working with me: my investment in being successful in treating her prevented me from truly hearing that part of what she was saying. The more empathic I tried to be, the more I was presenting myself as a substitute for Dr. R, and the more Marilyn had to reject me. If my own subjectivity had not prevented me from being more empathically attuned to the hopelessness of her dilemma, I might have responded to her differently, perhaps by verbally reflecting her sense of hopelessness about our working together and perhaps by wondering whether she thought we should consider discontinuing the therapy. If Marilyn had felt "heard" in her frustration and hopelessness about seeing me, in a way that I had been unable to hear her, perhaps she would have been better able to let go of her anger toward me, allowing us to move on together, or perhaps, we would have agreed that the therapy simply could not work and that we should go our separate ways. Her anger at me was about my not being Dr. R, but additionally, I think it was about my not being able to empathically understand the hopelessness she felt about trying to accept me as his replacement. My anger at her was about her attacking my professional self-image as an empathically attuned analyst, and frustrating my fantasy of being able to "win" her as a patient. As my anger mounted in the face of her unrelenting attacks upon my self-esteem, I tried harder to decenter and maintain my empathic stance. Unfortunately, my efforts at being empathic failed to establish a selfobject bond with her, her attacks increased, my anger increased, my ability to decenter from my anger faltered, and ultimately the anger was expressed by me. Had I been too empathic, not empathic enough, or just trying too hard to be empathic? I think all three were true.

With Helen, my empathic attunement to her from the beginning of treatment and her responsiveness to it fostered a very strong selfobject bond, and this bond allowed her to feel a sense of safety and trust rarely, if ever, experienced by her at any time earlier in her life. Her selfobject transference to me, as it unfolded, clearly became both idealized and eroticized, the result of the interaction between her subjective organization of experience (based on her history) and my provision of such an empathically sensitive milieu. In this empathic provision I see both the strength and potential danger inherent in the self psychological approach. It is inevitable that the patient, at some point, will experience the analyst as unable to fulfill the promise of perfect empathic attunement or availability, and the resulting severing of the selfobject bond will be experienced by certain patients as a mortifying narcissistic injury. The context necessary for the treatment to be able to survive this kind of crisis includes the availability of both co-participants to tolerate the experience of sometimes very dysphoric emotions while working together to reestablish the empathically based selfobject bond. The responsibility of patient and analyst is not equal: the analytic relationship is not symmetrical (Aron, 1996), and it is clearly the analyst's responsibility to "reach out" to reengage the patient. But the patient has to be receptive to such a reengagement. Fortunately, Helen was able to tolerate the expression of my anger and was able to "take in" the feedback I was able to verbalize to her along with my anger.

I certainly cannot say that the way things unfolded between each of these patients and me represents "optimal technique" on my part. I have to admit, in retrospect, that I waited longer to express my anger than I wish I would have. I believe this resulted from the complex interaction between my personality-based issues, including my tendency to avoid angry confrontations with others and my theoretically based beliefs, including my investment in striving to maintain sustained empathic attunement with my patients. There are many times when I feel perfectly comfortable making self-disclosures about a variety of aspects of my self-experience to patients; most of these I believe are largely responsive to my patients' needs and prove to be helpful for the therapeutic process. But I know I am reluctant to express my anger with my patients, and my efforts at decentering from my anger, if experienced intensely enough, may sometimes fail. It is becoming increasingly clear to me that there are times, in the face of certain patients' hostile and provocative behavior, when my maintaining a stance of empathic attunement to the patient's experience is not only impossible, but also represents my avoidance of the intersubjective issues that are most salient and pressing for us both to address at that particular time. As Mitchell (2000) noted:

> An all-out hatred or chronic, intractable resentment in the analyst toward the patient is incompatible with a constructive analytic process. Yet, episodic, even hateful exasperation is in some treatments a crucial and perhaps inevitable avenue into the patient's deepest struggles. It is part of the analyst's job to make continual judgments as to the nature of the patient's hatred and the nature of his own, and determine, as best he can, whether it is enhancing or impeding the analytic process [p. 139].

It seems to me that the ability of any analyst to make such judgments and act accordingly upon them is a product of the analyst's personal subjectivity and theoretical perspective and, simultaneously, of the specific intersubjective context co-constructed by both participants in the analytic relationship at that moment in the treatment. In retrospect, it is clear that consultation with a supervisor or colleague is strongly advisable at such difficult junctures during treatment.

In addressing these issues of anger and hate as they unfold in the analyst–patient relationship, the intersubjective perspective advocated by Stolorow and his colleagues shares a great deal in common with the views of relational analysts, including Hoffman, Aron, and Mitchell, but their emphases tend to differ. The intersubjective analyst's empathic focus on the patient's subjective experience permits the patient to feel relatively safe in revealing those aspects of self-experience that had to be withheld or dissociated in other relationships. On the other hand, the exclusive presentation of empathy by the analyst does not foster the development of the patient's ability to recognize and tolerate the separate subjectivity of the other, a developmental achievement that, I believe, cannot and should not be taken for granted, but that is certainly a goal of analytic treatment. In contrast, many relational writers seem to take for granted the patient's possession of the capacity to recognize and tolerate the subjectivity of the other. Indeed, some authors, including Benjamin (1990), advocate limiting the use of the term *intersubjectivity* to the achievement of this level of development. The relational analysts therefore tend to feel much freer to express their own subjectivity with what appears to be much less concern about the fragility and vulnerability of certain patients receiving such communications. The assumption that these patients can tolerate such expressions of the analyst's subjectivity is not always warranted, however, and some patients can experience such communications as traumatic assaults upon their tenuous sense of self-cohesion and psychic survival. Josephs (1995) expresses what he sees as the advantages of this approach when he states:

> I believe that a person can grow through confrontation with his or her own multiplicity and confrontation with the novel, multiple perspectives that others possess. I believe the boundaries of the self can be stretched and expanded to be more inclusive of what is self-dystonic. Kohut's approach tends to spare the patient an awareness of the patient's own egocentrism and in so doing deprives the patient of the self-enriching process of connection, confrontation, and interpenetration with that which is different from the self. It can be infantilizing of the patient to assume that he or she may be too fragile to usefully assimilate perceptions of the analyst's difference. I have found in clinical work that it is sometimes the more disturbed patient who benefits the most from confrontation with that which exists beyond the omnipotent control of the self [p. 137].

It is apparent, however, that either approach entails limitations and dangers. Ultimately, I believe that patients require us to provide both an empathic connection, upon which the patient's sense of relative safety is based, and our presence as a separate other, so that we can help the patient make the transition from the archaic level of solipsistic self-experience to the more mature level of reciprocally interrelated self-experience. This entails our including self-expression along with empathy in our repertoire of ways of being authentically in relationship with our patients. As always, timing is everything, but judging the timing of such communications is often extremely difficult and must be considered in relativistic and contextual terms, colored as it inevitably is by our own subjectivity within the intersubjective framework of the treatment relationship. The difficulty inherent in this process seems particularly pronounced when patient and analyst are engaged in a relational pattern involving mutual feelings of anger. There is clearly a difference between the analyst having the experience of feeling anger toward a patient and spontaneously acting upon that feeling by direct expression of the anger. If possible, it certainly seems "better" when the analyst can maintain the ability to experience his or her anger, reflect upon its possible meanings, and consciously decide whether and how to take action that would be "optimally responsive" to the patient's needs. However, I think it is important for us to recognize our own limitations as subjective beings and accept the reality that there will be times when we simply cannot maintain that "optimal" stance.

It seems clear to me that I am better able to understand and address the issues of what is going on intersubjectively in the treatment relationship when I am not extremely angry. I have no doubt that addressing my anger with my patient before it intensifies to such a level is preferable to waiting until I am furious, yet it occurs to me that sometimes, perhaps, I may have to get extremely angry and express it before both the patient and I can turn our attention to what has been unfolding between us. Sometimes, when the patient has had a prolonged experience of the analyst's empathy, the relationship can withstand such expressions of the analyst's authentic anger. Unfortunately, this is not always the case. On a personal level, I see that it is extremely important for me, as an analyst and as a person, to strive to become increasingly more comfortable with the experience and expression of my own anger and the anger of my patients, so I can find better ways of utilizing my anger therapeutically, which probably entails not waiting so long to risk expressing it.

As analysts, I believe, we are attracted to those theories that coincide best with our own personalities. The theories and technical approaches we choose to embrace tend to provide a framework that helps reduce the anxieties that our intense interpersonal relationships with our patients can engender in us and allow us to maintain a sense of emotional equilibrium and safety in the context of the often strenuous work that we do. In view of the fact that we analysts clearly do not all share the same personality pattern, it should not surprise us that competing paradigms exist within contemporary psychoanalysis and that we selectively divide ourselves among them. I think it is fortunate, though, that our old and usually comfortable approaches prove to have limitations, and so we are sometimes motivated to look further, to stretch our understanding, and perhaps even integrate alternative viewpoints into our personal and professional sense of self.

REFERENCES

Aron, L. (1996), *A Meeting of Minds: Mutuality in Psychoanalysis.* Hillsdale, NJ: The Analytic Press.

Atwood, G. & Stolorow, R. (1984), *Structures of Subjectivity: Explorations in Psychoanalytic Phenomenology.* Hillsdale, NJ: The Analytic Press.

Bacal, H. A. (1985), Optimal responsiveness and the therapeutic process. In: *Progress in Self Psychology, Vol. 1,* ed. A. Goldberg. Hillsdale, NJ: The Analytic Press, pp. 202–227.

Benjamin, J. (1990), Recognition and destruction: An outline of intersubjectivity. In: *Relational Psychoanalysis: The Emergence of a Tradition*, ed. S. Mitchell & L. Aron. Hillsdale, NJ: The Analytic Press, pp. 183–208, 1999.

Brandchaft, B. (1994), Structures of pathological accommodation and change in analysis. Presented at the Association for Psychoanalytic Self Psychology, March 12, New York City.

Frederickson, J. (1990), Hate in the countertransference as an empathic position. *Contemp. Psychoanal.*, 26:479–496.

Hoffman, I. Z. (1998), *Ritual and Spontaneity in the Psychoanalytic Process: A Dialectical–Constructivist View*. Hillsdale, NJ: The Analytic Press.

Josephs, L. (1995), *Balancing Empathy and Interpretation*. Northvale, NJ: Aronson.

Kohut, H. (1971), *The Analysis of the Self*. New York: International Universities Press.

——— (1977), *The Restoration of the Self*. New York: International Universities Press.

——— (1984), *How Does Analysis Cure?* ed. A. Goldberg & P. Stepansky. Chicago: Univeristy of Chicago Press.

Livingston, M. S. (1996), Countertransference and curative process with "nondifficult" patients. In: *Basic Ideas Reconsidered: Progress in Self Psychology, Vol. 12*, ed. A. Goldberg. Hillsdale, NJ: The Analytic Press, pp. 141–158.

Miller, M. L. (1997), The nondifficult patient and the nondifficult analyst: Resolving the impasse of intersubjective pseudoconjunction. In: *Conversations in Self Psychology: Progress in Self Psychology, Vol. 13*, ed. A. Goldberg. Hillsdale, NJ: The Analytic Press, pp. 125–145.

Mitchell, S. A. (2000), *Relationality: From Attachment to Intersubjectivity*. Hillsdale, NJ: The Analytic Press.

Orange, D. (1995), *Emotional Understanding*. New York: Guilford.

——— Atwood, G. & Stolorow, R. (1997), *Working Intersubjectively: Contextualism in Psychoanalytic Practice*. Hillsdale, NJ: The Analytic Press.

Ornstein, A. (1974), The dread to repeat and the new beginning. *The Annual of Psychoanalysis*, 2:231–248. New York: International Universities Press.

——— (1990), Selfobject transferences and the process of working through. In: *The Realities of Transference: Progress in Self Psychology, Vol. 6*, ed. A. Goldberg. Hillsdale, NJ: The Analytic Press, pp. 41–58.

Renik, O. (1993), Analytic interaction: Conceptualizing technique in the light of the analyst's irreducible subjectivity. *Psychoanal. Quart.*, 62:553–571.

Shane, M. & Shane, E. (1996), Self psychology in search of the optimal: A consideration of optimal responsiveness, optimal provision, optimal gratification, and optimal restraint in the clinical situation. In: *Basic Ideas Reconsidered: Progress in Self Psychology, Vol. 12*, ed. A. Goldberg. Hillsdale, NJ: The Analytic Press, pp. 37–54.

Stern, D. B. (1997), *Unformulated Experience*. Hillsdale, NJ: The Analytic Press.

Stolorow, R. & Atwood, G. (1992), *Contexts of Being*. Hillsdale, NJ: The Analytic Press.

——— Brandchaft, B. & Atwood, G. (1987), *Psychoanalytic Treatment: An Intersubjective Approach*. Hillsdale, NJ: The Analytic Press.

Teicholz, J. G. (1999), *Kohut, Loewald, and the Postmoderns*. Hillsdale, NJ: The Analytic Press.

Trop, J. & Stolorow, R. (1992), Defense analysis in self psychology: A developmental view. *Psychoanal. Dial.*, 2:427–441.

Chapter 5

Survival and Recovery: Psychoanalytic Reflections

Anna Ornstein

The Holocaust, the almost complete destruction of European Jewry in the years 1939–1945, has been extensively studied and written about from a historical, as well as a psychological, perspective. The psychological and psychiatric literature of this tragedy has primarily emphasized the psychopathological consequences of prolonged physical and psychological deprivations, humiliations, and the depression that followed the inadequate mourning of the survivors' losses of most or all members of their families. The helping professions had also become concerned with the transmission of this national trauma to the second and third generations. In this chapter, I shall question the exclusive attention on psychopathology in this patient population. No doubt, depression and other forms of mental illnesses were not infrequent consequences of the Holocaust. However, even then, as they struggled with their emotional pain and the challenges of building a new life, survivors, on the whole, retained the standards, principles and values by which the fundamental features of their personalities were formed. These psychological building blocks that have become established prior to their war experiences constituted the foundation of their post-Holocaust recovery. To understand the spontaneous recovery that many Holocaust survivors were able to make, it is also important to recognize the psychological mechanisms that may have been involved in the emotional survival of conditions that existed in concentration and extermination camps, in hiding and in labor camps. I believe that similar mental mechanisms may be at work in surviving and recovering from other forms of traumatic experiences.

CRITICAL REVIEW OF THE LITERATURE

Over the years, psychoanalysts in clinical settings and psychologists through empirical research have made repeated attempts to find a common denominator that would characterize and be specific for Holocaust survivors and their children. Because of considerable heterogeneity among survivors in their pre-Holocaust experiences and the great variety in the nature and degree of traumatization during the war, clinicians who interviewed the survivors shortly after the war were eager to adopt the one thing they believed to be observable in all survivors. The psychological features that were supposed to be independent of pre-war personality organization and were expected to be universally present in this population are contained in the now well-known label, the Survivor Syndrome: "pervasive depressive mood with morose behavior and a tendency to withdrawal, general apathy alternating with occasional, short-lived angry outbursts, feelings of helplessness and insecurity, lack of initiative and interest, prevalence of self-deprecatory attitudes and expressions" (Niederland, 1968, p. 12). To these features others have been added: "a severe and pervasive guilt complex, partial or full somatization, states of agitation, anxiety, insomnia, paranoid ideation" (p. 18). The syndrome also included "personality changes showing more or less radical disruption of the entire maturational development, behavior and outlook" (p. 22).

Though there were objections to the unquestioned acceptance of the universality of the survivor syndrome primarily because they were theoretically based and because of serious methodological shortcomings (Antonovsky et al., 1971), the label has stuck to this day and has become the common denominator for further studies and emendations focusing on the psychological problems of survivors and their children. Noteworthy in these early clinical reports is the fact that, although most of the investigators were psychoanalysts, they had dismissed the survivors' pre-Holocaust personality organization in their assessments (Ornstein, 1985, 1986). The massive nature of the Holocaust trauma was supposed to have "washed away" any individual differences among the survivors (Krystal, 1978). What at one time was supposed to have helped to receive restitution from the German government had become irrefutable truth, and the presence of the survivor syndrome on which the quality of survivor-parenting and the transposition and transmission of the Holocaust trauma was predicated was no longer questioned. What remained to be answered was only how the transmission occurred and how many generations were yet to be effected. This question was answered by the investigative analysts with a set of assumptions relative to the survivors' parenting abilities and by the extensive use of psychoanalytic concepts. For example, Levine (1982) postulated that, through a "child of survivor complex," similar to the Oedipus complex, the Holocaust trauma was transmitted in all survivor families, but while in some instances the pathology associated with the transmission became manifest, in others, similar to the Oedipus complex, it remained latent. The transmission of the Holocaust trauma was expected to be universal because the children of survivors were supposedly born into "ambivalence, despair and anger and at the same time, there existed hopes and expectations for these children that have frequently proved unattainable. It is small wonder that given the nature and extent of the Holocaust trauma, that it was passed on to the next generation. The psychiatric literature, while far from definitive, gives ample evidence of this fact" (p. 75)

However, parenting, as one of the most challenging and difficult tasks in adult life, has its own developmental history. As it is true for other parents, the empathic capacities of survivor parents would have to be traced to their original sources (such as the manner in which they were parented in their childhoods) and ought not have been viewed as the product of their Holocaust experiences alone. Still, generalizations persisted, such as the children being treated as "objects" and were viewed by their parents as replacements for lost members of the parents' original family members[1] or that they were expressions of revenge on the Nazis. There was a general agreement among these authors that, because these children perceived their parents' fragility, they suffered the consequences of a great deal of hostile aggression, which explains why so many display personality features that are similar to borderline and narcissistic disorders (Kestenberg, 1972).

[1] In order to discover this particular problem in survivor parenting, the question "After whom was the patient named?" was included in the questionnaires. The question was "posed with the idea that a child named after a grandparent or a sibling killed by the Nazis would indeed feel it a burden that reverberated with doom" (Bergmann & Jucovy, 1982, p. 140). This is an unfortunate assumption; it is a time-honored Jewish custom to name children after deceased members of the family.

In view of the absence of identifiable psychopathology and because all the mechanisms that were found in survivors' children were not necessarily shared by all such cases and were not unique to them, many investigators of the children of survivors settled for what they called a "psychological profile" of the Holocaust offspring. The profile that was considered to be characteristic for children of Holocaust survivors was supposed to consist of the following personality features: they are less differentiated from their parents; have less autonomy and independence; are experiencing elevated anxiety, guilt, and depressive mood; and are having more difficulties in regulating aggression than do their cohorts (Felson, 1998). Kestenberg (1982), one of the most devoted and persistent among the clinical investigators concluded that the children of survivors suffered not from the consequences of a simple transmission of trauma, but that the children of survivors "wanted to live in the past and harbor the dead within themselves" (p. 148). She called this phenomenon "the transposition" of trauma, a finding, resembling the description by Barocas and Barocas (1979):

> The children of survivors show symptoms which would be expected if they actually lived through the Holocaust. The children present a picture of impaired object relations, low self-esteem, narcissistic vulnerability, negative identity formation, personality constriction and considerable affective impairment. . . . These children wake up with terrifying nightmares of the Nazi persecution, with dreams of barbed wire, gas chambers, firing squads, torture, mutilation, escaping from enemy forces and fears of extermination" [p. 331].

In contrast to the clinical studies that were conducted at first by psychoanalysts who immigrated to this country before the Holocaust, much of the empirical research on nonclinical subjects was conducted by the children of survivors. The object of the study of this latter group was to ascertain whether there were consistent differences between survivor families and control families who sought help in clinical settings. The statistical studies failed to confirm the findings of the clinical investigations (Solkoff, 1979, 1991; Leon et al., 1981; Zlotogorsky, 1983). In other words, the empirical research failed to confirm the findings of the clinical investigators. However, the reports of the psychologists did not have the same "clout" as did the publications of the analysts and did not reach the same readership; their findings were dismissed by subsequent investigators. Literature published in the 1980s and up to the present continued to speak of a child of survivor syndrome that is supposed to consist of alienation from society, severe problems related to aggression, and "boundary blurring."

The only empirical study on the third generation was conducted by Sigal et al. (1988) in Montreal. This study started out to examine the hypothesis that "exposure to extended, extreme stress can have demonstrable negative psychosocial effects two generations after the exposure" (p. 207). However, on the basis of their data, they too concluded that, "While there may be individual exceptions, as a group the grandchildren of survivors are not distinguishable from other clinic children with respect to their mood, personality or behavioral items included in this study" (p. 210).

Some of the harshest criticism of the survivor literature came from Robert Krell, a child survivor himself. Krell (1984) suggested that the therapist's "inability to comprehend the extent of Nazi sadism has unwittingly led clinical researchers to attempt to understand the perpetrators by investigating the survivor" (p. 523). In Krell's view, and I agree:

> To equate the survivor's aggressiveness with Nazism, however it is expressed, continues the dehumanization of the survivor. This has not escaped notice by survivors whose reluctance to seek help personally or for their children, is at least in part due to awareness of generalizations from samples of survivors who have been psychiatrically investigated. . . . The failure to refine survivor terminology has at times misdirected treatment and obscured the remarkable adaptations and coping styles of the majority of survivor generation and its offspring [p. 521].

In view of the liberal generalizations by clinicians, it is instructive to review the literature that deals with the nonpatient population of Holocaust survivors. For example, Hartman[2] (n.d.) suggested:

> We have an obligation to hear out what each survivor has to say—even if, and perhaps because, their autonomy as human beings was jeopardized by the most brutal and systematic deculturation ever devised. Now that the stage of gathering information for writing the history of the Holocaust is considerably advanced, a further task emerges. We must refuse to intellectualize prematurely, or generalize about the mentality of either survivor or aggressor. Perhaps we can apply a lesson from a philosophical controversy of the Middle Ages and say, God knows these things only in their particular, never in their generality. Research should go on, must go on; but let us beware of creating a false science that tries to master this event by a professional deformation that flatters our competence as historians or psychologists, at the price of excluding the nearness and pathos of these individual stories.

[2] Professor of English and Comparative Literature at Yale University.

William Helmreich (1992), a professor of sociology and Judaic studies at City University, New York, interviewed 170 randomly selected survivors. The findings of this study are of importance because Helmreich primarily used psychological criteria for his conclusions and because he carefully avoided generalizations. In order to underscore a particular observation, he cited verbatim descriptions by individual survivors. This served to emphasize the uniqueness of each survivor's experience: the differences in their pre-Holocaust lives, their ages at the time of persecution, the length and severity of their camp—or hiding—experiences, and the extent of their losses. In spite of this diversity, certain "Jewish values" became evident in these interviews: already in displaced persons camps, while waiting for immigration, survivors set up schools and published newspapers, indicating a capacity to resurrect a value system that "had been nurtured and developed in the families and communities in which they were raised prior to the war" (p. 85). Vulnerabilities remained: the sight of a uniform, a knock on the door, dogs barking, or smoke from a chimney could provoke anxiety. However, none of the survivors considered this to interfere with their ability to pursue their goals and ambitions. Among those interviewed, only 18 percent sought professional help. At the time of the interviews, the children of survivors had excellent school records and there was relatively little crime and juvenile delinquency among the survivors and their children. As adults, a large number of the "second generation" had elected to go into the helping professions.

Auerhahn and Laub (1985) were equally critical of the liberal generalizations among psychoanalysts:

> What the researcher sees is neither universal themes nor syndromes but particular startling phenomena, which in a given individual, have a unique stamp. That is, trauma does not appear as a major personality organizer alone but. . . . it permeates life in fragments, in circumcised phenomena that are usually overlooked by those searching for trends and generalizations [p. 191].

I believe that one of the problems with the assessments of the survivors by the professionals was that they had made them from the perspective of civilized existence. Because it was indeed difficult, or maybe impossible, to put themselves into the shoes of people who were in hiding or lived in forests for years and because they could not comprehend life in a concentration camp, they ended up treating survivors as experimental subjects, totally different from themselves.

THE INFLUENCE OF THE HOLOCAUST LITERATURE ON THE TREATMENT OF SURVIVORS AND THEIR CHILDREN

Patients are no less eager for an explanation about why they are suffering or may have difficulties in living than are their therapists. Under these circumstances, the Holocaust works like a giant magnet that can explain just about everything for both participants. There is also something very reassuring about generalizations. If one can explain one's difficulties with a single fact, there is no need for further exploration. Survivors and their children accepted the experts' explanations readily. The problem was that these explanations frequently lead to a therapeutic dead end. One of the difficulties was related to the fact that many of these therapists–investigators failed to examine their expectable countertransference difficulties in treating this patient population. Danieli (1981) interviewed 40 psychotherapists to pinpoint the specific countertransference affects these therapists had experienced. They spoke of "bystander guilt," murderous wishes, fear of death, grief and mourning. The reactions varied in keeping with the therapists' background, whether they were Jewish or not, survivors or nonsurvivors. On the whole, Danieli found, survivors appeared to handle their affects better than nonsurvivors. In my view, the reactions Danieli describes were not countertransferences since they were not reactions to the patients' transferences. Rather, they appear to have been reaction to the content of the survivors' narratives.

In reviewing the literature regarding the treatment of survivors and their children, with few exceptions (Herzog 1981, 1982), there are no case reports that would include the therapist's attitude and responsiveness to their patients. Kestenberg (1982) offered a cogent explanation for this striking omission regarding the analyst's participation in the treatment process: "The analyst's own denial, inability to listen, or overinvolvement require a special study which has not been undertaken by our group" (p. 157). However, the therapists' total omission of themselves as agents of therapeutic action is particularly regrettable since these therapists may have been the only people in the survivors' lives who could have—potentially at least—provide a setting in which the survivors' efforts to recover could have been recognized and validated.

In the 1960s and 1970s, it was still believed that it was possible to maintain "analytic neutrality," and analysts feared losing their neutrality by responding with empathic understanding to their patients. However, in the 1980s and 1990s, it was no longer possible to consider that one could arrive at a meaningful understanding of the patient's inner world without recognizing that the therapist's mode of inquiry, mode of listening and responding had an impact on their observations.

But even in the early years of these "investigations," there were exceptions. In 1968, at the same time when Henry Krystal had successfully argued that Holocaust survivors, by and large, were untreatable because of the severity of their alexithymia and anhedonia, Emanuel Tanay (1968) gave a beautiful example of the impact of his own attitude and responses on the survivors' capacity to experience strong emotions. This is what Tanay writes:

> Once the flood gates opened up, emotions so intense would emerge that they appeared to threaten the patient's homeostasis. Whether such a development would take place or not would depend on my attitude and receptiveness. On the days when my capacity to endure such a session was very low, the patient obligingly maintained a defensive posture. I know of no question or technique, which will automatically turn on this process of expression of catharsis. But there is nothing easier than to turn it off. One question or even a glance which is out of tune and the psychological closing off is established [p. 225].

What Tanay described here is the importance that the empathic listening perspective has on the treatment process, how a glance or an ill-phrased question can interfere with an emotionally meaningful communication between the two participants. Empathy is frequently misunderstood; it is considered a form of kindness or tact, rather than a listening perspective that requires that therapists make an effort to put themselves into their patient's shoes. In fear of contaminating the analytic field and experiencing intolerable affects, the original investigators carefully avoided this mode of listening. Instead, they were concerned with the possibility that they may miss the survivors' repressed rage and identification with the perpetrators. They believed that it was crucial "to evoke the difficult phase in treatment when the therapist must be experienced by the survivor as a Nazi. . . . If the unconscious identification with the Nazi perpetrators is not to remain forever lodged in the unconscious of the survivor, it has to be reexperienced in the transference" (Bergmann, 1989, p. xi).

The oft-repeated generalizations and the manner in which they were handed down from one author to the next infiltrated and biased the attitudes of future generations of psychotherapists. When seeking professional help, many survivors and their children encountered unexpected difficulties. Two clinical vignettes shall serve as examples. Dr. A, a 30-year-old physician, had marital problems and had already consulted with two therapists before he discussed his dilemma with me. He told me that, as soon as he told the therapists that he was a child of survivors, all his difficulties were interpreted as the consequence of his parents' persecution. Attention from the nature of his relationship with his wife would shift to the discussion of his parents' Holocaust history: what, when, and how he knew about them. Believing these to be relevant data, he accepted their opinion that his problems were "typical problems of the second generation." Had he not told the therapists that he was a son of survivors, Dr. A would have had a better chance of benefiting from an unbiased, openminded listening perspective that every patient is entitled to.

Esther was a 22-year-old student of History. As a member of a nontherapeutic group of second-generation young people, she was telling the group about her mother's depression and how gloomy the home was in which she grew up. As a facilitator, I asked whether she knew the nature of her mother's depression. Esther was surprised; she thought I ought to know that the depression was the expectable consequence of her mother's Holocaust experiences. After the group meeting, she decided that she would take a chance and ask her mother about her childhood, about the way the family lived before the German occupation of Poland. Esther was surprised that her mother welcomed her question; nobody had asked her that before. The psychiatrist she had consulted asked only about the number of people she had lost in her family and in how many camps she had been. In subsequent conversations, Esther learned that several members of her mother's family suffered from depression and that her mother had a difficult childhood long before the war began. Esther regretted that, because the family was so ready to accept the psychiatrist's verdict, her mother was not only deprived of proper treatment but the children ended up treating their mother with a mixture of pity and rage. Esther found these conversations with her mother liberating for both of them. Most importantly, it seemed to have freed her from a vague responsibility that she should have done something for her mother to make her feel better but she did not know what. By speaking to her mother and securing proper help for her depression, she had done for her mother a great deal, indeed.

The extraordinariness of the survivors' experiences created a natural gulf between them and their therapist–investigators, a gulf that could be bridged only if therapists made an effort to empathically place themselves into the situation of which the survivors were speaking. For example, to an external observer, the inmates of concentration camps were not only helpless but passive as well; they were "like sheep going to their slaughter." Survivors appeared passive only to those who judged them in terms of their manifest behavior. To survive physically, survivors had to follow orders without protest and resistance; their behavior had to be passive in relation to the SS and their Jewish superiors. But survival was not possible in a helpless and passive state of mind. This required a great deal of activity and resistance in all aspects of camp life: not to fall asleep when standing in line for hours, not to sit down when totally exhausted, not to eat the piece of bread that was to last all day—all of these required extraordinary amounts of activity and alertness.

SURVIVAL OF EXTREME CONDITIONS

There are several factors that have to be considered in the assessment of Holocaust survivors and the way these influenced their recovery: constitutional resiliency, the pre-Holocaust personality organization, the mental mechanism that may have been at work that made adaptation to extreme conditions possible, and the fact that the Holocaust was a collectively rather than an individually, experienced trauma.

Resilience

Resilience is a poorly understood capacity of the human psyche. Research data regarding this particular property of the mind had been studied in various contexts: in the clinical situation, where unexpected improvement contradicted the prognosis based on the patient's diagnosis; in the practice of pediatrics where infants and children have been observed to recover from medical trauma or compensate for developmental disruption to a remarkable degree; and more recently, in observations made on premature infants in hospital nurseries. The nurseries provide the most reliable data because, in this setting, the infants could be observed under relatively identical environmental circumstances before the home environment affected their constitutional capacity for self-regulation. In terms of resilience, the study showed that many infants developed normal or typical state regulation capacities in spite of prolonged and early exposure to the chaotic and disruptive nursery. This indicated that constitutional, inborn capacities played a role in some infants' state-regulation, while in others, this capacity was not present (Fajardo, 1988).

Anthony's (1987) findings regarding resilience and invulnerability came out of his research of observing children whose mothers had suffered from a major psychiatric disorder and children who grew up "motherless." Similar to children who lived in ghettos and the few who survived concentration camps, motherless children exhibited unusual degrees of precocious competence;[3] "Motherless children, for example, begin to care for themselves and their bodily wants like little mothers. [This] adultomorphic behavior may break down under stress but it may also provide the child with a high degree of adaptive coping mechanisms (p. 22).

There was a small group of children who survived the concentration camps of Therezin and Auschwitz and were airlifted to London after the war. In a therapeutic nursery they were observed by psychoanalytically trained caretakers (Freud and Dunn, 1951). For several months after their arrival in the therapeutic nursery, the children remained suspicious of adults and aggressive toward them. In contrast to this, they were extremely protective of each other, the older ones taking responsibility for the younger ones. The airlifted children were tracked down and interviewed 38 years later (Moskovitz, 1983). Only one of these individuals required long-term hospitalization for psychiatric problems. These interviews do not provide depth-psychological data but considering the very early ages (some were infants, others less than three years old) at which these children were separated from their families, it is significant that 38 years later, most of them were married and were gainfully employed.

Collectively and Individually Endured Trauma

The foregoing would suggest that, regarding possible psychopathological consequences, distinction also has to be made between trauma that has been endured individually and in secret and trauma that has been endured collectively. Some of the most malignant consequences of childhood sexual abuse, for example, appear to be related to the fact that the trauma was afflicted by the very people who are responsible for the child's welfare, and under the threat to their lives, the children were sworn to secrecy. Adult patients who were abused as children suffer from a persistent sense of badness,

[3] Magda was a Hungarian-Jewish child. She was 12 years old when separated from her family. On her own, she helped two of her younger cousins survive the ghetto in war-torn Budapest. Airlifted to London after the war, in the orphanage, she behaved like a strict mother toward her charges, keeping them constantly in sight; eight-year-old Heidi had to carry six-year-old Fritz on her back because the younger child's legs were weakened by polio.

attachment to the abuser, and flashbacks associated with self-destructive behavior (Lewis, 1992). The secrecy surrounding the childhood abuse created a profound sense of emotional isolation in these patients while survivors of collectively endured trauma were able to share their experiences throughout the ordeal.

Holocaust survivors, as survivors of major collectively experienced tragedies, developed a special bond, compensating them, to some degree, for the lost members of their families. Rabinowitz (1976) describes this process well: "For years, they had pieced together the details of their pasts; what one forgot, the other remembered. . . . This group was small but they were close and when they talked about the camp, it was not only horror that drew them back, but also the memory of their youth" (p. 135).

Infantile and Adult Traumatization

The majority of Holocaust survivors were in their late teens or in their 20s or 30s after the war. This ought to have made it mandatory to include their pre-Holocaust personality organization in their psychological assessment. Adult traumatic experiences do not bring about the same kinds of psychological compromises that impinge upon the infant's and child's developing self. Krystal (1978) addressed this issue and reaffirmed the importance of distinguishing between the two forms of traumata both on theoretical and on clinical grounds. The adult, by virtue of the structure of the adult psyche, has the capacity to block emotions and constrict cognition, that is, to call on defensive operations in response to a "trauma signal." This capacity prevents the adult psyche from the life-threatening regression that is the likely outcome of significant (i.e., frequent and severe) childhood traumatizaton. Still, Krystal maintained that massive psychic trauma, such as occurred to the victims of the Holocaust, was expected to have similar consequences to those that followed significant childhood traumatizations. The assumption that the Holocaust had "bleached away" all childhood memories and had altered internalized values, as well as object relationships may well have been the reason why earlier reports on the psychology of survivors did not include the assessment of their pre-Holocaust personality organization (Krystal, 1978; Lifton, 1979; Grubrich-Simitis, 1984).

From a self-psychological perspective, I would argue, the distinction between the consequences of childhood and adult traumatization would have to be made because of the difference in the relative cohesion that the nuclear self had attained at the time of the trauma. Adult survivors whose prior development assured the establishment and consolidation of the nuclear self were able to retain their values and ideals in spite of the severe humiliation they had to suffer. The recovery of the Holocaust survivors depended on the presence of values and ideals that had become established in their childhoods.

The question has also been raised whether or not having survived extraordinary circumstances and having had to mourn the total or partial loss of one's emotional milieu had "hardened" the survivors of the Holocaust, making them less vulnerable to future, everyday stresses of life. There are only some anecdotal indications for this. Equally anecdotal, but more frequently heard, is that survivors of extreme conditions have an unusual degree of appreciation for the comforts and the pleasures of everyday life.[4]

Survival of Extreme Conditions and the Process of Recovery

Adaptation during the years of persecution and victimization constituted a link that could meaningfully connect the survivor's pre-Holocaust personality organization with his or her recovery and adaptation to new lives. Any effort to study the process of recovery following a traumatic experience of the magnitude of the Holocaust raises the question of how best to conceptualize the nature of this trauma. I am suggesting that the years of hunger, hard labor, chronic physical exhaustion, constant threat to life, the total absence of external support, and the loss of most or all family members constituted a strain trauma that was punctuated with shock traumatic experiences such as selections, beatings and other states of helplessness conforming to Freud's original definition of a traumatic state (1917a). When helplessness did not lead to the prisoner becoming a Mussulman,[5] the defense that would be successfully employed under these extreme conditions was disavowal, a mental

---

[4] A telling example of this can be seen in a dialogue in the movie *Harold and Maude*. Maude, a Holocaust survivor, says to Harold, a suicidal adolescent: "Dreyfus once wrote from Devil's Island that he would see the most glorious birds. Many years later, from Brittany, he realized that they had been just seagulls. For me, they will always be glorious birds."

[5] In concentration camps, people who succumbed to the state of hopelessness and helplessness were called Mussulmen. These were people who refused to eat, walked in a mechanical, apparently purposeless manner, and had a vacant look in their eyes; they looked but did not see. A Mussulman would die within days.

mechanism Freud (1895) described as a defense that is directed not against instinct, but against the dangers of external reality. Disavowal creates a state of mind in which emotional detachment, that is, numbing of affects, makes adaptation to traumatic conditions possible. Basch (1974) offered a useful description of this defense: "Disavowal manages to avoid a painful reality not by vitiating or denying the percept, but by creating two currents of mental life, a split that permits reality to be acknowledged while at the same time allowing a belief in a wished-for situation to co-exist" (p. 89). For example, some people knew the meaning of the sweet smell and the heavy black smoke in Auschwitz, but many did not. Mothers and older sisters were known to make up stories that "explained" the smoke and the smell to the younger ones; they reinforced disavowal, thereby protecting the younger ones from being prematurely exposed to unbearable terror.

In camps, while attention had to be directed toward the outside (one had to know from whence blows were likely to come and how to position oneself in the soup line)—at the same time, attention also had to be directed toward the inside, toward the preservation of the core of the self.

The core of the self, or "nuclear self" (Kohut, 1970) is a psychological configuration in depth that has continuity in time, a configuration that we experience as the "I" of our perceptions, thoughts and actions. This is how Kohut described it:

> In the clinical setting, we recognize the simultaneous existence of different and even contradictory selves in the same person with various degrees of stability and of various degrees of importance. . . . Among these selves, however, there exists one which is most centrally located in the psyche, one which is experienced by the individual as the basic one, and which is most resistant to change [pp. 9–10].

In camps, the preservation of the nuclear self, with its capacity to experience vigor and vitality and to maintain moral and ethical values and a modicum of self-esteem was made possible by the creation of small groups. These small groups, a social-psychological phenomenon that was prevalent in labor camps, had important depth-psychological significance for the individual survivor. The groups, consisting of three to four members or only of two people (a mother and a daughter, two sisters or cousins), provided the setting in which ordinary human affects, hostilities, jealousies, loyalty, love, and caring could be experienced and expressed. There were fights, disagreements, and reconciliations within these groups, and there was fierce commitment and much sacrifice, similar in its intensity to ordinary family life. The members of the group supported each other in every way possible (for example, on death marches, younger men would carry the weak and sick members of their group on their backs), but everyone outside of the group was viewed with suspicion.

Recovery and psychic continuity between pre-Holocaust organization of the nuclear self and the demands on the psyche after liberation also required the integration of traumatic memories into the fabric of the rest of the personality. Survivors had to recover sufficiently to be able to mourn the loss of all or most members of their families (Ornstein, 1994).

THE INTEGRATION OF TRAUMATIC MEMORIES AND THE PROCESS OF RECOVERY

From clinical and nonclinical experiences, it would appear that the integration of traumatic memories into the rest of the psyche is a psychological imperative. However, such an integration encounters an obstacle in that traumatic memories have a dialectic built into them: while they demand articulation, they are also felt to be unspeakable and unsharable, and they are feared because of their potential to bring back the originally disavowed terror. Another obstacle to the integration of traumatic memories is the fact that some of the most traumatic elements lack coherence; they only exist in fragments. The success of the integration of traumatic memories depends on where and when an empathic emotional milieu becomes available for this difficult psychological task. This may occur either in or outside of a therapeutic setting. When survivors speak of their experiences in an affectless, intellectualized tone of voice, this indicates that disavowal had to be left in place, that they had to protect themselves from retraumatization, which could occur either just by telling the story or because they feared that their narrative may meet with an indifferent reception. The affectless and hesitant delivery also indicates that it is not easy to find words that are adequate to describe their experiences. But it is important to find the right words and to help their listeners create images that approximate their experiences: survivors of traumatic experiences have to educate their therapists about the events of which they speak. And then again, therapists have to allow themselves to be educated.

Once psychic pain—anger, sorrow, and a profound sense of grief—replaces numbness and detachment, recovery is in progress. Only when one's self has become sufficiently cohesive can one experience potentially disruptive affects. This is the process whereby disavowal, the vertical split in the psyche, will be healed and grief and other painful affects may finally emerge. In the presence of an empathic other, when the responses to the survivor's narrative indicate that the listener either understood or made a genuine effort to understand, survivors, as all other patients, experience the feeling of being understood. It is the experience of feeling understood in-depth that facilitates the consolidation of a self that has been threatened with fragmentation—and it is the consolidated self that will be able to take possession of repressed or disavowed affects. The experience of painful affects is one of the most welcome experiences after a prolonged period of numbness. This is also the beginning of the grieving process. Now, it is possible to recreate details of the past that bring back the memory of the lost members of one's family and the profound grief that accompanies these memories. Repeated clinical experiences led me to question Freud's theory of this process, namely, that without giving up the "libidinal cathexis" to the old objects, no new relationship can be established (Freud, 1917b). Rather, this process appears to occur in reverse: only when new relationships become established and the self is experienced as firm and cohesive can the process of mourning begin.

For Holocaust survivors, each fragment of a memory was precious. In the absence of any material possessions (a piece of clothing, a photograph, a sample of handwriting), memories became "anchor points," they attained symbolic significance, and their value and significance increased with the passage of time. A clinical example[6] will demonstrate how a patient attempted and eventually succeeded in reassembling her childhood memories, beginning with the potentially most painful one—the memory of the last day she had spent with her family.

Clinical Example

Mrs. Halpern was referred to me because her duodenal ulcer failed to respond to a well-established regimen of diet and medication. The internist thought that the difficulty was related to the patient's current life situation bringing back painful memories from her Holocaust past. Though Mrs. Halpern was not sure of this connection, she followed up on the recommendation. Having survived several concentration camps, she married another survivor, and the couple had two teenage sons. One of the hypotheses the

---

[6] This clinical example was published in a different context (Ornstein, 1986) in *The Reconstruction of Trauma*, Workshop Series of the American Psychoanalytic Association.

internist maintained was that the older son was about to go off to college, reactivating Mrs. Halpern's separation anxiety since she was about the same age when she was separated from her family of origin.

During the camp years, when she considered herself lucky to have remained with a cousin and several girlfriends, she did not think much about her life before: hunger, sores on her body, and constant concern with physical survival preempted any thought she could have had about the past. Soon after arrival in the United States in 1948, she met her future husband. The young couple was generously supported by the local Jewish agencies, and in a few years, they were able to buy a home and have their first child. She was impressed with the kindness of the people in the United States and learned quickly that they were satisfied with a minimum of information about her past. Since they settled in a small community, she had very few contacts with other survivors.

Ever since the end of the war, Mrs. Halpern found herself trying to remember two things in particular: the color of the dress her mother wore when she last saw her and the name of the camp where she had briefly met a childhood friend and lost sight of her again. Looking back on this now, she was embarrassed by the "silliness" of her effort to try to hold on to such seemingly insignificant details. I said that I could see that she was trying to have a clearer image of her mother now because it may help her remember more about her family and what happened the last time she saw them. She was glad I did not think this was silly, and she had a good reason to want to remember more. When Mrs. Halpern succeeded in "seeing" her mother's dress (she never recovered the name of the camp where she last saw her friend), many of the other details of the last day she spent with her family came to mind: where her father was sitting and what her little brothers were doing on that day. She again asked me if I thought this was "sick" or "stupid" but said that remembering such details made her feel good. Pausing for a minute, she wondered whether trying to forget how they died would help her ulcer to heal. I told her that it would be impossible to forget how they died but that she now also wanted to remember how they lived. As if confessing, she said that, since she does not have a picture of her family, she was afraid that if she loses the memory of their faces, then she really would not have anything that would help her remember them. After her own sons were born, she was thinking of her family even more than before. She was afraid to tell anyone that she hoped that her sons would resemble her brothers. When I said that her wish made good sense because that way part of them would have survived, she began to cry. Her cry sounded more like a cry of relief than a cry of anguish. She asked me again why she feels good when she talks about these things. I said that feeling the profound sadness of their premature and cruel deaths and feeling her own irretrievable losses made her feel better because they signaled the end of the numbness, the end of an inner void.

After a brief silence during which she appeared to be deep in thought, Mrs. Halpern remembered the interview she had with a social worker soon after coming to this country. The social worker asked her if she felt guilty for being the only survivor of her family. She no longer remembered how she answered the question. For some reason, she was thinking about that question now. She thought that she felt very little, if anything, at the time, but she knew what she was feeling now: she felt a piercing ache around her heart, a tremendous desire to know what would have come of her brothers had they lived. Her feelings about her parents were different; she always remembered them better than her two younger brothers. There was a smile coming through her tears as she mused: "I can just see how my father would have enjoyed my boys, how he would play with them—I remember him playing with my brothers." The pain of their loss was now mixed with the joy of the picture she managed to recreate in her mind about her father playing with his two young sons. From here, more memories followed, each of them "bittersweet"—a mixture of joy and a sense of profound sorrow.

Mrs. Halpern and I never returned to the discussion of whether or not she felt guilty for having survived; however, I suspect that she was, in many ways, rehabilitated by being able to "fill in the gaps" in her memory that helped her reestablish a line of continuity between the way she experienced herself within her family of origin and the life she was living with her current family now. It would be unfortunate if Mrs. Halpern's desire to see features of her brothers in the faces of her sons would be considered to indicate that she viewed her sons as "replacements" of her brothers. Being able to remember and to mourn them increased her ability to make a better distinction between them; she did not confuse the identities of her sons with those of her brothers. Rather, Mrs. Halpern, as most survivors whose parents and siblings died without a trace (without a picture or a burial place where their names would appear), hoped that her brothers had left some traces behind that could indicate that they had ever lived.

Increased self-cohesion allowed previously treated affects, such as anger, to enter consciousness. To feel anger in this context, in my view, is an expectable response indicating that recovery is in progress;

justified anger is not to be confused with chronic narcissistic rage that could become the nucleus of severe personality disorders.

SUMMARY

In response to a concern that the impact of the Holocaust will not be recognized by psychotherapists treating survivors, several psychoanalysts who were refugees from Nazi Germany, devoted a great deal of time and effort to detail the psychopathological consequences of the Holocaust trauma. Considering the magnitude of the trauma, it was not difficult to find evidence for psychopathology. However, because of their almost exclusive emphasis on psychopathology, most of these investigators failed to recognize the particular manner in which survivors mourned their enormous losses and made an effort to integrate their painful memories into the rest of their personality. This meant the loss of an opportunity to learn about the process of recovery following severe traumatization.

The chapter also described a hypothesis regarding the psychological mechanisms involved in the adaptations to extreme conditions. In my view, this constituted a link in the survivor's effort to establish psychic continuity between her pre-Holocaust psychological organization and adaptations to a new life.

Unlike my colleagues, I do believe that integration of traumatic memories was possible as long as the survivors encountered an empathic listening perspective and their efforts to recover were validated. Survivors of trauma have every reason to expect that their stories will evoke fear, confusion, horror, and disbelief and that therapists will protect themselves from these affects by resorting to generalizations or praise for the survivor's heroism or special qualities. Such responses, however, make it impossible for survivors to proceed, and the affects associated with the traumatic memory may never, or only partially, enter the therapeutic dialogue. Once recovered and articulated, the memories are accompanied by grief and anger, indicating that an increase in self-cohesion, a healing of the vertical split, has allowed the previously feared affects to enter consciousness.

REFERENCES

Anthony, E. J. (1987), Risk, vulnerability, and resilience: An overview. In: *The Invulnerable Child,* ed. E. J. Anthony & B. J. Cohler. New York: Guilford, pp. 3–48.

Antonovsky, A., Maoz, B., Dowty, N. & Wijsenbeek, H. (1971), Twenty-five years later: A limited study of the sequelae of the concentration camp experience. *Soc. Psychiat.*, 6:186–193.

Auerhahn, N. & Laub, D. (1985), Knowing and not knowing the Holocaust. *Psychoanal. Inq.*, 5:191–193.

Barocas, H. A. & Barocas, C. B. (1979), Wounds of the fathers: The next generation of Holocaust victims. *Internat. Rev. Psycho-Anal.*, 6:331–340.

Basch, M. (1974), Interference with perceptual transformation in the service of defense. *Ann. Psychoanal.*, 2:87–92.

Bergmann, M. S. (1989), Foreword. In: *Healing Their Wounds*, ed. P. Marcus & A. Rosenberg. New York: Praeger, pp. xi–xii.

——— & Jucovy, M. E. (1982), *Generations of the Holocaust*. New York: Basic Books.

Danieli, Y. (1981), Countertransference in the treatment and study of Nazi Holocaust survivors and their children. *Victimology: An Internat. J.*, 5:45–53.

Fajardo, B. (1988), Constitution in infancy: Implications for early development and psychoanalysis. *Learning from Kohut: Progress in Self Psychology, Vol. 4*, ed. A. Goldberg. Hillsdale, NJ: The Analytic Press, pp. 91–100.

Felson, I. (1998), Transgenerational transmission of effects of the Holocaust: The North American research perspective. In: *International Handbook of Multigenerational Legacies of Trauma*, ed. Y. Danieli. New York: Plenum Press, pp. 43–68.

Freud, A. & Dunn, S. (1951), An experiment in group upbringing. *The Psychoanalytic Study of the Child*, 18:127–169. New York: International Universities Press.

Freud, S. (1895), Project for a scientific psychology. *Standard Edition*, 1:295–317. London: Hogarth Press, 1966.

——— (1917a), Introductory lectures on Psycho-analysis. *Standard Edition*, 16:243–463. London: Hogarth Press, 1963.

——— (1917b), Mourning and melancholia [1915]. *Standard Edition*, 14:243–258. London: Hogarth Press, 1957.

Grubrich-Simitis, I. (1984), From concretism to metaphor: Thoughts on some theoretical and technical aspects of psychoanalytic work with children of Holocaust survivors. *The Psychoanalytic Study of the Child*, 39:301–319. New Haven, CT: Yale University Press.

Hartman, G. H. (n.d.), *Preserving the Personal Story: The Role of Video Documentation*. Video Archives for Holocaust Testimony. New Haven, CT: Yale University.

Helmreich, W. (1992), *Against All Odds; Holocaust Survivors and the Successful Lives They Made*. New York: Simon & Schuster.

Herzog, J. (1981), Father hurt and father hunger: The effect of a survivor father's waning years on his son. *Geriat. Psychiat.*, 15:211–223.

——— (1982), A daughter of silence. In: *Generation of the Holocaust*, ed. M. Bergman & M. Jucovy. New York: Basic Books.

Kestenberg, J. (1972), Psychoanalytic contributions to the problems of children of survivors of Nazi persecution. *Israel Ann. of Psychiat. & Related Discip.*, 10:311–325.

——— (1977), *The Psychological Consequences of Punitive Institutions: Humanizing America*. New York: Knopf.

——— (1982), A metapsychological assessment based on an analysis of a survivor's child. In: *Generation of the Holocaust,* ed. M. Bergman & M. Jucovy. New York: Basic Books, pp. 137–158.

Kohut, H., ed. (1970), *On Courage. Self Psychology and the Humanities: Reflections on a New Psychoanalytic Approach.* New York: Norton.

Krell, R. (1984), Holocaust survivors and their children: Comments on psychiatric consequences of psychiatric terminology. *Comprehen. Psychiat.,* 25:521–528.

Krystal, H. (1978), Trauma and affects. *The Psychoanalytic Study of the Child.* 33:81–116. New Haven, CT: Yale University Press.

Leon, G., Butcher, J., Kleinman, M. & Goldberg, A. (1981), Survivors of the Holocaust and their children: Current status and adjustment. *J. Personal. & Soc. Psychol.,* 41:503–516.

Levine, H. (1982), Toward a psychoanalytic understanding of children of survivors of the Holocaust. *Psychoanal. Quart.,* 51:70–92.

Lewis, H. J. (1992), *Trauma and Recovery.* New York: Basic Books.

Lifton, R. J. (1979), *The Broken Connection.* New York: Simon & Schuster.

Moskovitz, S. (1983), *Love Despite Hate: Child Survivors of the Holocaust and Their Adult Lives.* New York: Schocken Books.

Niederland, W. (1968), The problem of the survivor. In: *Massive Psychic Trauma,* ed. H. Krystal & W. Niederland. New York: International Universities Press, pp. 8–22.

Ornstein, A. (1985), Survival and recovery. *Psychoanal. Inq.,* 5:99–130.

——— (1986), The Holocaust: Reconstruction and the establishment of psychic continuity. In: *The Reconstruction of Trauma; Its Significance in Clinical Work,* ed. A. Rothstein. Workshop Series of the American Psychoanalytic Association, pp. 171–191.

——— (1994), Trauma, memory and psychic continuity. In: *A Decade of Progress: Progress in Self Psychology, Vol. 10,* ed. A. Goldberg. Hillsdale, NJ: The Analytic Press, pp. 131–146.

Rabinowitz, D. (1976), *New Lives: Survivors of the Holocaust Living in America.* New York: Knopf.

Sigal, J., DiNicola, V. F. & Buonvino, M. (1988), Grandchildren of survivors: Can negative effects of prolonged exposure to excessive stress be observed two generations later? *Canad. J. Psychiat.,* 33.

Solkoff, N. (1979), Children of the survivors of the Nazi Holocaust: A critical review of the literature. *Amer. J. Orthopsychiatr. Assn.,* 51:29–4.

——— (1991), Children of survivors of the Nazi Holocaust: Critical review of the literature, *Amer. J. Orthopsychiatr. Assn.,* 63:342–358.

Tanay, E. (1968), Initiation of psychotherapy with survivors of Nazi persecution. In: *Massive Psychic Trauma,* ed. H. Krystal. New York: International Universities Press, pp. 219–233.

Zlotogorsky, Z. (1983), Offspring of concentration camp survivors: The relationship of perception of family cohesion and adaptability to levels of ego functioning. *Comprehen. Psychiat.,* 24:345–544.

Chapter 6

Selfhood and the Dance of Empathy

Jan L. Rieveschl
Michael A. Cowan

> Empathy serves . . . as a therapeutic action in the broadest sense of the word. That seems to contradict everything I have said so far, and I wish I could simply bypass it. But since it is true, and I've evidence for its being true, I must mention it [Kohut, 1981b, p. 530].

> Empathy is the spark of human concern for others, the glue that makes social life possible. It may be fragile but it has, arguably, endured throughout evolutionary times and may continue as long as humans exist [Hoffman, 2000, p. 3].

With the exception of self-psychological psychotherapists, there are relatively few practitioners of empathy-centered therapy today when compared with the heyday of client-centered counseling and psychotherapy in the middle of the 20th century. The vast majority of professionals across the spectrum of the helping professions have, however, been trained to regard empathy as one of the basic tools in the helper's kit. This is evidenced by the fact that, since the 1970s, empathy has gotten a chapter or a major section in all standard introductions to counseling and psychotherapy. Our agenda in this chapter is to break through this utilitarian understanding and kindle (or rekindle) our readers' imaginations regarding the significance and power of empathy. We do so by building on the rich legacy of self psychological theory while synthesizing it with aspects of several other pioneering modes of thought that gained currency in roughly the same period of time: philosophical hermeneutics (Gadamer, 1990), process philosophy (Whitehead, 1978), complexity theory (Waldrop, 1992), and the developmental psychologies of Piaget (1981) and Hoffman (2000). Empathy is our focal example and underlying concern throughout.

RECONCEIVING THE SELF

Moved by the paradigmatic shift in thinking over the past half century, often dubbed "postmodern," psychology is fundamentally revising its conception of the self. Rather than an intrapsychic entity apart, the self is increasingly understood as the constantly evolving organizing filter through which we receive, process, and express all our life experience. More process than structure, more verb than noun, the developing self, present in rudimentary form from very early on, constitutes the heart of the "assumptive world"—that tapestry of meaning woven cumulatively from ongoing experience without which we could not interpret our world or our life in it.

> In order to be able to function, everyone must impose an order and regularity on the welter of experiences impinging upon him. To do this, he develops out of his personal experiences a set of more or less implicit assumptions about himself and the nature of the world in which he lives, enabling him to predict the behavior of others and the outcome of his own actions. The totality of each person's assumptions may be conveniently termed his "assumptive world" [Frank, 1973, p. 27].

The self inevitably makes its contribution to everything we experience, observe, understand, and explain. There are no uninterpreted facts for human beings (Gadamer, 1990). One example of the many implications of this vantage point for psychotherapy is how it transforms our conceptualization of transference. Understood as the inevitable activation of some aspect of one's assumptive world for the purpose of interpreting the present, transference can now be understood not just as typical of some people some of the time, but of all people all of the time. Transference is constant. What varies is the extent to which one is open or closed to what might be new in the present. People might resolve particular transferences in the classical psychoanalytic sense, but the past always makes its contribution to the creation of meaning as we interpret and are interpreted in the present.

Recognizing the interpreting self's embeddedness in an evolving assumptive world is of a piece with postmodern psychology's ironic realization that the self is not self-contained but, rather, "independent" only in a relative sense. From its quickening after conception to its relinquishment at death, selfhood is constituted and sustained in relations with the surrounding world. Being a self is not reducible to the activity of an isolated thinking subject, despite our modern Western sense that that is precisely its defining character (Stolorow and Atwood, 1992). Psychological truth is relative and psychological selfhood is relational.

Nothing animate or inanimate evolves in isolation. "The Universe is not a collection of objects but a communion of subjects" (Berry, 1995, p. 96). All self-organizing systems, be they galaxies, hurricanes, animal species, or human selves, are interacting and co-developing with other complexly organized systems. The health of the self is realizable only within a web of relationships embodying particular qualities. Prolonged subjective disengagement from relationships, even for the purpose of self-preservation from threatening relational events, endangers the self's integrity and potential. Even though it may be the least detrimental alternative at certain moments, there is a psychic price to be paid for such disconnection. Like a plant pulled from the soil by its roots, the disengaged self will in time wither before our eyes. Once removed from the relational ground of its being, it cannot reliably sustain or actualize its unique potential, which will languish in the realm of possibility unless and until it is called forth again onto the ground of cocreative interaction.

What relational selfhood means is best illuminated by focusing pointedly on the qualities of dialogue that nourish the self's development when healthy and restore its viability when stunted. As sustaining and transformative dialogue approaches its fullest expression, it takes on qualities of mutually attuned responsiveness. This relational dance has two fundamental steps—one is having effects, the other receiving them. To be in relationship is to influence and be influenced. Contrary to our ordinary understanding of power as unilateral, philosophers have noted that the capacity to be influenced is as truly a sign of power as the capacity to influence (Loomer, 1976). Influencing and being influenced entail acts of interpretation, making meaning of what is transpiring relationally, whether in exercising influence or discerning how one has been influenced. Partners in a relationship do not have direct, unmediated access to their own or the other's intentions, but can act only on their respective interpretations of what is transpiring inside and between them. Self-expression and reception of another's self-communication are moments in a flowing, mutually interpretive process.

The dancers in a face-to-face relationship alternately shift their weight from the expressively interpreting step of influencing to the receptively interpreting step of being influenced. This process of mutual influence will tip toward synergy (wherein a relationship is enhanced) or entropy (wherein it is diminished). The whole of any particular relationship will tend at any point in time to be more or less than the sum of its parts. In its constructive form, empathy, which we define as a mode of interpretation based upon thinking and feeling one's way into the subjective experience of another, moves the dance named relationship toward synergy rather than entropy.

EMPATHY AS THE INTERPRETIVE KEY: KOHUT'S SELF PSYCHOLOGY

With the possible exception of the work of Carl Rogers (1951, 1980) and Martin Hoffman (2000), nowhere has the unique place of empathy in human development been as brilliantly illuminated as in the clinical and theoretical work of Heinz Kohut and those who continue to elaborate his seminal contributions. The paradigm shift that became self psychology began with the publication in 1959 of Kohut's first paper on empathy, "Introspection, Empathy, and Psychoanalysis: An Examination of the Relationship Between Mode of Observation and Theory." There he asserted that the mode of observation in any endeavor to understand and explain a phenomenon must be congruent with that phenomenon's character. He proposed that empathy was the most appropriate mode for the observation and interpretation of subjective, complex mental states. The assiduous, sustained application of this interpretive stance in his and his associates' clinical work led to a sequence of discoveries that, taken together, became self psychology and represented a sea change in psychoanalytic thinking. Among the core reformulations that emerged were the primacy of experience-near understandings over experience-distant interpretations, the importance of open-ended guiding theory as opposed to theory-drivenness, the central role of significant others in nurturing the developing self, the conception of self as a synergistic whole not reducible to its parts, the revised view of narcissism as a developmental line evolving (if supported) from archaic to mature expressions and not a threat to maturation (unless unsupported), the positing of intersubjective reality in distinction to the Cartesian concept of objective reality, the crystallizing of a radically different and more positive philosophical view of the human condition (with an accompanying change in guiding ideals and values), and the shifting of focus from the vicissitudes of the drives and instincts to those of self and selfobject evolution (Ornstein, 1978, 1990).

In his pioneering explorations of selfhood, Kohut came to conceptualize empathy as a kind of surrounding atmosphere without which the self progressively suffocates. Although the contemporary infant research of Stern (1985) supports the view that we enter the world with a readiness and ability for relational engagement and asserts that we are both shaped by and shapers of the conversation from our earliest days, it also agrees with Kohut that the absence of empathic parental attunement can thwart development of the nascent self. As a quality of creative dialogue, empathy appears indispensable. If relationship is a dance, the back-and-forth movement of influencing and being influenced, then empathic attunement choreographs it creatively.

In the years between his first (1959) and last (1981b) publicly presented papers on empathy, Kohut was unwavering in his commitment to the empathic mode of interpretation in his clinical work. Central to the profound shift that moved self psychology beyond the then prevailing conceptual framework of psychoanalytic psychology was his concept of the "selfobject" experience. By this, Kohut meant the subjective experience of another person as supplying or sustaining essential functions within the self. For example, the proud gleam in his or her parent's eye initially supplies the small child with self-esteem before it has become internally structured as a function within the child's self. After it has become progressively internalized, he or she can experience such proud looks as sustaining, rather than solely supplying, feelings of self-esteem and is more able to tolerate their absence. Kohut described an identifiable developmental sequence of selfobject strivings in normal development or selfobject transferences in the psychotherapeutic restoration of self: from mirroring to idealizing to twinship. He conceived the healthy self as developing through this sequence of self/selfobject relations, pursuing its unique trajectory from cradle to grave.

Substantial failures of responsiveness on the part of significant others put developing selfhood at risk of derailment, while their "good-enough" (Winnicott, 1962) attunement to the self's evolving needs and uniqueness increases the likelihood that the internal structuring of the self will be activated and strengthened. Kohut became convinced that a key difference between developmentally enhancing and developmentally thwarting relational events rests in the self's subjective experience of the quality of the significant other's empathy. Even in instances when a particular need cannot be gratified, the experience of being understood empathically can make the difference between a manageable frustration that still supports and, indeed, may further growth versus a traumatic one that derails it.

The subjective experience of another's empathy typically supports the self's continuing efforts to get what it needs from others and facilitates the development of healthy internal structure. By virtue of its tentative effort to approximate accurately the other's subjective experience, empathy nourishes what is unique in each person's perspective and, more deeply, in their nuclear life plan—that unique combination of skills, talents, ideals, and ambitions, the actualization of which becomes the main "drive" in each individual once his or her needs for recognition, inspiration, and accompaniment by significant others are met well enough. Although we never outgrow the need for such recognition, its role in facilitating and shaping our development gradually becomes internalized as we strive to actualize a viable life plan. This view sheds a self psychological light on the root meaning of the word *parent,* which is derived from the Latin verb *parere,* meaning "to bring forth" or "to call into being." The empathy of parents and other significant persons brings forth selves.

Kohut observed that empathic failures of significant others beyond the developing self's ability to cope lead to a defensive or, more aptly, self-preservative closing off of particular interpersonal needs and their associated developmental strivings. In this wounded sector of the self, deficit encroaches on health and, as an old proverb predicts, "Where there are empty spaces, demons come to dwell." These spaces form fertile ground for the eruption of secondary psychopathology in the form of internalized conflict, symptom eruption, character malformations, and so on. Kohut noted repeatedly that the health-restoring process of psychotherapy lay primarily in the remobilization of the self's previously thwarted developmental strivings through empathic nourishment. What had been closed off in the name of self-preservation needed to be reopened in the name of self-actualization. An interrupted dance had to be resumed, one that reengaged closed off and devitalized sectors of the self frozen in time and waiting, spring-loaded, to be remobilized by another's empathy. The inherent design of the self, nature, had to be brought into realignment with the stimulating and shaping influence of an empathically attuned other, nurture. Although Kohut focused primarily on the particular form of conversation named psychotherapy, we believe that his discoveries are relevant to all conversations between people aspiring toward well-being, creative transformation, and prosocial behavior in their relationships.

Kohut ultimately and reluctantly concluded that the very lens through which the psychotherapist observes—empathy (or "vicarious introspection")—could have a profound effect on the revitalization of selfhood. "Could have" is an important nuance because the relational process is not complete, the loop is not closed, until and unless the person being empathically understood experiences this. Recall that two selves in conversation are constantly in the process of expressive and receptive interpretation. The act of empathy entails not just one person's expression of understanding the other, but simultaneously the other's feeling of being understood. One can understand another who does not then necessarily feel understood; one can misunderstand someone who nonetheless feels understood. The presence of empathy on one or both sides of a relationship increases the likelihood of the kind of dance that sustains and vitalizes selfhood, while its absence can produce a deeply wounding interaction. Either way, we are dealing with a very powerful phenomenon that, as Kohut pointed out, can be used for destructive, as well as creative, purposes. While our focus here is on its creative expression, that is, on empathy guided by the intent to be constructive, we hasten to concur that an accurate empathic understanding of another also gives one the power to injure another deeply. Beware the enemy who understands you.

While Kohut's conception of the "selfobject" experience, with its relational and subjective connotations, had moved early on beyond modern objectivist and reductionistic scientific understandings of the self, his definition of empathy did not, in our view, until his last publicly presented paper entitled "On Empathy" (1981b). Until then, he sought to adhere assiduously to an epistemological definition of empathy as a mode of observation singularly suited to the study of complex subjective mental states. Later, he expanded this definition by describing empathy as an informer of appropriate action. In his final presentation, he struggled poignantly, as our opening quote depicts, to bring his conception of empathy firmly beyond the modern understanding of the self as an isolated Cartesian thinker. Underlining the essential importance of empathy in sustaining the human self, Kohut (1981b) urged an in-depth study of "the developmental line of empathy—from its early archaic beginnings, to such high levels as barely touching, as barely still having any trace of the original holding that communicates the empathic understanding" (p. 534).

AN EVOLUTIONARY, DEVELOPMENTAL PERSPECTIVE ON EMPATHY

As if in response to Kohut's call for an investigation of the developmental line of empathy, the extensive research of Martin Hoffman (1981) makes plain that, before becoming elaborated developmentally into increasingly sophisticated levels of empathic ability, the human predisposition to resonate with the experience of others is rooted in our genetic design. Within the first day of life, newborns have been observed to cry more at the sound of another newborn's cry than at a computer simulation of the same sound. It is evidently the humanness of the sound, not its quantitative intensity, that stirs archaic empathic vibrations (Sagi and Hoffman, 1976, pp. 175–176). Spitz (1965) noted the same phenomenon and employed the term *coenesthetic perception* to designate it as a primary openness to the affective states of the parenting other. The fact that we are inherently designed to sense and respond to the feeling states of other selves, in combination with our lifelong need for empathically attuned others, strongly suggests an evolutionary basis for empathy. In two fascinating papers, Kriegman (1988; Kriegman and Slavin, 1989) expands the conventional interpretation of evolutionary theory and challenges classical psychoanalytic theory by arguing that empathy and altruism toward one's kin, as well as unrelated others, have been built into the human design via natural selection, owing to the survival value such traits confer. Accordingly, the concept of fitness, most commonly associated with aggressive competitiveness, must be revised to include the evolutionary advantages of empathic and altruistic attunement to others.

> The tendency toward empathic union with others and altruistic behavior may not be a recent cortically based overlay in conflict with a more primitive biological core of self-serving sexual and aggressive drives, but rather may itself be based on a very primitive biological core [Kriegman, 1988, p. 271].

Taking optimal care of one's own increases the likelihood, not only of their physical survival, but also their psychological actualization and the passing on of the original caretaker's genetic endowment. This is a stunning reversal of prior classical psychoanalytic thinking with its focus on the primacy of intergenerational hostility. It calls to mind the profound philosophical shift offered earlier by Kohut (1981a) in his last publication focusing on empathy.

Shifting from the evolutionary to the developmental perspective, we note that, like our basic sensory modes of perception, empathy as a mode of interpretation evolves from its reflexive, genetic roots through stages of ever-increasing developmental complexity. Like Piagetian schemas or internalized structures, empathy interacts both assimilatively and accommodatively with that portion of the world to which it is most attuned, that is, the subjective states of other selves. Assimilation of the already familiar nourishes and strengthens the current schema's interpretive power. Accommodation, set into motion by the often disturbing, conscious recognition of something unfamiliar and unassimilatable, catalyzes a reorganization in the very structure of the schema itself, taking it to a higher developmental level of functioning.

An example of such developmental transformation from Piagetian research involves the young child's ability to discern accurately the emotional states of others, known as "affective role-taking" (Urberg and Docherty, 1976) or "egocentric empathic distress" (Hoffman, 2000). The one-year-old child will assume egocentrically that the other feels exactly what he or she feels and, in those situations where this happens to be true, all is well. Assimilation works and the existing schema is adequate for the interpretational task. But where accurate interpretation requires the child to decenter from his or her stage-appropriate egocentrism in order to realize that the other's feeling is different from the child's own, the child's empathy will falter. If such disjunctions stir the child's conscious recognition that something is awry, the balance tips from assimilation to accommodation, forcing a questioning of his or her own schematized assumptive world. In this instance, the child begins to understand that others have different experiences, feelings, and perspectives.

As the egocentric illusion is repeatedly challenged, the prior schema reorganizes, and new interpretational resources develop to fill the space previously occupied by egocentric assumptions. Empathic interpretation is now not only informed by the realization that others may have perspectives that differ substantially from one's own but also shaped by concurrently developing skills and knowledge that allow increasing effectiveness in ascertaining what these other perspectives might be. Empathic ability has evolved to a higher level in accordance with its own developmental line, and new worlds of meaning open to its increasingly sophisticated eye. The assumptive world in which empathy is embedded has been raised to a new level, where it will reside until and unless the phase-specific limitation inherent in this newly achieved level is consciously confronted. A more complex self has emerged.

Piaget (1981) employed the term *disequilibrium* to capture the conscious struggle that ultimately ensues when an individual perceives meanings that are discordant and thus not assimilatable to his or her current mode of understanding. This perturbation entails, not simply the cognitive dissonance that pulls for decentering and accommodative reorganization, but also the emotional turmoil that accompanies this effort. This can be seen, not only in individuals, but also in cultures as they are pitched, often with great upheaval, into the hard work of rethinking their vantage point, their theory, their working understanding of the world, and their place in it. "It was as if the ground had been pulled from under one, with no firm foundation to be seen anywhere, upon which one could have built" (Einstein, 1949, p. 45). Thomas Kuhn's (1996) magisterial work on how scientific paradigms emerge and are transcended by more inclusive successors suggests that something like such perturbation drives the very process of science's development.

> Scientific revolutions are inaugurated by a growing sense . . . that an existing paradigm has ceased to function adequately in the exploration of an aspect of nature to which that paradigm itself had previously led the way. In both political and scientific development the sense of malfunction that can lead to crisis is prerequisite to revolution [p. 92].

It is part of our premise that the introduction of novelty in a manner that is subjectively experienced as empathically attuned greatly facilitates the accommodative developmental process in bringing forth strengthened selves.

In a recent publication summarizing three decades of research, Martin Hoffman (2000) has proposed perhaps the most comprehensive conceptualization of the development of empathic capacity. His focus is the role played by empathic distress in the unfolding of prosocial behavior, caring, and justice. Thus, Hoffman's starting point can be seen as analogous to Kohut's second formulation of empathy as "an informer of appropriate action." However, while Hoffman's formulation resonates with Kohut's view of empathy as involving both cognitive and affective components in mutually shaping ways, he emphasizes that empathy is not just an informer but, more importantly, a motivator of appropriate or prosocial action. He views empathy as a vicarious affective response that is genetically based and motivational for prosocial cognition, defining it as involving "psychological processes that make a person have feelings that are more congruent with another's situation than one's own" (p. 30).

Hoffman details a line of empathic development from innate, preverbal forms to highly sophisticated manifestations of resonance with subtle and complicated human affective experience. This line embraces five modes of empathic arousal emerging in distinct developmental stages. Mimicry, classical conditioning, and direct association, the first three modes of arousal, are present in the neonate. They continue as foundational activators of empathy throughout life. They not only enable a person to respond empathically but, when another's distress is involved, compel a response and thus serve as the deepest motivational layer for prosocial behavior. With increasing cognitive development, two higher forms of arousal subsume and integrate the earlier basic modes. The first is mediated association, which supports the association of the other's emotional circumstances with similar experiences of the child's own. The second is other-focused role or perspective taking, which allows one to imagine how the other feels and how one would feel in the other's situation. These last two expand and deepen empathic capacity beyond face-to-face situations and facilitate empathy with others who are not physically present.

Hoffman (2000) posits five stages in the unfolding of the modes of empathic arousal as they progressively come "online." The first he terms "the reactive newborn cry," described above, wherein neonates cry instinctively at the sound of another infant's distress. The second (around one year of age) is the stage of "egocentric empathic distress" where the child can feel empathy for the feelings of another but with no realization of a distinction between self and other. The other's pain is experienced as one's own. Third, early in the second year, children become capable of "quasi-egocentric empathic distress" wherein they recognize that the distress originally belongs to another, not the self, but still confuse the other's inner state with their own. Although there are fairly wide individual differences, by the middle of the second year and in the context of significant cognitive advances and deepening life experiences, children enter the fourth stage, termed "veridical empathic distress." At this point, empathic understanding and resonance with the other is much more accurate because the child realizes that the other has inner states independent of the child's own. Finally, the fifth stage, "empathic distress beyond the situation," consists of the ability to empathize with another's experience beyond immediate circumstances. It is rooted in the emerging realization that other people have distinct lives, unique personalities, different group affiliations, private inner worlds, and so on.

> When a person has advanced through the five stages and encounters someone in physical, emotional, or economic distress, he or she is exposed to a network of information about the victim's condition. The network may include verbal and nonverbal expressive cues from the victim, situational cues, and one's knowledge about the victim's life. These sources of information are processed differently: Empathy aroused by nonverbal and situational cues is mediated by the largely involuntary, cognitively shallow processing modes (mimicry, conditioning, association). Empathy aroused by verbal messages from the victim or one's knowledge about the victim requires more complex processing by mediated association and role-taking. In the role-taking's most highly developed form, observers may act out in their minds the emotions and experiences suggested by the above information and introspect on all of it. In this way they gain understanding and respond affectively to the circumstances, feelings, and wishes of the other, while maintaining the sense that this is a separate person from themselves [Hoffman, 2000, p. 90].

The abilities and motivations that infuse and inform empathy are truly a complex result of both evolutionary and developmental processes.

RECONSIDERING EMPATHY

As the foregoing evolutionary and developmental analysis suggests, "to think and feel oneself into the subjective experience of another" as a definition of empathy implies far more than it articulates explicitly. As we begin to flesh out this potent process, we reiterate our conception of empathy as a transactional or relational process, that is, an interpersonal event, a dance wherein meaning is mutually created. Empathy entails not just one person's subjective experience of understanding the other and being understood, but simultaneously the other's feeling of being understood and understanding. Empathy is never something done to another who receives it passively in a simple linear sequence. Nonetheless, for the purpose of clarity, we approach the complex intersubjective reality of empathy by first considering each movement of the dance of empathy separately and then looking at the synergy of their co-creative effects.

Empathy Expressed

By *empathy expressed* we mean one person's effort to acknowledge another's experiences and feelings. One can never entirely think and feel oneself into the subjective experience of another because the empathic listener inescapably contributes to the joint construction of emerging meanings. We approximate understanding of others (and self) only partially, never fully achieving it. In their respective definitions of empathy, both Martin Hoffman and Kohut leave tacit space for the otherness of the empathic listener, for the fact that, despite people's effort to go where another is, they never entirely leave their own selves behind. Moreover, viewed through a postmodern lens, the act of observing or interpreting any phenomenon has the effect of altering that phenomenon such that something different, no matter how subtle, has emerged for our next approximation at understanding. The concept of boundary between observer and observed has become more arbitrary and far less objective. Indeed, even the ideal of objectivity has come into question. The uncertainty principle (Heisenberg, 1958) from quantum physics implies that the horizon of understanding something is always expanding just beyond our reach partly because of our very effort to grasp it. This recalls Whitehead's (1978) assertion that the truth of something can only be grasped asymptotically, never achieved perfectly. Indeed, Kuhn (1962) suggests that the quest for objective truth is inevitably illusory and that the progress of ever-expanding understanding is better measured by comparing its explanatory power to that of prior understandings, rather than to some absolute truth toward which we imagine ourselves to be going.

The self psychologist's hope is that an optimal empathic interpretation will be experienced by the one who receives it as resonant with his or her own self-understanding. But no matter how resonant, no matter how close to being accurately attuned to the subjective perspective of the recipient, such an understanding will always alter what is being understood because it will contain an element of "other" in it, that is, the imprint of the empathizer's assumptive world. Indeed, the experience of being understood by another can, in itself, be profoundly new to some people. This introduction of novelty, with its accompanying press for creative accommodation, is, as we are about to see, an indispensable part of the transformative power of empathic understanding.

As is true of any other complex human perceptual capacity, the development of empathy is both made possible and limited by the composition and configuration of one's assumptive world. Its specific aspects (e.g., one's personal philosophy of the human condition, one's guiding ideals, one's educational or professional training, the theory that informs one's interpretive vantage point, one's own psychodynamics, etc.) have powerfully facilitating and limiting effects. For example, to focus on theoretical orientation alone, it should be clear that empathy informed by cognitive behavioral or Bowenian family-systems theory would be different than a self psychologically informed empathy in regard to the configurations that it would bring to the foreground. As we noted in the opening of this chapter, whether acknowledged or not, almost all psychotherapeutic approaches utilize empathy as a mode of observation—some explicitly and extensively, some prereflectively and narrowly. This may, in fact, help explain why disparate therapeutic techniques can produce positive results. Could it be that the experience of another working to understand us as deeply as possible within our own perspective combined with our subjective experience of being understood is therapeutic in and of itself, as Kohut's quote at this chapter's opening seems to imply? The developmental research of Bavelas et al. (1987) suggests that even simple facial mimicry of another's emotional state, what those researchers call "primary empathy," evokes in the recipient a feeling of solidarity and involved caring on the part of his or her listener that typically results in a decided strengthening effect in the recipient's self-experience.

The hermeneutical perspective invoked here reminds us that, like any act of a finite interpreter, the expression of empathy has limitations. There can never be a pure knowing of the other's experience simply because, in order for knowing to be possible, the knower must engage his or her assumptive world, ability to interpret, and the self that encompasses both.

> If we believe that the therapist is involved in the construction rather than merely the discovery of the patient's psychic reality, we are confronted with the fact that there is no way to reduce one's involvement to merely being that of a facilitator of self-awareness or even integration. There is no objective interpretation and there is no affective attunement that is merely responsive to and reflective of what the patient brings to the situation. There is always something personal and theoretical that is coming from the side of the therapist [I. Hoffman, 1996, p. 110].

Empathy expressed inevitably reflects the light and shadows of the expresser's assumptive world, not just in the illumination and, perhaps, remobilization of the other's true self, but also in the codetermined shaping of that self. We are aware of the apparent contradiction of speaking of true self and codetermined self in "both/and" rather than "either/or" terms. However, we believe that while true self, analogous to genotype, sets potentialities, codetermined self is shaped relationally in highly unique ways, analogous to phenotype, as its possibilities are realized and expressed over a lifetime. As part of an extensive review of the nature/nurture conundrum (i.e., genetic determinism versus cultural or environmental influence), Ehrlich (2000) wrote:

> It would not have made sense evolutionarily to prevent development of the human capacity to make real choices by imposing strong genetic control over the "wiring" of every synapse; indeed it would defeat the purpose of the complexity. That wiring pattern in the hominid line evolved to change throughout life with learning and memory. After all, brains basically evolved as devices for dealing with environmental variation and uncertainty. Whatever are the exact physical bases of memory or thought, wiring the brain to store specific instructions for all prospective situations would be a serious "design mistake" unlikely to be made by natural selection even if the genetic code had the capacity to do the job [p. 125].

In short, we believe empathy both facilitates the unfolding of the self's inherent design and shapes the unique trajectory and expression of that self.

Empathy Received

As in the expression of empathy, the ability to receive empathically attuned understanding is a complex phenomenon. The novelty inevitably introduced by the interpreting other can serve to counteract tendencies in the recipient to remain fixated in an assumptive world dominated by assimilation by inviting creative accommodation. Bruggemann's (1999) concept of "othering" captures the transformational power of encountering the other. Shifting focus from the resonance of empathic understanding to the inevitable otherness that infuses this understanding, he cites the "dialogical principle" based on Buber's concept of I–Thou:

> The human self is not an independent, autonomous agent, but is always and necessarily preceded by a Thou, one radically other than us, who evokes, summons, authorizes, and "faiths" us into existence as persons. . . . This restless, unsettleable relation is the irreducible core of what it means to be human. . . . The enterprise of coming to terms with this other in a way that is neither excessively submissive nor excessively resistant is at the core of living a human life [p. 1].

There are echoes of Kohut's concept of the selfobject in this, but Bruggemann's emphasis is on the importance of otherness as a source of developmentally enhancing struggle. Kohut spoke of the struggles that arise when our needs for empathic recognition are frustrated. If such frustrations are manageable, the self grows incrementally. Bruggemann privileges "speaking the truth in love," while Kohut highlights empathic response to the other's disclosures. For both, truth is not objectively determined by one partner or the other but, rather, codetermined in conversation.

Anna Ornstein (1989) has suggested that human beings perch somewhere between hope and dread in their relationships. The more traumatized they have been, the more the balance between hope and dread is understandably weighted in the latter direction. It is here above all that the subjective experience of beneficial empathy is so essential in inviting the shift back from invariant assimilation toward hopeful accommodation and a new beginning. Those who have suffered significant trauma to the self tend to recoil from openness when it touches upon the wounded aspects of their self-experience. They close off outwardly to any event that stirs the dread of being once again vulnerable to traumatization and inwardly to the original needs and strivings that exposed them to trauma in the first place. These inner and outer walls are built in the name of self-preservation but result in fixated, malnourished, and closed sectors of the self's experiencing. Self-preservation then takes precedence over self-actualization.

In the psychotherapeutic endeavor to realign the balance between hope and dread toward self-actualization, Kohut (1984) delineated a two-step process, which he termed the basic therapeutic unit of understanding and explaining. While both steps are empathically informed interpretations of the patient's subjective experience, they differ with regard to how much "other" enters into the communication. Kohut considered the task of the first step, understanding, to be staying as near to the patient's subjective state as possible. Even though the therapist's own assumptive world inevitably plays its part in formulating understanding, the expression of his or her view is minimized during this phase. The focus of understanding is for patients to feel known, strengthened, and accompanied in a fashion that reawakens and nourishes their search for internal cohesion and constructive relationships with others. For very fragile people, Kohut believed that the understanding phase required the therapist's immersion in the patient's subjective experience for prolonged periods of time. Only with gradual cohesion in the patient's self can the therapist move to the second step, explaining, with the introduction of perspectives from the therapist's side of the relationship. Although still empathically informed, explaining is more distant from the patient's experience; it contains more "other," as the therapist reveals more about how the patient's world looks from the therapist's vantage point.

Kohut (1984) regarded this gradient from experience-near understanding to experience-distant explanation as a catalyst for change in the patient's subjective sense of self at many levels. Taking a page from normal development, he likened this process to what occurs between mother and child as the latter moves outwardly toward more independent functioning and inwardly toward internalized structuring of previous optimal relational experiences. As the mother accompanies her child on this developmental journey toward enhanced separation and individuation, her empathic holding shifts from immediate physical modes of securing and nourishing to those that are expressed from a greater distance and more abstractly, usually via language. In so doing, the mother is both staying with and inviting the child's evolving strivings for positive relationships with others. Her interpersonal move is paralleled by a developmental shift in her child's self-experience and the kind of reaching for empathic recognition that sustains it. In the patient–therapist relationship, just as in the mother–child dyad, the shift from understanding to explaining is not a simple transition at one point in time but, rather, a tentative and complexly interwoven movement back and forth between the two levels of empathy. The shift from understanding to explaining and back again typically occurs numerous times before the invariant forces of derailment have diminished and the progressive forces of development have consolidated sufficiently. Only then does the next psychic task open itself to the process of understanding and explaining, thus taking the sequence to the next level.

The overall effect of this nuanced expression of empathy by the therapist on the side of empathy received is for the patient to feel held, be strengthened, and reengage strivings for constructive relationships from the point at which they had become frozen in self-protecting defensiveness. Through the therapist's judicious empathic deployment of understanding and explanation, both inward and outward self-preservative walls are opened once again to the process of accommodation. Inwardly, previously walled-off aspects of selfhood reenter into conscious conversation and active participation in the patient's life. "The analyst's empathy serves to open the patient's mind to a greater breadth and depth of his own thought and feeling, leading in time to an integration of previously disavowed experience and to an increased robustness of self" (Teicholz, 2000, p. 35). Outwardly, previously warded-off needs for recognition by significant others can be sought in a world of presently available resources. Invariant organizing principles are raised to consciousness, explored, and, via gradual opening to a new balance of assimilation and accommodation, renegotiated. The patient's evolving realm of experience with significant others has resumed its development. The variety and maturity of his or her capacity to engage the world of relationships has increased, and life goes on in more meaningful and satisfying ways.

Those who have traumatically experienced the pain of failed or destructive empathy do not open easily to being understood no matter how much they may desire it. More than anything else, it is their listener's sustained, good-faith empathy that creates for them the chance of the balance tipping from dread to hope, from self-preservative closing to self-actualizing opening, from self-experience based on fixed toxic assumptions to one based on principles open to ongoing reorganization, and, finally, from thwarted to remobilized selfobject strivings. One of our clients, who had just achieved such a shift in her own inward journey, summed it up succinctly, "I used to believe I didn't want to share all this bad stuff about me with other people; now I don't want to share these parts of myself with bad people." Her previously fixated notion of essential badness had been renegotiated, and she had remobilized her strivings for constructive relationships informed by a new, more open assumption: There were others whose empathy she could trust and whose understanding was central to her healing and growth.

In our opinion, the contention regarding the primacy and distinction between invariant organizing principles versus the developmental vicissitudes of selfobject strivings has been drawn rather too sharply. Ornstein's (1999, pp. 215–227) and Stolorow's (1999, pp. 229–232) discussions based on case material presented by Kindler (1999, pp. 197–205) are examples. It seems to us that the perpetually denigrating mother described by Kindler's patient was not only experienced as failing her daughter as a sustaining selfobject but, simultaneously, as inculcating an invariant organizing principle into her child's self-experience. Both facets are important to address therapeutically as each comes to the fore in the patient–therapist conversation. The factor that does not shift is the primacy of the empathic mode of interpretation, which allows the therapist to respond to whichever configuration is in ascendancy at any given moment.

Change and growth involve an optimal degree of opening one's self experientially to what is different. Those capable of growth are open to accommodation, receptive to the otherness of the one who addresses them, not just to the empathic echoing of their experience no matter how securing that may be. The balance can be delicate—too little other tilts one toward the fixation of closure and too much other tilts one in the opposite direction of intolerable intrusion, disruption, derailment, and the defensive reactions that cement fixation yet again. The latter has the effect of once more closing the developmental process off via defense mechanisms that ward off the new and permit only assimilation in the name of self-protection from a world interpreted as unmanageably destabilizing. Empathy as a mode of interpretation invites an opening in the one being understood, not for the imparting of an objective or authoritative "truth," but for the mutual exploration of co-created subjective understandings within an atmosphere of psychological safety.

Believing that one of the hallmarks of a healthy relationship was an openness in both partners to mutual understanding and that the core of cure consisted in the mutual creation of "a path of empathy" between self and others, Kohut considered the expansion of his patients' empathic capacity toward self and others to be one of the most important indicators and outcomes of a successful psychotherapy (Kohut, 1984, p. 52). Empathy begets empathy.

Empathic Synergy

What happens when we view empathy expressed and empathy received in the back-and-forth movement of conversation? What happens when we shift from the modern, reductionistic interpretation of relationship as external association between two separate individuals to a postmodern focus on the mutual transformation that results from the mode of relationship called conversation? Distinguishing empathy expressed and empathy received in the two previous sections allowed us to consider the steps of the dance of empathy separately. As we move now to look at them as a relational whole in motion, we find immediately that there is literally much more at play here than meets the eye. Analysis of ultra slow-motion video of simple conversations shows that, when two people talk to each other, they engage in an intricate dance that is mutually shaped and includes their themes and words but goes far beneath this into the prereflective realm of their physical gestures, speech patterns, and conversational rhythms (Condon, 1982).

> Two people may arrive at a conversation with very different conversational patterns. But almost instantly they reach a common ground. We all do it, all the time. Babies as young as one or two days old synchronize their head, elbow, shoulder, hip, and foot movements with the speech patterns of adults. Synchrony has even been found in the interactions of humans and apes. It's part of the way we are hardwired [Gladwell, 2000, pp. 82–83].

When two people talk, they quickly and unconsciously negotiate a physical, cognitive, and affective choreography, which contextualizes and conditions the verbal content of their communication. The predisposition to this dance shows itself within the first days of life (Stern, 1985; Bavelas et al., 1987) and evolves to higher and higher levels with maturation. Ogden's (1994) concept of the "analytic third" captures well the form this mutual choreography can take in psychoanalytic psychotherapy where, in the context of their intersubjective explorations, patient and therapist create a third process that is co-authored by both participants and not independent of either.

Authentic conversations are not conducted, but cocreated, with the outcome being more than the sum of the parts of each participant's original expectations. Whether this striving for mutual attunement will work its way upward to include higher forms of empathic understanding will depend perhaps upon other variables. But suffice it to say that the relational character of selfhood pulls for a continuum of empathic attunement from the most unconscious, reflexive levels to the most consciously intricate levels of understanding. And the experience of empathic attunement is essential to the activation of the strivings for confirmation, accompaniment, and being uplifted by significant others that underlie healthy development in the self. As alluded to above, this tropism toward attunement is perhaps the human version of a universal physical principle: All mutually influencing organized systems in the known universe appear to sustain a delicate balance between the forces of attraction and repulsion, between collapsing into each other and pulling apart, between individuality and togetherness. In the human world, constructive empathy can be seen as a manifestation of our tendency to come together for the purpose of sustaining the self-organizing capacity so essential to ongoing development and wholeness while also respecting the need for optimal, self-preservative distance.

Postmodern complexity theory arose from the study of such nonlinear phenomena as weather patterns, stars, and sand dunes (Waldrop, 1992). It attempts to explain what happens when we exchange the reductionistic mode of observing one variable at a time while controlling all related variables for the observation of multiple variables interacting simultaneously. Shifting emphasis from the laboratory to the natural world, the early pioneers of complexity theory were barely prepared for what they saw. The interaction of all related variables results in astonishing arrays of synergistic patterning where the only "controls" are mutually established, dynamic equilibria among interacting systems. Unfortunately, the term they chose to designate these relationally organized phenomena, "self-organization," which was meant to capture the intricate dynamic integrity of the entities that emerged to their observing eyes, obscures the main thrust of their discovery that all "self" organization is contextual.

Dynamic phenomena do indeed reorganize themselves continually, but all such reorganization is rooted in the mutually shaping interplay of all the contributing entities, and ultimately, all contributing entities encompass all things. For example, the swirling self-reinforcing nature of a hurricane is shaped by the available energy of a sun-heated ocean whose water vapor rises into multiple thunderstorms that interact synergistically and, in concert with the rotational spin of the planet, form the spiraling cyclone of the hurricane. Like the human self, the hurricane process cannot be understood as an entity unto itself, arising in isolation from the surrounding phenomena that shape and sustain its organization and identity. Here we might aptly invoke the words of cosmologist and theologian Teilhard de Chardin (1968): "My matter is not a part of the universe that I possess totally; it is the totality of the universe possessed by me partially" (pp. 12–13). Just so with everything that is real, including the reality named "self." Properly—that is, relationally—understood my self is not a private, isolated phenomenon possessed by me totally; rather, I compose and recompose myself continually on the basis of all the relational effects that I receive from everywhere in nature, society, and culture. My story is not a part of history that I possess privately; it is all of history affecting me partially. All self-organization unfolds within a web of constitutive relationships. "Nothing is itself without everything else" (Berry, 1999, p. 181).

The profound shift in worldview embodied in complexity theory is based on an observational stance that accepts the integrity of phenomena on their own relational ground, rather than viewing them as discrete objects to be separated and controlled into yielding up their secrets. The authentic character of something is only recognized when its inherent, irreducible relationship with all else (including the observer) is appreciated and unbroken. Self-organizing systems can only be truly understood in context. This is compellingly reminiscent of Kohut's original breakthrough realization that, when it comes to the complexity of human experience, the self is more than the sum of its parts, that it is imbedded in relationship, and that empathy must be our primary mode of observation. He emphasized that empathy, more than any other mode of interpretation, is uniquely well suited, not only for the exploration of complex internal mental states, but also for its recognition and acceptance of what it perceives and its own role in shaping self-experience. Kohut was a complexity theorist and didn't know it, perhaps because this paradigm-shifting vantage point was in the process of emerging all around him, particularly at the University of Chicago, during his most productive years at the psychoanalytic institute in that same city. As in other times when the foundations of thought were shifting, complexity theory was "in the air" but not yet widely articulated.

The synergism of the dance of empathy can be illuminated by two core principles of complexity theory: "the edge of chaos" and "increasing returns" (Waldrop, 1992). The former describes how systems evolve to higher or lower levels of organization within certain limits. If their inherent structure is too rigid, they tend to remain in a steady state or to degrade. If their inherent structure tends toward randomness, they dissipate by virtue of being unable to organize. Somewhere in between too much structure and too much randomness is the creative zone known as "the edge of chaos." Here the forces of prior organization are sturdy enough to maintain identity (assimilate) and yet flexible enough to be open to new influences (accommodate). More interesting still is the fact that self-organizing systems perched on the edge of chaos tend to reorganize, not so much through a series of quantitative steps, but rather, with the nonlinear emergence of substantially and, at times, surprisingly new configurations. Gladwell (2000) speaks of the "tipping point," Stegner (1971) of the "angle of repose," Piaget (1981) of "disequilibrium," and Kuhn (1962) of "paradigm shift" in their respective attempts to describe how one seemingly small influence—the proverbial straw that breaks the camel's back—can result in a profound reorganization, whether it be in the incipient spread of an epidemic, the birth of an avalanche, the unfolding of lives, or the cognitive paradigm shift that begins with one bit of incongruent information and ends by moving a child or a culture from one developmental worldview to another. In the dance of empathy, very small effects can have very big consequences akin to what occurs at the narrow transition points between state changes in physics or chemistry. For example, one degree of heat added to frozen water makes no substantial difference until one reaches 31 degrees Fahrenheit, where the addition of one more degree changes everything. The moments in human discourse when creative disequilibrium reaches critical mass are similar, but given the complexity of the psychological self, not remotely as predictable.

The principle of "increasing returns" describes how systems evolve by influencing each other via mutual feedback in the form of organized energy, that is, information. The output of one system becomes input to the other, which processes this information and feeds it back as altered input to the first. For evolution or creative accommodation to take place, such feedback must be useable by each recipient yet must also contain something new. No feedback, no self-organization, no evolution. In terms of this chapter, the classic example of such co-creative feedback is the interactive process in which empathy expressed becomes empathy received, and empathy received affects subsequent empathy expressed. We realize that our schematic separation of these two steps in a fundamentally flowing process has the liability of making it seem that something material is transferred from one partner in the dance to the other. This is an artifact of the structure of our presentation and could obscure one of our emphases that nothing more (or less) substantial than meanings are shaped and interchanged in this relational process. In empathically attuned conversation especially, such meanings are literally (in)formation. Postmodern self psychologically informed empathy is respectful of the co-evolving process in which meanings are formulated, appreciated and negotiated between people. It is adept at avoiding the traps and dangers inherent in the unilateral imposition of meanings disguised as objective truths. Evolved empathic communication is an exquisite mutual feedback process, the dance that is human discourse at its best.

Constructive empathy invites people in conversation to dance on the creative edge of chaos both intra- and interpersonally more potently than any other mode of communication. In its inherent tentativeness and respect for the self's and the other's uniqueness and limited knowability, as well as in its continual willingness to be surprised, empathy is itself neither too rigid nor too chaotic. At its best, empathy is an open-ended endeavor to understand by approximation another's ever-expanding and changing narrative, one that implies an acceptance that the empathizer's understanding is likewise perpetually expanding and changing. In its aim of understanding the other as much as possible within his or her own perspective, empathy has the quality of accepting, securing, and strengthening fragile aspects of the self. Selves thus strengthened are more open to the new, which invites further creative transformation. In its inevitable introduction of the new, empathy invites opening, flexibility, and sometimes perturbation. This is not necessarily a function of someone's intent to change the one being understood but, as stated previously, the result of the irreducible otherness of the one who empathizes and the effect that such understanding has in both challenging invariant organizing principles and simultaneously awakening or reawakening developmental forces in the one who feels understood. As two people dance on the edge of chaos, a cycle of increasing returns is born.

There are no uninterpreted truths in human interaction. Inevitably guided by his or her theory (and more), the therapist who leads with empathy respects the "theory" embraced by the client (i.e., the client's understanding of why they are seeking treatment, all that means to them, and more). The empathically attuned therapist is constantly crystallizing and recrystallizing his or her own theory via an understanding of the client's theory—and the client is doing the same. These theories, these two assumptive worlds, have entered into the space of mutual influence. Evolved empathy includes and integrates the subjective truths (invariant or otherwise) of both participants as these emerge in a conversation wherein new configurations of subjective truth can be negotiated and co-determined. These meanings are not unilaterally established, but rather, involve the practice of relational power, of mutual influence, rather than the one-sided effect of one person's subjectivity on another's.

In the psychotherapeutic version of this dance, the balance is ordinarily weighted in the direction of the client's subjective truth, which, as the main area of mutual exploration, is properly privileged as the center of empathic understanding for both partners. The conversation between them is inevitably accompanied by conversations within each partner as aspects of their own self-experience are stirred. For the client especially, this often leads to crisis, the proverbial dangerous opportunity. Psychological stagnation and suffering arise from disturbances in the relational dance by traumatic failures of empathy on the part of significant others resulting in defensively sequestered and fixated facets of self. The assimilative bias of self-preservation runs counter to the accommodative openness that feeds self-actualization. The client's experience of the therapist's empathic attunement and ability to articulate the wounded aspects of selfhood is crucial in remobilizing and renegotiating these previously thwarted developmental strivings. The steps in this empathic dance are not always graceful or well choreographed. Missteps and stumbles are possible yet still inherently part of the codetermined rhythm. We are not privileging evolved empathy as the only mode of communication capable of facilitating developmental or therapeutic change in human beings; we believe, however, that it is the most optimal.

Not least among the fruits harvested by self psychology is the realization that defense and resistance arise in the service of self-preservation and not primarily as efforts to defeat others, including therapists. Regarding this insight, Kohut (1984) wrote:

> It is only when we recognize that the patient has no healthier attitude at his disposal than the one he is in fact taking that we can evaluate the significance of "defenses" and "resistances" appropriately. The patient protects the defective self so that it will be ready to grow again in the future, to continue to develop from the point in time at which its development had been interrupted. And it is this recognition, deeply understood by the analyst who essentially sees the world through his patient's eyes while he analyzes him, that best prepares the soil for the developmental move forward that the stunted self of the analysand actively craves. Such recognition serves the patient better than anything else the analyst can offer, however deeply ingrained his traditional "realism" may be at such moments [p. 141].

Self psychology places empathy at the center of the relational process named selfhood and empowers practitioners in all the fields of human service with new assumptions about the vicissitudes and possibilities of ever-emerging relational selves. It has not invented a new kind of empathy but, rather, brilliantly illuminated and enhanced empathy's transformative power.

REFERENCES

Bavelas, J., Black, A., Lemery, C. & Mullett, J. (1987), Motor mimicry as primitive empathy. In: *Empathy and Its Development*, ed. N. Eisenberg & J. Stryer. New York: Cambridge University Press, pp. 317–338.

Berry, T. (1995), *Befriending the Earth*. Mystic, CT: Twenty-Third Publications.

——— (1999), *The Great Work: Our Way into the Future*. New York: Bell Tower.

Bruggemann, W. (1999), *The Covenanted Self*. Minneapolis: Augsburg Fortress Press.

Condon, W. (1982), Cultural microrhythms. In: *Interaction Rhythms: Periodicity in Communicative Behavior*, ed. M. Davis. New York: Human Sciences Press, pp. 77–102.

de Chardin, P. T. (1968), *Science and Christ.* New York: Harper & Row.

Ehrlich, P. R. (2000), *Human Natures: Genes, Cultures, and the Human Prospect.* Washington, DC: Island Press.

Einstein, A. (1949), Autobiographical note. In: *Albert Einstein: Philosopher-Scientist,* ed. P. A. Schilpp. Evanston, IL: Open Court, p. 45.

Frank, J. (1973), *Persuasion and Healing,* rev. ed. Baltimore, MD: Johns Hopkins University, pp. 27–35.

Gadamer, H. (1990), *Truth and Method.* New York: Crossroad Publishing.

Gladwell, M. (2000), *The Tipping Point.* New York: Little, Brown.

Heisenberg, W. (1958), *Physics and Philosophy.* New York: Harper & Row.

Hoffman, I. (1996), The intimate and ironic authority of the psychoanalyst's presence. *Psychoanal. Quart.,* 65:102–136.

Hoffman, M. (1981), Is altruism part of human nature? *J. Personal. & Soc. Psychol.,* 40:121–137.

——— (2000), *Empathy and Moral Development: Implications for Caring and Justice.* Cambridge: Cambridge University Press.

Kindler, A. (1999), The case of Joanna Churchill. In: *Pluralism in Self Psychology: Progress in Self Psychology. Vol. 15,* ed. A. Goldberg. Hillsdale, NJ: The Analytic Press, pp. 197–205.

Kohut, H. (1959), Introspection, empathy, and psychoanalysis: An examination of the relationship between mode of observation and theory. *J. Amer. Psychoanal. Assn.,* 7:459–483.

——— (1981a), Introspection, empathy, and the semicircle of mental health. In: *The Search for the Self, Vol. 4,* ed. P. Ornstein. New York: International Universities Press, pp. 537–567.

——— (1981b), On empathy. In: *The Search for the Self, Vol. 4,* ed. P. Ornstein. New York: International Universities Press, pp. 525–535.

——— (1984), *How Does Analysis Cure?* ed. A. Goldberg & P. Stepansky. Hillsdale, NJ: The Analytic Press.

Kriegman, D. (1988), Self psychology from the perspective of evolutionary biology: Toward a biological foundation for self psychology. In: *Frontiers in Self Psychology: Progress in Self Psychology, Vol. 3,* ed. A. Goldberg. Hillsdale, NJ: The Analytic Press, pp. 253–274.

——— & Slavin, M. (1989), The myth of the repetition compulsion and the negative therapeutic reaction: An evolutionary biological analysis. In: *Dimensions of Self-Experience: Progress in Self Psychology, Vol. 5,* ed. A. Goldberg. Hillsdale, NJ: The Analytic Press, pp. 209–252.

Kuhn, T. (1962), *The Structure of Scientific Revolutions.* Chicago: University of Chicago Press.

Loomer, B. (1976), Two conceptions of power. *Process Studies,* 6:5–32.

Ogden, T. (1994), *Subjects of Analysis.* Northvale, NJ: Aronson.

Ornstein, A. (1989), The dread to repeat: Comments on the working-through process in psychoanalysis. *J. Amer. Psychoanal. Assn.,* 39:377–398.

Ornstein, P. (1978), Introduction: The evolution of Heinz Kohut's psychoanalytic psychology of the self. In: *Search for the Self, Vol. 1,* ed. P. Ornstein. New York: International Universities Press, pp. 1–106.

——— (1990), Introduction: The unfolding and completion of Heinz Kohut's paradigm of psychoanalysis. In: *Search for the Self, Vol. 3,* ed. P. Ornstein. New York: International Universities Press, pp. 1–82.

——— (1999), The centrality of the selfobject transferences: A discussion of Alan Kindler's "The case of Joanna Churchill." In: *Pluralism in Self Psychology: Progress in Self Psychology, Vol. 15,* ed. A. Goldberg. Hillsdale, NJ: The Analytic Press, pp. 215–227.

Piaget, J. (1981), *Intelligence and Affectivity: Their Relationship During Child Development.* Palo Alto, CA: Annual Reviews.

Rogers, C. (1951), *Client-Centered Therapy.* Boston, MA: Houghton Mifflin.

——— (1980), *A Way of Being.* Boston, MA: Houghton Mifflin.

Sagi, A. & Hoffman, M. L. (1976), Empathic distress in the newborn. *Develop. Psychol.,* 12:175–176.

Spitz, R. (1965), in collaboration with C. Coblinger. *The First Year of Life: A Psychoanalytic Study of Normal and Deviant Development of Object Relations.* New York: International Universities Press.

Stegner, W. (1971), *The Angle of Repose.* New York: Penguin Books.

Stern, D. (1985), *The Interpersonal World of the Infant.* New York: Basic Books.

Stolorow, R. (1999), Antidotes, enactments, rituals, and the dance of reassurance: Comments on the case of Joanna Churchill and Alan Kindler. In: *Pluralism in Self Psychology: Progress in Self Psychology, Vol. 15,* ed. A. Goldberg. Hillsdale, NJ: The Analytic Press, pp. 229–232.

——— & Atwood, G. (1992), The myth of the isolated mind. In: *A Decade of Progress: Progress in Self Psychology, Vol. 10,* ed. A. Goldberg. Hillsdale, NJ: The Analytic Press, pp. 233–250.

Teicholz, J. (2000), The analyst's empathy, subjectivity, and authenticity: Affect as the common denominator. In: *How Responsive Should We Be? Progress in Self Psychology, Vol. 16,* ed. A. Goldberg. Hillsdale, NJ: The Analytic Press, pp. 33–53.

Urberg, K. & Docherty, E. (1976), Development of role-taking skills in young children. *Develop. Psychol.,* 12:198–203.

Waldrop, M. (1992), *Complexity: The Emerging Science at the Edge of Order and Chaos.* New York: Simon & Schuster.

Whitehead, A. (1978), *Process and Reality: An Essay in Cosmology,* ed. D. R. Griffin & D. W. Sherburne. New York: Macmillan.

Winnicott, D. W. (1962), *The Maturational Processes and the Facilitating Environment.* New York: International Universities Press, 1965.

Chapter 7

Psychic Survival versus Psychic Freedom: Reflections on Symington's Theory of Narcissism

Michael Shoshani
Batya Shoshani

Our aim in this chapter is to develop a dialogue with some of Symington's ideas about narcissism as presented in his works over the years.

PART 1

Neville Symington is the president of the Australian Psychoanalytic Society. He was trained in the British Independent School, of which he is a senior member. Deeply influenced by Alfred Bion, he developed his own original theory of narcissism. His studies in theology and philosophy and his extensive psychoanalytic experience with narcissistic patients were the background for the development of what might be termed an existential psychoanalytic conceptualization (Grotstein, 1993).

Out of his many rich ideas, we chose two that stood out as the most important concepts in his theory of narcissism: (1) *the idea of the*

We wish to express our gratitude to Bat Sheva Adler and Raanan Kulka for their helpful ideas and their generous teachings over the years and to Paul Ornstein, James Fish, Meir Winokur, and Moshe Halevi Spero for their insightful comments and encouragement.

lifegiver object, defined as the unconscious acceptance or refusal of life and (2) the notion of the antithesis between what he termed the ontology of survival, on the one hand, and the ontology of freedom of thought and feeling, on the other hand.

The Lifegiver Object

Symington (1999a), building upon Bion (1967), underscored the role of early "psychological disaster" (trauma) in the etiology of narcissistic personality disorders. This idea has already been absorbed in the literature, but Symington's contribution centered on his notion of a *lifegiver object,* which he proposed in order to account for an element of personal choice in the development of this disorder. The concept of the *lifegiver,* although intuitively makes a lot of sense to us, is not easy to define. Following Symington's use and applications of the term in his clinical examples, we agree with Grotstein's understanding of it. He described it as an internal, phantasmal, transitional-like object that is composed of aspects of the self and of the external life-supporting object. Thus, according to Symington, a central feature of pathological narcissism is what he termed the turning away from and repudiation of the lifegiver object. The infant makes an unconscious choice, either toward the lifegiver (spontaneity, Winnicottian living, hope, and authenticity) or to the disavowal of it. The narcissistic patient repudiated the lifegiver and restored to the use of magical pretense in order to evade psychical reality and to avoid the pains of external and internal reality. This process is not a total process, but a partial one that results in a split within the self, as Symington (1993) explained:

> The intentional core of the self is able to turn against the object that I have named the lifegiver. It is able to repudiate it, to turn its back upon it. ′. . . If one accepts the idea of the lifegiver as being the source of emotional life and also the source of biological survival—that the two are linked—then the self can never effect a total repudiation, and so a split takes place, with one part of the self turning against the lifegiver. As the lifegiver is incorporated into the self, a division and a repudiation of the self's own nature occurs, resulting in an anti-relational position being taken. . . . This turning away from the lifegiver forms the core of narcissism [p. 39].

The reader may find it helpful to think of the relationship between the narcissistic personality and the lifegiver object through viewing the relationship between a prisoner and his warden. This relationship entails high levels of dependency with extraction of the biological needs of life, on the one hand, and rejection, hostility, and repudiation, on the other.

This conception of a lifegiver object, emphasizing the possibility of a voluntary acceptance or refusal of it, is a creative and illuminating concept at three different levels. The first level is *epistemological/metapsychological:* the concept of a lifegiver object at this level turns the heated discussion around conflict versus developmental deficit into a controversy based on a false dichotomy. Both conflict and deficit are seen to play a role in the development of narcissistic disorders. These are seen to result from the interaction between trauma in infancy or childhood and the ways in which the subject has chosen to cope with the trauma.

The second level is experiential: at this level the concept of a lifegiver object helps us recognize and give meaning to experiences of lifelessness and emotional death in the transference–countertransference (Ogden, 1995).

The third level is technical: at the technical level this concept has what may be termed considerable "resuscitory power," in that it provides a foundation for the birth of hope in the course of therapy.

We would now like to illustrate these ideas with a clinical example (taken from Michael Shoshani's practice).

Danna, a young professional woman aged 31, came to see me after she had sustained two previous long-term therapies over a number of years with two different female therapists. She said that, while both therapists had been very pleasant and understanding, the therapies nevertheless had not really helped her. The complaints that she presented focused on lack of vitality and interest in life, an inability to maintain long-term relationships with members of the opposite sex, and various dilemmas concerning her professional future. She struck me simultaneously as a beautiful, intelligent, and arrogant woman. I felt that everything she said and did was aimed at one goal: to elicit my admiration. There appeared to be a very desperate, life-or-death quality to this need, as I sensed that she was determined to squeeze admiration out of me at all costs. This desperate quality also epitomized her descriptions of how she pursued and conquered men and women with whom she came in contact with. In her words: "Everything that breathes is suitable prey for my hunting instinct—anyone, a taxi driver, a petrol attendant, an army commander, or a female university professor."

At the end of the second session, I said to her that, although I could *hear* the contents of distress, I could not *feel* her distress or pain. Her immediate response was, "I can assure you that it will take a good few years before I let you feel my distress."

Approaching the third session of the intake, I began to feel pushed away and rejected by her. Everything I told her was already "known" to her. I began to have severe doubts about whether I had anything to offer her. I began to experience myself as shrinking and shriveling up inside. During the third session, she told me that the only long-term relationship she had had with a man lasted one year. This relationship was aborted by David, her partner, and she quoted what he had said to her on the occasion of their break-up: "You don't want a boyfriend or a partner, what you want is a 'fan-heater' and I am not willing to be that." This unsolicited image of a fan-heater fit the "admiration fan" role she had allocated to me all too well.

In this session I insisted on hearing a bit more about her parents and her relationship with them, and the story that I shall bring reflects the central organizing principle of my understanding of her.

Danna described her parents as educated people who enjoyed their occupations and, at the same time, had invested a lot in their children and in her in particular as an only daughter among brothers. She received a great deal of love, affection, and indulgence from her mother whom she said had reduced her work load by half after Danna was born, in order to invest more time taking care of her new infant.

At the young age of seven, Danna clearly decided to break off all emotional contact with her mother and stopped sharing anything of emotional significance. She stopped all discussion with her about clothes, friends, studies, and the like. She maintained the relationship only at the level of technical exchange, and this severance has continued to the present. All her mother's entreaties for closer emotional contact have been sharply dismissed by her. As Danna went on to describe the details of her mother's desperate and rejected attempts to get close to her, I felt my heart drop ("Is that what I have in store for me?" I wondered). Perhaps the most painful event in her description was when, at age 15, her mother asked her for the umpteenth time why she was unwilling to be close to her. Her mother then departed from her usual format of questioning and asked: "Why is it that you do relate to father?" Danna's response was to cut off relations with the father so that, in her words, the mother would have "no case."

In order to better understand the picture, two issues warrant emphasis. The first has to do with Danna's reasons for the breakoff of relations. In trying to find out these reasons, at one point I asked her directly, and she replied that she did not know why she did that. After some hesitation, she added that while it was true that her mother did much for her and gave her a great deal, her feeling throughout the years was that this effort did not emanate from maternal caring and concern for her, but from her mother's own need to feel and claim to be a "good mother."

It was my impression that Danna's mother was herself an extremely anxious person and more so as a mother who was struggling with her *own* traumatic past and therefore functioning on a survival level.

The second issue worth emphasizing is that, while Danna recalled these interactions with her mother without any signs of pain or sadness, she repeatedly emphasized her fear that ultimately it was she (Danna), who was without feelings. She also let me know that at those times when she was indeed accused of being feelingless by various people, she would feel intensely guilty and wish to die. I did not perceive any sense of such guilt, but I did believe her. That gave me hope for the possibility of my being able to help her.

Later in the course of that session, I said to her that what I understood from what she had told me was that at age seven she had decided to dismiss her mother from her role as mother. I added that, certainly, she had good reasons for this and if we decide to work together, we would want to understand these reasons. For instance, I continued, her feeling that her mother was mothering her only for her own needs, and not for her child's, would be very important for us to understand. At this point, there was a distinct silence in the room. I added that it seemed that, with David, her previous boyfriend, there was something similar, as if she had fired him as her boyfriend and had left him only in the role of "fan-heater." I went on further to say that in my contact with her during the three sessions that we had spent together, I felt that she had done something similar with me, not on purpose or consciously, but that I had felt that she was expropriating me of my role as her therapist. I proceeded with examples from the sessions. After a long silence, she contemptuously let me have it. She told me in no uncertain terms that I was talking nonsense and that what I said simply could not be true: first, because I don't even know her; second, because neither of her previous therapists had ever said anything like that to her; and third, how could such a little girl possibly decide something like that. No, she insisted, from her point of view, "Mother is responsible, and Mother is the guilty party."

At the end of the session, I asked her if she wanted to schedule another appointment. She angrily said, "Well, okay," and we set a time. After the session I thought that perhaps I had been too sharp with her and that quite possibly she would not come to the session we had set. And if she would come perhaps it would only be in order to formally dismiss me as her therapist.

The appointed time came, and to my surprise, so did Danna. She began her session by telling me of a terrible tragedy that had befallen her family about a year before (for reasons of confidentiality, details cannot be shared with the reader). At a certain point, I said that our previous session had not been an easy one and asked her how she had felt and what she had thought. *She answered that, for the first time in years, she felt hope.* And when I asked her why, she replied that, if it was true that she had *decided* to fire her mother, then she can also change the decision. I was quite excited and responded: "That's true; that's how I also see and think about it." I added that I saw in what she had said a good basis for our work together and if she decided that she wanted to work with me, I would be glad to work with her.

It seems that the intervention concerning Danna dismissing her mother, emphasizing the element of Danna's choice, resonates with Symington's conceptualization of the lifegiver object. We contend that this patient developed a severe narcissistic disturbance as a result of infantile trauma and a particular personality organization. In deciding to reject her mother as a lifegiver object, she unconsciously chose to turn her back on life. We think that, when Michael told Danna that she decided to "fire" her mother, a psychic process was begun that could allow the transformation of a concrete fact into a feeling and a symbol. In other words, this dialogue initiated a hermeneutic process that enabled the gradual transformation process from concrete entity into experiential feeling and the capacity to choose a symbolic impression over literalism. One can describe it as a movement from a situation of *forced suffering* to *chosen suffering* (Valliant, 1993). In this process, Danna could become, following Symington, the possessor of a sense of agency, an active ego, and not a passive entity that reality could merely sculpt.

Survival versus Freedom

Symington's claim is that the philosophy of the narcissistic personality disturbance is one of survival, whereas the philosophy of the healthy personality is one of freedom and creativity. Furthermore, Symington suggests that, as therapists, we have not achieved sufficiently positive results in treating narcissistic problems because we have been working with the inappropriate model. We work on the basis of an ontology that assumes that the aim of the psyche is survival, when we should be working on the basis of an ontology that assumes that the aim of the psyche is freedom and creativity. In Symington's (1999b) words:

> One reason why we do not solve the problems that are presented clinically through narcissism is that we are working with the wrong model. The false model is the belief that survival is the goal of the human endeavor. The philosophy of the narcissistic personality is survival; the philosophy of the healthy personality is the achievement of emotional freedom [p. 5].

In the second section of the chapter, we shall discuss and question these assumptions and present some alternative viewpoints. We are, however, in full agreement with Symington that, in personality disorders with an archaic structure, like narcissistic disturbances, questions of survival as opposed to freedom are of utmost importance. For this reason, we wish to present a later session with Danna and illustrate the importance of identifying and teasing out these ontologies for an in-depth understanding of the narcissistic disturbances. The example is taken from a session that took place about a year and a half after the beginning of the therapy. During these 18 months, I was shoved around, treated with contempt, repeatedly threatened with termination, and dried out emotionally and sometimes intellectually. Perhaps the image that best expresses my experience is of Danna as a tyrannical play director and of me as a mere actor who is continually castigated for not playing his part in strict accordance with the script. Retrospectively, using Symington's lense, I would say that, during this period, I was primarily concerned with survival, often through compliance in response to Danna's coercion and occasionally by defiance. Since she was so vulnerable, my somewhat pathetic efforts at self-assertion petered out soon enough.

In the session under consideration, Danna told me how she had lured someone at work into her net that week, using all her charms. She described her as sublime, distant and inaccessible. Every now and then, she would glance at me as if to say: "So what do you think?"

Further along in the session, she came out with the following: "So, why don't you say anything? You know how difficult it is for me. . . . You are probably not saying anything because you feel that I am trying to impose my will on you and that's why you are silent."

I said, "I notice a feeling of rising desperation in your voice."

Danna said, "I don't know why you don't give me what I so much need. . . . You are so unempathic with me."

At a certain point I said, "I am empathic with the Danna I see and hear."

Danna responded, "I don't know what you mean; I just want you to tell me what you think about what I told you; your silence drives me mad." She fell silent and after a while asked me to explain to her what all that meant, what I meant, since she knows only one Danna.

Then I said: "It sounds to me that the Danna that you are talking about, and in a way, the Danna whom you are speaking for now, is a Danna that needs very particular kinds of food in order to satisfy her hunger. She needs constant contact with the other; she needs physical contact at night, there must always be a body touching her. As you recently told me . . . or contact through words, there shouldn't be even a moment's silence: the kind of food that this Danna needs is 'fast food' or 'quick fix.'" (This is a term taken from the language of drug addicts in urgent need of a drug, and Danna has often used the term.) I was silent for a moment, and Danna said that the metaphor of food and hunger really said something to her and asked if she had ever told me that she had eating problems. I answered that she hadn't and added, "The problem is that, when you provide that Danna with the 'quick fix' that she needs (through conquests, one-night stands, uncontrolled amounts of marijuana) and through mobilizing me to talk incessantly, you are satisfying the one Danna, while starving the other. The kinds of food supplies that the other Danna needs are different. . . . For instance she doesn't need admiration, but love and authenticity . . . and unlike adulation and conquests, love and realness are the kinds of food that take time to prepare." She was quiet for a while and then answered that it was true but that, if she feeds the other Danna, she is afraid that she would remain hungry. The session approached its end, and she quietly said, "I am less hungry now; I received food that will keep me going until next week."

I said, "There is a feeling of closeness and togetherness here and now in the room and perhaps this is also the kind of food that the other Danna needs." Danna was quiet, and I saw, or perhaps I just imagined seeing, tears in her eyes, and this was the way the session closed.

This session signified the beginning of a turning point in the therapy. For the first time, Danna had a bit of space allowing her to function not only at the survival level. At the same time, the therapist had a bit more freedom to put his thoughts into words and give room to the Danna who may operate on the principle of freedom and authenticity.

We believe that the increased freedom for both Danna and the therapist in this session would not have occurred without the long period in which the therapist was a survivor, in a role that was fashioned for him by her.

This is a good point at which to begin to indicate the differences between Symington's ideas and ours. We turn now to the second section of the chapter where we shall present a different point of view on a number of topics.

PART 2

From Symington's writings, it appears that he presumes that the two ontologies of survival and freedom comprise goals that stand in a contradictory and mutually exclusive position vis-à-vis each other. We would like to raise a question regarding this assumption. Initially, we also conceived of these two ontologies as opposite poles on a single continuum; however, on the basis of life experience and experience with our patients, we have come to the conclusion that this is a somewhat *unidimensional* presentation of things. At this point, we believe that it is more worthwhile to think of this as *a dialectic between two basic and contradictory needs within a single ontology.* Our position is that people have two basic needs out of which two basic fears emerge. It was Otto Rank who first conceptualized this. According to Rank (1945), people have two basic needs: the first is for union and merger from which dependency, love, and belonging derive. The second need is for autonomy and separateness out of which the need for freedom and creativity derive. With the first need for merger comes the fear that Rank calls *death fear,* which involves loss of identity caused by the merger into others. The second need, for autonomy and separateness, brings the fear of loneliness and alienation that Rank calls *life fear*. Rank believes that, from the time of our birth to our death, we have to cope with these contradictory fears. In our opinion, the aim of life is to learn to maintain a dialectic relationship between being a separate and a simultaneously connected person in a state of relatedness. This dialectic is fundamental to human existence. When this dialectic breaks down from the direction of the life fear pole (that is the fear of loneliness and alienation), we respond with enslavement, restricting ourselves to merely surviving and foregoing the freedom to think and create. When the dialectic is ruptured from the direction of the pole of the death fear (i.e., the loss of identity by becoming lost in the other), we will respond by distancing ourselves from others and isolation and will function on the basis of the autarchic illusion of self-sufficiency. Michael Balint (1959) refers to this dialectic, proposing the *Ocnophil* and *Philobat* personality organizations. Other authors, noticeably Winnicott (1971), Mahler, Pine, and Bergman (1975), and Modell (1993), also described this dialectic in their own manner. Each pole of the dialectic represents a *need* in its own right and, at the same time, functions as a defense, limiting the expression of the opposite pole. That is to say, *merger is a need as well as a defense against separateness, and separateness is a need as well as a defense against merger.* Benjamin (1995), in her discussion of recognition and destruction in the processes of discovering objectivity, offers an interpretation of Winnicott and Mahler in the language of subjectivity. She concludes, "Then separation is truly the other side of connection to the other" (p. 41). In confronting different psychoanalytic psychologies, we all too often discover divisions based on false dichotomies. The Kleinians and the ego psychologists paradigmatically extol the need for autonomy and separateness. They place autonomy and separateness at the highest level of human development. In contrast, self psychologists paradigmatically place great importance on the need for merger. This is reflected in Kohut's locating the need for a selfobject at the center of his theory of human existence and development as well as in his theory of the curative forces in psychoanalysis.

Symington seems to place himself among those who emphasize separateness and otherness. His position is clearly illustrated in his discussion of the myth of Cassius (Symington, 1993). In this myth a young man called Cassius was lost in the outback and was unable to find his way back to human habitation. He arrived at a fertile glade that provided all his needs and desires with the help of a nymph that appeared upon his wish. The nymph supplied Cassius with shelter, food, drink, music, literature, and sexual satisfaction. The nymph vanished when Cassius fell asleep. He passed his days in a blissful abandon and felt himself to be the luckiest man in the universe. After about a year, he woke up one morning with a headache and realized that he was longing for a friend. The nymph was unable to fulfill his wish. Since he knew the myth of Narcissus, he went to look at himself in the water but still felt lonely. Then he decided to walk in search of a companion. He then encountered Miriam, a girl rowing her boat on a stream. He asked to join her and be her friend. She agreed only on the condition that Cassius give her a baby and work hard to provide the needs of the child and herself. Cassius was also asked to leave his sanctuary forever and burn the boat that could lead him back to the glade. Cassius was reluctant, and the nymph appeared. While conning him, she promised him everything Miriam had offered previously, without leaving the glade. Cassius was tempted by the nymph. While feeling lonely, he called out the name of "Marian," intending to call out Miriam's name. Cassius lived with Marian, the nymph, until one day she vanished. Only then did he remember Miriam and looked for her once again. When Cassius heard that it was too late and that Miriam had found a man who gave her a baby, he drowned himself in the well.

"Marian" is a golden fantasy, a nymph, who fulfills every need before it becomes a wish and her raison d'être is Cassius's ultimate satisfaction. "Miriam," on the other hand, is another human being, a separate individual, with a separate self and her own needs. It is clear that for Symington a mature and healthy person would have the courage to choose "Miriam" and to give up "Marian" forever.

In our opinion, both of these opposing camps see with one eye only, and in this situation, even if one's vision is excellent, it is only by the simultaneous use of both eyes that one can see three dimensionally. Transposing this to our current topic, we may say that we are born into and live with the dialectic between these two needs. We all make Faustian bargains with the devil. For instance, for the sake of fulfilling our needs for love and belonging, we forego a little separateness and freedom and pay with a bit of enslavement, and for a little emotional freedom we'll pay with loneliness and some of the risks of nonconformity.

With regard to narcissistic disorders, our position is similar to that of Winnicott (1960). The false self is that part of the personality that functions according to the principle of survival. It offers a compromise solution, but a compromise that is humanly legitimate. In certain personality constellations, the false self is a choice preferable to psychotic disintegration. This compromise allows for the existence of the true self and its protection. One can find support for this position in Fairbairn (1940) and Guntrip (1980) who have similarly emphasized the value of survival even when this is at the expense of freedom and creativity. Thus, the main pathogenic factor in archaic personality disturbances, including narcissistic disorders, is not necessarily a preference for an ontology of survival over an ontology of freedom, but *the inability of such persons to cope symbolically with the paradoxes of human existence and interpersonal relationships.* The great paradoxes of life that we are all acquainted with are separateness versus merger, self versus other, male versus female, omnipotence versus impotence, and mortality versus immortality (Bach, 1994).

According to Winnicott's dictum, which we find most compatible with our experience, these kinds of human paradoxes cannot and should not be resolved. *They should be accepted without questioning; that is, they should be contained.* Any attempt to resolve them would inevitably be at the expense of human complexity.[1]

The conceptualization of the dialectic outlined here has implication of utmost importance to questions of technique and the theory of technique. The main question of technique as we see it, and which troubles Symington as well, is how we are to work with patients with narcissistic disorders who experience threatening feelings of envy and greed in a way that does not lead them to feel condemned and attacked? This question has a bearing on the subject of survival versus freedom. It seems that the answer does not lie in the traditional distinction between external and internal reality. Alternatively, the answer lies in the distinction between a psychic reality sustained by clearly

[1] For a similar discussion, yet different perspective, see Erlich (1998).

differentiated internalized representations and *subjective–experiential reality* (Kulka, 1991).

When we, as therapists, are attentive to our patients' subjective experience *(this resonates with Kohut's concepts of "empathy" and "experience-near")*, we often need to accept the ontology of survival as an integral part of their mental deployment, even if only as an expedient. The psyche, with impoverished capacity to cope, when faced with significant threats from either the inside or the outside, will automatically, without choosing, perform the acrobatics required for its psychic survival. One could conceptualize this kind of mental activity as *psychic alchemy* (Valliant, 1993), rather than as unilateral (Bionian, Kleinian) hatred for, or murder of, reality. Obviously, these two alternative formulations, psychic alchemy versus hatred of reality, reflect different values. John Steiner (1993) echoes Kohut's thesis when he says that such patients have neither the time nor the mental stamina to understand but have a desperate need *to be understood*. The therapist who holds to this therapeutic stance suspends his own self by seeing reality almost exclusively through the eyes of the patient, or in Britton's (1998) terms, the therapist keeps his point of view to himself and communicates to the patient his understanding of the patient's point of view. From the Winnicottian point of view, we provide the patient with an illusion of union, an illusion that he creates the breast, that it is he who brings the other and the world into being.

On this subject, Kohut (1977, 1984) taught that, when we suspend our selves and listen to the patient's subjective experience, the patient's feelings of shame, humiliation, and insult come to the center of the patient's mental stage. It is this same attitude of attending to the patient's subjective experience that will allow these feelings, in the course of time, to subside and leave the center of the stage. In our experience, it is after this phase that intense feelings of guilt, related to contents and feelings of greed, envy, and vengefulness, begin to emerge. The therapist's suspension of his self and attention to the patient's experience creates an emotional context within which there is an increased possibility that the patient will get in touch with and understand threatening feelings without feeling blamed or condemned. In this situation, there is an increased likelihood that patients will take the risk of revealing themselves and their threatening feelings as we, as therapists are experienced as allies against their internal condemning and attacking parts.

Since Symington's classical article, "The Analyst's Act of Freedom as Agent of Therapeutic Change" (Symington, 1983), and throughout his future works, he repeatedly suggests that the essence of the therapeutic act is in the therapist's declaration of otherness. We would like to use one of Symington's examples in order to question this idea. This example is taken from his text *Narcissism: A New Theory* (1993). The description is of the treatment of a patient who has had a psychotic episode. For months, according to Symington, it appeared to him that he had been a very patient therapist, gradually crafting understandings and coherent meanings out of the patient's bewildering communications. However, the price he paid was of becoming an accomplice. This went on until one day he said to his patient: "You want me to build this into a meaningful structure because you think that you are unable to do it yourself" (p. 67). Symington adds that until this time, the atmosphere in the room was warm and empathic. From this time on, the atmosphere became stormy and hostile. From what he describes, we can understand that this session was a watershed in his conceptualization. When Symington points to the importance of declaring his freedom and otherness, we hear the ring of classical theory:

"It is the failure of omnipotence which forces the child to reality" (Novick and Novick, 1987, p. 376). We find ourselves deeply resonating with this statement. Alongside this viewpoint, Winnicott's and Ballint's positions and Kohut's later one, which speak to the importance of listening to the patient's subjective experience, relies on an opposite conception: *"It is the failure of reality which forces the child to turn to omnipotence"* (Novick and Novick, 1987, p. 376). Since we are in full agreement with this statement too, we find ourselves once again with the dialectic that we have outlined previously. At this point, one can say that a good-enough mother or a good-enough therapist needs to be in a relationship with the patient that incorporates a dialectic between oneness and twoness (Ogden, 1990). At the beginning of the therapy with Danna, Michael, like Symington in relation to his patient described above, was in a state of relatedness characterized mainly by oneness, without noteworthy expressions of otherness and freedom.

Gradually, as therapists (or mothers) sense that the patient moves apart even slightly and minimal space is established, they should find a way to place themselves in a position to meet the patient in the space that has been created. The significance of this moment is in the therapist's declaration of otherness in a dosage that parallels the capacity of the patient. It should be noted that a good-enough therapist will feel the change on the basis of internal cues such as feeling calm versus impatient and not only on the basis of information coming from the patient.

In the course of many years of work with patients with archaic personality disturbances, we have learned that our feelings before giving an interpretation are the best diagnostic indication of the patient's state and progress. Sometimes, over very long periods of time, even years, we feel that we risk a severe disruption of the atmosphere and the therapeutic relationship right before any interpretation that we give. If or when we begin to feel gradually that we do not need to prepare a shelter before giving an interpretation, we have come to know that this reflects the patient's growth and development in the direction of separateness and freedom to be himself and let us be ourselves. These processes of mutual influence represent the essence of the conception of a two-person psychology. They also provide the essential foundation of intersubjectivity. Both in Symington's example and our own example of Danna, it seems that, if there had not been work at the pole of oneness, that is, accepting the principle of survival, a premature declaration of otherness and freedom would have had antitherapeutic consequences and resulted in a therapeutic retrogression. Following Symington's conception, the therapists in both cases had ceased to experience themselves as having the freedom to respond to the patient but felt that they could only react. In his discussion, Symington (1990) draws a dichotomy between responding and reacting and advocates against the position of reacting because it is based upon accepting the principle of survival for the patient. We would argue that in both cases it was a sound therapeutic decision to agree to give up the freedom to respond until time was ripe to move on to the position of responding. Thus, therapists need to place themselves neither in the position of subjective object nor objective object, but to be in a constant play, in potential movement between the two. It seems that Mitchell (1997) struggled with the same dilemma, although from a somewhat different angle, when he suggested "that the central feature of the therapeutic action of psychoanalysis is the emergence of something new, from something old. It cannot be there in the beginning, because you have to find yourself in the old to create the proper context for the emergence of something new" (p. 59).

We would like to suggest an additional angle to the question of therapeutic technique in working with narcissistic disorders. In our experience, one of the foci of disturbance in such patients is on what might be called the dimension of precocity, "too big too soon." Indeed, these patients as children somehow "jumped" from child to adult status without really growing up (similar to going from third grade to twelfth grade in one leap). This reminds us of two patients with severe narcissistic features. The first had a repeated dream that he is in twelfth grade and about to take his final examinations. He is in terrible anxiety when, suddenly, members of the school administration come to him and tell him that there is nothing to worry about, that he doesn't need to take the examination because he has already been tested long ago and he is, in fact, already in the second year at University. The second patient stole his father's car at night and drove around when his father was abroad on business. This went on for many years, since he was 10.

The phenomenon of the jump in time and size can occur and be maintained only if the psyche undertakes two acrobatic operations in what might be termed the framework of psychic alchemy. The first operation is to be "big." As a child imagines grown-ups, he sees them as people who aren't frightened, envious, embarrassed, or dependent. That is to say, the imagined "bigness" is actually a caricature of a grown-up, which is perceived as being "blown up" like a balloon. Thus, the child develops in his mind, an equation between being big and being "blown up." The most malignant result in this case is that there is no need to grow up and develop; the person has already, so to speak, "passed his final examinations"; he has already been driving for years and, therefore, has no need to "learn to drive or to be tested."

The second operation involves the splitting off of parts of the true self. These parts, according to the Kohutians, contain feelings of insult, inferiority, smallness, shame, and humiliation. According to the Kleinians, these parts contain feelings of envy, greed, and hatred. In our view, whichever the case may be, these are intolerable feelings that are connected to premature awareness of separateness and otherness. The only way out for a child in such a position is to cut himself off from these parts. This results in constriction of the true self and contributes to its impoverishment. These split-off and rejected parts may then be replaced by false parts with chameleon-like qualities with high survival values, which take over the personality. It is not surprising that such a person does not only feel a little dishonest and a little imitative, like most of us, but that all of his self-experience is dominated by feelings of fraud, falseness, and being an imposter.

The translation and application of these understandings to our clinical work requires the concepts of regression and reversibility. Regression is the process through which access may be gained to what Winnicott (1954) defined as "the failure of reality frozen." Kohut (1959) translates and applies this understanding to the transference: "The analyst is not the screen for the projection of internal structures, but a direct continuation of an early reality that was too distant or too rejecting or too unreliable to be transformed into solid psychic structures" (p. 219).

In the context of the precocity dimension that we have just described, regression allows access to the situation that led the child to jump from third grade to twelfth grade or the situation that led Danna to fire her mother at the early age of seven, become a mother to herself, and develop all the defensive features necessary to maintain this psychic alchemy. Our claim is that the process of regression enables the creation of a dialogue with parts of the true self. The false self that functions on the principle of survival serves as the gatekeeper and, only after being secured by the therapist, allows the contact with parts of the true self that are in "deep freeze." If we succeed in "defrosting" these frozen parts of the true self and in bringing them out of hiding, we will succeed in changing the balance between the two principles (survival versus freedom) and tip the balance in favor of the part of the psyche that aims toward life freedom and creativity. We are reminded of a patient who became ill with cancer at the age of 10, and for many years his life was in danger. He referred to various time periods during the years of his illness as "silent movies without emotional subtitles." Following on Bollas's (1987) "unthought known," we have come to call this phenomenon "unfelt-experienced." The only way to defrost these parts is to be there as a transformational object willing to share the constant burden of intolerable emotional intensity. The therapist felt the pain with this child sick with cancer. He also feared and cried with him. He shared with him the experience of the shame of being defective, the insult of being deviant, and together they got through this holocaust. The patient went through the Holocaust for a second time, but lived it for the first time. It is important to note that this process includes a phase of total dependence on the therapist and his idealization. This implies that both dependence and idealization are developmental phases and not only defensive operations.

Before we conclude this chapter, we would like to point out several theoretical issues that arise from our previous discussions. We chose not to elaborate on these profound issues since we believe they merit a separate article.

(1) We realize that a thorough comparison between Symington's and Kohut's theories is required. In this context, we wish to mention three points that stand out in our presentation.

- First, Kohut and Symington seem to share the same view when emphasizing the role of external (real) trauma in the etiology of narcissistic patients; however, their views sharply diverge on issues of responsibility. Symington emphasizes the element of personal choice and thus the patient's responsibility for his psychic organization, whereas Kohut emphasizes the responsibility of the external environment in that it failed to fulfill the selfobject needs of the patient.
- Second, it would seem worthwhile to compare and contrast Symington's idea of rejection of the *lifegiver object* with Kohut's

(1977) idea of the *dread to repeat* the trauma. In this light, one might question whether the patient (in our case, Danna) rejects the *lifegiver object,* or rather is it that in the patient's experience it is actually the *deathgiver object* that the patient rejects?

- Third, one could compare and contrast Symington's (1999b) psychic goal of freedom and creativity to Kohut's (1966) psychic goal of self-cohesion.

(2) Concerning the issue of the theory of technique, it is a crucial question whether one sees and describes the therapist (Michael with Danna) as a survivor who struggles to maintain his separateness and otherness, even if it is not openly declared, or as actively suspending his own self for the benefit of his patient. This issue touches upon the important question of how the therapist understands and employs the countertransference feelings that are evoked within him.

(3) The idea of unconscious choice that is central to Symington's theory is complex and deserves a separate discussion of its epistemological status and meaning.

We would like to conclude with two tales that bear on the theme of psychic survival versus psychic freedom, with which we have struggled throughout the chapter. The first is a story told of a great Kabalistic Hasidic leader, Rabbi Nachman of Breslav, who used to say: "Wherever I travel, I travel to the Land of Israel, and for the time being I am a shepherd in Breslav." This is how we see our situation as therapists and patients. All our lives we travel toward truth, freedom, and creativity. We try to follow Socrates' dictum "know thyself." But in the meantime, we are a bit occupied with self-deception and, more than occasionally prefer not to know ourselves. The same idea, from a somewhat different angle, is expressed by the concept of "journey." There is a "way" and a "destination" in all journeys. In the language of the "Myth of Cassius," the destination is "Miriam." This destination is simultaneously highly desirable and highly threatening. In our experience, in contrast to Symington's view, what strengthens a person's resolution to try to reach a destination is, paradoxically, his knowledge of the operation of the principle of reversibility. In the language of the myth, one needs to know that the boat has not been burned and that one can return to "Miriam" if one's psychic life is threatened. As we see it, unlike Symington, the choice between Miriam and Marian is never absolute. Marian is never forsworn for the sake of Miriam, but rather, there is a back and forth between the two on the journey toward Miriam.

The second is a personal story. Five years ago a close friend of ours died of lung cancer after six months of terrible agony. The encounter with the way in which he had coped with his impending death turned everything upside down for us. Throughout the 32 years of our friendship, he was seen to us as the symbol of a free man. We had always envied his courage to live his life truthfully with uncompromising freedom from social expectations, as well as his willingness to pay the social price that accompanies such freedom. His last months were horrendous from the point of view of his suffering and physical deterioration. His behavior, until his dying day, showed no indication that he accepted or was even aware of the fact of his impending death. He behaved until the last moment as if he were certain that he would defeat the illness and it was clear that he expected from those around him to participate in what we surely thought must be a massive self-deception. We asked ourselves how to view this phenomenon. In this context, did the choice of not knowing and not accepting his impending death express an ontology of survival or an ontology of freedom? Is this a choice at all or, rather, an enormous fear of death that dictates massive self-deception. As Sartre would claim, our friend, in his inability to face death, lost his autonomy and freedom.

Or is it perhaps an expression of the freedom to choose and fight to the last moment out of the belief in his basic right to struggle against all odds? Is this what Plato meant when he said that a person who accepts his death ceases being a person?

REFERENCES

Bach, S. (1994), *The Language of Perversion and the Language of Love*. Northvale, NJ: Aronson.

Balint, M. (1959), *Thrills and Regressions*. London: Marsfield Library.

Benjamin, J. (1995), *Like Subjects, Love Objects*. New Haven: Yale University Press.

Bion, W. R. (1967), *Second Thoughts*. London: Maresfield Books.

Bollas, C. J. (1987), *The Shadow of the Object: Thoughts on the Unthought Known*. New York: Columbia University Press.

Britton, R. (1998), *Belief and Imagination*. London: Routledge.

Erlich, H. S. (1998), On loneliness, narcissism, and intimacy. *Amer. J. Psychoanal.*, 58:135–162.

Fairbairn, W. R. D, (1940), Schizoid factors in the personality. In: *Psychoanalytic Studies of the Personality*. London: Routledge & Kegan Paul, 1952, pp. 3–27.

Grotstein, J. (1993), Foreword. In: *Narcissism: A New Theory*, ed. N. Symington. London: Karnac Books, pp. ix–xvi.

Guntrip, H. (1980), *Schizoid Phenomena, Object Relations and the Self*. London: Hogarth Press.

Kohut, H. (1959), Introspection, empathy, and psychoanalysis. In: *The Search for the Self*, ed. P. Ornstein. New York: International Universities Press, 1978, pp. 205–232.

——— (1966), Forms and transformations of narcissism. *J. Amer. Psychoanal. Assn.*, 14:243–272.

——— (1977), *The Restoration of the Self.* New York: International Universities Press.

——— (1984), *How Does Analysis Cure?* ed. A. Goldberg & P. Stepansky. Chicago: University of Chicago Press.

Kulka, R. (1991), Reflections on the future of self psychology and its role in the evolution of psychoanalysis. In: *The Evolution of Self Psychology: Progress in Self Psychology, Vol. 7,* ed. A. Goldberg. Hillsdale, NJ: The Analytic Press, pp. 175–183.

Mahler, M., Pine, F. & Bergman, A. (1975), *The Psychological Birth of the Human Infant.* New York: Basic Books.

Mitchell, S. (1997), *Influence and Autonomy in Psychoanalysis.* Hillsdale, NJ: The Analytic Press.

Modell, A. H. (1993), *The Private Self.* Cambridge, MA: Harvard University Press.

Novick, K. K. & Novick, J. (1987), The essence of masochism. *The Psychoanalytic Study of the Child,* 42:353–384. New Haven, CT: Yale University Press.

Ogden, T. H. (1990), *The Matrix of the Mind.* Northvale, NJ: Aronson.

——— (1995), Analysing forms of aliveness and deadness of the transference–countertransference. *Internat. J. Psycho-Anal.*, 76:695–709.

Rank, O. (1945), *Will Therapy.* New York: Knopf.

Steiner, J. (1993), *Psychic Retreats.* London: Routledge.

Symington, N. (1983), The analyst's act of freedom as agent of therapeutic change. *Internat. Rev. Psycho-Anal.*, 10:283–292.

——— (1990), The possibility of human freedom and its transmission (with particular reference to the thought of Bion). *Internat. J. Psycho-Anal.*, 71:95–106.

——— (1993), *Narcissism: A New Theory.* London: Karnac.

——— (1999a), Bion and trauma transformed. Lecture given at the conference on Bion and Narcissism. Bar-Ilan University, Tel Aviv.

——— (1999b), The core of narcissism. Lecture given at the conference on Bion and Narcissism. Bar-Ilan University, Tel Aviv.

Valliant, G. E. (1993), *The Wisdom of the Ego.* Cambridge, MA: Harvard University Press.

Winnicott, D. W. (1971), *Playing and Reality.* New York: Basic Books.

——— (1954), Metapsychological and clinical aspects of regression within the psycho-analytical set-up. In: *Collected Papers.* New York: Basic Books, 1958, pp. 278–294.

——— (1960), Ego distortion in terms of true and false self. In: *The Maturational Processes and the Facilitating Environment.* New York: International Universities Press, 1965, pp. 140–152.

II

Clinical

Chapter 8

Working with Adolescents: A Time for "Reconsideration"

Mark D. Smaller

I was about nine years old when I attended my last summer of day camp, which was, for me, preparation for the big time of overnight camp the following summer. Camp Optimist provided excellent activities and counselors for the three summers I attended. That last summer, I had a counselor named Mike, who, in my mind, almost walked on water. This guy really could start a campfire barely using one match; hit bull's eyes at the archery or shooting range; and could teach basketball, baseball, and swimming, not only with great sensitivity, but also by example. Most important, he maintained absolute authority and commanded respect. We would start cutting up at the lunch table, and he needed only to give us a look and we would immediately shape up. The guy could do no wrong. One day, I had a dental appointment that meant I would not take the camp bus home, but stay at the "Y" until my mother arrived to pick me up. The counselors used to hang out after putting the kids on buses home and usually played some pool or ping-pong. I sat quietly near the front door waiting to get picked up and remember feeling quite privileged listening to the banter of unwinding counselors in the next room. Suddenly, I heard, with great alarm and utter disbelief, my counselor Mike swearing, I mean really swearing, while playing pool. To this day, I could not tell you what words flew around the corner banging my ears, but I can tell you, and with certainty, they were bad. Mike used *those* words? I was stung, devastated, and disoriented. When my mother finally arrived, after what seemed to be hours, but which was probably a few moments,

I remember saying something to her like, "I can't wait to go to overnight camp next summer—this camp is for little kids." But to myself, I knew the real reason I never wanted to return. Camp Optimist would never be the same.

It would be misleading to suggest that this camp experience became the organizing trauma of my life. However, it serves as an example of the many inevitable disappointments that occurred later on during my adolescence, experiences that involved either the disappointment in admired others or my disappointing those admired others or myself.

As we witness these kinds of ongoing and inevitable disappointments with our adolescent patients, we see that these dissapointments do, in fact, significantly impact character and are often the scenes needing to be discussed and understood when the adolescent arrives at our office for help.

Adolescence is a significant time for emotional, physical, and cultural development, but then, which phase of development isn't? Middle age also involves coming to terms with physical changes in one's self, integrating certain disappointments with one's self and others, and attempting to sort out that which has occurred previously in order to move on toward the future (Galatzer-Levy, 1984). More psychological structure often helps. However, does not every stage of development, from infancy through older age, involve coming to terms with emotional, physical, and cultural changes in one's self? Similar to middle age, does adolescence have to be the volatile time we have all read about in psychoanalytic literature over the years, that children and parents must go through this difficult time and hopefully survive enough to proceed to young adulthood and, for the parents, middle age? I wonder.

Freud (1905), Erikson, and Blos write about adolescent volatility. For example, Erikson (1963), attempting to take the focus off drives and describe the development of identity, writes:

> The growing and developing youths, faced with this physiological revolution within them . . . are concerned with what they appear to be in the eyes of others. . . . In their search for a new sense of continuity and sameness, adolescents have to refight many of the battles of earlier years, even . . . appoint perfectly well-meaning people to play the roles of adversaries [p. 261].

Like Freud, Erikson relies on the language of battle and revolutions describing this period of development and conflict. Although drives are no longer central, he remains focused on the internal state of the adolescent, "appointing well-meaning people" to be adversaries and assuming those real significant others are "good enough."

Blos (1962) focused on drives and the Oedipus conflict: "Instinctual urges of early childhood make themselves felt again. . . . Drives are intensified, new instinctual aims emerge" (p. 16). Blos gives rich clinical examples and emphasizes the second stage of individuation accompanied by feelings of isolation, loneliness, and confusion. We often observe these feelings in our adolescent patients, but are they developmental givens?

Is it the developmental phase, or possibly the parental response to that phase, that creates these "battles and revolutions"? As Kohut pointed out, the acts of Oedipus killing his father and marrying his mother must be considered in the context of his history. As an infant, Oedipus was taken by his father to a desolate rocky side of a mountain, tied down by his ankles, and left to die. It is reasonable to assume that this trauma could create understandable problems later on in Oedipus's adult life and family, especially in the areas of aggression and sexuality.

Our theoretical views impact how we respond to clinical material. If we view adolescence as a reawakening of or regression to intense oedipal conflict over sexual and aggressive drives or a repetition of unresolved separation anxiety left over from an earlier time, therapeutic responses will be offered in a particular direction. Interpretation would be the primary form of technique and would be curative.

I would suggest that one of the central (but not the only) concerns of adolescence is working through severe and mild, inevitable disappointments with admired others and with one's self (for more general self psychological perspectives, see Palombo, 1988; Lage, 1997; Shane, Shane, and Gales, 1997). This allows for the integration of ambitions and ideals creating a strong and cohesive self. As Wolf (1988) points out, "Cognitive development leads to a recognition of parental defects, with the inevitable outcome of a rapid de-idealization of the early idealized selfobjects" (p. 58). Since the adolescent cannot survive in a vacuum, Wolf underscores the importance of the adolescent turning toward "the peer group, idealized heroes of literature, history or the current teenage subculture in order to sustain a self and develop values" (p. 58). He also echoes the need for and sometimes ambivalence toward the adolescent "moratorium," which Erikson described in his writings on identity.

Webster's (1976) defines moratorium as a time sanctioned by some authority where there is a "suspension of activity during a time of reconsideration" (p. 256). Treatment might be considered a moratorium. This view underscores the usefulness and impact of analysis for the adolescent unable to connect to a responsive selfobject peer, group, or family milieu in order to create time or space for reconsideration. The relationship with the real, genuine or authentic person of the analyst becomes critical, which enables the adolescent to remain connected to or develop his or her own authenticity.

Based upon the self psychological view of adolescence being a period of rapid de-idealization of early parental selfobjects, treatment would naturally focus upon these disappointments. These would include disappointments as they occur in the adolescent's past and current life outside the treatment, in the transference, and within the adolescent's self. I am not suggesting that other dynamics are not present, important, or influencing functioning, but these areas of disappointments with the self, parents, teachers, admired figures, and sometimes the analyst often become the primary focus. Although earlier issues are present, the analysis, if conducted with the appropriate responsive ambience, will provide a corrective optimal experience (Bacal, 1985), facilitating the working through of disappointments at a gradual, nontraumatic pace that allows the adolescent self to be reorganized, cohesive, creative, and thriving.

I don't believe adolescence has to be a volatile time if an appropriate and responsive selfobject milieu is in place. As Cohler and Galatzer-Levy (1993) point out, "Many researchers doubt that the turmoil and distress are necessary or that the moratorium is inevitably part of healthy adolescence" (p. 188). Focusing on external behavior rather than on the experiential world of the adolescent can be misleading. Many adolescents may appear quite rebellious on the surface, but remain connected to their parents and the family's values as long as the parents can tolerate certain adversarial behavior.

The following clinical examples will describe how a self-psychological perspective influenced my responses during the initial phases of treatment with two adolescents and how a responsive selfobject analytic milieu in the third case provided an adolescent girl enough space to strengthen a fragile self amidst some typical adolescent concerns. This perspective has emerged over the last 25 years after listening to my adolescent patients and learning to take them at their word. They have taught me how useful or curative empathic and appropriate responses can be in helping them get back on a personally satisfying self-trajectory in their lives.

I have also been able to let go of old ideas I was taught years ago about treating the so-called difficult, resistant, involuntary, untreatable, psychotic, borderline, impulsive, or unmotivated adolescent patient. This transformation occurred in various settings: home visits through the juvenile court, an outpatient clinic, an elementary school, a state hospital, and a private practice.

By the time adolescent patients make it to our office doors, even when it appears they have been dragged there by their parents or forced by a school or the court or a hospital upon release, I believe they want more than anything to be there. They are hungry for meaning, responsiveness, validation, and healing. Only their terror of traumatic disappointment by yet another adult claiming care and reliability makes them want to bolt.

LISA

Lisa was 12 when she first arrived at my office. Although physically mature in her looks, she seemed a bit younger in manner. She explained that she was not doing well in school, would often lose her appetite, was preoccupied with certain private thoughts, and was certain her stepmother hated her. She explained that her father had recently remarried after having been divorced from her mother for about five years. When Lisa was seven, her mother had announced to the family that she was leaving. She moved out of the house and, for a while, settled in Europe. Lisa felt she had accepted what had happened regarding the subsequent divorce, but now her problems were about her stepmother.

Initially, and for some months, Lisa came in and talked about the activities of her day, about her horrible stepmother and stepsister, and about her anger with her father for marrying such a woman. Although complaints often focused upon daily routines and habits of her new family, her most frequent complaint about her stepmother was that she tried to suggest what Lisa was feeling. "She's in therapy, my brother and stepsister are in therapy, and so is my father, and they all want to make interpretations about me."

Lisa began drawing, mostly faces, but always the same face, which I only came to recognize when I finally met with her mother. These faces were drawn over and over again, sometimes faces on models with particular clothes Lisa designed on paper. Occasionally, I commented that drawing and redrawing the face resembling her mother's might have been an attempt to somehow make or remake her mother since she had experienced such disappointment with her. Lisa would smile politely and say, "That's a psychological interpretation, right?" Then she would laugh and say, "I'm just drawing, really." She went on to talk about the latest movie she had seen, book she had read, or restaurant where the family had eaten. Even while talking about a movie, she would warn, "Now don't start reading anything into it about me."

Although I believed my interpretations were accurate and even suggested Lisa's need to protect herself from the enormity of her disappointment and hurt with all her parents, I tried to take Lisa at her word. She seemed most responsive talking about clothes, movies, restaurants, and TV shows, with intense interest in my opinions on these matters, which I willingly shared. She asked for advice about how to handle problems with family and friends. The drawings of her mother's face soon faded and were replaced by drawings of elaborate floor plans of houses. Lisa was open about the meaning of these drawings—she was designing the perfect home, where she would live when her father would finally divorce her horrible stepmother. I was often struck and troubled by her stepmother's lack of understanding of Lisa, which I openly shared. I also felt this woman did not stand a chance in the face of Lisa's understandable mistrust of mothers, a view I also shared with her.

After a few months in a twice-a-week treatment, Lisa's symptoms subsided. She began doing better in school, appeared less anxious, and reported rarely losing her appetite, even though her stepmother told her she was becoming anorexic. There was no evidence for this, although when upset, Lisa would temporarily lose her appetite. I became aware that interruptions early on in the treatment were difficult. Lisa dreaded going away on family vacations because of the family tension, but also because of the absence from therapy. When I suggested this, she would again politely smile and say, "Well, maybe," but then launch into a series of complaints about her stepmother, her chronic criticism, her double standards for Lisa and her brother, and her treatment of her father. It was around these disruptions, however, that symptoms would reemerge, often causing overreaction of the parents. Obsessive thinking and mild panic about walking down the street alone became problematic and, then, almost magically subside once Lisa and I returned to a normal schedule. These difficulties also emerged when a school year ended, or began, and were not only related to the treatment interruptions.

Lisa found therapy most useful as a place to come and talk about whatever was on her mind and not feel intruded upon by interpretation or by any comments that left her feeling like someone was reading her mind. Therapy was a "moratorium" for Lisa, a place and time for "reconsideration." One could present a convincing argument that Lisa was suffering from the traumatic impact of her mother's temporary abandonment, the subsequent divorce, and remarriage, as well as the onslaught of adolescence. She was in some ways overly involved with her father and felt competitive with her stepmother for his attention. She talked with little apparent anxiety about wanting to rid the family of this woman and live happily ever after with her father and brother. Her anger and sometimes helpless rage was painful and disruptive, but would subside with comments about how upsetting it was that her stepmother turned out to be such a disappointment. Lisa eventually shared her secret wish that her stepmother might have become the mother she never had or at least one who would not leave. Later in treatment, as Lisa was more secure in our relationship, she began talking about her disappointment with her father, who complained to her about the marriage and how unhappy he was. The overstimulation of these conversations was not about being too close to her father, but was about the disappointment with her father's self-absorption and inability to understand her experience of his difficulties. His chronic complaints about his life left her feeling helpless and angry.

As these disappointments were more fully understood and integrated, Lisa slowly developed a more thoughtful perspective on her parents, both marriages, and herself. She became less preoccupied with getting all A's at school and more accepting of her limitations without the previous loss of self-esteem. Symptoms of anxiety, depression, isolation from friends, and loss of concentration and motivation at school subsided, as disappointments about all her parents were understood. By the time Lisa was 16 and finishing her treatment, she was doing well at school, had a comfortable group of friends, was thinking about dating, and talked about her college ambitions.

Severe disappointment or de-idealization of her parents was directly connected with symptoms. Was it the volatility of Lisa's adolescence or understandable reactions to her parents' inability to provide an appropriate empathic or responsive milieu? Interpretation was rarely used with Lisa unless she chose to interpret something about herself. She often described her work with me as someone to talk to about school, movies, friends, and neat places to go in Chicago. "It was," she once said, "not really being in therapy." Although treatment addressed internal dynamics, dynamic formulations and responses were organized around the real disappointments in Lisa's life and her most conscious concerns. Yet such a focus created the opportunity for much of Lisa's unconscious, or subjective, organizing principles to become known to both of us.

TOM

I first learned about Tom from his mother. She explained over the phone that her 19-year-old son had just been released from the hospital with a diagnosis of manic depression. The precipitant for his hospitalization was a fistfight between Tom and his father on the front lawn of the family home, which resulted in the police being called. Tom was unable to calm down and was arrested and taken to the hospital. The mother went on to explain that Tom was refusing to come for help so the parents would have to bring him to my office.

At his first appointment, Tom and his parents marched into my office before I had a chance to suggest I see Tom alone. Tom sat between his parents. His mother, the apparent spokesperson of the family, again described why they had come, followed by Tom and his father arguing again about who had started the fight. I became a bit anxious, since Tom was bigger than his father and me. Both appeared muscular and athletic, and both were in a rage. As the intensity of the argument grew, I finally intervened. I said I worried that the fistfight would be reenacted in my office, and since I was clearly the least muscular of the three of us, I would not be able to break them up like the police had. I added that I had only been in three physical fights in my life, resulting in two draws and one loss. They both laughed, to my great relief, and calmed down. I asked the parents to wait in the waiting room while Tom and I talked alone.

Tom quickly explained that he did not need help and that it was his parents who did. He said his father could never talk about anything, favored his older, more athletic brother, and was disappointed that he had dropped out of college a few months before. He described his mother as also never wanting to acknowledge family problems. His mother "babied" him and was overprotective ever since the accident when he was 11. Tom was on the back of a friend's mini-bike when a car hit them and the friend was killed. Tom's leg was severely injured but saved, and after extensive rehabilitation, he walked with a slight limp.

"If you want to help me, you'll see my parents. They need the shrink." Toward the end of the first visit, Tom shared more important information. He explained that the week before the fight with his father, he had picked up one of the phones at his father's office and heard his father talking to a woman with whom he was having an affair. When I commented to Tom how devastated he must have felt, he said that, although he had suspected this, he would never forgive his father. I wondered if he had talked with anyone about this, and he said he had not. No one at the hospital had asked about why he had been so angry with his father.

I did see Tom for a short time, but as we began talking more about his parents, the accident, and other painful matters, Tom, on an impulse, left town. He traveled with friends out West to work and ski, lived for a while in a small town in Texas, and moved later to New Orleans, where he worked in various restaurants and bars. I did suggest maintaining weekly phone contact, to which Tom agreed. He called but kept repeating that, if I really wanted to help him, I should see his parents. At one point he mentioned also that he was confused about his sexuality and that maybe he was gay. He was considering returning to Chicago to sort this out with me.

I finally listened and responded more directly to Tom and his view of things and set up some appointments with his parents. I explained to them that their son believed I should be meeting with them. Tom had confronted the parents about his father's affair, which precipitated his leaving town. The parents agreed to come in and did so for two months. My seeing the parents appeared finally to validate Tom's view, and eventually he returned and began seeing me regularly. As long as I stayed focused with him on the disappointment with his parents, I was able to engage him in treatment.

Once engaged, Tom's need for an idealizing selfobject relationship emerged. When he returned and saw how much better his parents appeared to be with each other, he figured I must be "the best therapist in town." He asked for advice about everything: girls, sex, friends, work, school, career, and exercise. The confusion about his sexuality faded as his fear of being close to men or women was more fully discussed. The issue of his leg and accident became central and related to his and his parents' reactions. Although this event had been traumatic in and of itself, the parental responses and Tom's reaction to those responses were at the source of Tom's difficulties with his anger, anxiety, loss of motivation in school, and isolation from others.

Tom discovered that I was a runner after his father had seen me at a local race and began running himself, which was not good for his leg and back. After learning I was running in a marathon, he made plans to run with little training and did not mention this plan during sessions. Tom completed the 26-mile race but ended up in the medical tent dehydrated and with severe leg pain. He later explained that he had run because he felt certain I would be proud of him and, if he had not finished, I would be disappointed. Those thoughts kept him going for the six hours it took him to finish. I was direct in expressing my concern about his not taking care of himself and wondering why he could not talk to me about his plans before. We were able to connect his thoughts to how upset and disappointed he had imagined his father was with him after the accident. Although his father had withdrawn, unable to integrate emotions connected to the near loss of his son (his father had described these feelings in the parent consultations), Tom had perceived this withdrawal as an expression of his father's anger toward him. He worried that he had taken up too much of his mother's attention during his rehabilitation and was now disabled and therefore inadequate because he was no longer athletic like his father and brother. Much doubt about himself as a person and a competent man was connected to his fear of his father's disappointment with him and his own disappointment with his father.

Tom's difficulties exemplify how normal oedipal feelings during adolescence were intensified by a tragic accident. His subsequent disability and understandable anxious and depressive reactions by the parents created a developmental phase filled with tension that interfered with the proper selfobject milieu Tom needed. The focus of our work was on severe disappointment with the parents and their responses before and during Tom's late adolescence. Tom had imagined, ultimately, that he was the cause of his parents' marital problems and his father's affair. Was the affair another expression of the father's withdrawal like before? As he began to integrate his parents' and his own limitations through the use of an idealized selfobject experience in the treatment, he could get back on track in his life with appropriate self-esteem, ambitions, and goals.

Although interpretation ultimately was useful and helpful to Tom, my willingness to take him at his word and work with his parents at the beginning of the treatment was critical. This technical decision validated Tom's view of his problems. Already overwhelmed with feeling, such a validation offered Tom needed control and less helplessness. Tom's sense of me as a real person, his knowledge of me, and aspects of my personal life facilitated trust in the therapeutic relationship.

ANGELA

After three years in analysis, Angela, a 16-year-old girl, was absorbed with concern about sex and becoming a young woman. She felt confused and nervous and somewhat hesitant to discuss her discomfort. Angela had come to treatment following a suicide gesture resulting in a brief hospitalization. At the time, she too made it clear that her difficulties followed the discovery of her father's alcoholism and subsequent sobriety two years before, her parents' individual problems, and their marital difficulties. She had been depressed and isolated from others and had lost interest in school or activities, even in her painting, which was so important to her.

Angela was a very bright, articulate, and creative girl who quickly became engaged in a four-day-per-week analytic treatment and showed great motivation and gains early on. When she began the treatment and throughout, I was struck by how quickly and effectively she used the analysis to climb out of a severe depression and involve herself in an active and satisfying adolescent life. One may have mistaken, as her parents almost did early on, that her turnaround meant she was finished with treatment after only a few months. What became clear was that analysis offered her a reliable and consistent experience focused upon her concerns that strengthened her self, like consistent exercise strengthens a heart. Problems with parents, friends, sex, values, school, hobbies, and so on. could be discussed and explored with me in a nonthreatening way, allowing Angela's own feelings, thoughts, wishes, and convictions to be known. Only temporary disappointments with me and my inevitable lapses in understanding, the interruptions by her or my vacations, or missed appointments would disrupt Angela's fragile self. The material below describes her concerns during the late middle and ending phase of her treatment. It may illustrate the confusion and sorting out confronting many adolescents, as well as their parents.

This period was introduced by the following dream. "I dreamt I was a boy and was with two other guys, older, maybe 30 years old. We were smoking. The joints looked more like cinnamon sticks. I didn't know who I was, if I was one of the guys or with both of them as boyfriends."

Angela said the dream embarrassed her because she remembered when she was younger she was happy not to be a boy. Boys asserted themselves, she thought, and she remembered her fear of doing that. She also explained that, if she were a boy, then she wouldn't have to talk about what it felt like to be a girl or talk about sex. "It's [sex] too personal. I'm afraid I'll look silly in front of you. You know all about it, and I'm so confused."

Later on in the treatment, Angela became involved in a steady relationship with a boyfriend and began talking about her confusion about whether to have sex or not. While reading a biography about Oscar Wilde, which was recommended by her father, she expressed her worry that she was no longer depressed like Oscar Wilde. "I used to be depressed like him, but now I can only think about being happy and whether to have sex or not." She reported that, as she became more interested in sex, her boyfriend had started to feel more Christian and was considering remaining celibate. She also worried that I would become jealous of her relationship with her boyfriend, as her dad was of her boyfriend and me. The two older men in the dream became clearer. Angela's father often teased her about how important analysis was and, more recently, about her boyfriend. Her parents' marriage still troubled her as she attempted to sort out her feelings about being a young woman and about sex. "I asked my mom if she still liked my dad after 24 years of marriage. She said 'No.'"

Angela described feeling depressed about this, but no longer angry as she had been in the past. She also recognized that she would never be like her sister who was more like her mother, but that she, Angela, no longer wanted to be like her mother. "I want to be able to assert myself and not be passive like my mom."

When I suggested that her confusion about sex appeared more about asserting herself, even if it meant expressing her uncertainty to her boyfriend, she agreed. She worried, as she always had, that others would not like her were she to express her true feelings. She knew having sex meant responsibility, and she did not feel ready. She joked about sounding too much like the health books at school. "And how much influence are you supposed to have on me?" she asked one day. " Maybe you should be more like my parents, or maybe you'll be disappointed that I don't have sex." She described many of her friends as having sex, but saw them as insecure and more uncertain than she was. "How important are you supposed to be in my life?" she wondered.

Angela's apparent concern about sex gave way to a more profound concern about being true to herself and what price she was willing to pay to be liked. She talked about wanting to be liked, like her best friend who was more social and liked by others. At the same time her individuality was essential to her. Sex, as other important aspects of her self had been previously explored in the treatment, was now the arena where the strength and cohesion of her self was being tested.

Angela and I discussed her fear that she could not tell me, her boyfriend, or her parents what she did or did not want. In the past she had worried about being uncertain or appearing foolish. Her precocious behavior protected her from that fear. Could she express herself without too great a fear of losing her self, as had been her concern when she began treatment? Her suicide gesture had been a desperate and painful attempt to let her parents and those around her know she was in serious trouble, disconnected from her self, her parents, and her peers. Killing herself seemed the only way out. Now, amidst concerns about sex, self-assertion, ambitions, and goals, she could risk not knowing, disappointing, and even making mistakes in her attempts to feel more solid and cohesive.

I was impressed with Angela's thoughtfulness and capacity for self-observation amidst difficult decisions confronting her. My role and technique primarily involved listening at this point in the analysis; however, at times, my impulse and subsequent countertransference reactions took the form of parental responses. When Angela was trying to decide whether to have sex or not, at times, I became too active out of my anxiety that she would decide to do something before she, or I for that matter, were ready. What she finally made clear was that the issue of sex was not about an impulse to act upon a drive but, rather, an old reflex to ignore her own feelings, convictions, values, and thoughts about her life. She had witnessed both parents in careers and a marriage about which they openly and chronically complained, but did little to change. The pain of disappointment for Angela was separating her own aspirations from her parents and coming to terms with their limitations.

During the termination phase of the analysis, similar feelings emerged in the transference and were exacerbated by a serious illness in my family. Although Angela rarely asked directly about anything in my personal life, my cancelling appointments at short notice often forced me to explain my circumstances outside the treatment. Witnessing me experiencing a difficult time in my life tested Angela's gains and also served as an opportunity to witness genuine empathy on her part. Coming to terms with my limitations, her parents', and her own and the limitations of the analysis created the opportunity for her to grow and move on beyond the treatment into a new phase of her life. At last report she is enjoying her college experience.

DISCUSSION

Angela, Lisa, and Tom all struggled with wanting to change their parents and make them more like they wanted or needed them to be. All three had experienced normal early childhood idealization of their parental selfobjects and, later, experienced an abrupt rupture of those selfobjects by life events and subsequent disappointing parental responses. The parents could not be used in the way their children needed, not out of a lack of concern or love for their children, but because of their own limitations. The consequences of these limitations, in combination with other factors, resulted in painful and sometimes severe symptoms. Treatment provided an opportunity, a moratorium or time of reconsideration, that the family, peer group, high school or college experience, or adolescent cultural group or activity temporarily could not.

The focus upon real disappointment and disillusionment with parents and the responses of other admired persons in these young persons' lives dictated a technique that, at first glance, might appear more interpersonal than intrapsychic in its focus; however, interpretation could only be useful if followed by an initial phase of responding in more direct and active ways. I was used as a responsive, sometimes advice-giving, flexible selfobject experience, creating a corrective optimal and reliable experience desperately needed by these troubled adolescents.

Many of my responses occurred in reaction to affect. When Lisa talked of clothes, restaurants, and movies, she was the most animated and engaging. Another patient talking of such things might feel distant. When Tom spoke of his accident and related family matters, it was as if the accident had occurred the week before, rather than years before. The terror, sadness, and helplessness were very much alive in the present. When Angela discussed her painting, she too became a different person, no longer the distant, depressed, and anxious girl that initially walked through the door of my office. It was that creativity that later allowed her to look at herself in some of the most thoughtful ways.

In response to these patients' openness, I found myself noticeably connected to them and to what they were saying. Countertransference experiences were those moments when I suddenly became more parental—directive, anxious, provoked, or adversarial. Although these responses and subsequent disruptions and restorations sequences (Wolf, 1988) are inevitable, how they are handled with adolescents, or with any patient, is critical.

With Lisa, my identification with her rage at her stepmother could, at times, lead us away from our exploration of her (and my) disappointment and helplessness. The stepmother could never make up for the overwhelming loss associated with the mother's leaving the family when Lisa was seven. With Tom, my impulse to be both protective like the mother and provoked by his need for distance mirrored the parents' reactions. With Angela, her chronic complaints about family, friends, and boyfriends sometimes produced an irritation within me about the intensity of her demands. And with all three patients, my disappointment with myself amidst their disappointments with me, when they could not temporarily use me or make me feel useful to them, created temporary impasses in the process.

As Kohut (1976) described, it is not what a parent does that so affects a child but, rather, who the parent is. I believe this is applicable with much of what goes right and wrong in treatments, especially with adolescents. As they struggle to connect to who they are becoming in the most genuine and honest ways, they need to feel they have a clear sense of who the therapist is in order to move on in their journey toward adulthood.

We have much to learn from treating children and adolescents with significant implications for treating adults. Decisions about technique must be considered in response to our patients, and theories must be the proper guides. Regardless of one's theory, adolescents demand that the analyst recognize the real loss of responsive adult empathy in their lives. The fear of being retraumatized can only be matched by the intense longing to connect. In this sense, they are no different from our other patients or, for that matter, any of us.

REFERENCES

Bacal, H. (1985), Optimal responsiveness and the therapeutic process. In: *Progress in Self Psychology, Vol. 1,* ed. A. Goldberg. Hillsdale, NJ: The Analytic Press, pp. 202–227.

Blos, P. (1962), *On Adolescence: A Psychoanalytic Perspective.* New York: The Free Press.

Cohler, B. & Galatzer-Levy, R. (1993), *The Essential Other.* New York: Basic Books.

Erikson, E. (1963), *Identity and the Life Cycle.* New York: Norton.

Freud, S. (1905), Three essays on the theory of sexuality. *Standard Edition,* 7: 130–243. London: Hogarth Press, 1953.

Galatzer-Levy, R. (1984), Adolescent crisis and midlife crisis. In: *Psychoanalytic Perspectives on the Older Adolescent,* ed. D. Brockman. New York: International Universities Press, pp. 29–51.

Kohut, H. (1976), *Restoration of the Self.* New York: International Universities Press.

Lage, G. (1997), Self psychology perspectives on adolescents. *Adolesc. Psychiat.,* 21:305–316.

Palombo, J. (1988), Adolescent development: A view from self psychology. *Child & Adolesc. Soc. Work J.,* 5:171–186.

Shane, M., Shane, E. & Gales, M. (1997), *Intimate Attachments: Toward a New Self Psychology.* New York: Guilford.

Webster's Dictionary (1976), New York: Gramercy Press, p. 245.

Wolf, E. (1988), *Treating the Self.* New York: Guilford.

Chapter 9

A Case of Sexual (Dis-)Orientation with Thoughts on Sexuality, Sexual Orientation, and Psychoanalysis

Jeffrey Stern

This chapter discusses the case of Watt, who was in doubt as to whether he was gay or straight and hoped that psychoanalysis would provide the answer. He thought at first that I would see through to the truth of his inner nature much as a radiologist sees through the body to bone. Of course, I had no idea whether Watt was gay or straight—how could I know?—and I wondered why he thought I should, and why he didn't know himself.

In a recent paper Arnold Goldberg (2001) takes up a question that seemed at least partly to animate Watt's anxiety, and that was the question of whether or not homosexuality is a pathology. Goldberg argues that as psychoanalysts we can't possibly offer a simple answer because for some of our analysands homosexuality may be expressive of pathological self-structure; for others, it may be the expression of a healthy and vigorous self, and for still others, it may be first one and then the other. Richard Isay (1989) believes that homosexuality is genetic and either neurotic, if the father responds with hostility to his small son's erotized love, or normative, if the father's response is warmly loving. For Kohut (1971), homosexuality represents the sexualization of a structural deficit, meaning that, if a boy's phase-appropriate desire to merge with his spiritually idealized father is traumatically frustrated and his subsequent self-development damaged as a result, he might attempt to achieve the thwarted relation by merging sexually with a physically perfect homosexual lover. Goldberg (1995) thinks that at least some defensive and neurotic homosexualities may become structurally compensatory—and thus serve the cohesiveness of the self—if the subject's longing for the original idealized object can be reanimated in the transference relation and the idealized object eventually de-idealized and transmuted into psychic structure. He argues that both hetero- and homosexualities are capable of being either salutary or perverse and bases the distinction on the use sexuality plays in the constitution of any given self: if driven, compulsive, and functioning principally as a hedge against fragmentation, sexuality in whatever of its forms is perverse; if the expression of a vigorous and cohesive self, it's salutary. Finally, research, especially on the sexuality of women, suggests that our familiar essentialist notions of bedrock sexual identity, the conviction that people are either fish or fowl—gay or straight—may be deeply flawed (Baumeister, 2000). These studies indicate, rather, that sexuality may be a fluid and variable response of the self to its position in a potentially changing psychological universe. One may have different orientations at different times of one's life.

Watt said he hoped he was straight because he wanted to have a conventional married life and very much wanted to be a father, but he felt he'd have no problem being gay if it turned out that he was, as indeed he thought more likely. The problem was being stuck in the middle and living as it were in an equal opportunity hetero- and homosexual closet. He'd had one brief homosexual fling as a teenager and one fairly long-term heterosexual relation as an adult in his mid-twenties. He'd enjoyed both forms of sexual expression, but both relations had ended unhappily. The faithless boy had left him, and he'd broken up with the cloyingly needy young woman. His sexual fantasies and dreams were generally homoerotic, which was why he imagined he was gay, but still, he wasn't sure.

Watt had consulted briefly with a gay therapist who believed he was gay, irrevocably and genetically, and that his problem was in learning to accept the hand that nature had dealt him, and also with a straight therapist, who felt the answer to Watt's question could be determined mathematically by assigning numerical values to his sexual fantasies and activities and coming up with a "scientific" score that would settle the issue once and for all. Watt found that both of these approaches merely spiked his anxiety and hoped a third opinion might prove the charm. I told him that I had no answer: I could see that sexuality was a source of anxiety for him, but it was clear after we'd talked for a few hours that he was anxious about many things. He had panic attacks when he found himself in unfamiliar places, couldn't sleep at night unless the television was on, found it nearly impossible to regulate both money and food, smoked three packs of cigarettes a day, and although nearing 30, had no idea what he wanted to do when he "grew up." He was imposingly large physically, but inside he felt like a small child. That he didn't know who he was sexually seemed merely an aspect of his overarching sense of confusion. I thought that to try to answer the question of his sexuality as if it were distinct from his doubts about himself generally would simply make no sense.

I told him I didn't know what form his sexuality might take, but that if we were to look into his thoughts and feelings in an unhurried and open-ended way, he might begin to come to terms with his deepest longings in a manner that hadn't been possible previously in his life. He thought this sounded like a good idea and so we began.

HISTORY

Watt's family history seemed like the stuff of *Bonnie and Clyde*. He had never met his father, a man he thought might be a sheriff "somewhere out west," and who had left his 20-year-old wife (and Watt's 2-year-old half-brother Nick) shortly before she was arrested for driving the getaway car for a new boyfriend who robbed banks. Watt spent most of the first five years of his life living with his mother's stepparents who were concerned that her wildness and the months she spent in prison made it impossible for her to provide a proper home for her sons. Watt recalled repeatedly dreaming as a child that he was naked except for his shoes and socks and running crying through a housing development along curving streets. "I was looking for my mom and dad; people were laughing," he said.

Watt's grandfather was an angry and stingy man who worked in a baking factory. He was obsessed with money and continually hoarding what little he had. He preferred Nick to Watt because Nick was athletic and conventionally masculine. Watt wasn't interested in aggressive play or sports. He never felt close to his grandfather, who spanked him with a willow switch when he misbehaved, but somehow, inexplicably, bought Watt exactly the bicycle he wanted one year for Christmas and never refused to take Watt in when he needed a place to stay. Watt remembered his grandmother fondly as "a good mix of sweet and sour." Ordinarily submissive to her old-country husband, she nevertheless repeatedly stood up to him in Watt's defense. When one day the old man called Watt a "sissy boy," she told him she'd leave him if he ever said it again. Watt felt loved by her and protected, and she was able to soothe him when he was troubled.

When Watt was four, his mother married for a third time, a union that produced a third son, Jessie, when Watt was eight. Like Nick's father, this husband was an alcoholic. "My mother was an asshole magnet," Watt said, as a way of accounting for the procession of drunken losers she was always either married to, planning to marry, or breaking up with. His mother boasted that she never spanked her sons, but Watt remembered that unlike his grandmother she never protected him or his brothers either. He was thus often cruelly disciplined by frightening men he scarcely knew. He thought his mother weak-willed, depressed, and oppressively needy, often clinging to him desperately to shore herself up.

In school Watt did well until the fifth grade, when his mother moved them unexpectedly to an especially unwelcoming neighborhood. Watt had difficulty making friends at the new school, found the work boring, and began to cut classes. He didn't like being teased about being fat. By eighth grade he was cutting all the time. While his mother was at work he'd practice the guitar and watch cooking shows on TV. They lived in a studio apartment, and his mother brought men home to sleep with, dividing her bed from those of her sons with a sheet she hung across the room like a shower curtain. Sometimes Watt would wake up and have to pee, requiring him to pass her and her boyfriend to get to the bathroom. Then he'd eat candy and cookies he hid under his bed to distract him from the things that were always going bump in the night. He never slept well.

Watt dropped out of school at 16, eventually earning a diploma by taking the GED exam. When he was 18, he found a job with a company that owned tour boats that cruised the lake. The couple who owned the company took Watt under their wing and became an enduring source of stability and attachment for him. At first he worked as a deck hand and maintenance man, but his bosses saw his potential and trained him to become a captain. He passed the licensing exam and was extremely successful in his new role, although the daunting task of piloting a large vessel filled with tourists through a maze of powerbooks and sailboats led to his first panic attacks. He also got a job as a houseman for a professional couple with two young children. These people virtually adopted Watt and provided him with his first experience of life in a stable family, as well as access to cultural experiences he never knew existed.

PART I

During his first hour on the couch, Watt reported a dream. He looked in the mirror and discovered to his astonishment and joy that all of his hair had grown back. (Though still in his twenties, Watt was completely bald.) He wondered what it meant. I said I thought the dream contained his hope for the analysis, namely, that something within his head—within his mind—that had been lost would be restored, that he would begin to grow again emotionally. He also reported that on the previous evening he had rented the Andy Warhol film *Flesh*. He said that he'd wanted to see it because he was turned on by the beautiful hero, Joey Delsandro, which proved he must be gay. I asked him which part of the movie he liked best. "The scene where Delsandro is naked on the floor holding his infant son. He's very tender playing with him as he feeds him. That's my favorite," Watt said. I said it was interesting that the scene he liked best was about a father lovingly nurturing his little boy, precisely the sort of experience he had so painfully missed growing up because his father had abandoned his mother before he was born. Watt was surprised; he hadn't thought of that at all.

The image of the beautiful father playing with his child made me think that idealization would play a crucial role in the transference. I imagined Watt hoped the analysis would reanimate and permit us to work through his longing for a strong, tender, and nurturing father who would wish to be with him—unlike his own perpetually absent father—and who would want to touch him emotionally, a father who would be unafraid to let his own feelings show—Delsandro's nakedness—and who would lovingly teach him to be a man. The physical perfection of the movie star brought to mind Kohut's idea of the moral perfection Watt longed to merge with in a father who might provide an antidote to his confining emotional attachment to his weak, depressed, and depreciated mother. I thought Watt's confusion about whether he was gay or straight probably spoke to his question about whether he would be doomed to experience himself as depressed, which by his lights meant *like a woman*, like his mother, or whether he could come to feel energetic and competent, which for him meant *like a man*.

On the surface Watt was open, friendly, and at ease, but beneath this, there was something in his manner both opaque and guarded. He seemed to trust, but trusted no one. Indeed, it became clear before long that he assumed, as a matter of course, that I would soon want to be rid of him. He was, after all, a low-fee patient, and although I might need to use him for a while in the service of my training, I'd kick him out the first moment I could or the first moment he pissed me off. He'd been a "charity case" all his life, relying, like Blanche Dubois (in *A Streetcar Named Desire*), on "the kindness of strangers." But such kindness had strings attached. Everyone wanted something in return. The question for Watt was, What did I want? He was sure that if he didn't come up with whatever it was soon enough, he'd find himself back on the street. He had many dreams of fellating powerful men, never with his own pleasure as the motive, but rather in an effort to placate and control them. He believed these dreams proved he was homosexual, but to me they seemed to have little to do with sex. What they suggested instead was the sexualization of Watt's hunger for the substantiality of a father and his view that masochistic submission was the only way he might maintain his connection to such a selfobject. That such fantasies occurred most often during breaks in our schedule or after small derailments in our rapport further suggested that they functioned chiefly to ward off anxiety and depressive affect.

From the outset Watt found the basic rule of free association terrifying. He didn't want to say what came to mind; he wanted to tell me what I wanted to hear. He assumed that I wanted to hear that he was straight, and he soon began telling me how attracted he was to various female television and movie stars. Then he began seeing and sleeping with his former girlfriend, Ann. After a while he reported a disturbing "Freudian" dream. In it he and Ann were having sex until Ann began to metamorphose into his mother. He described waking up in horror. "I guess you'll say the dream is about my sick Oedipus complex," he said. But I said nothing, so he went on. "After we have sex, Ann always wants to talk about her problems, and I mean for hours. And she expects me to give her advice. Like I have any. I just want to go to sleep!"

I said, "It sounds like your dream came true." He didn't follow. "Ann metamorphosed into a depressed woman," I said, "who wanted you to solve her problems, just like your mother. No wonder you worry about getting involved with women!" He was surprised. He'd never thought that he rejected women: only that they rejected him because he was fat, bald, and had a too-small penis. But maybe it was true that he worried that women were finally all like his mother. He remembered reading *Portnoy's Complaint*. Portnoy told his shrink he could never escape his mother, that as a child he'd leave her in the morning only to discover at school that she'd somehow morphed into his teacher so that she could give him grief all day before flying home at three o'clock like a witch on a broomstick in order to bust his balls all night. Now that he thought about it, Ann was always needy and depressed and did seem a lot like his mother. Even the woman in whose home he worked, a woman who was cultivated, energetic, and rich—in short everything his mother wasn't—became completely helpless and in need of rescue whenever a drain backed up or the electricity shorted out. No wonder he longed to be close to strong, competent men. Women could be so seductive and manipulative! He bitterly recalled being offered the holiday weekend use of a cabin cruiser by a woman who was a friend of his employers' at the boats. He'd accepted gratefully and with great excitement—vacationing on a boat had been one of his dreams—but when he picked up the keys, the woman handed him a list of repairs she said she was sure he wouldn't mind making and that wouldn't take him long. As it turned out, he barely had time to do anything but these chores and was still unable to finish everything on the list.

Of course he feared the analysis would prove to be the same sort of experience: one sold as a wonderful opportunity for him, but really something that was going to be good only for me. So he did his best to hold me at arm's length, which served also to protect him from the beckoning whirlpool of the transference. He was fearful that if he became truly emotionally engaged he'd fall apart. His friends thought him easy-going and laid back; he was always the one calm enough to play shrink to them when they were upset. They didn't know about his panic attacks or his insomnia and fear of the dark or that to soothe himself enough to go to bed every night he had to eat an entire box of Oreos and drink a quart of milk.

He recalled that when he was 10 his mother decided to move for a while to the West Coast. She arranged for Watt, Nick, and Jessie to live with Nick's mean father and his meaner wife. The night their mother left, Watt wouldn't get up from the floor where he was watching TV to say goodbye to her. His mom's girlfriend misread this as Watt's "cool" and told her not to worry because Watt would hardly notice she was gone. But Watt said that he kept his eyes on the set to keep them from filling up with tears. He remembered thinking that if he hugged his mom, he wouldn't be able to let go and her friends would have to pry him off her.

After 18 months or so, he broke up with Ann and didn't attempt to date other women for a long time. Nor did he get any closer to me.

PART II

Watt became very upset on a Saturday morning two years into the analysis because the following day was Father's Day, and he alone among his friends had no plans. He said he had a giant black hole where all the Dad stuff was supposed to be. He didn't want to be with his friends on Father's Day, and he didn't want to be alone. It would be a nice day to be dead, especially inasmuch as he imagined I would be having a great time with my children. The Monday after Father's Day he didn't show up, explaining on Tuesday it was because his alarm clock failed to go off, a frequent explanation for missed morning sessions. He was sorry to have screwed up. I said I thought his alarm was working, but that it was an internal alarm that directed him to sleep through the session so that he wouldn't have to think further about not having a father. He was surprised; he'd completely forgotten that we'd talked about Father's Day. He didn't like thinking that things like the alarm clock not working happened to him because of feelings, things that were beyond his control. I made it sound like his life was a dream in which he stumbled about blindly and without a clue. He thought analysis was supposed to make his life less painful, but it was making the pain worse! What was the point of dredging up awful feelings from the past when there wasn't a damn thing he could do about them in the present, he said to me hotly. This was the first time he became really upset with me and with the analysis. His outburst frightened him, and he retreated for some weeks into his default position of guarded pleasantness. Nonetheless, a cat had been let out of the bag.

The following Christmas I was to be away for two weeks on vacation. Watt insisted that a break from the analysis would be a relief rather than a problem because it would allow him to sleep in and relieve him of the burden of getting to my office and trying to think of things to say. A week later he called me at the resort where I was vacationing to report that he had tripped while descending a flight of stairs and broken both arms. We came to think of this fall as his "Freudian slip," that which gave the lie to his claim of self-sufficiency and dramatized the regressive helplessness he felt when our connection was interrupted. His inability to acknowledge how "dis-armed" he felt when I left had manifested itself entirely literally, as if to prove Lacan's maxim that what is suppressed in the Symbolic Order of language returns in the Real. Willy nilly, as we came to see, he had fallen down the rabbit hole of the transference and into the regressive wonderland of the analysis in which the feelings he had tried so hard to keep, as it were, at arm's length increasingly forced their way into his actions and then into his consciousness.

After the casts were taken off Watt required extensive physical therapy to regain the use of his hands and arms. He loved physical therapy because he was infatuated with his physical therapist, Marie. Being with her made Watt think of a baby's interactions with a loving and patient mother. The feeling of being touched and manipulated and for a while even fed reminded him of Joey Delsandro's baby in *Flesh*. Suddenly he was himself the envied baby, experiencing a sort of polymorphously perverse pleasure in response to Marie's touch, voice, and smile. Watt had never known a woman like her. She was infinitely patient and encouraging; he struggled to please her when they were together and exercised faithfully according to her instructions between sessions. He realized he was thinking about her all the time. She was lively, intelligent, and funny and up on current events, and she liked his favorite movies and bands. Her competence, devotion, and delight in his progress lifted his spirits, and like a schoolboy with a crush on his teacher, he found excuses to extend their time together a minute here, two minutes there. As the weeks passed, he found himself noticing how attractive she was, and he began to wonder if she might have more than professional feelings for him too, especially when she showed up at a bar one night to hear him sing with his band.

Marie reminded Watt of Ted, who had been his best friend and roommate for four years while Ted was in graduate school. Ted had worked summers with Watt on the boats and was an inspiration to him. He encouraged Watt to lose weight, work out, stop smoking and think seriously about his education and future. Watt did all of these with increasing enthusiasm, until one day out of the blue Ted announced he was moving out of their apartment so that he could live with his new girlfriend. Watt was devastated: he admired Ted—indeed he secretly felt he was in love with him—and then Ted had just dumped him. Watt gained back all of the weight he'd lost, went back to smoking three packs a day, and quit the health club where he and Ted had exercised together. These memories frightened Watt because he worried Marie might tell him that she, too, had someone else. As indeed she did once Watt found the courage to ask her out. He was heartbroken and again he crashed, losing interest in the exercises he was doing to strengthen his arms and shoulders and the diet he'd undertaken to make himself more attractive to her. Bad as he felt, however, he was encouraged to think that his attraction to Marie was real, unlike any sexual longing he had ever felt for a woman. Indeed, in contrast to his relation with Ann, which in its most recent incarnation seemed largely staged for my benefit, Watt had clearly loved Marie and painfully lost, his intense sexual feelings arising out of his idealization of her, as had his romantic feelings for Ted.

I wondered what all of this meant from the point of view of Watt's sexuality. Was he bisexual or, rather, one who lacked the psychological structure to neutralize idealizing feelings and thus sexualized the displacement of the transference that his relation to Marie represented? I didn't know.

Watt almost never reported having sexual thoughts or fantasies involving me, but after breaks in our schedule, he often dreamed the familiar dreams of fellating older men, which I thought pointed to his disillusionment with me for abandoning him and his regressive wish for enlivening contact with father figures as a way to ward off his anger, loneliness, and depression. Again he worried that such dreams meant that he was homosexual, but again, I was convinced only that they spoke to the need he felt to manage his disappointment. The fact that Watt's dreams weren't accompanied by feelings of arousal lent plausibility to the thought that their manifest sexual content wasn't where their chief significance lay.

This phase of work on the idealized figures who briefly lifted Watt up before failing him and causing him to crash began to make sense of his fear of flying. Merely thinking he might have to travel somewhere in a plane was sometimes enough to bring on a panic attack, and he practically had to put himself in an alcoholic stupor before actually boarding a flight. He realized that flying meant putting his life in the hands of a pilot he didn't know but had absolutely to trust, which of course he found impossible. Ordinarily not trusting wasn't a problem because he was good at looking trusting when the situation called for it. But with flying the issue wasn't about convincing the pilot that he trusted him; it was about convincing himself. I imagined that his anxiety about airline pilots spoke as well to his worries about me. His doubts were hardly surprising: none of the people who'd been charged with his care had been up to the task except his grandmother, and he found he was safest in most situations when he was on his own. He remembered the story of the little red hen who learned she would get no help from others and as a result decided she preferred doing everything all by herself.

He realized that he'd managed generally to split off his awareness that his idealizations of people, me included, were at best partial and more often wholly superficial and false, yet he was finding it increasingly difficult to resist his growing longing to believe in me. He began watching sports. He'd never been interested in them, but because he knew I was, he began taking note of the scores and finding ways to tell me he was keeping up. Then he began watching games on television and would ask me questions about rules and strategy as he headed for the door or before he settled himself on the couch. After a while I said I thought he was trying to connect with me in these liminal moments before and after our sessions as sons connect with fathers. This made him feel a bit shy, but he said he guessed so. I enjoyed answering his questions and soon began having countertransference fantasies of taking him to ball games or teaching him to throw and catch properly, as my dad had taught me and as I'd enjoyed teaching my daughter and son. I didn't know what this had to do with his sense of sexuality, but it surely seemed connected to his sense of masculinity, and for long stretches of time the question of whether he was gay or straight didn't come up.

Watt began gradually to feel more secure. His fantasies of fellating powerful men stopped being part of his regular discourse, and his nightly bingeing on cookies became limited to the aftermath of specific disappointments, rather than functioning as an automatic means of making it through the night. He began to sleep better and to find effective ways to manage his time and money. Perhaps more importantly, he became increasingly able to experience and talk about what he thought were unacceptable affects. He no longer slept through his alarm clock when he was upset about something that was happening between us; rather he would dream of oversleeping but come in and tell me about the dream. This made it possible for us to talk about the feelings that had given rise to the dream, rather than splitting them off as he had done formerly.

A major breakthrough occurred in the transference relationship after Watt saw a movie in which a prison guard helps a prisoner to write his life story by providing him with paper and pens although doing so is forbidden. The prisoner, a brutal murderer, is transformed by writing about his life and knowing the guard will read what he writes. Watt was struck by the analogy of the television drama to the analysis. The prisoner who makes a story of his life comes to see his experience—including his crimes—as effects of the violence that had been done to him rather than as evidence that he is an inhuman monster—as he'd always believed. Everything turns for the prisoner on the fact that the guard takes an interest in his present life as well as in his past and future—like a father. Watt thought that telling me about his life not only gave it a shape that it never had before, but somehow and for the first time made his life seem his own. The fact that I wanted to know and that I remembered what he told me helped him find words for what he had lived through, and he could see that the words were producing a history that we held between us. What he'd suffered could never be undone, but that his suffering for the first time had meaning and an enduring form changed everything. Where he'd felt empty, he began to feel substantial. His sense that I was watching over him and remembering him made him feel held and held together.

His sense of coherence in time past and present carried with it a sense of possibility about the future. He decided he wanted to go to college and get his degree so that he could become a therapist and work with children. Until this point his only thought of the future was that his little bar band would be signed by a major recording label and he'd become a rock star. His failure to publicize the few gigs the group ever got made the enormous odds against such fortunes even longer, as well as making it impossible for his friends to come and see him play. He considered their failure to show up proof that they really didn't care about him and that everyone in the world was just like the dad who'd abandoned him. Writing songs had been especially important to him because he felt that in his music he could share emotions that he couldn't express in any other way. As he began to be able to come to terms with his feelings in the office, the rock star fantasy began to fade. He continued to write songs, but his daydreams of being adored by countless "fans" and pursued by women who would dig him because he was famous started to seem adolescent to him. He thought he'd need a day job that he loved and that, if he could play music in bars for his friends, it'd probably be enough. Grandiose fantasies, however, tend not to go gentle into any good night, so occasionally he'd dream of being offered the chance to open for Bruce Springsteen or Aerosmith. Then he'd laugh and say, "naahhh."

The thought that he might become a child therapist became more real to him and more exciting every day. His chief responsibility in the household where he worked was child care, which he was terrific at and loved. He was friend and confidant not only to his own two charges but also to many of their friends and even friends of their friends, who came to talk with him because they'd heard he was someone who could help a kid in trouble. It moved him to think that his suffering might not have been entirely in vain after all; clearly it was the source of his connection to children in pain.

The major work of this long middle phase of the analysis continued to center around the question of Watt's willingness to experience rather than to split off his affects: primarily his rage, but also his feelings of longing and love. His characterological defense in the face of feelings had been to suppress them as much as he could by eating, smoking, and buying himself presents he couldn't afford. Then he'd berate himself for being weak and disgusting, someone no one would want to be around. Everything, he said, was his own damn fault. I said that blaming himself in this way was useful in that it transformed what he couldn't help—the traumatic disappointments he'd suffered as a child—into things he could. Rather than face the fact that there had been no father to love or care for him in his world and only a very inadequate mother, he could sustain a split-off idealization of both parents by imagining that they hadn't failed him, but that he'd failed them. If he'd only change, the love he'd been denied would still be forthcoming.

His approach in the transference was the same. He wouldn't let himself see that he felt hurt or angry because I had disappointed him; he'd simply announce that he was furious with himself for some sin of indulgence or sloth for which he deserved a whipping. Invariably it was possible to link these excesses to some recent failure of mine that he barely remembered or considered irrelevant to his distress, like my being late for a session or my not picking up on the name of one of his friends. But he refused to believe I'd disappointed him; he wasn't mad at me he insisted—he was mad at himself, and not for anything I'd done but rather because he was so weak. It took a long time for him to see that the things he did that humiliated and angered him represented his attempts to soothe himself when he felt I had let him down. He would announce that he was feeling better because he was, say, sticking to his diet and smoking less or feeling worse because he was not sticking to his diet and smoking more, and I would say that I thought his varying ability to stay with his diet or not to smoke had everything to do with his feeling that I was either there for him and that we were connected, or that I had failed him and we were not.

He didn't mind telling me that he was angry with his mother or his bosses. They clearly needed him and weren't about to forsake him, but he was terrified to be anything but appreciative and good-natured regarding me. His mother could tolerate his negative affects because she was so cow-like and out of it that she scarcely noticed that he was upset even when he was trying to tell her off, and because like a bad penny, even when she disappeared she always turned up again. His father, however, was a different story. The way Watt understood his father's incomprehensible absence from his life was to think that his father had from the first understood that Watt would burden him oppressively with his needs if he didn't flee before Watt was born. Watt was certain that it was merely a matter of time before I came to see things in the same way and followed suit. To forestall such an eventuality, he did whatever he could to appear agreeable. He feared that if he betrayed the depression and rage he felt over even the most venial of my sins, sins that he thought couldn't properly even be called sins, I'd abandon him in disgust and rage. So the idea of being real with me was virtually out of the question. What was more distressing was that his negative affects were for a long time so split off where I was concerned that he didn't even experience them himself. Indeed, what I most disliked about the treatment were the many sessions when Watt was blandly friendly and apparently intent on merely filling up our time until it ran out. He'd come in a few minutes late, kill another minute or two taking off his coat, and then tell me jokes he'd just heard or the plot of some television show or movie I hadn't seen or the state of the world according to the editors of *People Magazine*. At such times I felt we were living in the movie town of *Pleasantville*—numbed by Watt's friendliness to which I reacted countertransferentially by feeling sleepy or bored or angry at my helplessness to do anything other than mirror his "false self" blandness with a similar version of my own. For a while I was no less caught up than he in the grip of an enactment in which each of us felt we should be "nice" and not upset the other. Eventually I'd realize I was ready to scream and would finally make an interpretation along the lines of how, when we were merely pleasant with one another, we were colluding to keep strong feelings out of the room—perhaps like his mother who always wanted to think things were all right—thereby confirming his conviction that neither of us could handle them. Such interpretations gradually allayed the anxiety that becalmed us, and we began again to move ahead.

PART III

As we worked on Watt's getting in touch with the feelings he would try to split off, for instance by discussing the relation of his bingeing behavior to a weekend absence or a canceled appointment, Watt began dreaming of horrible beasts on rampages destroying everything in their path. I said that the beasts were his feelings, and he would say no, they were just dream junk, nonsense, but after a while he could see that the dreams followed sessions that had upset him as those preceding his self-indulgent behaviors had and that they were offering to us a vision of angry emotions he'd not known how to acknowledge. He bought himself a copy of Maurice Sendak's *Where the Wild Things Are* to celebrate his evolving willingness to tolerate the idea that the wild things were in his heart.

On a day when I announced I needed to be away unexpectedly the following week, he couldn't conceal his rage from either of us. "Don't I matter at all?" he fumed. "Couldn't you have given me more notice? This is really going to fuck me up!" I said I was glad he felt able to let me see how betrayed and angry he felt. The next day, however, he missed his session because he had so frightening a panic attack that he drove himself to a hospital emergency room, certain he was having a coronary and was about to die. I said that the heart attack was an apt metaphor for his feeling that because he had attacked me I would banish him from the analysis which would break his heart and kill him. We remembered that when he was angry with me a couple of years before he had said nothing but fell and broke his arms. This time he was able to express his anger, but doing so had terrified him. Watt's becoming angry with me—and, more important, our coming to terms with the panic his anger inspired in him—seemed to both of us a crucial breakthrough. From totally denying he had negative feelings, he had come to agree that such feelings were concealed in his various actions and dreams, then to thinking his dreams and symptomatic behavior were indeed affect-laden, and finally to experiencing feelings of rage and depression directly.

Watt also found that he was able to express loving feelings. He began talking about how much he wanted to be special to me, indeed, how much he wanted to belong to me. He had always been treated well by those who had taken him in, as had both of the families he worked for, but as much as they were fond of saying he was "one of the family," he knew he wasn't. He remembered reading the *Uncle Remus* stories. In one, Brer Rabbit gets caught by Brer Fox who tricks him with the tar baby and, to escape, begs Brer Fox not to throw him in the briar patch, which he pretends is the place he is most afraid of. Brer Fox falls for the trick and sets Brer Rabbit loose in the briar patch where of course he escapes because the briar patch is his home. Watt said the office felt like the briar patch to him, and he wished he could somehow belong to me. If he did, I could never send him away. Then he said that in normal families kids have rooms and, when they are bad, they get sent to them, but they don't get sent away. He'd never had a room of his own and had always been sent away, but if the office were his room, it wouldn't matter how mad he got, or how bad he was, because we'd just talk about it next time in my briar patch office that was his room.

He began to feel that he finally had what he needed to grow up. He remembered his grandmother and recalled being safe as a small boy, huddling under the bridge of her legs when she rested them on the ottoman in front of her chair. His sexual fantasies about fellating physically strong men had all but disappeared, replaced by a longing he felt to incorporate what he saw as my moral strength into himself. He began to stand up to his bosses over matters of conscience, although he feared doing so would get him fired. At the boats he witnessed a near disaster when a crew member came to work drunk and carelessly left a hatch open on deck through which a small boy fell. Luck saved the child from serious injury or even death, yet the boss, worried about staffing during the brief high season, let the man off with a warning. Watt told the boss he'd quit on the spot if the man was allowed to work even one more trip. Doing so made him think of how his grandmother told his grandfather she'd leave him if he ever called Watt a "sissy boy" again. The boss fired the deckhand and thanked Watt for bringing him to his senses. After this incident Watt told his other employers that they were copping out on their children by too often expecting Watt to discipline them. Again his stance met with gratitude rather than anger. When Watt's troubled 19-year-old nephew asked if he could stay with him over the summer and work on the boats, Watt took him in and got him a job because the boy promised to get himself together. But he was soon busted for smoking pot at work, and Watt caught him stealing money from his wallet and prescription drugs from his medicine cabinet. When it was clear to Watt that giving him second chances was only leading to more of the same bad-ass behavior, Watt told him he'd have to leave, and despite the boy's pleading, stood his ground. It was painful to say no, but Watt was proud of himself for sticking to his guns. He could see that he was no longer the desperately needy person he'd been, the one who had always been willing to sacrifice his integrity for the sake of maintaining relationships. He remembered the story of "Pinocchio," one of his favorites as a child. It was funny to think of the little marionette's metamorphosis from wood into a flesh-and-blood "real" boy. Watt's changes seemed to be taking an opposite course. He'd always been too fleshy and soft, yet now it seemed he too was metamorphosing into a real boy—a real man—with a solid backbone. The masculinity he'd dreamed he could only take into himself sexually and briefly from another was something he now felt had become a permanent part of himself.

After a long period of failed efforts at dating, each against a terrible gradient of anxiety that he would be rejected, Watt began to date Quinn, a woman he really liked. She was a new hire at the boats who seemed energetic and kind and who made it clear that she was attracted to him. He could see that the relation would soon become sexual and worried about having to expose his naked body to her and perform in the role of a lover. What if she found him repellant or anxiety wilted his erection? What if she thought he wasn't any good in bed? He decided to get himself a prescription for Viagra—which it was soon clear he didn't need—while we discussed his anxieties in the office. The idea that he was "performing" for his girlfriend led to talk about whether lovemaking was something he was doing for her—even as he had long felt analysis was something he was doing for me—or something he was doing with her, but for himself. The matter was relevant to the idea of our terminating because he worried I would feel rejected were he to leave, rather than delighted that we had reached a desired end together. As the relation to Quinn grew in importance, Watt returned to the idea that what had kept him from connecting with women wasn't, as he'd imagined, that he was unattractive, but rather that he was afraid of being subjected to the neediness and depression he was afraid they all shared with his mother, and his helplessness to maintain a firm sense of himself in the face of it. But Quinn seemed completely different from his mother, as Marie had been, lively and funny and hopeful, rather than depressed. But then her older sister attempted suicide and she seemed completely undone. For days she was unable to think about anything else and talked to Watt about it from morning till night. He began to feel uncomfortable. She didn't want him simply to listen; she wanted him to tell her what to do, and he didn't know. Finally he told her that he couldn't be a shrink to her; he could only be her boyfriend and that she should get into therapy. She did so, and they grew closer. It was the sort of thing he had been unable to say to Ann years ago.

PART IV

Around this time he had a dream he thought important. He was driving his car in an unfamiliar mountain region. The weather was stormy, and he was worried about what might happen if he got stuck. No one else seemed to be around. On a hairpin switchback turn, one of his front tires ran slightly off the road and sent the car into a skid. Watt didn't feel panicky as he was sure he would have in the past but expertly slowed the car and then discovered that all of the equipment he needed to fix the damage was in the toolkit. He thought the dream pretty much announced the state of his self. He was feeling that he didn't have to worry about derailments in life because he had the wherewithal to set things right. He'd always dreaded the thought of termination, but now it seemed like a manageable step because he believed it wouldn't mean the end of our relations, just their taking a new form.

He was full of plans and happy to think of his future and of what we had accomplished. He realized that he had come to feel that the office did seem like his room, even if I had other patients, and he joked that he was planning to build a replica of it in his apartment so that he could go there whenever he needed me or just when he wanted to feel peaceful. But in fact, he said, the calm place was already inside him. This was why he was no longer afraid of flying. He trusted the calm in himself because we had worked through his assumption that anyone he might rely on would fail him. I had stayed with him even when he was certain I wouldn't, and now he thought I was in some ineluctable and permanent way his. "It changes you," he said, "having someone that you have come through with. I'm more than I was." And this was true. He was full of hope for the future and had become a college student. He had a girlfriend he really cared about and had made a point of the fact that his decision to stay in the relation or move on to another would be based on his sense of how happy he was with Quinn, not on a wish to please me, or for that matter, her. He could see that his dream of being the father he had never had was going to come true. He felt he wasn't entirely free of homosexual longings, but these occurred rarely, usually when he was upset with Quinn or with me, and he didn't think they were likely to disrupt his life. He'd learned not to be afraid of his feelings, so if he was inclined to gaze more longingly than the next guy at a male model's washboard stomach in an ad on the side of a bus, so what? He loved Quinn's body and didn't have homosexual fantasies when they were making love. He rarely had homosexual dreams, and when he did, they were no more a problem to his relation with Quinn than the fleeting heterosexual attraction he felt to women he encountered in the world every day. Indeed it occurred to him that anyone in a committed relationship—whether homosexual or heterosexual—was going to be attracted to other people at times, and those who were happy in their relations lived with those attractions as a matter of course. Feeling attracted to a person outside the relation but not acting on that attraction didn't mean you were living a lie; it meant you were committed. He no longer worried that he was gay or even bisexual, although he thought Freud had it right in insisting such potential exists within us all.

As we moved into the final days of the analysis he had three dreams. In the first, he saw himself with dreadlocks. This reminded him of his first dream on beginning analysis, the one in which he had hair. He guessed the dreadlocks suggested the idea of dread: he was confidant about being without me, but a little anxious nonetheless; and the idea of strength: dreadlocks suggested the hair of a warrior. He wasn't afraid; he was one to be feared. Well, maybe he was both. In the second dream he found himself in an old hotel. His computer was set up in his room, and with it he could somehow look into the other rooms that housed strange and lonely souls he felt he knew and didn't know. He thought they were his family and all of the people he'd lived with and been abandoned by growing up, even forgotten aspects of himself. The computer was his memory, which he could use to access his history and the people he had known. He didn't need to be with them, and he didn't have to wall them off to keep the feelings they inspired in him from overwhelming him with despair and rage and dread. The third dream was again about his car. He was driving and noticed the ashtray was filling up with oil. There seemed to be a leak somewhere. He thought the leaky ashtray meant sadness. The car was wet with tears. He said he felt sad to be leaving me but happy because the sadness was sadness: it wasn't depression. And it meant he was growing up: so he felt sad and happy all at once.

As did I.

THOUGHTS AND CONCLUSIONS

What conclusions can be drawn regarding the question with which this analysis began, that of Watt's sexuality? I think it was clear that his sexuality was not something that he'd lost and that we found as it were by digging through layers of repression like treasure hunters.

Rather, his sexuality seemed a developmental potential that evolved as the analysis progressed and Watt's self became increasingly cohesive. Could I have answered his question as to whether he was straight or gay when he began treatment—as he hoped I would—my words would have had no meaning for him because the problem wasn't crucially that he didn't know, but rather that he couldn't function in a sexual context until his self was sufficiently structuralized to allow him to manage the affects attendant on sexual relations. "Not knowing" what he was sexually was his way of trying to explain his panic over the idea of having to carry on adult relations—thematized as sexual relations—given the trauma he had been exposed to in childhood, trauma that Freud would say had been organized largely around the primal scene. In other words his doubt about his sexuality was akin to his fear of flying, a means to avoid experiences that would cause him to crash and burn.

I do not wish, however, to suggest that Watt's difficulties were essentially oedipal. I don't think that his homoerotic feelings marked a negative oedipal retreat from women based on his fear of a castrating father-imago to whom he became submissively homosexual. He didn't appear principally to fear punishment for forbidden sexual desire despite the explicit primal scene experiences he had been subjected to as a child. Rather he worried obsessively about being ridiculed, rejected, and abandoned, all threats to his narcissism. He feared that women would humiliate him by finding his body too large and penis too small or worse, obliterate his sense of self boundaries by engulfing him within the enslaving circle of their own, like the mother of Mr. Z (Kohut, 1979). There never seemed reason to think his symptoms represented a regression from a developmental level he had reached but had been unable to sustain. Rather, they seemed the result of a developmental arrest. The issue for us wasn't the "restoration" of his self, but the restoration of self-development to allow a cohesive and structuralized self to come into being.

Initially Watt's sexual feelings were predominantly homoerotic and pointed both to his longing to take the strength and power of an idealizable father figure into himself and his wish to control such a figure. His sexual activity was almost exclusively masturbatory because the idea of actually engaging in sex with another person was too fraught with anxiety (i.e., of impingement, humiliation, and abandonment) for him to risk. Goldberg (1995) would describe his use of sexual fantasy as "perverse," because it functioned to protect his depleted self from the experience of unbearable affects and the threat of fragmentation.

Because sexual attraction for Watt represented the erotization of idealizing feelings and because his idealizations had a narcissistic cast—

he idealized people whom, as Lacan (1971) says (i.e., of the preoedipal child's relation to the phallus) he wanted to *be* rather than those he wanted to *have*—his desire was predominantly homosexual, but for exclusively heterosexual men. Homosexual men were, in his eyes, tainted with effeminacy: he saw them as nonfathers, hence essentially as women who needed from men precisely what he needed. They were thus incapable of providing him with what he lacked. His idealization of me during the analysis, however, wasn't accompanied by increased homosexual feelings (indeed it was drive-neutralizing in the homosexual sphere) but rather by his increasing sense of (heterosexual) masculinity and attraction to women. I didn't think his attraction to women was simply a displacement of an erotized transference to me (although I did think there was an element of this in his brief relation to his physical therapist Marie) but rather a spontaneous effect of his experience of increasing self-cohesion. What this suggested was that he had tended to turn away from his heterosexual feelings not because he was essentially gay, but because of the threat they posed to his sense of self.

As he gradually de-idealized me and came to feel integral, competent, and strong, as, in a word, he became structuralized, his dream of becoming the sort of family man and father he had always longed for seemed suddenly within his grasp, and the question of his sexual identity ceased any longer to be in doubt. His sexuality began to express a newfound capacity for intimate relatedness. He no longer saw women as essentially depressed and degraded; rather he began to see them as lively, capable, and self-sufficient, "vir"-tues he had formerly associated only with certain heterosexual men. Women thus stopped seeming to him creatures who would only use him and use him up and began to appear as sources of vital and vitalizing energy, which, of course, he desired.

This change in his vision brings to mind the love of the Duke Orsino in Shakespeare's *Twelfth Night* for Viola, who wins his heart while disguised as a boy before revealing her true identity. Interestingly, prior to falling under her spell, Orsino pays fruitless court to the Duchess Olivia who has no interest in his love because she is perpetually mourning a deceased brother, that is, because she is depressed. Shakespeare frequently suggests that men need a way to transform their vision of women in order to love them, because they see them initially as dangerously engulfing mothers—as did Watt. The seduction of such men by women who briefly disguise themselves as boys enacts the transformation Joel Fineman (1985) calls "The Turn of the Shrew."

It remains then for us to ask whether the case of Watt suggests anything generalizable about the nature of sexuality, and if so, what?

It seemed that Watt's sexuality was the product neither of nature nor of nurture, an effect of neither his genes nor his education (no one "taught" him to be one way or the other), although it's reasonable to think that both nature and culture pushed him as they would anyone more or less forcefully along converging or conflicting lines of sexual development. Rather I think Watt's sexuality is the construction of his experience of both nature and nurture, of what he made of living in the particular physical and relational world he alone finally occupied. In other words it was about meaning: "sexuality as texuality" in Bonnie Litowitz's (2002) fine phrase.

Sexuality was problematic for him because the homoerotic desire he felt clashed with what he experienced as a deep and abiding but perhaps unrealizable wish to function heterosexually. The analysis suggests that his homoerotic desire was symptomatic of his depleted and fragmentation-prone self and his need for idealized self-structure. For him such desire was perverse, not because there was any essential reason to regard homoerotic desire this way, but rather because for Watt homoerotic desire functioned essentially to shore up the depleted self and defend it against unendurable affect. He might have made exactly the same use of heteroerotic fantasy and function but didn't because for him heterosexual desire was associated with frightening primal scene fantasies of paternal violence, maternal engulfment, and the collapse of self-boundaries: that is, it was a source of terrifying anxiety. And again, not because heterosexuality is inevitably and essentially a source of such anxiety, but rather because it was a source of such anxiety for him.

If there is a lesson to be learned from this case, it may be that sexuality is more problematic and complex than even we who are the heirs of Freud are inclined to think. That it might arguably be useful to think of ourselves as having "sexualities," rather than merely sexuality, which, again, I think is something Shakespeare—Freud's teacher after all—passionately believed: think in addition to *Twelfth Night* of *The Sonnets*, *A Midsummer Night's Dream*, or of the play he punningly called *As You Like It*—to offer but a few examples of what for him was a nearly obsessive theme. But to continue. We assign definitive names to sexual orientation limited by language in possibility to but a single or at most a pair of binary alternatives: we are either gay or straight, or perhaps bi- or at the very limit asexual. But these more or less stable signifiers contain and condense vast complexities of feeling and meaning because the valences on anyone's desire and the pull of conflicting desires is completely individual, idiosyncratic, and potentially unstable. This is to say that behind the unitary signifier that names our desire as heterosexual or homosexual or bi- or asexual is a vast signifying chain of cultural and personal meanings that may have essentially the relation to such names as Freud's infinitely complex dream thoughts have to the comparatively few words and images that combine and condense them in the manifest dream, just as in Freud's beautiful metaphor the mycelia become indecipherably complex beneath the single mushroom they body forth (Freud, 1900). All of which is to suggest that our sexual sameness may be merely the stalking horse of our infinitely complicated sexual difference.

When analysis transformed the way Watt understood himself in the world, it transformed the registry of his desire. The fact, however, that self-cohesion made possible for Watt a move from homosexual fantasy to heterosexual fantasy and function doesn't mean that there is anything essential or necessary about such a move or its directionality. The analytic sea change might have been from archaic and perverse homosexuality to the homosexuality of a coherent and cohesive self; that is, from the driven, defensive, and self-reparative sexualizations of Watt's preanalytic self to the sexuality that represented the mature goals, ideals, and wishes of his nuclear self. Or it might have been from the archaic and perverse use of heteroerotic desire to the nuclear self's goal of mature homosexuality, or from perverse and driven heterosexuality to heterosexuality as the expression of a vigorous self. What the analysis cured wasn't his homoerotic feelings per se, but rather the fragmentation-prone self that used sexualization as a defense against anxiety and depressive affect. The reason then that for Watt heterosexuality was the choice seems to me not to have to do with some a priori notion of what is "good" or "normative," but with the fact that heterosexuality offered him the best solution to the complicated problem of defining his existence in his own uniquely significant world.

When and by exactly what alchemy a self constructs its goals, ideals, and aspirations is unclear, but early in Watt's life he came to have a vision of himself as a husband and especially a father, crucially to fill the missing place of the father he had never known, a vision that remained constant both before and after the analysis. Despair accompanied his fear that this profound inner goal might never be realized, even as a profound sense of joy followed the awakening of his sense that such a future could indeed be his. The same despair and joy follows the impossibility and realization of other of the nuclear self's goals, as when, for instance, one becomes strong enough to leave the career that means never fulfilling an inner dream and ventures bravely forth to pursue it. Those able finally to do what they feel they were "born" to do, or to live as they believe they were "born" to live, feel a special sense of "at-homeness" in the world, of being where they are "supposed" to be, of being lucky, even blessed.

This is why I don't believe that Watt's heterosexual resolution could be called an idiosyncratic effect of the particular intersubjective context that was his analysis with me. The achievement of self-cohesion allowed the heterosexual plan of Watt's nuclear self to come into being, but not, I think, to be rewritten or co-constructed as it were out of whole cloth. Had his analysis been conducted by, for example, Richard Isay, I believe the results would have been the same. But again, this is not to insist that sexual orientation might never be co-constructed in an analysis, merely to say that it seemed not to be in this case. The potential for sexuality is highly variable within every self, as Freud taught us, and for some, sexual orientation might indeed emerge in response to the particular opportunities for "self-fashioning" (Greenblatt, 1980) offered by a given analyst's personality within the self–selfobject context of the analysis.

The design then of the nuclear self in the sexual sphere might be for homosexuality, or heterosexuality, or perhaps bisexuality or asexuality, or it may allow for the more fluid move from one of these positions to another, perhaps with a view toward maintaining specific sorts of self–selfobject ties regardless of sexual lines, or despite them, across the life curve. I have no reason to think that one or another position is more "natural" or basic or loved by God. Each, like other compromise formations perhaps, represents a given self's efforts to solve the problems that confront it as it develops, and in so doing, rules various possibilities for vitalizing experience "in" while ruling others "out" as the self's cost of doing business with the world. We will know more as we share with one another what our patients teach us as they struggle to inscribe us within the circle of their humanity.

REFERENCES

Baumeister, R. F. (2000), Gender differences in erotic plasticity: The female sex drive as socially flexible and responsive. *Psycholog. Bull.*, 126:375–380.

Fineman, J. (1985), The turn of the shrew. In: *Shakespeare and the Question of Theory,* ed. P. Parker & G. Hartman. London: Methuen, pp. 138–159.

Freud, S. (1900), The interpretation of dreams. *Standard Edition,* 4 & 5. London: Hogarth Press, 1953.

Goldberg, A. (1995), Homosexuality as compensatory structure. In: *The Problem of Perversion: The View from Self Psychology.* New Haven: Yale University Press, pp. 97–118.

——— (2001), Depathologizing homosexuality. *J. Amer. Psychoanal. Assn.,* 49:1109–1114.

Greenblatt, S. (1980), *Renaissance Self-Fashioning.* Chicago: The University of Chicago Press.

Isay, R. (1989), *Being Homosexual.* New York: Farrar, Straus & Giroux.

Kohut, H. (1971), *The Analysis of the Self*. Madison, CT: International Universities Press.
——— (1979), The two analyses of Mr. Z. In: *The Search for the Self: Selected Writings of Heinz Kohut: 1950–1994, Vol. 4,* ed. P. Ornstein. Madison, CT: International Universities Press, 1991.
Lacan, J. (1977), *Ecrits*. New York: Norton.
Litowitz, B. (2002), Sexuality and textuality. *J. Amer. Psychoanal. Assn.,* 50: 171–198.

Chapter 10

The Case of Patient J and Discussions: Introduction

Estelle Shane

I will begin with a few comments about the question most pertinent to this panel, a question often raised and seldom answered to complete satisfaction: What is a relational perspective? The first point made by many in this regard is that there is no single set of descriptors or guidelines by which anyone who chooses this label for his or her clinical work must be confined; individuals holding to a number of diverse theoretical frameworks see themselves as relational analysts. However, we can use the clinical points delineated by Lewis Aron (1991) as one way to delineate the relational approach to the clinical process and, in any case, it serves as a good beginning for approaching a relational understanding. Aron includes in that article 10 points, which, for the purpose of my introduction here, I will paraphrase and shorten, as follows:

(1) The analytic situation is constituted by the mutual, though asymmetrical, regulation of communication between patient and analyst, a communication in which each is vitally affected by the other.
(2) The analyst's subjectivity is an important element in the analytic situation, and the patient's experience of it should be made conscious.
(3) Patients seek to connect to and to know their analysts.
(4) The analyst's self-revelation is inevitable and continuous, but direct self-revelation may interfere with the patient's capacity to recognize the analyst's subjectivity.

(5) Establishing one's own subjectivity in the analytic situation is essential, yet problematic, because the analyst is as complicated as the patient, and his or her self-awareness is limited. We are thus not in a position to judge the accuracy of our patient's perceptions of us, and therefore we cannot validate such perceptions.
(6) It is useful to ask patients directly about their perceptions of the analyst, but it is best to get at this perception through analytic exploration; however, the analyst's insistence on asserting too exclusively his or her own subjectivity leads to reversal in the relationship and doesn't permit an intersubjective exchange. Finally, these perceptions must be seen as only one aspect in the totality of the therapeutic relationship.

I can add to these points describing relational analysis by my own observation that, in the relational framework often the principal focus, though, of course, not the exclusive focus, is on the two-person, here-and-now aspect of the analytic relationship, as opposed to the genetic, there-and-then aspect. And emergent in that relationship, the relationalist expects to discover and experience transference phenomena, pathological symptoms, enactments and countertransference expressions.

Obviously much that has been written by Robert Stolorow speaks clearly and consistently to some of these same issues identified by Lewis Aron. Specifically, Stolorow, like Aron, views the patient's subjectivity, the analyst's subjectivity, and their confluence in the intersubjective field as crucial to analytic process. He also contends that we, as analysts, are not in a position either to validate or to disconfirm patients' perceptions of us. These productions must be explored and understood, as with any other, for their personal, subjective meanings to the patient. These ideas are commonplace in Stolorow's relational perspective wherein he emphasizes that the transference relationship, in both the repetitive–conflictual and the developmental dimensions, must be explored interpretively as the major intervention in the analytic process. Stolorow asserts in his discussion that follows that he has been writing and speaking about the role of the relationship in the therapeutic process for some 25 years, beginning with his first conceptualization of the therapeutic dyad as an intersubjective system formed by the reciprocally interacting, experiential worlds of patient and therapist. Because space is short, I will restrict this review of relational analysis as written about by Aron and Stolorow to these few points and turn to Joye Weisel-Barth's discussion of her analysis of J.

REFERENCE

Aron, L. (1991), The patient's experience of the analyst's subjectivity. *Psychoanal. Dial.*, 1:29–51.

The Case of Patient J

Joye Weisel-Barth

J came to see me six years ago in distress about violence. She was in a destructive relationship with an alcoholic and compulsively unfaithful man. Her encounters with this man had become increasingly violent, violence in which she participated by baiting him and hitting him in their drunken rages.

J is a middle-aged beauty with patrician features; dark, well-cut hair; and hazel eyes. Her dress is either casual urban chic—good slacks and Armani jackets with the sleeves rolled—or raggedy blue jeans and boots, her "cowgirls-get-the-blues" look. She brings her big old dog to sessions, a loving black retriever. A year and a half ago, J agreed to be an analytic control case and come to treatment four hours per week.

J grew up on an isolated farm with her intact family: parents, an older sister, and two younger siblings, a boy and a girl. Her father, charming and charismatic, was also an alcoholic womanizer. Many people from political, literary, and theatrical circles visited the farm. J says, "There were two different groups of people at our home: interesting artists and intellectuals and vicious alcoholics. The same people belonged to both groups depending on the amount of alcohol consumed." In the grip of alcoholic states, the father and mother physically battered each other, violent encounters that J and her siblings witnessed. The father also beat the children in unregulated rages.

Her mother, the daughter of a socially prominent family, suffers from schizophrenia. J remembers her childhood mother as drunk, ineffective, violent, and not much involved in child-rearing. Once, during J's adolescence, the mother went on a rampage and trashed

J's bedroom. Her father was kinder to her, and as a child J identified with her father's strength. When she was a teenager, her parents divorced. The mother now lives in a transient motel.

J's childhood was socially isolated and largely unsupervised. In addition to the domestic violence, she suffered from many early traumatic experiences. These included several sexual molestations by her uncle, neighbor boys, and drunken family friends; an automobile accident that sent her (alone at four years old) to a hospital for several weeks; and a public school tenure in which her classmates, poor rural farm children, treated her as a social pariah. J wandered the farm to comfort herself and found an imaginary friend. Set into the stone wall bounding the farm was a medallion of a little deer. J imagined that the fawn would come alive to play with her and protect her. She believes she saw it move and look at her on several occasions. This fawn has been a kind of talisman for J in her life.

J left home early, left college early, and then became a model and actress. She also became a jet setter, involving herself sexually with a roster of fast, famous, and powerful men. She participated in orgies. The history she described is one of sexual exploitation, heavy drug and alcohol use, and occasional physical violence. Initially, she defined her life as moments of intense drama and of narrow escapes. Now she identifies her sexual experiences as "spaced out," devoid of feeling, episodes of dissociation.

When J was in her mid-twenties, her younger brother committed suicide, an act she blames on her father's brutal treatment but for which she also carries deep grief and feelings of guilt.

At 28 J married a man known equally for artistic genius, destructive drug use, and reckless behavior. During the marriage, he beat and sexually abused her. She fought back. Although divorced now, they still maintain close personal and business ties.

THE TREATMENT

During the first stage of our psychotherapy work, J tested me. How shocked was I by graphic depictions of her sexual exploits? Could she seduce me with her tales? Sometimes! Could I stand her impulsive behavior, temper tantrums, and sometimes foul mouth? She would watch me, head cocked to the side with the smile of a naughty child, as she narrated some outrageous incident. She was surprised and touched when I commented at every opportunity on her strengths: her generosity, her senses of justice and loyalty and humor, her street smarts, her kindness to animals, and her ultimate self-restraint—the ways in which she played at its edges but never let herself fall into the abyss. In fact, our closest therapeutic moments have occurred when I have surprised her expectations, when instead of criticizing her, I have gotten beneath her narrative to find tender meanings.

After about a year and a half, J became "a very good girl." She would report those occasions on which she contained her anger or said "No" to some powerful man. She even broke off her relationship with the alcoholic for a while. In return, she expected perfect therapeutic behavior from me. She became very sensitive to and critical of my every word. She frequently accused me of clumsiness and obtuseness in dealing with her. For example, with respect to her alcoholic lover, she felt I disapproved of the relationship and did not respect the depth of their mutual feelings. She scolded me for weeks "for not getting it right." There have been many disruptions of this sort in our relationship. I acknowledge here that usually she reads my deepest attitudes correctly.

When I presented her the offer of an analysis, she accepted immediately. (Parenthetically, J had left a classical analysis with a male analyst in early adulthood.) Later, she wanted assurance that I would not become cold and clinical. She also insisted on my choosing a woman supervisor. She argued that no man would comprehend her story. In her view, even if a woman supervisor missed something or was mistaken about something, at least a woman can admit a mistake and rectify an error.

The expansion of therapeutic space has enabled J to slow down and elaborate her narrative of early deprivation, neglect, and abuse. Telling the story slowly allows the emergence, not only of long-buried incidents, but also of long-buried sorrow. Particularly in relation to her dead brother, J has expressed profound grief.

Feeling pain is difficult for J, and she has a number of avoidant and protective strategies to distance herself from emotion. For example, she often cancels the session following an intense analytic hour. At times, she wants a phone session from her bed. Then, J brings her dog to analysis to guard her. Together, we have observed that the animal does, in fact, regulate and modulate her feelings. If she is angry, distressed, or crying, the dog lumbers over and nuzzles her or licks her hand. J also relieves intense feeling by changing the subject. For example, she might abruptly shift from a painful memory to some superficial observation about my hair or clothing. I sometimes feel annoyed at the resulting choppiness in the flow of our sessions.

In addition to these strategies, J protects herself from painful emotion by isolating narrative content from feeling. To illustrate: J has horrible dreams in which demonic men pursue, threaten, or sexually attack her. In different dreams these men assume different guises: "machete men," "gangster men," "murderous men of color," menacing men, faceless or masked, and sexual predators, unknown and renowned, wielding all kinds of lethal weapons. In these dreams her places of refuge are compromised. They have broken door locks or fissures in the walls where the men can enter. When I appear in these dreams, I am far away, out of earshot, or somewhere across a dangerous catwalk, certainly beyond J's hope of help or rescue. Early in our work J reported these terrible dreams to me matter-of-factly, sometimes with puzzlement, sometimes in a cheerful tone, sometimes even with a joke.

Now I'm going to describe several therapeutic incidents that will convey the ways in which J's issues emerge and are enacted in our analytic sessions. These incidents contain emotionally charged moments: "now moments." Here is the issue I'd like to address: how to convert these moments into encounters that expand the analytic horizon.

(1) J told me she had shown a picture of her mother to her friend A. "What a loser!" A commented. In that moment, J said she "wanted to kill A." A few minutes after relating this incident, J said she had meant to bring me the picture, but "I forgot it." I suggested maybe there was a reason she had forgotten the picture. She was quiet and then agreed. She said she worried that I might also criticize her mother.

J continued to forget the picture. Then, after about two weeks, right in the middle of a session and *a propos* of nothing, J handed me a photograph. It took me a second to realize this was *the* photo. "Another test," I thought. J was watching my face. The woman in the photograph had the vague look of a deteriorating schizophrenic. She stood stiffly and without expression, a slightly plump woman with a puffy face, swollen eyes, and facial skin sprinkled with small brown growths. Her hair was slightly disheveled, but her clothes were clean and the room spare and orderly. This is J's mother looking quiet and childlike, the lifelong fire of her mental illness having finally cooled.

Feeling sad for the two women, the one in the picture and the one in the room with me, I said that I appreciated J's bringing the photograph. It clarified for me how ill her mother must have been when J was a little girl. I also noted the effort her mother had put into fixing the room and dressing herself nicely. J's face lit up as she proudly pointed out the curtains in the room, which her mother had sewn. That was all. She took back the photo and changed the subject. At the next session, she thanked me for recognizing her mother's suffering. "I figured you would, " she said and then added,

"Usually I can't stand Mother, but since our session I've actually felt some kindness toward her."

(2) Last spring, J described staying up all night watching a tornado disaster on TV. She confessed that she took pleasure in seeing the body count rise. She was shy about telling me, worried that I would think her a "freak, perverse, horrible, and disgusting." She wasn't far off; my first reaction was of horror. She went on to say that she particularly liked it when fat "wonderbread" people died. The only thing that bothered her about the tornado was that innocent animals also suffered.

Remembering the farm children who had tormented her, I asked about "wonderbread" people. "You know," she said, "all blown up with air—no substance, stupid, no culture." She compared them to the terrible men she has loved. "They're like 'wonderbreads,' too, except for being sicker and more twisted, smarter and . . . much more interesting."

Then, J wondered about how I judged her perverse pleasure. She said, "If I were you, I'd think me horrible and disgusting." When I didn't respond, she looked me directly in the eye and asked point blank, "Okay Joye, what do you think of me wanting the death toll to go higher?"

There is something wonderfully risky in how squarely, how authentically J puts herself into our relationship, in how directly she confronts me. This willingness to risk invites me also to risk, to enter her world more boldly than I might otherwise. And so, as in this instance, she pulls my imagination into her life, into her memories, feelings, and current experience. In order to understand what would cause her to celebrate human catastrophe, I imagine myself as little J, lonely, frightened, and hyperaroused; as J, the victim of neglectful and violent parents; as J, the butt of ridicule from the farm children who were her classmates; and as J, the object of sexual degradation.

I said to her, "I think you've been terribly disappointed with people, enormously hurt by them." She became teary and silent. For several of the following sessions, she alluded to what I had said and commented a few times, "That was right. People have hurt and disappointed me."

(3) J still brings her bulky old dog to our sessions. One day, he turned over a small table, shattering the glass top and knocking over a vase of flowers. The glass collapsed on itself in a neat pile of long shards. "Damn!" I first thought. Then, I caught sight of J. She had blanched and soon became panicky and distressed, rushing around the room looking for something with which to soak up the spilled

water and, all the while, apologizing: "I'm sorry, I'm sorry!" As her emotions heated, I noticed myself becoming cool and still. Surprised and curious, I watched her panic mount. Then I saw her bend down, about to pick up the sharp glass strips, heedless of the danger to her bare hands. While I didn't mind water on my Oriental rug, I really didn't want blood, and I didn't want J to hurt herself. So at that point, I stepped in. In my best mother voice, I told her to sit down, assuring her that I had cleaned up much worse in my day. After that, she did settle onto the couch, bent, her head bowed, looking for all the world like a sullen child in the principal's office.

When I had finally disposed of the mess, an amazing thing happened. J's demeanor utterly changed. She pulled herself into an adult posture, raised her chin, and assumed the same maternal voice I had just used with her: "It's Okay, Joye, you don't have to get so excited, you know. Settle down now, and chill out. You're overreacting, honey." Then her body relaxed, her shoulders fell, and her emotional state again visibly shifted. As though amused by what she had just said, her face softened; she laughed and said to me in her familiar joking way, "Pay attention, Joye, I want my appointment now, damn it!"

Confused by these changes, I asked her what had just happened. She replied, "I got scared and acted overexcited. I thought you'd be so mad at me." I realized that I had just witnessed an episode of dissociation and recovery. The episode was complete with alterations in J's facial expression, body posture, language style and voice intonation.

Following this enactment and in subsequent sessions, J remembered many childhood instances of merciless and irrational punishment. Willful childish misbehavior, minor self-assertions, simple accidents, and acts of God—any of these earned beatings in J's family. Later, as an adult, J continued to expect "without-rhyme-or-reason violence." In fact, for J, physical pain is an integral part of intimate relationships and generally precedes resolution of conflict.

"How did you stand the pain?" I asked. J described first trying to avoid brutal treatment by "making nice," that is, by being helpful and ingratiating. If that didn't work, she could numb herself so that she "didn't feel anything." She also fought back physically and verbally. Then, she added, "I always looked ahead. I knew when the fight ended, there would be peace." In light of all this, J and I reexamined the broken glass accident. We saw that she had enacted with me her whole dynamic of violence: the expectation that I would attack her, the panicky effort to placate me, and the willingness to injure herself in order to resolve the conflict. All of this had occurred in a procedural state, a state of dissociation.

(4) As part of her business, J receives first-run movies on videotape. In past years she has brought me some videos to see. This year, she described watching new movies on tape and repeatedly said in an offhanded way, "I'll bring [this or that film] for you to see." She didn't. Recently, when she again vowed to bring a movie, I commented, "You've mentioned bringing movies here several times, but you haven't." She stuttered nervously, "Oh . . . Oh, I'll bring some movies next time." When I asked if maybe she didn't want to bring movies, she thought for a minute and then answered that, indeed, she didn't want to, but she felt selfish admitting it.

Then, she started talking, excitedly and with rising anger, about all the people who exploited her, and not just with the movies. None of the exchanges in her life were reciprocal or fair. She began to catalogue—and this time sadness laced the anger—how often she has let herself be used and exploited and how seldom anybody has actually met her needs. I observed that she didn't want to feel that way about me. She wanted me to respect her boundaries and not to exploit her. She left the session happy, and since has referred frequently to my willingness to let her be a "selfish bitch."

(5) I blew my nose in a session, and it began to bleed. I excused myself and went over to my desk until the nosebleed stopped. The session resumed. At the beginning of the next hour, J said she felt angry and rattled off a number of small life events that had "pissed her off." I asked if she was also angry with me. Her face hardened. "I'm furious about the nosebleed," she said. It had taken away from her appointment time, and it was disgusting that I hadn't left and gone into the bathroom to bleed. She was very offended by my rudeness and lack of caring about her.

I was floored. I certainly never anticipated this, and I felt defensive. But I kept inquiring about her feelings. It seemed my handling of the nosebleed was a breach of boundaries. The sessions are for her, and I shouldn't burden her with my problems or imperfections. She felt embarrassed to tell me these things (they confirm what a "selfish bitch" she is) but I needed to know them.

I related these "nosebleed" feelings to the movie tapes. I said that analysis was the only place where she could express herself and claim her rights, even if they felt selfish and unreasonable, as they had to both of us in this instance. Any infringement on my being available for her made her angry. When I inquired about whether it worried her to see me bleed, she didn't answer and changed the subject.

Next day, after the nosebleed confrontation, J recounted that she had had the most frightening experience of her life. She had dreamed her familiar "demonic man" dream, and this time it was her ex-husband who was sexually debasing her. The configuration of the dream was familiar but the emotional experience completely new. In the dream and then on waking, a deep and wrenching sadness had overpowered her. She felt heartsick and cried for a long time in the analytic session. "What's happening to me?" she finally asked, and I answered, "You've connected normal feelings to your horrible dream. You're feeling your experience." For me this was a shining moment. Of course, after the intensity of the session, J called to cancel the next appointment. Her voice message: "I need a vacation."

I know that J is a difficult person and, by most standards, a difficult patient. At times, she infuriates me, and at times, she exasperates me. Her impulsive acting out behavior, about which I've said only a bit, worries me. It also draws out a part of myself that I dislike: my judgmental and "teachy-preachy" self. In spite of all this, J is not a particularly hard patient for me. Here are some reasons why. I love and admire how immediate and real she is in her wildness and spunkiness. I love how she struggles to use in her life the reflective skills she is learning and practicing in our analysis. I love that J and I track each other affectively so that we are able to mend—in a fairly easy and continuous way—the recurring breaches in our relationship. And I love that over time J has come to trust that I read her pretty well. Finally, I am awed that, even without verbal cues, J reads me quite accurately in return. She will say things to me like, "I know what you're thinking. You're thinking, Oh no, J, you didn't do *that!*" or "Joye, you look so cool, but your impatience with me is noisy today." And she also sometimes says, "I know you love me." She reads me quite right.

A Ruthless Examination of an Empathic Clinical Presentation:

A Discussion of Joye Weisel-Barth's Clinical Case

Lewis Aron

My task is to examine the role of the relationship in the therapeutic process, and Dr. Joye Weisel-Barth has provided us with some moving clinical material that is not only interesting and engaging, but that also lends itself quite well to this purpose. In order to approach and open for discussion some difficult, controversial, and, perhaps, some unresolvable theoretical and technical questions about clinical psychoanalysis, I will utilize this material ruthlessly. I do not know Dr. Weisel-Barth (as I write this chapter, we have not yet met), but my sense is that the clinical work is going well, in its own troubled way, and I will draw on the data presented to show precisely why I am encouraged about this analytic process. To express my rationale in Winnicottian terms, it may be because I do have this good feeling about the work that I trust myself to "use" the clinical report in this "ruthless" manner, rather then simply to "relate" to it in a kinder, but more superficial, way (Winnicott, 1971). In beginning my discussion by recognizing and acknowledging the excellent quality of aspects of the treatment and of the presentation and by following up with a critical and perhaps at times aggressive engagement with the material and by encouraging us all to articulate our reactions to this engagement, I hope to enact in the here-and-now something of the quality of what I would look for in the analytic relationship.

At the beginning of the chapter, Weisel-Barth begins her clinical presentation to us with J's initial clinical presentation to her, so that the continuing systemic operations of enactment, identifications, role reversals, and other such processes have, as always, already begun. We first hear about a destructive, violent, alcoholic, compulsive relationship. We are immediately introduced to an archetypal sadomasochistic relationship.[1] Soon we learn, but already we could not be surprised, that J's family background, going back multiple generations and both witnessed and experienced by her directly, is characterized by drunken violence, physical and sexual abuse, and betrayal. Next, we learn that, socially and developmentally, J has been the object of sexual molestation by family, friends, and social acquaintances; unsupported, lengthy separations from her family at an early age; physical trauma; and teasing and social humiliation by peers. Not surprisingly, her adult intimate and casual relationships continue to be sadomasochistic, including a marriage to a drug addict who beat and sexually abused her. Just for the record and just to be sure that we do not in any way underestimate the complexity and difficulty that we would all expect in the treatment, let me not omit her mother's schizophrenia, her own report of childhood hallucinations, and her adult report of dissociative episodes.

With a case study so *dominated,* if you will, by sadomasochism, my first thought as a clinician is to wonder where and how this sadomasochism will emerge in the analytic relationship. This is not because I expect it to come up "in the transference" in the old-fashioned sense, meaning as a distortion of the patient's, in which she perceives the analyst as abusive or submissive, but rather because with Ed Levenson and others, I expect that what is talked about in analysis—simultaneously played out between patient and analyst—is the analytic relationship, that what is talked about and what is enacted are isomorphic transformations of each other (Levenson, 1991). So clinically, I would begin to wonder how I as analyst (or for that matter as supervisor or discussant) would get caught up in

[1] By sadomasochism I mean a relationship dominated by themes of dominance and submission. I am not using the term *sadomasochism* as embedded in a traditional theoretical context of drive theory, but rather, descriptively, from a relational perspective, where mutuality (mutual recognition and reciprocal trust) is impossible and the only option available is one form or another of sadomasochism (see Frankel, 1993; Bach, 1994; Aron, 1996).

sadomasochistic scenarios. Please understand that I would not assume that this could be avoided, but I would hope to be able to catch myself, sometimes before and sometimes only after engaging in these engagements, or at least I would hope to be open and receptive to feedback from the patient, a supervisor, or a colleague about this form of participation. I would not expect that the patient would or could usually tell me about this in any direct manner; rather, I would expect to hear about this indirectly in the form of allusions and references in the patient's associations.

But one way or another, if a patient's life has been hell, if their childhood was hell, if their adult relationships have been hell, then I sure expect their analysis to be hell, and I expect to have to burn there with them, as their tormenter, fellow sufferer, witness, and rescuer. I do not expect that I could maintain my cool for very long in this situation. And if I do, then I can't imagine how the analysis will progress beyond the superficially supportive. Davies and Frawley's (1994) book on the treatment of adult survivors of sexual abuse is an excellent introduction to this clinical approach, mapping out how patients and analysts mutually enact a wide assortment of roles and scenarios.

So here, too, I would expect that, in one way or another, our participation on this panel will include some enactment of sadomasochistic themes, as well as defenses against assuming these unpleasant roles, and I do not believe that being forewarned regarding this likelihood will be enough to prevent their occurrence, even if it may temper or modulate our participation. Furthermore, I would expect that some unconscious performance along these lines might lead to didactically and even to clinically productive dramatizations.

So with that, let's look at what we're told about the process of the analysis and the construction and unfolding of the analytic relationship. The very first thing that Weisel-Barth reports about the first stage of the therapy is that J tested her to see if Joye could stand her admittedly outrageous and provocative behavior. How does Joye respond to J's opening gambit, as Steve Mitchell (1988) called such an initial interpersonal move? Does she confront her provocative behavior, point it out, interpret it, question it, or share her feelings about being so challenged? No. Nor does she respond aggressively or in any obvious retaliatory way; rather, she surprises J by commenting on her strengths, generosity, sense of justice, loyalty, humor, kindness, and self-restraint. Weisel-Barth then reports, "In fact, our closest therapeutic moments have occurred when I have surprised her expectations."

Well, it's no surprise why J is surprised. She knows her provocative and outrageous behavior better than to expect this response from those with whom she interacts; she knows something of her impact on others even before they respond. So what would she make of Weisel-Barth's response? That Weisel-Barth is an angel, a perfect empath who is beyond being provoked? Is she to believe that here in psychotherapy she has finally found her "new good object," her "good mother"? Or might she suspect that something else is going on? That her analyst is playing a particular role, responding with a particular stance, or perhaps is avoiding or resisting taking on certain roles?

The very next thing that we are told is that, in response to these surprise interventions, J became "a very good girl." Here, I believe, we see the typical and predictable switches and role reversals where, in response to and identification with her therapist's good object role, she adopts a good patient role, at least superficially. But in the next sentence we learn that, "in return," J becomes incredibly sensitive, demanding, and entitled, expecting "perfect therapeutic behavior" from Weisel-Barth. In my reading, it's as if she says, "All right, is this the game here? We're going to both be good girls to each other; then let's see just how very good you can really be. Now I'll tyrannize you in your "'good mother' role!" as J scolds Weisel-Barth and challenges her repeatedly.

Next in the sequence: And I hope that you will notice that I am sticking to a close reading of the text of the clinical report in sequence, as if it were associative data in an analysis. Since I do not know anything about the analyst here other than what I have in the text, I am trusting my own affective reactions to the flow of the text, as well as inferences based on contiguity, continuity, narrative coherence, and sequencing to construct my own interpretive reading (see Arlow's classic studies, 1991).

So, next we are told, as an aside, that from Weisel-Barth's point of view, J usually reads Weisel-Barth's deepest attitudes correctly. Well, what are we to make of this acknowledgment coming at just this point in the narrative sequence? Of course, I agree with Weisel-Barth that it is always useful to consider what a patient says about the analyst as an important perspective on the interaction, as one plausible construction about the analyst. I elaborated on just this point in my early work on "the patient's experience of the analyst's subjectivity" (Aron, 1991). Why does she tell us *now* that J reads her deepest attitudes correctly? She is in the midst of reporting that despite her best efforts to be the good object, she is still under increasing attack for not getting it right. So why when under attack does she respond by protesting how well she is understood? One possible take on this, and one that I believe fits the narrative coherence of the report and that fits what I know of work with sadomasochism, is that Weisel-Barth is adopting a masochistic defense in response to these attacks. Rather than maintaining her own independent perspective about her clinical work while under attack, while considering her patient's view as one interesting and important perspective, she submits to the patient's perspective and owns it as if it were her own. It is just this giving up of one's own perspective in favor of the other's that I regard as at the heart of sadomaochism. In theoretical terms, empathy involves seeing things from the patient's perspective while maintaining one's own point of view, whereas to adopt another's perspective and to give up one's own is not empathy but masochism. (This was a significant feature of Ferenczi's mistake in his mutually analytic work with RN reported in his *Clinical Diary* (Ferenczi, 1932). See Aron, 1996, for further examination of Ferenczi's treatment of RN.)

Next in sequence, still under attack, Weisel-Barth offers J the gift of an analysis, I suspect at a reduced fee although we are not told anything about this, and J insists on a woman supervisor while demanding assurance that Weisel-Barth would not become cold and clinical. Again, my reading is that J rightfully fears that sooner or later a role reversal will take place. She knows full well that, sooner or later, all human beings respond to attacks and provocations with counterattacks and/ or defenses against such attacks. Since, as Sullivan (1953) said, analysts are all more simply human than otherwise, J is right to expect this sooner or later. But what does Weisel-Barth report as her first observation about the expansion of the therapy to an analysis? Although she tells us that J continues to act provocatively by missing sessions, requesting (or I suspect demanding) sessions from her bed (just like RN by the way), avoiding affect, bringing in her dog to guard her, nevertheless Weisel-Barth's interventions emphasize her pain, sorrow, and grief. Weisel-Barth continues to avoid any confrontation or aggressive response, instead empathizing with J's vulnerability, while avoiding her sadism.

Here, about halfway through the chapter, I note a sign that brings me some relief. Weisel-Barth tells us finally that she "sometimes" feels annoyed at the "choppiness" of the sessions. Thank God, I think. For me, here is some initial, cautious acknowledgment by Weisel-Barth that she can own some of the inevitable hostility being evoked continuously in this treatment. The sessions are certainly choppy, and it is Weisel-Barth who is being continuously chopped. J repeatedly dreams of "demonic men," "machete men," "gangster men," "murderous men of color." But while she has been careful to keep all men away from the analysis in reality, in psychic reality, isn't J deeply identified with these men and doesn't she relate to and attempt to elicit these roles in her analyst as well? Isn't this one aspect of her cheerful tone and joke making as she reports on these demons?

In order to leave myself some time to reflect on all of this clinical material, I have to move quickly through the several clinical vignettes presented, but I will say enough to give you a sense of my approach. In the first, J presents Weisel-Barth with the photo of her mother without warning. J recognizes this as a test, but I would go further and call it both sadistic and provocative, in addition to whatever other more benign motivations were at play. While recognizing that she is being tested, Weisel-Barth chooses to pass over this aspect of the interaction and, instead, expresses appreciation, again reframing what may be seen as a sadistic interaction into something exclusively positive and affirmative and owning only her sadness, but not responding overtly to the part of her that felt tested and put on the spot.

Vignette two is wonderful. Here we have a vivid image and description of J's inner rage, sadism, and explosiveness. She confesses that she takes pleasure in the body count following the tornado. Why, after several years of therapy and analysis, would Weisel-Barth be at all surprised by her own horror? J stays up all night watching the disaster because it is such a pleasure and relief for her to externalize her own inner violence and disaster area. J is the tornado and its victims, its rescue hero and its witness, and, by now, so is Weisel-Barth. Both Weisel-Barth and J need to be able to identify with all of these roles and their affective repercussions. J knows that Weisel-Barth is horrified; who wouldn't be? But J continues to put Weisel-Barth on the spot with this, challenging her reactions directly. Does Weisel-Barth respond with any annoyance or report on how manipulative and sadistic this is? No, she describes it in terms like, "wonderfully," "squarely," "authentically," "risky," and "This willingness to risk invites me also to risk." Again, Weisel-Barth reflects back to J only her sadness and disappointment, keeping her identified only with the role of the vulnerable, hurt victim. But what about her murderous, sadistic, demonic tornado? Where is the body count in this analysis?

In the third vignette J's big, bulky, old dog knocks over and breaks her vase. J begins to pick up broken glass with her bare hand, in my mind going to great lengths to bring blood and guts into the analytic space more concretely. As if to say, I think, "When are you going to see and acknowledge the bloody mess? Why don't you see my sadism and masochism and talk to me about it directly?" Weisel-Barth jokingly tells us "While I didn't mind water on my Oriental rug, I really didn't want blood." Now, once again, I felt some relief, in that in emphasizing her concern for her carpet, Weisel-Barth expressed some sadism in that remark. Of course, I understand that literally none of us wants our vases broken or blood-stained carpets, but I think we need to hear this on a metaphorical level as well. Weisel-Barth is resisting getting blood on her hands, as well as on her carpet. She deals with violence and bloodshed, tornadoes and abuse by "putting on" her "best maternal voice." No wonder that this precipitates a dissociative episode with dramatic role reversals, but that very fluidity of roles and the dramatic quality of the enactment leads to further recall of violent memories in which J avoids brutal treatment by making nice, by being helpful and ingratiating.

Here, I think that J and Weisel-Barth together are getting to the crux of the transference–countertransference interlock. Increasingly, as we have moved from vignette to vignette, we have seen some recognition by Weisel-Barth of her own negative, hostile, or sadistic reactions. Gradually, I believe that some space is being created for Weisel-Barth to own roles other than that of the good mother, good object, good analyst. I think that the heart of the analytic relationship consists of Weisel-Barth's deep identification with this aspect of J, namely, that they share a tendency to avoid brutal treatment by "making nice," that is, by being helpful and ingratiating. So in my reading, it is not an accident that in the next vignette, Weisel-Barth directly confronts J, for the first time that we hear, when she points out to her that, in spite of repeatedly offering, she, in fact, does not bring her the videos. Again, it's no accident that this confrontation frees J up to express her own anger more directly about being exploited and to own her character as a selfish bitch even directly toward Weisel-Barth.

In the final vignette, once again, real blood flows in the consulting room. This time, I think luckily, Weisel-Barth does not hide or take the blood out of the room. Her own needs inadvertently enter the office, and Weisel-Barth owns them and deals with them even while continuing to empathize with J's need not to be burdened by Weisel-Barth's own bloody and bodily needs. This contact with real blood in the analysis leads to J's coming into better contact with her own bloody, affective experience.

Finally, in the concluding paragraph, Weisel-Barth acknowledges that J is indeed a "difficult person and by most standards, a difficult patient." She ends the report with increased recognition of what I see as the crux of the analysis, that the difficulty in the analytic process is based on her reluctance to identify with an aspect of the patient, her sadism, because she dislikes that aspect of herself so very much. It "draws out a part of me I dislike: my judgment and teachy-preachy self." I see this insight as critical, although obviously, I am trying to develop it and elaborate on it here.

In order to deepen the analytic process, we have to face our most difficult obstacle. There are always aspects of the patient that remind us of ourselves. Some of these aspects of our character we deeply wish to deny. In order to keep them at bay in ourselves, we often deny these aspects of our patients as well, and in doing so we cannot help our patients deal with them. Analytic stalemates and impasses arise when we join in counterresisting along with our patients, so that we meet anxiety with counteranxiety, resistance with counterresistance, and transference with countertransference. I have quibbles with some of the technical terms that I have just used, but I think that they nicely capture the nature of "transference-countertransference interlocks" as Ben Wolstein (1959) put it. Namely, we have to maintain the fluidity of being able to identify with all aspects of our patients, even the ones we are most frightened of in ourselves. Our patients help us to do that over time, as I think it is clear that J is helping Weisel-Barth. But this affirmative reading of J's helpfulness should not obscure her sadistic and destructive side.

So while I do believe in the mutual love between J and Weisel-Barth, I remain troubled that Weisel-Barth emphasizes only this side of the relationship. I would gradually want to make more room for the dark side of the relationship to emerge on both sides of the couch. It doesn't have to lead to real bloodshed, but it sure as hell isn't all affirmative and loving.[2] Being a good object or a new object, surprising the patient with our consistent benevolence is insufficient. As Greenberg (1991), among others, has proposed, the analyst must also be experienced as the old object, often the bad object, and sometimes the traumatizing object among other roles. To briefly relate this to the theoretical realm of contemporary self psychology, analysts need to attend to and be available for the selfobject, developmental, or reparative dimensions of transference as well as

---

[2] It may be worth adding that the analyst may be affirmative, appreciative, and even celebratory of the patient's dark side. As an example, the analyst might have not only tolerated or accepted the patient's enjoyment of the body count following the tornado, but also might have welcomed this as an increasingly direct expression of sadistic ideation, thus helping the patient appreciate and value the pleasure that may accompany aggressive fantasy.

its repetitive dimensions, to both needed and repeated aspects of the therapeutic relationship. Philip Ringstrom (1998) has been very helpful in clarifying this bidimensional, cotransference system developed by many in the contemporary self psychology community. Stern's (1994) essay on needed and repeated relationships is an important contribution to this topic. The impossible profession demands empathy with all aspects of the patient, including and perhaps especially with those characteristics that we have most trouble with in ourselves.

A final word: The purpose of my discussion has been to utilize my own subjective reactions, including the theoretical background that I favor, my clinical experience, and my personal, affective reactions to the clinical presentation in order to highlight salient aspects of the analytic relationship. I do not believe that there is any one, singular best way to work with J or any other patient. I certainly do not believe that I can tell Weisel-Barth how she should work. What she has already accomplished with J is quite impressive in its own right. It is my responsibility, however, to utilize myself and my own reactions fully, in the service of bringing new perspectives to light and increasing the complexity and depth of our thinking. There cannot be any universal "standard technique" or "basic treatment model" that prescribes just the right balance of old and new object experience, love and hate, positive and negative affects and motivations (see Aron, 1999). For one thing, and it is not the least, different analysts tolerate love and hate from and for their patients differently and to different extents. Some of us may enjoy our patients' hatred of us more than others. Some of us enjoy their love, while others are made uncomfortable when patients express their love too directly. And each group believes that the other needs more analysis. Our theories of technique need to make room for these individual differences among analysts, as well as among patients. I hope that I have not only repeated some old, bad, traumatic engagement, but also that I have provided some needed, developmental experiences and even some nurturing food for thought.

REFERENCES

Arlow, J. A. (1991), *Psychoanalysis: Clinical Theory and Practice.* Madison, CT: International Universities Press.

Aron, L. (1991), The patient's experience of the analyst's subjectivity. *Psychoanal. Dial.*, 1:29–51.

——— (1996), *A Meeting of Minds: Mutuality in Psychoanalysis.* Hillsdale, NJ: The Analytic Press.

——— (1999), Clinical choices and the relational matrix. *Psychoanal. Dial.*, 9:1–30.

Bach, S. (1994), *The Language of Perversion and the Language of Love*. Northvale, NJ: Aronson.

Davies, J. M. & Frawley, M. G. (1994), *Treating the Adult Survivor of Childhood Sexual Abuse*. New York: Basic Books.

Ferenczi, S. (1932), *The Clinical Diary of Sándor Ferenczi*, ed. J. Dupont (trans. M. Balint & N. Z. Jackson). Cambridge, MA: Harvard University Press, 1988.

Frankel, J. B. (1993), Collusion and intimacy in analytic relationship. In: *The Legacy of Sándor Ferenczi*, ed. L. Aron & A. Harris. Hillsdale, NJ: The Analytic Press, pp. 227–248.

Greenberg, J. (1991), *Oedipus and Beyond: A Clinical Theory*. Cambridge, MA: Harvard University Press.

Levenson, E. (1991), *The Purloined Self*. New York: Contemporary Psychoanalysis Books.

Mitchell, S. A. (1988), *Relational Concepts in Psychoanalysis: An Integration*. Cambridge, MA: Harvard University Press.

Ringstrom, P. (1998), The pursuit of authenticity and the plight of self deception: Commentary on paper by Slavin and Kriegman. *Psychoanal. Dial.*, 8:285–292.

Stern, S. (1994), Needed relationships and repeated relationships: An integrated relational perspective. *Psychoanal. Dial.*, 4:317–346.

Sullivan, H. S. (1953), *The Interpersonal Theory of Psychiatry*. New York: Norton.

Winnicott, D. W. (1971), *Playing and Reality*. London: Tavistock

Wolstein, B. (1959), *Countertransference*. New York: Grune & Stratton.

On the Impossibility of Immaculate Perception—There Is No Relationship without Interpretation, and There Is No Interpretation without Relationship: A Discussion of Joye Weisel-Barth's Clinical Case

Robert D. Stolorow

Participating on this panel has created a difficult conundrum for me. My collaborators and I have been writing and speaking about the role of the relationship in the therapeutic process for more than 25 years now, beginning with our first conceptualization of the therapeutic dyad as an intersubjective system formed by the reciprocally interacting experiential worlds of patient and therapist (Stolorow, Atwood, and Ross, 1978). What can I possibly have to say about this subject that you haven't read or heard before? In order to avert the danger of putting both you and me soundly to sleep, I have decided to draw on an aspect of my personality that has made me particularly beloved here in Chicago. I shall play the role of irritating gadfly, questioning and challenging the philosophical assumptions that embed Weisel-Barth's clinical presentation.

The dichotomy between interpretation and relationship in the therapeutic process is directly descended from and a perfect mirror image of Descartes's philosophical dualism, which bifurcated human experience into cognitive and affective domains. Such artificial fracturing of human subjectivity is no longer tenable in a post-Cartesian philosophical world. Cognition and affect, thinking and feeling, interpreting and relating, these are separable only in pathology, as can be seen in the case of Descartes himself, the profoundly isolated man who created a doctrine of the isolated mind (Stolorow and Atwood, 1992), of disembodied, unembedded, decontextualized *cogito*. Examples of such separation of cognition from affect also abound in the case of J, Weisel-Barth's patient who initially reports horrifying nightmares without showing any trace of painful affect, a clinical feature to which I will soon return.

The endless debate in psychoanalysis over the role of insight through interpretation versus affective bonding with the analyst in the process of therapeutic change keeps alive the Cartesian dinosaur upon which it rests. The dichotomy is revealed to be a false one when we recognize that the therapeutic impact of analytic interpretations lies not only in the insights they convey, but also (and Kohut, 1984, knew this well) in the extent to which they demonstrate the therapist's attunement to the patient's affective life. Interpretations do not stand apart from the therapeutic relationship; they are an inherent, inseparable, and, to my mind, crucial dimension *of* the therapeutic relationship. In the language of intersubjectivity theory, interpretive expansion of the patient's capacity for reflective awareness of old, repetitive organizing principles occurs concomitantly with the emotional impact of ongoing relational experiences with the therapist, and both are indissoluble components of a unitary therapeutic process that facilitates the establishment of alternative principles for organizing experience, whereby the patient's experiential horizons can become widened, enriched, more flexible, and more complex.

Going back to the article in which we first introduced the concept of an intersubjective field (Stolorow et al., 1978), my collaborators and I have long contended that a good (that is, a mutative) interpretation is a relational process, a central constituent of which is the patient's experience of being understood. More recently, I (Stolorow, 1993) suggested that it is the specific transference meaning of the experience of being understood that supplies its mutative power, as the patient weaves that experience into the tapestry of mobilized developmental longings, enabling thwarted developmental processes to become reinstated and new organizing principles to take root. Whereas good interpretations tend to take on meanings that strengthen and expand the selfobject or developmental dimension of transference, bad interpretations—those that leave the patient feeling not understood or misunderstood—lend themselves to meanings that bring the repetitive/conflictual/resistive dimension into the foreground,[1] making it more available for analytic investigation. A similar heightening or entrenching of the repetitive dimension may result when transference interpretations that would benefit the patient go unformulated by the therapist.

As I read through Weisel-Barth's presentation, I felt at several points that J would have benefited from a more active, interpretive approach to her transference experiences. This seemed particularly so with respect to her aforementioned consistent pattern of averting painful affect: by canceling sessions or physically distancing by using the phone, by bringing her guard dog to analysis, by changing the subject or shifting attention to some detail of her analyst's appearance, and so on. J has recurring nightmares in which dreadful, demonic men pursue, threaten, or sexually attack her, but she reports this grisly imagery to her analyst matter-of-factly, even cheerfully, sometimes with jokes. When the analyst appears in these nightmares, she is far away from J, out of earshot or separated from her by some dangerous expanse. Weisel-Barth does not appear to see a connection between the dream images of an unbridgeable gulf separating her from her patient and J's pattern of isolating ideational content from painful feeling. From my perspective, it is not so much that Weisel-Barth is pictured as beyond J's hope of help or rescue. It is more that J—daughter of a very ill, schizophrenic mother—cannot dare to hope for a close and stable bond with her analyst in which traumatic affect states would be welcomed, heard, and held and, thereby, could be safely and fully felt. I believe the therapeutic relationship would have significantly deepened, had Weisel-Barth been able consistently to interpret this aspect of the repetitive dimension of the transference. In the session after the nosebleed incident, J does connect one of her nightmares with a feeling of wrenching sadness, but still she cancels the next appointment, and still no transference interpretation is reported.

---

[1] In lived experience, the various dimensions of transference are indissociably amalgamated with one another.

My hunch is that the relative scarcity of the kind of interpretations I would favor may reflect Weisel-Barth's adherence to a theoretical assumption that privileges provision of positive new (that is, transference-free) experiences with the analyst (Shane, Shane, and Gales, 1997) over investigation and interpretation of repetitive aspects of transference as the primary source of therapeutic action. I infer this from her noting that she comments at every possible opportunity on J's strengths, as well as from her claim that the closest therapeutic moments occur when she surprises J's expectations. Weisel-Barth's approach with J seems to be working very well. Clearly, there is a "good enough" fit between the two psychological worlds to facilitate considerable therapeutic transformation, and it is difficult to argue with success. As a cautionary tale, however, I offer a brief vignette from my own practice, in which a similar attempt on my part to surprise my patient's expectations resulted in a therapeutic disaster.

Kevin, a cinematographer in his mid-twenties, came to see me for treatment months after leaving his former analyst of several years. On the basis of some of the former analyst's behavior and interpretations, which I recognized as interpretations of projective identification, Kevin had come to the conclusion that this analyst was having fantasies of sodomizing him. Remaining in this humiliating situation had become intolerable for Kevin, even though he felt the analyst had helped him in many ways.

Kevin's was a history filled with unspeakable abuse and horror. From his accounts, it seemed to me that his mother was floridly psychotic, subjecting him as a child to systematic torture in the form of grotesque "experiments" and to violent beatings if he protested in any way. He had relived much of this history with the former analyst, in the form of frightening and violent dissociative episodes during the sessions, wherein the analyst and the mother of Kevin's childhood became indistinguishable.

During what I initially thought would be a nodal point in the analysis with me, Kevin was describing his longing for an "advocate." His parents had divorced when he was an infant, after which he never saw his father. His stepfather largely stayed away from the home and, when he was there, remained on the periphery, disengaged and unapproachable. There was no one, Kevin said, to "bear witness" to the tortures to which his mother subjected him and to intervene protectively on his behalf, and he had yearned for a father who would do this for him. I was deeply moved by this material—as a boy I had wished that my own loving, but very reserved, mother had been strong enough to protect me from my father's rageful tongue-lashings—and I recognized within myself a strong desire to be the advocate for whom Kevin yearned. I thought of a recent episode of the television series *ER*, in which a father brought the son he had severely beaten to the emergency room, and the pediatrician was so outraged by the abuse that he punched the father in the face. Unaware of the difficulty I was having staying with the painfulness of Kevin's unmet longing, I decided to disclose this association to him as a way of indirectly expressing my wish to be his advocate.

In the next session Kevin told me how he had assimilated my disclosure. He said that it proved to him what he had known all along, that no one would want to have anything to do with the horrors of his childhood and that his longing for an advocate was doomed to rejection. He declared angrily that I had brought the *ER* pediatrician into the session to substitute for myself, because I could not tolerate being close to his experiences of being tortured. Kevin then revealed that what he really wanted was for me to be his advocate in relation to his former analyst, whom he likened to his mother—to report the analyst to the licensing board so that he would be barred from experimenting on other victims. What most irked Kevin, I learned, was that, although I seemed to grasp what he had experienced with this analyst, I refused to do anything about it. This refusal, rooted in part in my inability to have a God's-eye view of what "really" happened in his earlier treatment, had for Kevin confirmed a central, dooming organizing principle dominating the repetitive dimension of the transference. It was the confirmation of this principle by my refusal and its being pushed into the foreground by my disclosure about the *ER* doctor that made a bad situation turn ugly. A strong possibility, which did not occur to me at the time and therefore was not investigated, was that Kevin's intensifying demand that I report the former analyst was a concretizing attempt to restore the hope, shattered by the meaning of my disclosure, that I could be the advocate/father for whom he yearned.

Kevin left the treatment abruptly, although several months later he sent me a letter thanking me for the understanding he had received from me. In retrospect, it seemed to me that perhaps he had left in order to preserve the developmental dimension of the transference in the face of a crushing repetitive aspect that seemed unresolvable.

My collaborators and I (Stolorow, Atwood, and Orange, 1999) have been sharply critical of the Kohutian concept of empathic immersion and, especially, of the contention that such empathy can be neutral and objective, a claim that is saturated with philosophical assumptions once again inherited from Descartes. One isolated mind, the analyst, enters the subjective world of another isolated mind, the patient. With his or her own psychological world virtually left outside, the analyst gazes directly on the patient's inner experience with pure and preconceptionless eyes. From my perspective, any such doctrine of immaculate perception entails a denial of the inherently intersubjective nature of analytic understanding, to which the analyst's subjectivity makes an ongoing, unavertable contribution. How often do we hear it intoned that, by immersing himself in his patients' experiences, Kohut "discovered" the selfobject transferences, as if these were virgin clinical facts simply to be unearthed? But Kohut, like the rest of us, could only immerse himself in his own intersubjectively configured experience of his patients' experiences, and the selfobject concept, like all analytic understanding, could only be constituted intersubjectively, in the interplay between his own and his patients' experiential worlds (Atwood and Stolorow, 1993).

A way out of the fallacy of immaculate perception and of the false dichotomy between interpretation and relationship can be found in the philosophical hermeneutics of Hans-Georg Gadamer (1975), whose striking relevance for psychoanalytic theory was first brought to my attention by my friend and collaborator, Donna Orange (1995). Gadamer's revolutionary contribution to hermeneutics was to make the hermeneutical situation ontological, that is, to place the phenomenon of understanding at the very heart of human being-in-the-world. Understanding is always relating-in-the-world, and relating-in-the-world centrally involves understanding. Since all human understanding is mediated by interpretation, the dichotomy between interpreting and relating collapses. Interpretation *is* relationship, and relationship *is* interpretation. Furthermore, interpretation can only be from a perspective whose horizons are shaped and delimited by the historicity of one's own organizing principles, by the fabric of preconceptions that Gadamer calls "prejudice." There can be no understanding without prejudice, no relationship without "effective history" or transference. Immaculate perception of anything or anyone is impossible.

In a curious swing of the epistemological pendulum, Weisel-Barth seems to attribute the capacity for immaculate perception not to herself, but to her patient. Early in her presentation, she contends that J usually reads Weisel-Barth's own deepest attitudes "correctly." Toward the end, after describing what she loves about J and about their way of relating to each other, she discloses that she is awed by how "accurately" J reads her, even without verbal cues. In her use of the objectivist words *correctly* and *accurately,* Weisel-Barth reveals that she, at times, views her patient as an unembedded Cartesian subject, capable of attaining clear and distinct ideas that are beyond prejudice or doubt, or questioning through dialogue. It is apparent that J has benefited from this nondefensive and appreciative idealization of her empathic capacities, probably organizing it as validation and admiration yearned for since childhood. The danger here is that, in the idealizing innocence of "eyes wide shut,"[2] the prejudices shaping J's perceptions of her analyst's feelings may go unnoticed, unexplored, and uninterpreted, thereby obscuring and attenuating an important dimension of the therapeutic engagement. Ultimately, it may be more salutary to cultivate an attitude of fallibilism (Orange, Atwood, and Stolorow, 1997) toward the perceptions and understandings held by *both* participants in the therapeutic dialogue.

In closing, I would like to express my appreciation for Weisel-Barth's presentation of a fascinating analytic process currently in progress, along with my hope that she will forgive me for using her good work for my own purpose of pointing the way toward a radical "Descartesectomy" for psychoanalysis.

REFERENCES

Atwood, G. E. & Stolorow, R. D. (1993), *Faces in a Cloud: Intersubjectivity in Personality Theory*, Northvale, NJ: Aronson.

Gadamer, H.-G. (1975), *Truth and Method*, trans. J. Weinsheimer & D. Marshall. New York: Crossroads, 1991.

Kohut, H. (1984), *How Does Analysis Cure?* ed. A. Goldberg & P. Stepansky. Chicago: University of Chicago Press.

Orange, D. M. (1995), *Emotional Understanding: Studies in Psychoanalytic Epistemology*. New York: Guilford.

——— Atwood, G. E. & Stolorow, R. D. (1997), *Working Intersubjectively: Contextualism in Psychoanalytic Practice*. Hillsdale, NJ: The Analytic Press.

Shane, M., Shane, E. & Gales, M. (1997), *Intimate Attachments: Toward a New Self Psychology*. New York: Guilford.

Stolorow, R. D. (1993), The nature and therapeutic action of psychoanalytic interpretation. In: *The Intersubjective Perspective*, ed. R. D. Stolorow, G. E. Atwood & B. Brandchaft. Northvale, NJ: Aronson, 1994, pp. 43–55.

——— & Atwood, G. E. (1992), *Contexts of Being: The Intersubjective Foundations of Psychological Life*. Hillsdale, NJ: The Analytic Press.

——— ——— & Orange, D. M. (1999), Kohut and contextualism: Toward a post-Cartesian psychoanalytic theory. *Psychoanal. Psychol.*, 16:380–388.

——— ——— & Ross, J. M. (1978), The representational world in psychoanalytic therapy. *Internat. Rev. Psychoanal.*, 5:247–256.

[2] I owe this metaphor to Dr. Julia M. Schwartz.

Reply to the Discussions

Joye Weisel-Barth

> Our childhood sages
> Taught us that
> There are many ways
> To skin a cat

THE CRITIQUES

Robert Stolorow and Lewis Aron present persuasive polemical statements, both of which suggest that each knows a better way—be it a more sophisticated or more confrontational or more enactive or more interpretational, certainly a less Cartesian, way—to treat my patient J. To respond to them, I shall first describe some similarities in their theoretical positions. Then I'll reply to each critique and add a few ideas of my own.

Although they identify different origins for their ideas, both Stolorow and Aron share many theoretical assumptions, assumptions that underlie a range of thinking known as "relational" psychoanalysis. The chief of these assumptions pertains to what is going on in the therapeutic setting. Stolorow and Aron both believe in what analysts call a "two-person psychology." The central idea here is that the analyst is as much a player in the analytic encounter as the patient, that she and the patient mutually affect each other and what happens in the consulting room. Every particularity and peculiarity of the analyst affect what happens in treatment. Such things as physical appearance, age and dress, voice quality and vocabulary, what clinical material she attends to, how she thinks, what she says, what limits she sets, her personal preferences, her very presence, in short, all of these factors make the old notions of analyst anonymity, of analyst as "blank screen," absurd.

This does not mean that analysis is symmetrical. The patient's interests and concerns are always central. But the analytic relationship is mutual—this sounds like a tautology—because in relational theory mutuality defines relationship. Indeed, for relational psychoanalysts, mutuality is key to all human interaction and development. Mind only develops in relation to other minds; mind only develops contextually and interpersonally.

In the relational school, particularly as practiced in New York, analysts are quite open about being real and separate people. In the analytic encounter, they frequently make explicit their own life experiences, thoughts, and emotional attitudes, in hermeneutical terms, their "prejudices." These become a part of the analytic meeting. Relational analysts inquire about how patients perceive them—their analytic thoughts, interventions, and behavior (Aron, 1996). And, at times, they disclose personal attitudes and ideas when they deem such disclosure relevant to analytic process. Reading some of the relational literature and the central place in it for the analyst's feelings, classical analysts and traditional self psychologists sometimes ask, "Whose treatment is this anyway? Is the analyst making too much noise here? Is she leaving the patient enough space in the analytic process? Is she being self-indulgent at the patient's expense?"

Stolorow and Aron also agree that psychoanalysis is not about a patient learning objective truths about herself from a rational and knowledgeable analyst. They dismiss the old Freudian concept of a perfectly rational analyst as an illusion. Rather, they believe that patient and analyst form a unit, and what emerges from that unit transcends the individuality of the two participants. Analyst and patient bring their "prejudices," their separate attitudes, life experiences, and presences to the encounter. There they construct together or, more accurately, create a meaningful story about the patient's world. A good analytic story is inclusive and feels authentic. It reflects the affective tone of the patient's world with the intermingling color and overtones of the analyst's presence in that world. Nevertheless, the story is not "true" in any objective sense.

The story is not true on several levels, two of which I'll mention here. First, we know from neuroscience that memory is deceptive and slippery. Memory is not a fixed, stored item in our brain as we have conventionally thought. We do not retrieve a memory as we might a piece of jewelry locked in a household safe. Instead, every memory represents an ingathering of traces of sensory data, traces that are scattered throughout the brain. What traces we choose and how they come together and combine—these depend, among other things, on the interpersonal context and the intensity of emotion at the time of retrieval. Our affective environment forms and informs our memories to a larger degree than common wisdom has taught. Memories are interpersonal constructions or creations, which rest on feelings and not objective facts.

The second level has to do with the complexities of both subjectivity and the meeting of subjectivities. Contemporary theorists note that just as patients are limited in their self-awareness, so, too, are analysts. Gone, sadly, is the old Freudian analytic omniscience. As fallible creatures, our perceptions of ourselves, of our patients, of our patients' perceptions of themselves and of our patients' perceptions of us are all, unhappily, fallible. Yet perceptions are all we have to go on. Therefore, we inquire of ourselves and of our patients about our differing perceptions. The stories we concoct from these inquiries represent a series of best mutual guesses, the guesses based on two emotionally engaged minds examining together and negotiating together in the here and now their shifting and disparate perceptions of the world. The created stories are necessarily unpredictable and unique. They, again, are not truth in any objective sense. The logical conclusion from these relational ideas is that each analytic couple is wholly original.

How does all of this look, how does it express itself in the psychoanalytic hour? Stolorow and Aron have different answers to this question, and their responses to my work with J reflect some of these differences. I'll turn now to the case, using it to clarify my agreements and disagreements with the two men.

While both Stolorow (2000) and Aron (2000) contend that I fail to make important interpretations about J's behavior toward me "in the transference," each man has a different view about what kind of interpretation I fail to make. Stolorow thinks that I fail to confront J when she avoids painful affect, that is, when she cancels therapy after emotionally wrenching sessions—and that I do not adequately interpret the "repetitive dimension" of the transference. For example, J dreams of a dangerous breach that separates the two of us. Stolorow interprets this dream as reflecting J's hopelessness about the therapeutic connection. Based on experience with her schizophrenic mother, he believes, she despairs of creating a safe, sheltering and stable bond with me. He would say that this expectation of being alone, endangered and unprotected is an "organizing principle" of J's psychological world.

Stolorow argues that identifying these central relational constellations—in the context of an attuned analytic relationship—is at the heart of analytic change. Interpretation of and reflection on the patient's organizing principles allow the analytic couple to make the principles conscious and therefore subject to emotional revision and resolution.

In his comments, Stolorow argues, like Freud, that interpretation is the primary instrument of therapeutic action. Unlike Freud, however, he underlines the importance of emotional attunement as integral to a good interpretation. He rails against the false dichotomy, rife, he believes, in dualistic psychoanalytic thinking, between a rational interpretation and affect attunement, suggesting that the impact of well-formulated interpretations "lies not only in the insights they convey, but also . . . in the extent to which they demonstrate the therapist's attunement to the patient's affective life." He concludes, as in the following statement, that the mutative power of therapeutic action rests on verbal interpretive formulations, formulations that give the patient an experience of being understood.

> In the language of intersubjectivity theory, interpretive expansion of the patient's capacity for reflective awareness of old, repetitive organizing principles occurs concomitantly with the emotional impact of ongoing relational experiences with the therapist, and both are indissoluble components of a unitary therapeutic process that facilitates the establishment of alternative principles for organizing experience, whereby the patient's experiential horizons can become widened, enriched, more flexible, and more complex.

Aron thinks that sadomasochism is the dominant issue in J's clinical material and that I should have continuously interpreted J's sadistic and masochistic interactions with me and mine with her. In contrast to Stolorow, Aron is as interested in behavioral enactments as he is in interpretation. The analytic consulting room becomes a space for the analytic couple to mix it up and duke it out. For example, even though the dog upended the table in the broken glass incident, Aron somehow sees the episode as an expression of J's sadistic behavior and my response as a masochistic enactment:

> I expect that what is talked about in analysis—simultaneously played out between patient and analyst—is the analytic relationship, that what is talked about and what is enacted are isomorphic transformations of each other. . . . So clinically, I would begin to wonder how I as analyst (or for that matter as supervisor or discussant) would get caught up in sadomasochistic scenarios. . . . If a patient's life has been hell, if

> their childhood was hell, if their adult relationships have been hell, then I sure expect their analysis to be hell, and I expect to have to burn there with them, as their tormenter, fellow sufferer, witness, and rescuer.

Is it possible that, after reading my presentation, Aron got caught up in playing out his own sadistic role with me?

Both men also criticize my noninterpretive interventions. The general sense is that they think I am much too nice and, perhaps, more than a touch naive. Stolorow, for example, guesses that I privilege "provision of positive new experiences" with the analyst over "investigation and interpretation of repetitive aspects of transference as the primary source of therapeutic action." I know what Estelle Shane and colleagues (Shane, Shane and Gales, 1997) mean by the term *positive new experience* but am unclear what Stolorow means by the expression. Judging from the context, it is not a good thing. It is probably something like supplying "provisions," a dirty word in psychoanalytic circles. To "supply provisions" means the analyst actually tries to satisfy a patient's developmental longings, rather than simply investigating them. Such a goal is, of course, impossible to effect. Yet, even if I could supply J with provisions, such an act would, in my view, preempt her psychological process.

Aron is clearer about my proclivities to "make nice." He urges for space in the analysis for me to "wear roles other than that of the good mother, good object, good analyst." He states "that the heart of the analytic relationship consists of Weisel-Barth's deep identification with [a certain] aspect of J, namely, that they share a tendency to avoid brutal treatment by 'making nice,' that is, by being helpful and ingratiating." Elsewhere he says, "The difficulty in the analytic process is based on [Weisel-Barth's] reluctance to identify with an aspect of the patient, her sadism, because she dislikes that aspect of herself so very much."

MY RESPONSE

In thinking about my work as an analyst, I remember a story from my Jewish tradition. It describes the required conditions for priests who, on the holiest day of the year, enter the Holy of Holies, the most sacred space in the Tent of Meeting. In preparation, these priests must engage in purification rituals of body and spirit; they must cleanse themselves of everyday grime, venal deeds, distracting thoughts, and social artifice. They must train and focus their attention on the sacred encounter. If they fail to do it right (as in the story of

Aaron's sons) they get zapped by Divine Fire. As a child, I tried to imagine what the really pure priests, the ones left standing, found in that holy and awesome space.

Not being very religious, I don't know much about holy space. The closest I come to such geography is in my intimate relationships, especially in the carefully created intimate space of a long-term analysis. To be in this space the analytic partners also have to prepare, to come clean with each other humanly, to be their authentic selves. Experiencing and examining the many and manifold meanings of such encounters are at the heart of the analytic pursuit. When the analyst slips up and does it wrong—when she turns away or backs off from the other's pain—there are hurtful and dangerous ruptures, sometimes even the threat of zapping the whole enterprise. The vulnerability of holy space is exquisite. The rewards are too: the privilege of knowing another human being in all the messy complexity of herself, of her secrets and shame, of her treasure stores and sacred strivings.

How do I conceptualize my meetings with J? In relation to Stolorow and Aron and in relation to other analytic ideas, where do I place myself as a contemporary psychoanalyst? I'll answer these questions in the process of answering the respondents, and then I'll add a short personal reflection.

First, Stolorow. I'll begin my response to Stolorow by speaking about myself as a self psychologist. Kohut's ideas are meaningful to me as a person and analyst. His thinking about the interpersonal sources of human development, about the trajectory of growth in self-cohesion and expansiveness, is congenial to me. So, too, are his notions about empathy and selfobject experience as keys, not only to human psychological development, but also to therapeutic action and process. Finally, Kohut's beliefs about the nature and place of aggression in human affairs conform to my clinical and life experience. His argument that aggression is primarily an expression of interpersonal history suggests the possibility for healing in the analytic relationship. My clinical practice, then, uses many ideas from self psychology.

I appreciate Stolorow's refinement and augmentation of many Kohutian ideas (Stolorow and Atwood, 1979, 1992; Stolorow, Brandchaft and Atwood, 1987; Stolorow, 2000). His two-person, intersubjective emphasis, his understanding of the importance of psychological organizing activity and his conception of affect attunement in the analytic relationship, all are notions that help me greatly in my work with patients. Simply put, I admire his contributions to psychoanalytic thinking. So, disregarding theoretical impurity, I also think of myself as an intersubjectivist, having no argument with Stolorow's theoretical ideas and greatly respecting his clinical inclinations.

Yet I wish he were not so enthralled, or should I say, held in thrall, by his philosophical speculations. I understand the confidence and certainty that a coherent intellectual structure confers. However, in my opinion, some of Stolorow's philosophical positions seem limiting or confining. They seem to distract and contract him. They seem both to lure him away from his enormous strengths as an imaginative clinician and to hem him into a logically consistent, but humanly constraining, corner; however, in spite of that, I am in basic agreement with Stolorow, as far as he goes.

Where else would I like to see Stolorow go? Because I respect his capacities so much, not just as a thinker, but also as a clinician, I wish he would extend his explorations into the nonverbal, noninterpretive dimensions of the analytic relationship. I believe this is a fertile field, a field where budding psychoanalytic insights will flower. Yet Stolorow remains focused on interpretation as the primary vehicle for therapeutic action. While he acknowledges other sources of therapeutic benefit, he (Stolorow, 2000, personal communication) says, "I have been most interested in conceptualizing the therapeutic action of verbal interpretation precisely because it's an opportunity to deconstruct the false dichotomies between cognition and affect, and between interpretation and relationship and so on."

We know that vigorous, established flowers can crowd and strangle new and beautiful, but less hearty, blooms. So, in this case, I wonder if Stolorow's prodigious intellect, and his reliance on that intellect, might also be a limiting factor in his clinical work with a trauma survivor like J. The history of psychoanalysis certainly teaches us how theory may serve defensive functions, how interpreting from the safety of theory may provide the analyst refuge from the pain and helplessness and desperate longings of the traumatized other (see for example, Breger, 2000).

That reservation aside, I want to assure Stolorow that much of my work with J involves verbal exploration of her affective states and of our interactions. It also includes the articulation of organizing principles and the interpretation of patterns in the repetitive pole of the transference. What Stolorow missed in his response to J's case was the nature of the incidents I chose to present. They mostly depict highly charged affective moments between J and me, moments of primitively organized emotional states. At these moments J shifts from her customary attachment styles with me—usually engaged but, at times, avoidant—into more disorganized states. She becomes distressed and hyperaroused. Her emotional features resemble postraumatic stress disorder (PTSD) responses. Sometimes she panics, and sometimes she dissociates. As both Stolorow and Aron recognize, J is a severely traumatized woman. She has survived two different kinds of trauma: first, intense and acute, life-punctuating traumas from such experiences as molestations and physical beatings and, then, continuous "stress" or "strain" traumas throughout her life. The latter kind of trauma derives from such conditions as chronic parental alcoholism, environmental chaos, violence and mental illness. At moments when J is affectively aroused or in a dissociated state, a well-wrought interpretation has about the same impact and healing value as that forcefully hurled, proverbial old "snowball in Hell."

When J is in such a highly charged state, I look for helpful responses, ones that work to contain and hold her distress. I want to provide her with a selfobject experience. By this I mean I want to respond in ways that are contingent to and congruent with her expressed feelings. Fonagy (2002) presents a relevant concept. He speaks of "marked mirroring" (pp. 9–10), the experience a baby has with a caretaker who can convey deep understanding of the child's distressed affect and, at the same time, can also communicate that she is not herself anxious. She is one who "decouples her expression from her dispositional state and tells the infant, in effect, 'This is not how I feel, this is how you feel'" (p. 9). Caretakers who can "mark" the baby's affect, that is, those who can combine vocal or facial imitation of the infant's distress while at the same expressing more positive emotion appear more successful in soothing and comforting their babies.

With J, I try to "mark" her distress, and often, I do this nonverbally. Of course, I'm not always successful in my efforts. But when I do succeed, it's generally because I have found a way to resonate with J's disorganized affect state and also to respond to some deep developmental longing. Sometimes I do nothing more than sit quietly and attentively watch her. I try to keep my facial and vocal expressions in the general range of her own in an effort to convey that I connect with her experience. Sometimes, I say something simple and tuned to an unrealized wish. My strategies have nothing to do with "making nice" or "supplying provision." They are, in a word, instrumental. They simply work better than anything else I have found to do.

I can and do anchor these strategies in contemporary psychoanalytic theory, particularly in the work of the infant researchers and the attachment theorists. If I have any strong criticism of Stolorow and

Aron, it is that they did not attend to this important body of theory in responding to my work with J. I want to cite here infant researchers, for example, Daniel Stern (1985), Beatrice Beebe (1998), and Beatrice Beebe and Frank Lachmann (1994, 1998) for their enormously helpful ideas about multimodal and cross-modal matching in dyadic interaction. Beebe's ideas about parental mid-range responsiveness (1998) and Beebe and Jaffe's ideas about mutual affective coordination (1992a, 1992b) also support my reactions to J's disorganized emotional states. I also rely on the work of Mary Main (1995, 1999), Arietta Slade (1999a, b), Karlen Lyons-Ruth (1998, 1999), and Peter Fonagy (2002; Fonagy et al., 1991, 1997) in understanding the complex mechanisms of implicit affect communication and emotional regulation. These researchers also help me to conceptualize the transmission of attachment styles across generations and to recognize enduring attachment behavior in my consulting room. The Process of Change Study Group in Boston provides a model for me as its members struggle to extrapolate findings from infant research that apply to psychoanalysis with adults. And I can and will address some of Frank Lachmann's ideas below. Yet, in truth, my therapeutic ideas and strategies emerge primarily, as any good theory emerges, from my life and from almost 30 years of work as a psychologist.

The great pleasure and challenge of analytic work for me begin with my own personal reactions. I most value those moments in which I am deeply engaged with another person. In those moments I learn what interactions work humanly and learn to distinguish between interventions that undermine process and those that advance development and healing. It is also in the context of such interpersonal moments that I can best use psychoanalytic theory: that I can draw from it and distinguish what harmonizes and what clashes with my experience.

At base, then, I am an empiricist, yet an empiricist who loves theory. I love theories that validate, illuminate, and expand on my clinical observations. If clinical experience is a simple form embedded in a marble block, then good theory provides the chisels and tools that help define the emergent form, which release it to reveal its details, its complexity of angles and expanses, and its lights and shadows.

I will continue now with some illuminating theory. Kohut describes two kinds of interpretations: "trailing edge" and "leading edge" interpretations. Trailing edge interpretations identify the dynamic and early-life determinates of a person's motivations and defenses. They frequently describe and explain the patient's pathology and neurotic constructions. Trailing edge interpretations are a familiar feature of our cultural climate. They are the staples of classical psychoanalysis as well as of old Hollywood shrink movies like *Snake Pit, Bedlam,* and *Spellbound.* Leading edge interpretations speak to the person's developmental longings and strivings. Good interpretations usually include both leading and trailing edge qualities. When J is affectively aroused, however, if I say anything at all, I try to address two things: her leading edge longings and her efforts to be an actor in her own life. J carries the pride, as well as the guilt, of a survivor. At the best of times, she has trouble hearing about her past suffering, an aspect of trailing edge interventions. When she is highly distressed, she has no tolerance for her own pain—for thinking, talking, or hearing about it.

I have many and fundamental differences with Lew Aron and what I consider his proposed trailing edge analysis of J. I'll begin, though, with an area of agreement. Aron presents a plausible story, which has as its monothematic premise and focus J's sadomasochistic proclivities. I agree that sadomasochism is an apt term, although I don't much like it because of its classical drive theory associations. Yet much in J's history and social behavior fits a sadomasochistic attribution, and in our long relationship, J and I have certainly explored this S-M configuration. As J puts it, "Ray Charles could see it."

Aron asserts, after Davies and Frawley (1991), that a valid treatment of adult survivors of sexual abuse requires both analyst and patient to enact all roles involved in the abusive drama: perpetrator, victim, witness, and rescuer. What's more, he insists, any analyst worth her salt—any authentic analyst, that is—could never remain cool in the face of a patient's provocative or sadistic strategies. The mother in me wonders if Dr. Aron has never seen parents remain cool in the face of a child's temper tantrum?

Oddly, Aron seems not to realize that his absolute, categorical statements, delivered in a tone of authoritative certainty, clash with basic tenets of relational psychoanalysis. Relational analysts, after all, believe that theories and techniques are merely reflections of individual analysts and of their interactions with a limited number of individual patients. Such interpersonally derived ideas are not the absolute truth about anything. Relational thinkers also believe that each working analytic couple is a unique joint creation. Presumably, what works in one dyad might not in another. However eccentric and strangely tinged a given couple may seem, it nevertheless has its own integrity. Simply put, nobody has the corner on truth; differences are okay; and theories are best held lightly in an open palm. There are, indeed, many ways to skin a cat.

In any case, if Aron were working with J—if she stayed in treatment with him, that is—they would likely create a story that has sadomasochism as its focus. I can also imagine them getting into some scrappy enactments. We certainly know that expectations are predictive: what we expect to happen or to find, we usually create/discover. Furthermore, J is an accomplished street fighter, quick to angry, disorganizing outbursts. In fact, many dissociated episodes in her life involve such violent eruptions. For J, the memories of these eruptions are like pools of shame. I expect that diving into and swimming in those pools with her analyst would likely retraumatize her. Provoked in this way, I also imagine she would abort the treatment. However, I could be wrong. Fortunately, J is my patient, and together we are creating a very different story. Ours includes sadomasochism but places it in the narrative exposition, not in the foreground or unfolding of the action. Before I describe our story, however, I want to discuss several of Aron's assumptions.

Aron's first assumption is that, when working with traumatized patients, "It is not enough to be a good or a new object; one must be an old, a bad, or a traumatic object, as well." Shane (this volume) states, and I concur:

> I would disagree that, in work with such a severely traumatized patient, one has to assume the role of the bad or traumatic object or that such a view of the analyst must inevitably emerge in the patient's mind. It may pervade the patient's experience of the analyst . . . but it is not always the case; just to assume the emergence of that transference configuration runs the risk of iatrogenically provoking it.

"Iatrogenic" originally referred to medical treatment that creates more disease. In current psychoanalytic parlance, it means problems manufactured in the analytic dyad. To expand briefly on Dr. Shane's statement: I wonder if Aron's emphasis on enactments and role-playing may not also constitute an evasion of the pain of trauma, a way to escape from its anguish into action and confrontation.

The second assumption has to do with the place of aggression and destructiveness in a person's life. This discussion is at least as old as the Biblical story of Adam and Eve and Original Sin and as the theological Problem of Evil. Leaving aside philosophical musings about such inexplicably evil people as Iago and Hitler, I would like to present two contrasting psychoanalytic streams of thought about aggression. Aron suggests that aggression is a primary force and must be "ruthlessly" confronted in analysis. He shares this assumption with classical and many object relational analysts. I, on the other hand—along with attachment theorists Bowlby (1969, 1973, 1980, 1985), and Main (1995, 1999) and self psychologists Kohut (1971, 1977, 1984), Shane, Shane, and Gales (1997), and Lachmann (2000)—understand aggression, not as a primary drive, but as a complex response to a number of factors. These factors include frustration from trauma, neglect, separation, and insecure attachment as they interact with such influences as parental, social, and cultural models and possible neurological anomalies.

Lachmann adds to the argument the idea that the absence in early life of any contingent responsiveness may produce the conditions for extreme violence. No "contingent responsivness" means that parents and caretakers (and, perhaps, the culture) have failed to respond to the child's very being, failed to recognize or provide for the child's needs, and failed to provide soothing for her pain or regulation for her physical and emotional arousal. At the same time, these same caretakers have prevented "the organization of the other [motivational systems] such as attachment, exploration, and sensual and sexual pleasure" (Lachmann, 2000, p. 143). The child who receives such treatment dies psychologically. Lachmann notes that common to all serial killers is "some variant of deadness," lifelessness, and lack of affectivity. Violence for them may serve an arousing and enlivening function, an antidote to existential nothingness. Finally, Lachmann speaks of the central role of shame in the motivation toward violence. He reports studies that show humiliation and disrespect and the loss of pride and self-respect as antecedent to many antisocial acts. Many contemporary analysts, myself included, view aggression as essentially reactive and a derivative of some combination of constitutional predispositions and painful lived experiences.

These differing understandings about violence express differing belief systems about human nature and have implications for analytic treatment. For example, if all patients are born with a reservoir of rage, then the regulation of aggression—its control, containment, and sublimation—becomes a primary treatment goal. This certainly was true for Freud and for Melanie Klein. I do not subscribe to the "reservoir of rage" concept. Therefore, the evaluation of a patient's aggression, its intensity and meaning for the person, becomes the therapeutic goal. Attaining the goal requires an understanding and exploration of the sources of that aggression.

For my patient J, neglect and shame are bedrock, foundational to her hostility. Incidents and interactions that feel insulting or disrespectful to her can cue her rage reactions. I understand this about her and try—mostly with success—to avoid comments that she might construe as disrespectful. The times when I have inadvertently shamed her, J has certainly let me know. Besides, I genuinely respect J and am a responsible partner in our relationship, with minor lapses, of course. These factors account, I believe, for the absence of significant anger between us.

I have a final quibble with Aron. I believe his conception of J's case is too static, too anchored in a single trailing edge formulation. Healthy, established analytic relationships are always moving and changing in a forward direction. We know from nonlinear dynamic systems theory (Edelman, 1992; Thelen and Smith, 1994; Cilliers, 1998; Damasio, 1999; Edelman and Tononi, 2000) that the analytic dyad constitutes a complex system, a system that obeys the principles of organization for complex systems generally. These principles are all about change and expansiveness: they track changes in a system's organization, in its discontinuities, and in its reorganizations. Development is embedded in a complex context, including the influence of a respectful, attentive analyst, and it is keenly sensitive to that context. Even small changes in existing contexts (complexity theorists call them "perturbations") may trigger the emergence of new and larger contexts. These, in turn, produce new system organizations and sometimes radical transformations. With all this emphasis on movement and change, Aron's critique seems rather cramped and anemic, far too focused on the fixed there-and-then rather than on the dynamic here-and-now and the exciting what-may-be.

Before concluding this response, I want to relate an incident that occurred at the Self Psychology Conference in Chicago in 2000. After the plenary panel where I presented my work with J, elated and feeling very full of many things, I headed for the ladies room. There I had the most surprising and affecting encounter, my own "now moment." The assembled women—and after sitting for almost three hours at the plenary session, there was a swarm of them waiting in line—turned toward me in what seemed like a single movement. Then, practically in unison, they gave me a rousing and affirming "*Yesss!*" Somehow, it seems, I had spoken for them. I think they were cheering, in part, a feminine version of David surviving the giant. By some unintentional accident, Estelle Shane and I, on one side, and Stolorow and Aron, on the other, had inadvertently aligned ourselves across complicated gender lines.

Later, many women approached and thanked me for "getting it," and a few men accused me of blindness to J's innate aggression. For example, with respect to the incident of the picture of J's mother, several men chided me for not recognizing and confronting the hostility in J's testing of me. On the other hand, Marian Tolpin, a well-known self psychologist, said of the incident, "Of course, the girl wants to love her mother and doesn't know how. You gave her a way to appreciate her mother. Those men just don't get it."

Such encounters caused me to reflect about gender issues in J's case. Without wanting to slide into a sexist swamp, I nevertheless recognize a feminine spirit hovering over and informing my work with J. To begin with, everyone involved with the case is female: J, Estelle Shane, I, and the invisible muse in this enterprise, my analyst, Janet Hadda.

What, then, are the features that stamp this case as particularly feminine? The answer, I think, is twofold: content issues and therapeutic approach, both of which have a feminine flavor. With respect to the feminine content issues, from the outset, sprinkling our sessions were the familiar topics of female small talk (opinions about clothes, hair, plastic surgery, other women, and the eternally imperfect female body), the small talk out of which women's relationships spring. Also, early on, I watched and felt J sizing me up as a woman, nonverbally, of course, although I heard the unspoken questions. How does this shrink decorate her office and herself? What kind of taste does she have? What's her history with men? How does she take care of herself? How's she holding up in the age department? Much later in our relationship, J laughed as she admitted that I had, indeed, heard these unarticulated questions correctly. Without reducing their complexity, I believe these deliberations functioned in part to help her decide if she could identify with me, trust me, and ultimately create with me a reparative bond of a maternal/feminine nature.

But mainly, weaving through all our sessions are the themes of J's history as a woman with men, her need to tell the story, and her longing to be empathically comprehended. Her history reflects a continuing effort to assert herself with powerful men in a man's world and the ensuing frustration and rage at failing. Despite brutal and exploitative treatment by male figures—beginning early with her father—she has used her beauty, brains, brassiness, and sexuality in a lifelong struggle to equalize power and establish a place for herself in their world. To that end, she has played many and varied roles: tomboy, sex kitten, femme fatale, spitfire, and vixen. Unfortunately, she has repeatedly chosen the same kind of man, demonic and brutal and, consequently, has repeatedly suffered the same pattern of frustration and failure. The fact that, after childhood, J became a cocreator of these dark, repetitive relationships does not diminish their pain.

J's story, while extreme in its brutality, is part of a larger feminist story, a story to which her analyst and her analyst's consultants are no strangers. While not always as violent as J's encounters, sexism (its cruel inequalities and injustices) takes many forms, wears many guises, and inhabits many worlds, including the worlds of marriage, academia, and even psychoanalysis. Shared suffering deepens understanding and creates compassionate community. I think this particular compassion—feminine compassion—has been a crucial feature in my relationship with J.

As important as the content issues is the analytic approach in this case. I have aimed to create with J a holding environment in which she might feel safe and free with another person, probably for the first time in her life. To accomplish this aim requires nonverbal attention and engagement that is responsive to J's affect states as mediated through my own subjectivity. I express this attention and engagement with J in physical ways, using such gestures as assenting head nods, continuous visual scrutiny, facial expressions that match J's emotions, and body extensiveness that is, leaning into her at heightened moments. Vocally, I notice myself making frequent nonlinguistic responsive sounds. Clicks, sighs, and many "hmm's," "tsk's," and "uh huh's" pepper our interactions. This nonverbal approach, validated by ideas from Winnicott, attachment theory, and early childhood research, clearly has a feminine/maternal character, regardless of the analyst's gender.

Gerhardt and Beyerle (1977), in an essay on gender differences in psychoanalytic process, speak of such gestures as "acknowledgment tokens." They remark on the softening of boundaries, that such markers promote:

> Such use bespeaks a mode of relatedness in which the separation of the therapist and patient is less well defined. It is as if in using these markers the therapist is in the "experiencing-self" (Bollas, 1992) mode of engagement with the patient, in which she sustains a relatively more interdependent way of being, and thus experiences her own reverie as a product of the intersubjective situation [p. 405].

This approach is as notable for what is background as for what takes center stage in the analysis. Conflict and confrontation in the analysis, for example, have been minimal, a surprising fact given J's stormy relational history. In our work, there has also been little attention paid to some usual therapeutic agenda items, and I refer here to serious and important items like forging an intimate relationship if the patient is single. One day in supervision, for example,

Dr. Shane asked me if I thought J would ever be able to sustain a relationship with a man. I was surprised at the question and surprised at my surprise. While I realized that I had a quick response to the question ("I'm not sure, but probably not") I also realized I hadn't ever thought about the question. During all the years, my work with J has focused on creating with her the trustworthy therapeutic space, a place to breathe easy and just "be" with another human being, and the difficulties of doing this. I believe this is the important analytic task; yet, it does keep us cocooned, in a space analogous to one occupied by a mother and child at an early developmental stage. We deal with issues of adult life, of course, but they are not at the heart of our work together.

What remains to write about my patient J and about our psychoanalysis? Certainly, I have indicated that J and I have created a story together. It is a story of a constitutionally strong person who, though seriously wounded, survived a neglectful, abusive, and traumatic childhood. Entrained with the childhood pain, her adult relational patterns, which mirror the early traumatic configurations, have left her with problems of esteem, self-regulation, and entitlement. Gifted with health, intelligence, and beauty, until recently, she has short-changed herself in personal transactions. After several years in treatment, she still struggles with feelings of worthlessness and failure. Her emotional fuse still trips easily. She works herself to exhaustion. She still takes care of her ex-husband and sick friends and probably gives too generously and indiscriminately of her time and money. She rescues stray animals, and at the end of the day, she still finds herself in debt.

Yet J would say her life is much improved from our first meeting. She hasn't engaged in a destructive sexual relationship in years, and self-interest now, at least, figures into her life plans. J no longer feels all alone and credits our relationship for making a great difference in her life.

Why? Roger Hastings, my colleague and teacher at the Institute of Contemporary Psychoanalysis (ICP), provides for me something of an answer. He commented recently on the amazing personal impact of his psychoanalytic training. While studying infant developmental research, he had a transforming insight about psychological growth. I'm going to paraphrase his insight in my own words because it also epitomizes what I have learned from conducting the control case and from my reading, supervision, and personal analysis. For me it reaches to the heart of contemporary psychoanalysis:

> Everything important in psychological development happens outside what we have traditionally called the mind. Even though, like Freud, I always thought it happened inside—in the psyche or whatever—I see now that everything important in psychological life happens in the shared space between me and another person.

I would add this corollary to Hastings's insight:

> In addition, feeling suffuses and infuses every important event and process in psychological development.

REFERENCES

Aron, L. (1996), *A Meeting of Minds: Mutuality in Psychoanalysis.* Hillsdale, NJ: The Analytic Press.

——— (2000), The role of the relationship in the therapeutic process. Presented at the 23rd International Conference on the Psychology of the Self, November 9, Chicago, IL.

Beebe, B. (1998), A procedural theory of therapeutic action: Commentary on the symposium, "Interventions that Affect Change in Psychotherapy." *Infant. Mental Hlth. J.,* 19:333–339.

——— & Jaffe, J. (1992a), Mother–infant vocal dialogues. *Infant Behavior & Devel.,* 15:48.

——— & ——— (1992b), The contributions of infant responsibility to the production of infant attachment. *Infant Behavior & Devel.,* 15:113.

——— & Lachmann, F. (1994), Representation and internalization in infancy: Three principles of salience. *Psychoanal. Psychol.,* 11:125–165.

——— & ——— (1998), Co-constructing inner and relational processes: Self- and mutual regulation in infant research and adult treatment. *Psychoanal. Psychol.,* 15:480–516.

Bowlby, J. (1969), *Attachment and Loss, Vol. 1.* New York: Basic Books.

——— (1973), *Attachment and Loss, Vol. 2.* New York: Basic Books.

——— (1980), *Attachment and Loss, Vol. 3.* New York: Basic Books.

——— (1985), *A Secure Base.* New York: Basic Books.

Breger, L. (2000), *Freud: Darkness in the Midst of Vision.* New York: Wiley.

Cilliers, P. (1998), *Complexity and Postmodernism.* London: Routledge.

Damasio, A. (1999), *The Feeling of What Happens: Body and Emotion in the Making of Consciousness.* New York: Harcourt Brace.

Davies, J. M. & Frawley, M. G. (1991), Dissociative processes and transference–countertransference paradigms in the psychoanalytically oriented treatment of adult survivors of childhood sexual abuse. In: *Relational Psychoanalysis: The Emergence of a Tradition,* ed. S. A. Mitchell & L. Aron. Hillsdale, NJ: The Analytic Press, pp. 269–299.

Edelman, G. (1992), *Bright Air, Brilliant Fire.* New York: Basic Books.

——— & Tononi, G. (2000), *A Universe of Consciousness: How Matter Becomes Imagination.* New York: Basic Books.

Fonagy, P. (2002), Interventions with individuals at risk of developing serious personality disturbance. Slides from a presentation at the conference on Attachment: From Early Childhood Through the Lifespan, March 10, Los Angeles.

——— Steele, M., Steele, H., Moran, G. S. & Higgit, A. C. (1991), The capacity for understanding mental states: The reflective self in parent and child and its significance for security and attachment. *Infant. Mental Hlth. J.*, 12:201–218.

——— & Target, M. (1997), Attachment and reflective function: Their role in self-regulation. *Develop. & Psychopathol.*, 9:679–700.

Gerhardt, J. & Beyerle, S. (1997), What if Socrates had been a woman? The therapist's use of acknowledgment tokens as nonreflective means of intersubjective involvement. *Contemp. Psychoanal.*, 33:367–410.

Kohut, H. (1971), *The Analysis of the Self.* New York: International Universities Press.

——— (1977), *The Restoration of the Self.* New York: International Universities Press.

——— (1984), *How Does Analysis Cure?* ed. A. Goldberg & P. Stepansky. Chicago: University of Chicago Press.

Lachmann, F. (2000), *Transforming Aggression: Psychotherapy With the Difficult-to-Treat Patient.* Northvale, NJ: Aronson.

Lyons-Ruth, K. (1998), Implicit relational knowing: Its role in development and psychoanalytic treatment in infants. *Infant Ment. Hlth. J.*, 19:282–289.

——— (1999), Two person unconscious: Intersubjective dialogue, enactive relational representation, and the emergence of new forms of relational organization. *Psychoanal. Inq.*, 19:576–617.

Main, M. (1995), Atttachment: Overview, with implications for clinical work. In: *Attachment Theory: Social, Developmental, and Clinical Perspectives,* ed. S. Goldberg, R. Muir & J. Kerr. Hillsdale, NJ: The Analytic Press, pp. 407–474.

——— (1999), Epilogue: Attachment theory: Eighteen points with suggestions for future studies. In: *Handbook of Attachment: Theory, Research and Clinical Applications,* ed. J. Cassidy & P. R. Shaver. New York: Guilford, pp. 645–887.

Shane, M., Shane, E. & Gales, M. (1997), *Intimate Attachments: Toward a New Self Psychology.* New York: Guilford.

Slade, A. (1999a), Attachment theory and research—Implications for the theory and practice of individual psychotherapy with adults. In: *Handbook of Attachment,* ed. J. Cassidy & P. R. Shaver. New York: Guilford, pp. 497–519.

——— (1999b), Representation, symbolization and affect regulation in the concomitant treatment of a mother and child: Attachment theory and child psychotherapy, *Psychoanal. Inq.*, 19:797–830.

Stern, D. (1985), *The Interpersonal World of the Infant.* New York: Basic Books.

Stolorow, R. D. (2000), On the impossibility of immaculate perception: There is no relationship without interpretation, and there is no interpretation without relationship. Presented at the 23rd International Conference on the Psychology of the Self, November 9, Chicago.

——— & Atwood, G. E. (1979), *Faces in a Cloud: Subjectivity in Personality Theory.* Northvale, NJ: Aronson.

——— & ——— (1992), *Contexts of Being: The Intersubjective Foundations of Psychological Life*. Hillsdale, NJ: The Analytic Press.

——— Brandchaft, B. & Atwood, G. E. (1987), *Psychoanalytic Treatment: An Intersubjective Approach*. Hillsdale, NJ: The Analytic Press.

Thelen, E. & Smith, L. (1994), *A Dynamic Systems Approach to the Development of Cognition and Action*. Cambridge, MA: MIT Press.

Commentary on Discussions by Stolorow and Aron

Estelle Shane

I want to begin with one comment on each of these discussions individually before I look at them more closely to compare them with one another. First, Lewis Aron makes a strong case for the overwhelming presence of sadomasochism in Joye Weisel-Barth's case material. He notes that, with a report so dominated by sadomasochism, his first thought as a clinician is to wonder where and how this will emerge in the relationship and then demurs that it is not because he *expects* it to come up in the transference, in the old-fashioned sense, but rather, that what is talked about in analysis is simultaneously played out between patient and analyst. I want to emphasize something I am sure Aron will agree with: when we, as analysts, wonder where and how, not whether, any particular material will emerge in the transference, then we will surely see it emerge. It is by now commonplace that what we expect to find, we will find. Aron, then, expects to find sadomasochism as a dominant theme in the transference relationship, but neither Weisel-Barth, nor Stolorow for that matter, were impressed or overwhelmed with its presence; at least, neither mentioned it. Perspective determines vision.

Turning now to Stolorow's discussion, I can't disappoint him by choosing to ignore his irritating gadfly role, that is, the challenge he mounts to the erroneous philosophical assumptions he finds of fractured human subjectivity in Weisel-Barth's patient, J, who reports nightmares without reporting the presence of painful affect. I know that in the example of J, Stolorow recognizes the pathology that divides J's subjective experience.

But now I want to look at the two discussions of Weisel-Barth's case material together, noting a fascinating juxtaposition of perspectives shared by Aron and Stolorow, for while they approach this clinical material from widely different theoretical–relational perspectives, each privileging his own distinct conceptualizations, they both can be understood to share an overarching common concern with the clinical work, and in addition, at various points in their discussions, they remark on the same areas in Weisel-Barth's presentation wherein they disagree with her approach to, and with her understanding of, her patient.

First, the overarching concern uniting their discussions would seem to be that each feels that Weisel-Barth has failed to interpret significant aspects of the patient's experience in the transference. Stolorow and Aron contend that Weisel-Barth appears to prefer noninterpretive interventions, interventions that differ in kind from the interpretive ones they prefer. Aron argues, as I have said, that both the history of the patient and the clinical material presented here is dominated by sadomasochism. He sees Weisel-Barth as having failed to recognize and to interpret this sadomasochism in the relationship between J and herself. Instead, when J tests her analyst with outrageous and provocative behavior, Weisel-Barth comments only on J's strengths. In this way, Aron says, Weisel-Barth has chosen to play "the good object" in relation to J. Further, in her identification with J, Aron sees Weisel-Barth as sharing with J a tendency to avoid brutal treatment by "making nice," by being helpful and ingratiating, and he says that Weisel-Barth seems reluctant to identify with another aspect of J, her sadism and destructiveness, perhaps because it is something that Weisel-Barth dislikes in herself and is therefore less able to see in J. Aron sees evidence of this dislike of sadism, both in her patient and in herself, in a comment Weisel-Barth makes that it "draws out a part of me I dislike: my judgmental and teachy-preachy self." Now, while Aron sees this insight as critical, I am not so sure that Weisel-Barth conceptualizes what she calls her "judgmentalness and preachiness" as sadism. Maybe Weisel-Barth can comment on this, but in any case, Aron contends that it is not enough to be a good or a new object; one must be an old, a bad, or a traumatic object as well. I would disagree that, in work with such a severely traumatized patient, one has to assume the role of the bad or traumatic object or that such a view of the analyst must inevitably emerge in the patient's mind. It may pervade the patient's experience of the analyst, and it may do so more or less, but it is not always the case; just to assume the emergence of that transference configuration runs the risk of iatrogenically provoking it.

For his part, Stolorow makes the point that he feels J would have benefited from a more active, interpretive approach to her transference experience, particularly in the repetitive dimension of the transference. He supports this assertion with a series of examples taken from Weisel-Barth's material. Stolorow notes, for example, that J demonstrates a consistent pattern of averting painful affect and that Weisel-Barth doesn't appear to see the connection between J's frequent dream images depicting an unbridgeable gulf separating herself from her analyst and J's pattern of isolating ideational content from painful feeling. Stolorow speculates that, because J's mother was so ill, J cannot hope to have a stable bond with her analyst in which J's traumatic affect states would be welcomed, heard, and safely felt. This fear is neither explored nor interpreted in the transference. Stolorow wonders whether the scarcity of transference interpretation might reflect Weisel-Barth's adherence to a theoretical assumption privileging positive new experience with the analyst over investigation and interpretation of repetitive aspects of the transference. Stolorow bases this inference on Weisel-Barth's having commented frequently on J's strengths and on the therapeutic value of surprising J's expectations.

I would like to make two points here. First, it should be said that a well-timed transference interpretation in itself may constitute a positive new experience, that is, as I would define it, an experience in the relationship that is experientially new, that is, different from what the patient had remembered experiencing in the past and one that advances the patient's development. But of more relevance here, I would argue that the absence of transference interpretation in the material presented for discussion here does not necessarily mean that such interpretation was altogether absent in the analysis. I believe what Weisel-Barth has emphasized in the material presented for us is the necessity for affectively attuned responsiveness to a patient who dissociates and who has been severely traumatized, as well as the importance of providing a calming, soothing selfobject experience to enhance self and interactive regulation in the dyad. While Stolorow draws a parallel with his own patient, Kevin, whose painful affect states he couldn't tolerate, I think that Weisel-Barth does manage to maintain an engaged connection with J through a full range of affect expression.

But to return to the discussants, both Aron and Stolorow are concerned with the paucity of transference interpretation in Weisel-

Barth's clinical work, though it is important to emphasize that they view differently the *content matter* of the transference they find to be present, but not attended to by Weisel-Barth. Also, both are concerned that Weisel-Barth's focus is on the patient's strengths, on playing "the good object" in Aron's terms, and on privileging the "positive new experience," in Stolorow's. So I would ask, how does Weisel-Barth feel about Aron's "good object" characterization of her, and how does she understand the stance she has taken with J? And, in relation to Stolorow's commentary, I would ask, is he correct that her approach is based on a privileging of positive new experience over interpretation of the repetitive conflictual dimension of the transference? In what way does Weisel-Barth conceptualize her own focus on that which she finds admirable and valuable in J to be working to her therapeutic advantage with this patient?

Weisel-Barth is correct in her approach to J. To my mind, to work effectively with traumatized patients such as J requires an exquisite resonance with their archaically organized affect states, which Weisel-Barth demonstrates beautifully in her work with this patient. Both Aron and Stolorow also take some exception to Weisel-Barth's assertion that J "reads her right," but I wonder if Weisel-Barth believes that her feelings of being understood by J preclude Weisel-Barth's following up with explorations of their meanings to J or would preclude Weisel-Barth's offering interpretations of those meanings to J? I certainly wouldn't think so, but we do have the advantage of hearing from Weisel-Barth herself, her own responses and clarifications on these questions.

I want to end by thanking these authors, and again, I want to thank Joye Weisel-Barth for sharing her clinical work with us, taking the risk of revealing her innovative approach to this highly traumatized patient. No one can, or did, argue that this treatment is not going well, so all that remains for me is to congratulate Joye for her good, caring, and successful treatment and for demonstrating a well-functioning analytic relationship.

III

Applied

Chapter 11

Death in Venice: A Selfobject Perspective on Thomas Mann's Homolimerence

Richard M. Childs

Heinz Kohut's first psychoanalytic paper was titled "*Death in Venice* by Thomas Mann: The Disintegration of Artistic Sublimation." It was written in 1948, long before self psychology. In this early article, Kohut interpreted Mann's novella from the perspective of traditional psychoanalytic theories that prevailed at mid-century.

Death in Venice (Mann, 1912) is the story of an aging writer, Gustav von Aschenbach, who becomes fatally fascinated with a handsome adolescent boy named Tadzio. Near the end of this long short story, Aschenbach has a climactic nightmare that Kohut (1948) interpreted as "the undisguised emergence of a primal-scene experience" (p. 126) in which the child was traumatized by observing adult sexual activities. Kohut went on to declare "There is little doubt, too, that [Aschenbach's] homosexual desires and fears must have originated during such experiences—that the child must have been partially identified with the mother and must have wished for the sexual love of the father" (p. 126).

At best, Mann's text offers scant support for Kohut's primal scene interpretation. This chapter suggests that Kohut's later notion of the selfobject experience offers a more interesting perspective from which to view this celebrated story and from which to understand

Thomas Mann's own lifelong vulnerability to repeated episodes of homolimerence.

LIMERENCE AND HOMOLIMERENCE

The words *limerence* and *homolimerence* were coined by Dorothy Tennov in her 1979 book *Love and Limerence: The Experience of Being in Love*. Tennov wanted a new term that would convey certain aspects of what is commonly meant by the words *love* and *sex*, and she wanted a term that would be free of the conflicting implications that have long burdened these two deceptively simple words. She sought a completely new term that would better distinguish the particular kind of intense emotional reaction to another person that is sometimes called a crush or lovesickness. Moreover, she sought a concept that did not necessarily imply sickness or abnormality—a goal consonant with self psychology's nonpathologizing approach. She created the word *limerence* out of whole cloth. It is not derived from or related to any existing word. She thought *limerence* had a suitable sound, and it was easy to pronounce.

Although the terms *limerence* and *homolimerence* do not yet appear in standard dictionaries, they are already accepted by a number of authors. The word *limerence* appears in *Textbook of Homosexuality and Mental Health* from the publishing division of the American Psychiatric Association (Cabaj and Stein, 1996). Whether one likes the word *limerence* or not, it is increasingly used by credible authorities to refer to a distinct psychological phenomenon that deserves a name of its own.

According to Tennov, limerence consists of a compact constellation of feelings and thoughts that consistently occur together. Reciprocated limerence can be the occasion for such profound ecstasy that it becomes life's central experience, whereas unreciprocated limerence, or rejection, can cause abject suffering. Limerence is often borne in silence, and even those nearest the one who experiences it may be unaware of his inner emotional state.

For the purposes of this chapter, I have summarized Tennov's criteria for limerence into the following four items:

(1) The limerent person experiences intrusive thinking about the object of his or her fascination. Tennov calls this person the *limerent object*, or LO, for short. The limerent person experiences a general intensity of preoccupation and feeling that leaves most other concerns in the background.

(2) The limerent person longs for reciprocation. His or her mood depends on how he or she reads the LO's behavior. He suffers an ache in the chest when he feels no mutuality; he walks on air when he feels there is even the slightest hope that his feelings may be reciprocated.
(3) The limerent person has a remarkable ability to see only what is admirable about the LO and to overlook anything negative or problematic.
(4) Limerence is often long-lasting (years or decades), yet one can react limerently to only one person at a time.

Tennov (1979) wrote:

> Why some people feel limerence and/or sexual attraction for members of their own sex and why others do not are mysteries thus far unsolved by scientific analysis. But it would appear that at least some homosexuals, maybe the majority, might more accurately be called "homolimerents," [because they find] an LO among [their] own sex, [and] it appears to be limerence rather than mere sexuality that is primarily involved [p. 225].

Limerence and sexuality clearly share some common ground. Making the distinction between them, however, can improve our understanding of an important category of human relationships. Many homosexual or gay men do not experience limerence at all; other men seem to be homolimerent much of the time. A man driven to cruising for anonymous sex with other men would obviously be homosexual but probably would not be homolimerent. Homolimerence represents a particular kind of affect and selfobject need, which may or may not result in physical sex or the intense desire to have it.

The experience of limerence has many self psychological implications. The coherence and vitality of a limerent person's self-experience is at times governed entirely by his perception, or his fantasy, of how his LO responds to him. Homolimerence can be seen as the signal for a selfobject encounter that has the potential of strengthening the homolimerent's inner masculine self. Not necessarily every instance of homolimerence has a significant selfobject dimension. Thomas Mann's stories depict examples of homolimerence that show differing degrees of selfobject relevance. This chapter will discuss how, in *Death in Venice,* the aging Gustav Aschenbach is unable to respond effectively to his homolimerence and thus dies, whereas in *The Magic Mountain* (1924), the young Hans Castorp's homolimerence is transformed into a self-enhancing experience. Here the consideration of homolimerence is limited to that which occurs in men. Homolimerence does, of course, occur in women, but the psychological factors that underlie it are different in the two genders. Homolimerence in girls and women would be the topic of a different paper.

The Venn diagram in Figure 1 attempts to represent the complex human phenomena of love, sex, and limerence in a simple sketch. A diagram with the categories of *spirituality*, *behavior*, and *affect* would present similar, but not identical, distinctions. Some blurriness and rather arbitrary compromises are unavoidable in any such representation, but this difficulty does not eliminate the usefulness of trying to make complex distinctions. Just as distinguishing between mirroring, twinship, and other types of selfobject experiences can deepen our understanding, so can distinguishing between homolimerence and homosexuality. Making the distinction can focus our insight, facilitate our information gathering, and deepen our empathy.

HOMOLIMERENCE IN *DEATH IN VENICE*

In 1911, Thomas Mann, along with his wife Katia and his brother Heinrich, made a trip to Venice. While staying at the famous Hotel des Bains on Venice's Lido beach, Mann became fascinated by a young Polish boy staying there with his family. This boy became Tadzio in his novella *Death in Venice*, which he completed in 1912. For a long time afterward, he tried to insist that his story had nothing at all to do with pederasty. He claimed he had used Aschenbach's predicament only as the vehicle to illustrate an older man's *Entwürdigung*—his loss of dignity.

Despite Thomas Mann's obfuscation about the implications of *Death in Venice*, he could scarcely have made Aschenbach's homoerotic attraction to Tadzio any more explicit than he did. Mann apparently did not regard himself as homosexual; his erotic attractions led him only to intense and prolonged visual observation. In denying that there was anything homoerotic in the story, he was either in deep denial (unlikely) or he was simply trying to maintain his respectable façade as a public figure. A reviewer once noted that Mann practiced absolute physical repression of his same-sex impulses while he indulged in an ongoing public fantasy about them in his writing.

Before he died in 1955, Mann directed that his personal diaries remain sealed for 20 years after his death. They contained information about his private life that he had never publicly disclosed.

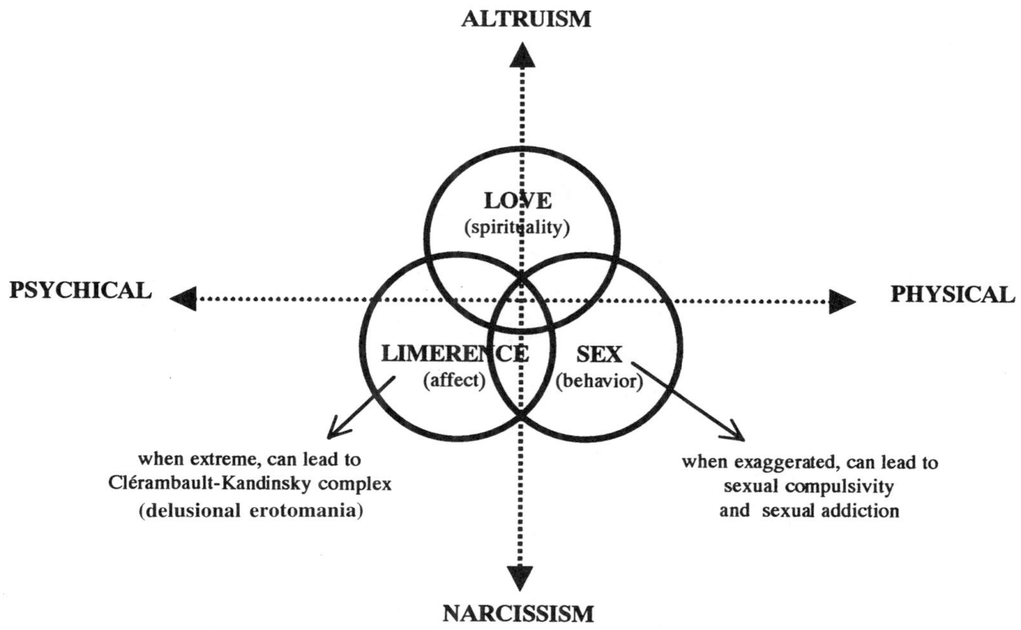

Figure 1. This Venn diagram is a visual allegory for the overlapping of love, sex, and limerence. It does not represent the extent or constancy of any particular area of overlap, all of which may change from moment to moment.

It was only after the publication of this revealing material in the 1980s that we could see how closely Mann himself was like the many men and boys in his fiction who became profoundly homolimerent for other males.

ASCHENBACH'S DIONYSIAN DREAM

When Heinz Kohut (1948) gave his primal scene interpretation of the big dream from *Death in Venice,* he paid too little attention to the fact that the dream's central image is actually a giant carved wooden phallus. In the Dionysian orgies of ancient Greece, those who carried these phallic images were called *phallophoroi,* or phallus bearers. The image they carried was worshipped as a god. Mann's text connects this godlike phallus directly to Tadzio by noting that, as its wooden image entered the old man's dream and was uncovered for the worshipers to see, the dreamer hears "shouts with a long-drawn-out-*u*-sound at the end." This refers to the boy's name "Tad-zi-uuu" when his mother called to him from a distance.

The giant phallus in Aschenbach's dream can be understood as representing everything that is specifically masculine or male. It is conventional to use the Greek spelling *phallos* (φαλλος) instead of the more familiar Latin spelling *phallus* when referring to this all-inclusive masculine domain. *Phallus* is a penis, and *phallos* represents masculinity in general. The dream equation *Tadzio* = *phallus* = *phallos* suggests that an unfulfilled longing to be connected to a more comprehensive masculinity is central to the dreamer's predicament.

Homolimerence may begin with the fascination a man or boy feels when he sees in another male any signs of masculinity that trigger his anxiety about his own completeness as a man. Such anxieties and misgivings are common. The culture's focus on image and celebrity keeps icons of idealized masculinity constantly in view and unavoidably accessible for self-comparison. For countless ages, limerence has been both lamented and glorified in song and story. The lyrics of contemporary country music often celebrate the ecstasy of reciprocated limerence, but more often, they bemoan the suffering when limerence is unreciprocated or no longer reciprocated.

Homolimerence is a more common experience than is generally acknowledged, yet it occupies a neglected region on the broad spectrum of human encounters. Part of this neglect is because of current cultural aberrations. The hypocritical homophobia and the sanctimonious religiosity that burden today's culture devalue homolimerent experiences by mislabeling them as immature at best and as perverse or sinful at worst. Consequently, many men who experience homolimerence are reluctant to let themselves be mindful of such feelings, let alone talk about them. This failure to give homolimerence the attention it deserves has several undesirable consequences. In the first place, men who do not understand the meaning of homolimerent fascination are more likely to stumble into its potential pitfalls, as did Gustav Aschenbach from *Death in Venice*. Men who have insight into their homolimerence are better able to transform any and all of their relationships with other men into more flexible, nuanced, and mutually beneficial encounters.

HOMOLIMERENCE AS A DISTINCT TYPE OF SELFOBJECT EXPERIENCE

This chapter suggests that limerence—and particularly homolimerence—can usefully be viewed as a potential and distinctive kind of selfobject experience, one that deserves a special name of its own. A *homolimerent selfobject experience* is not necessarily a more immature or a more problematic selfobject experience than other similar ones that involve friendship, affection, love, sex, or any combination of these. But the affects generated by homolimerence are sometimes so acute and intense that they have a long-lasting effect on a man's feelings, motivation, and judgment. Mismanaged homolimerence can produce chronic self-pity and depression and can lead to disastrous judgment.

THOMAS MANN'S REPEATED EPISODES OF HOMOLIMERENCE

Thomas Mann lived from 1875 to 1955; he received the Nobel Prize for literature in 1929 for his novel *Buddenbrooks* (1901), which had been written years earlier. Mann's diaries indicate that he experienced repeated episodes of homolimerence throughout his long life. In his last years he was still ogling handsome young waiters like Franz Westermeier, who became the model for Felix Krull in his final novel, written in 1954.

His 1903 novella *Tonio Kröger* describes the homolimerence of its 14-year-old protagonist Tonio Kröger for his handsome Nordic schoolmate Hans Hansen. Tonio loved Hans not only because he was so "extraordinarily good-looking and well built, broad in the shoulders and narrow in the hips, with keen, steely blue eyes" (p. 136), but more important, Tonio loved him because Hans seemed to him to have all the enviable phallic qualities Tonio felt he himself lacked. The story's narrator tells us that Tonio often felt a deep pain in his chest when he contemplated his relationship with Hans. This description fits one of Tennov's criteria for limerence. During one of his many bouts with homolimerent suffering, Tonio lamented, "If I could be like you [Hans Hansen]! If only I could begin all over again and grow up like you, decent and happy and simple, normal and at peace with God and the world" (p. 186).

Tonio feels something is lacking in himself, and he projects this missing something onto Hans. Although he does not speak in the language of self psychology, Tonio appears to be saying that what he needs is an empathic, mirroring, twinship selfobject response from his friend. And in the story, Hans does care deeply for Tonio, but Tonio does not recognize that what he sees reflected in Hans are actually latent and undeveloped qualities in his own psyche. Tonio would need a change of inner perspective with respect to his mirroring selfobject before he could take advantage of his relationship with Hans to actualize his own inner phallos. Tonio would have to view both Hans and himself from a different perspective before transmuting internalization could take place.

Tonio's predicament is not unlike that of Narcissus, who also had not learned to negotiate the complex intrapsychic geometry that governs mirrored images of one's own inner self. The boy or man who has difficulty achieving a satisfying masculine self-realization is likely to become exquisitely sensitive—even acutely vulnerable—to certain manifestations of masculinity that he sees in other men. Each man looks for his own particular "Mr. Right." A man's search for the phallic ideal can sometimes evoke painful states of envy and longing. If he tries to acquire these unactualized masculine qualities by fusing himself with the other man who appears to embody them, then he will lose his own individual masculine identity, like a droplet of liquid mercury that merges into a larger drop and vanishes.

At the conclusion of Mann's novella *Tonio Kröger,* we find that Tonio has grown up to be an unfulfilled adult, still painfully hung up on his long-ago relationship with Hans Hansen. In a paroxysm of self-pity, he cries out: "I never forgot you Hans. . . . If I could be like you! If only I could begin all over again and grow up like you, decent and happy and simple, normal and at peace with God and the world" (p. 186).

Thomas Mann's diaries reveal that the biographic original of Hans Hansen was his schoolmate Armin Martens. Thomas wrote poems to him and confessed his love, but Armin did not know how to respond. Tennov notes that LOs often do feel puzzled or overwhelmed by the very intensity of someone's limerence for them, and they just don't know how to handle it. They may care a great deal for the person, but this fact alone cannot compensate for the distorted psychological geometry inherent in some types of homolimerent mirroring experiences.

Near the end of his long life (he lived to be 80), Mann wrote about Armin Martens in a letter to a friend: "He was really my first love, and a more tender, more pleasurably painful love was never to be granted to me again. Something like this is unforgettable, even if seventy eventful years supervene. It may sound ridiculous, but I cherish the memory of this innocent passion like a treasure" (cited in Hayman, 1995, p. 97).

Thomas Mann was 28 when he wrote *Tonio Kröger*. He had not yet married or achieved the great fame that was yet to come. For most of his life, Mann was generally unhappy if not outright depressed. He considered suicide several times.

The protagonist in his 1897 short story, "The Clown" ["Der Bajazzo"], referred to the young men for whom he became homolimerent as "children of light, with the radiance of the sun reflected in their eyes, they float their way through life in an effortless, confident and amiable way, while everyone surrounds them, admires them, flatters them, envies them, loves them" (cited in Hayman, 1995, p. 127). Thomas Mann never felt that he fully belonged to this fraternity of men blessed by such phallic radiance and splendor.

His expression "children of light with the radiance of the sun reflected in their eyes" can be seen as a metaphor that represents a blinding and unsuccessful mirroring selfobject experience. In some cases the metaphorical mirror may simply appear too numinous—so bright with phallic radiance that its glare blinds and overwhelms, instead of illuminating, the observer's inner masculine self. Perhaps the mirror itself is wrongly positioned, so instead of providing a useful view of the object that stands in front of the viewer, it reflects back the overwhelming source of its illumination ("the radiance of the sun"). Thus, the seeker after a needed phallic role model is psychologically blinded by the experience.

It can be helpful for the homolimerent man to step back from his feelings and reflect upon what they might tell him. Knowing that other men, including fictional characters like Gustav Aschenbach, have had similar feelings can sometimes improve the outlook for a man whose homolimerence might otherwise cause him to fall victim to self-pity and poor judgment. This wider perspective can help some afflicted men gain the emotional distance and extra psychological wiggle room they need in order to adapt more comfortably. This benefit can be enjoyed even though no change in sexual orientation is anticipated.

"OBJECTS IN MIRROR ARE CLOSER THAN THEY APPEAR"

Men must learn from experience how to use the selfobject mirrors that help guide them on their path to manhood. Selfobject mirrors—unlike those slightly convex, passenger-side rearview mirrors—do not inform the user that the reflected image he sees represents something closer to him than he thinks—his own self-potential. When a boy or man has no insight into how mirroring selfobjects operate within his psyche, then other males can become for him a source of painful longing and confusion instead of being role models and facilitators of masculine individuation.

As psychotherapist Peter Schellenbaum (1991) points out, "das Spiegelbild ist nicht der Spiegel" [the image in the mirror is not the mirror itself] (p. 84). Schellenbaum suggests that men who are particularly sensitive to the phallic "signal" sent out by other males need to learn to interpret it as an *Individuationssignal* (a signal or opportunity for individuation) instead of responding to it exclusively as a *Beziehungssignal* (a relationship signal or an imperative call for a physical relationship with the other man).

The boys who fascinated young Thomas Mann all had a strongly developed sense of their own masculine self. But instead of being able to recognize his own phallic self-image reflected in the faces of these boys and men he saw and loved, Mann was dazzled and misled by the bright radiance of maleness they presented to his intrapsychic view. Although his own phallic potential was in fact closer to him than he felt, he could not transform it into his own masculine experience.

Thomas Mann did not have the kind of childhood that taught him how to see his own phallic masculinity in the selfobject mirror. He never learned how to experience other men as accessible role models and potentially transmuting selfobjects. Instead, they were a source of painful homolimerent longing that he did not understand.

His first great novel, *Buddenbrooks: The Decline of a Family* (1901), tells of the decay through several generations of a bourgeois North German merchant family not unlike his own. In this novel, he lays out for all to see the troubled selfobject milieu of his own formative years. The fact that both of Thomas Mann's own sisters committed suicide supports the notion that his family's psychological dynamics were seriously out of balance. In addition, two of Mann's own three sons also died by suicide. One of them, Klaus Mann, was gay. He was a gifted novelist and writer who, during World War II, enlisted in the U.S. Army. He served overseas as a correspondent for the Armed Forces newspaper *Stars & Stripes*. Klaus Mann committed suicide in 1949. Mann's daughter Erika was lesbian. She married the gay Anglo-American poet W. H. Auden for the purpose of helping him acquire United States citizenship.

As with the Buddenbrook family, the Mann family's psychological dysfunction was intergenerational and tended to repeat itself in succeeding generations.

DEATH IN VENICE: FRAGMENTATION INSTEAD OF TRANSMUTING INTERNALIZATION

Like Thomas Mann himself, the protagonist of *Death in Venice* was in a psychically vulnerable state when he arrived in Venice for his much needed vacation. As the plot unfolds, we watch helplessly while Aschenbach's masculine self undergoes its fatal fragmentation. Here is how the narrator describes the older man's reaction to his first glimpse of Tadzio from across the hotel lobby:

> Aschenbach noted with astonishment that the boy was perfectly beautiful. . . . He had a straight nose and a lovely mouth and wore an expression of exquisite, divine solemnity. It was a face reminiscent of Greek statues from the noblest period of antiquity; it combined perfection of form with a unique personal charm that caused the onlooker to doubt ever having met with anything in nature or in art that could match its perfection [Mann, 1912, pp. 21–22].

The inflated expressions "divine solemnity" and "perfection of form" suggest that it is an impersonal dimension of Tadzio's attractiveness that is compelling the old man's attention. Nothing about the object of his fascination—nothing about his LO—escapes Aschenbach's notice. In particular, he observes and is deeply affected by the earnestness and grace of the boy's movements. How the youth walks, holds his head, and smiles are all experienced by the watcher as events of awesome beauty and great portent.

The things about Tadzio that seize Aschenbach's attention involve how the boy appears (i.e., how he appears to Aschenbach) to feel about himself as a male and about his relationship to the world. Aschenbach is profoundly affected by the coherence and energy of the boy's connection to a source of male energy that Aschenbach himself desperately longs to experience. Aschenbach's yearning is largely sublimated in his intellectual activity as a writer. He is particularly sensitive to the boy's body and physicality. For example, at the beach he rapturously notices Tadzio's armpits and the hollows behind his knees. Because these areas are usually covered by clothing and are not seen, they may substitute for the also unseen but more specifically phallic, part of Tadzio's anatomy that the old man dare not allow himself to contemplate.

Aschenbach is able to soothe himself and overcome his feeling of self-depletion only so long as he can keep his eye on the attractive boy. When Tadzio is out of his sight, the old man's feelings of emptiness and despair return. An important aspect of Aschenbach's vulnerability was that he did not know how to find any common or sharable ground upon which to build an ordinary relationship of give-and-take mutuality with Tadzio. At the single instance when he came close to speaking to Tadzio, he was precipitated into a veritable panic with palpitations and shortness of breath. He was unaware of his predicament of homolimerence and thus unable to reflect upon its consequences. In this context, homolimerence ceases to function as a true selfobject experience.

THE GREEKS KNEW THE DANGERS OF HOMOLIMERENCE

Thomas Mann was well acquainted with the literature of classical Greece that celebrated the culturally accepted and highly institutionalized relationships between young adult men and older adolescent boys. In an episode where Aschenbach was watching Tadzio play with some other boys at the beach, he saw an older boy kiss Tadzio on the cheek. The sight of this greatly energized him. He smiled and shook his finger at the older youth and said out loud to himself: "Let me give you a piece of advice, Kritobulos. Take a year's journey. You will need at least that much time for your recovery" (Mann, 1912, p. 27) (i.e., recovery from your homolimerence for the boy you have just kissed). Mann is referring here to a dialog from Xenophon's *Symposium*. Xenophon was a contemporary of Plato whose more famous dialog, likewise called *Symposium*, was also a celebration of homolimerence in male–male relationships. Xenophon's character Kritobulos was in the throes of a visually induced homolimerence for the boy Clinias, whom he extols in this fashion. Emphasis is added to the words that relate to the act of seeing.

> I would rather *look* at him than anything else in the world. I would cheerfully agree to be *blind* to all other objects [read: selfobjects]. I resent sleep because it removes him from my *sight*. I am grateful for *daylight* when I can *behold* him. . . . His *image* is deeply engraved in my psyche and I can reproduce it exactly even when he is out of sight [cited in Flacelière, 1962, p. 71].

In the language of self psychology, Kritobulos (Xenophon) could as well have been saying, "I have internalized his image as a selfobject that favorably transforms my own masculine self-experience."

In yet another of his writings, *Memoirs of Socrates*, Xenophon tells how the great philosopher had warned him about the disastrous consequences of kissing handsome boys, alerting him, so to speak, to the fact that homolimerence could be a dangerous business. Socrates told Xenophon:

> "Poor thing! Do you have any idea what will happen to you once you have kissed a handsome boy? Without a doubt, you will become an instant slave instead of a free man, you will spend lots of money on harmful pleasures, and you will be forced into pursuits even a madman would try to avoid." Hearing this, Xenophon trembled and cried out: "Hercules! What terrible power you ascribe to kissing a boy!" [cited from Davidson, 1998, pp. 194–195].

The Greeks understood very well the risks of intense homolimerent selfobject experiences. Davidson (1998) indicates that Socrates' comment to Xenophon was the origin of "an alarming infinitive to describe the economic effect of homosexual liaisons. *Katapepaiderastēkenai* means 'to have wasted an estate in affairs with boys'" (p. 195).

Aschenbach, like Kritobulos, spent a lot of time intently gazing at his LO. On one occasion, Tadzio smiled directly back at him. This caused the old man to fragment even more. He did not know how to respond to an authentic overture and could not contain the intense affect generated by the openness and acceptance he saw in Tadzio's smile.

Very soon after this disturbing encounter, Aschenbach had the dramatic dream that climaxes with the appearance of the symbolic wooden phallus. This is how the story's narrator tells it:

> That night he had a terrifying dream. . . . It began with . . . fear and desire. . . . From afar there approached a mixture of noises. . . . All this was accompanied . . . by the gruesomely sweet tones of a flute playing a cooing, recklessly persistent tune that penetrated to the very bowels, where it cast a shameless enchantment. . . . [S]mooth-skinned boys used garlanded staves to prod their goats . . . shouting with joy when the goats sprang. . . . [T]he ecstatic band howled the cry . . . with a drawn-out *uuu* sound on the end [Tadzio pronounced as "Tadzi-uuu"], a cry that was sweet and wild at the same time. . . . Fumes oppressed the senses: the acrid smell of the goats, the emanation of panting human bodies. . . . [H]e was overcome by a numbing lust, and his soul longed to join in the reeling dance of the god [whose] obscene symbol [the phallus], gigantic, wooden, was uncovered and raised on high. . . .

> [T]hey stimulated each other with lewd gestures and fondling hands . . . [and] began an unfettered rite of copulation in sacrifice to the god. [Aschenbach's] soul tasted the lewdness of frenzy and surrender. The afflicted dreamer awoke unnerved, shattered, a powerless victim of the demon [Mann, 1912, pp. 56–57].

After suffering this dream, he began to detest his own aging body and his sagging features. He dyed his hair coal black and put on garish cosmetics. He no longer cared who saw him following Tadzio about and leering at him. He yielded to a lustful and shameless pursuit of the boy at every opportunity.

Near the end of the story, when he learns that the Polish family is soon to leave the hotel, he knows that he will never see Tadzio again. One last time he goes to the beach to watch the boy whom he now sees as a "charming psychagogue [psychagogue = soul guide = selfobject] . . . beckoning to him . . . hovering before him in an immensity full of promise" (p. 63). As he sits in his beach chair watching Tadzio, his head falls on his breast, and he dies.

A story like *Death in Venice* can always be interpreted in more than one way. The view suggested here is that the story is about a man whose difficulty incorporating a satisfying masculine experience into his own self predisposed him to an archaic kind of selfobject experience that had no chance of leading to transmuting internalization. Aschenbach's difficulty coming to terms with phallos made it impossible for him to derive any benefit from his encounter with Tadzio, let alone pick up again the dropped threads of his own phallic development.

HANS CASTORP'S "INWARD GOOD" AS AN EXAMPLE OF TRANSMUTING INTERNALIZATION

As he grew older, Thomas Mann seems to have gained a broader perspective on the developmental and healing potential inherent in a male's intense attraction to another male. At the time he wrote *Tonio Kröger* and *Death in Venice,* he was able to foresee only self-pity and death as the consequence of his protagonists' homolimerence. Several of his later novels, however, give evidence that, in his later years, he had developed a more resilient self. The abject self-pity and bitterness of his youth yielded to an ability to reflect upon his own inner state with more insight and empathy.

Hans Castorp, the protagonist of *The Magic Mountain* (Mann, 1924), seeks to be healed by visiting a mysterious sanatorium in the

Swiss Alps. In an engaging episode shortly after he arrives at "the magic mountain," he falls into a trance and has a prolonged reverie in which he revisited his schoolboy fascination with Pribislav Hippe. He recalled how he looked forward each day to seeing the object of his fascination at school. Mann celebrates Hans's powerful feelings of homolimerence for Pribislav.

> Hans Castorp had had his eye on young Pribislav for a long time, had chosen him from among all the boys in the bustling schoolyard, had . . . followed him with his eyes . . . with ever-growing interest and sympathy [p. 118].

Mann notes that Hans Castorp, unlike Aschenbach, reflected usefully upon the nature and potential of his experience with Pribislav Hippe although he was reluctant to put a label on his feelings.

> Hans Castorp did not worry about the intellectual or emotional basis of his reaction to Pribislav, or even to question what name he would give it if he called it anything. . . . Indeed, he did not think that the experience could be grasped by language at all. Besides, to give it a name would have meant, if not to pass judgment on it, at least to define it, to classify it as one of life's familiar, commonplace experiences; whereas Hans Castorp was thoroughly convinced at some subconscious level that an inward good of this sort was above all to be guarded from definition and classification [p. 118].

The protagonist recalls the climactic event when he took the great risk of speaking to Pribislav. It was the one and only time the two boys ever spoke to each other.

> And this is how it came about. The drawing class was next, and Hans Castorp found himself without a pencil. With a joyous impulse of his entire being he determined to seize this opportunity to ask Pribislav if he might borrow a pencil. It was a rather odd thing to do . . . but this escaped him in his recklessness. So there he stood face to face with Pribislav Hippe, there among the bustling crowd that filled the brick schoolyard. And he said to him: "Excuse me, could you lend me a pencil."
>
> Pribislav looked at him . . . and spoke in his pleasantly husky voice. . . . He said "Glad to. But be sure to give it back to me after class." And he pulled a pencil from his pocket, in a silver-plated holder with a ring you had to push up to make the reddish pencil tip emerge from its metal casing. As he explained its simple mechanism, both their heads bent down over it together.
>
> They looked at each other and smiled. . . . That was all there was to it. But Hans Castorp had never been happier in all of his life than

> during that drawing class when he sketched with Pribislav Hippe's pencil. . . . He even took the liberty of sharpening the pencil a little, and he kept three or four of the red-lacquered shavings in a drawer of his desk for a year or two—anyone who might have seen them would never have guessed their significance [p. 120].

The psychological significance of the pencil, the ritually preserved shavings, and the restorative effect it had upon Hans Castorp revolves about his need for a specifically phallic type of sustenance in his self-development. The incident represents a homolimerent selfobject experience that was more successful than those experienced by the two earlier protagonists, Tonio Kröger and Gustav Aschenbach. Hans Castorp understood well that, outwardly, his encounter with Pribislav may have seemed trivial, but inwardly, it was a momentous occurrence for him, a turning point in his life. His homolimerence had evolved into a transformative selfobject experience.

Thomas Mann's last novel, *The Confessions of Felix Krull, Confidence Man*, completed in 1954—the year before he died—is written from the perspective of the LO himself, rather than from the perspective of the one who is limerent. Felix, the handsome and charming young con man, reacts with insight and empathy to an older man who falls into a pitiable state of homolimerence for him. Mann makes it unmistakably clear that the character of this older man represents the author himself. The respect, humor, and tolerance with which Felix treats the older man demonstrates a mature insight and a finely tuned empathy not found in any of Mann's other characters.

MANN ANTICIPATED KOHUT'S SELFOBJECT CONCEPT

In 1936 Thomas Mann was invited to speak at a symposium held in honor of Sigmund Freud on his 80th birthday. In his remarks, Mann (1936) referred to the profound importance to psychoanalysis of what we now call the selfobject process:

> [It is] the solemn and novel confrontation of object and subject [read: object and self], . . . their mingling and identification, the resultant insight into the mysterious unity of ego and actuality, of destiny and character . . . and thus into the mystery of reality as an operation of the psyche—it is just this confrontation [i.e., the confrontation of self and object] that is the alpha and omega of all psychoanalytical knowledge [pp. 411–412].

It would be difficult to find a more comprehensive preview of Heinz Kohut's selfobject concept than these words spoken in honor of the founder of psychoanalysis by the author of *Death in Venice.*

REFERENCES

Cabaj, R. P. & Stein, T. S., eds. (1996), *Textbook of Homosexuality and Mental Health.* Washington, DC: American Psychiatric Press.

Davidson, J. (1998), *Courtesans and Fishcakes: The Consuming Passions of Ancient Athens.* New York: St. Martin's Press.

Flacelière, R. (1962), *Love in Ancient Greece.* New York: Crown.

Hayman, R. (1995), *Thomas Mann: A Biography.* New York: Scribner.

Kohut, H. (1948), *Death in Venice* by Thomas Mann: A story about the disintegration of artistic sublimation. In: *The Search for the Self, Selected Writings of Heinz Kohut: 1950–1978, Vol. 1.* New York: International Universities Press, 1978, pp. 107–130.

Mann, T. (1897), "The Clown." In: *Tonio Kröger and Other Stories,* trans. D. Luke. New York: Bantom Books, 1970.

——— (1901), *Buddenbrooks: The Decline of a Family,* trans. H. T. Lowe-Porter. New York: Vintage Books, 1984.

——— (1903), Tonio Kröger. In: *Death in Venice and Other Stories by Thomas Mann,* trans. D. Luke. New York: Bantam Books, 1988.

——— (1912), *Death in Venice,* trans. C. Koelb. New York: W. W. Norton, 1994.

——— (1924), *The Magic Mountain,* trans. J. E. Woods. New York: Knopf, 1995.

——— (1936), Freud and the future. In: *Essays of Three Decades.* New York: Knopf, 1968, pp. 411–412.

——— (1954), *Confessions of Felix Krull, Confidence Man,* trans. D. Lindley. New York: New Amsterdam Library.

Schellenbaum, P. (1991), *Homosexualität im Mann: Eine tiefenpsychologische Studie.* Munich: Kösel-Verlag.

Tennov, D. (1979), *Love and Limerence: The Experience of Being in Love.* New York: Stein & Day.

Chapter 12

John Adams and Benjamin Rush Exchange Dreams

Miriam Elson

John Adams, the second president of the United States (1797–1801), for some years (1805–1813) had been engaged in correspondence with Dr. Benjamin Rush (1746–1813). At some point, Rush suggested that they exchange dreams, to which John Adams agreed (Ellis, 2001, p. 214). Rush, a distinguished physician and educator, had long been interested in dreams. To his students he suggested that "dreams should be allowed to 'sport themselves idly' in their brains. Observed, dreams could provide useful inferences" (McCullough, 2001, p. 600). Rush had already related several dreams and then reported to Adams a dream prompted by a breach in friendship that had arisen between Adams and Thomas Jefferson.

In his dream, Rush had been reading the history of America written at some point in the future. On a particular page, the most extraordinary event of the year was the renewal of friendship between the two former presidents, Adams and Jefferson. According to Rush's dream, it was Adams who rekindled the old friendship, addressing a short letter to his friend, Mr. Jefferson, in which he congratulated him upon his escape to the shades of retirement and domestic happiness. This letter "did great honor to Mr. Adams, for it disclosed a magnanimity known only to great minds" (Schutz and Adair, 1966, p. 171). Mr. Jefferson reciprocated with "expressions of regard and esteem. . . . These letters were followed by a correspondence of several years" (p. 171).

Adams was delighted by Rush's "good-natured performance" (persisting in efforts to reestablish communication between these two) and replied, "A dream again! I wish you could dream all day and all night, for one of your dreams puts me in spirits for a month. I have no other objection to your dream but that it is not history. It may be prophecy" (Schutz and Adair, 1966, p. 173).

OF DREAMS AND DREAMING

From Adams's response, it is clear that dreams are regarded as reporting "history" (what has already happened) and prophecy (what the future might hold). However, from a distance of almost 200 years, these dreams lend themselves to the lens of self psychology, both as self-state dreams and as dreams in which the importance and vitality of the self–selfobject bond enters the regulatory and developmental process served by dreams and dreaming (Tolpin, 1983; Kohut, 1984; P. Ornstein, 1987; Fosshage, 1988).

I do not at this point choose to burden the reader with the lengthy history of dream theory and its application to the treatment of the individual by way of interpretation and the transference to the therapist (Freud, 1900). However, a brief description of Kohut's (1977) view on dreams is in order. Kohut identified basically two types of dreams:

> Those expressing verbalizable latent contents [drive wishes, conflicts, and attempted conflict solutions] and those attempting, with the aid of verbalizable dream imagery, to bind the nonverbal tensions of traumatic states [the dread of overstimulation, or of the disintegration of the self (psychosis)]. The very act of portraying these vicissitudes in the dream constitutes an attempt to deal with the psychological danger by covering nameless processes with nameable visual imagery. . . . [It] is the analyst's task, with regard to the first type of dream, to follow the patient's free associations into the depths of the psyche until the formerly unconscious meaning has been uncovered. In the second type of dream, however, free associations do not lead to unconscious hidden layers of the mind; at best they provide us with further imagery which remains on the same level as the manifest content of the dream. The scrutiny of the manifest content of the dream and of the associative elaborations of the manifest content will then allow us to recognize that the healthy sectors of the patient's psyche are reacting with anxiety to a disturbing change in the condition of the self—manic overstimulation or a serious depressive drop in self esteem—or to the threat of the dissolution of the self. I call these dreams "self-state dreams." . . . Associations to these dreams did not lead to any deeper hidden meaning, but tended to focus on the diffuse

> anxiety that had been part and parcel of the dream in the first place [pp. 108–110].

Thus my interest is the manner in which the dreams of these two outstanding representatives of the American Revolution reflect the state of the self. As they share their dreams, the sense of fragmentation yields to coherence, and fragility yields to sturdiness. The inner experience that each as selfobject provides the other is that of being calmed, soothed, affirmed, and energized. There have been many contributors to theoretical formulations with regard to self-state dreams, but this may be the subject of another paper!

In his 1983 paper, Tolpin suggested that "if one were to require a term for self psychological dreams that would differentiate them from dreams associated with the framework of classical structural analysis, one might designate them self–selfobject dreams" (p. 270), thus indicating the crucial role of the "relationship" of the self to the selfobject. To seek one who listens empathically and who responds may then return the self to its coherence and vigor. Kohut coined the term *selfobject* to describe the inner experience of validation and inspiration. As we shall note, in the case of Adams and Rush, their use of each other as selfobjects provides the inner experience of being deeply understood, of calming and soothing. Through a strengthened self, ambitions and goals are effectively reestablished. To be deeply understood may be the equivalent of being lifted and comforted in childhood (Elson, 1986; Ornstein and Ornstein, 1996).

In the classical mode of dream interpretation, wish fulfillment is viewed as the basic stimulant for dreaming. Sexual, aggressive, and narcissistically related processes may have been stimulated but insufficiently modulated during the day. In the revised model, wish fulfillment is no longer viewed either as a defensive process or as a fantasied gratification of libidinal or aggressive impulses with the primary function of discharge but, rather, as an avenue of regulation and management. As Fosshage (1988) sums up, in principle, "Dream mentation not only serves to maintain organization but contributes to the development of new organization . . . and management of affective cognitive experiences" (p. 164).

As we reflect on the self-states of Adams and Rush at this time, both had confided an arousal of anger and the experience of depletion by reason of the current histories being written both by those who had participated in the formation of the nation and those who had no contact with events. "Both men had labored too long and accomplished too much to let posterity go on uninstructed and ignorant; posterity must do them justice. With this impulse, Adams renewed an acquaintance that had grown cold by distance and difference of opinion and suggested a regular correspondence" (Schutz and Adair, 1966, p. 5). Adams's ambitions were high and reflected grandiosity and assurance: the letters were to be in the classical style with "Cicero primarily in mind." There were not infrequent episodes when each instructed the other to burn the letters but "knowing full well that these letters must be saved so that posterity could have a 'truthful account' of the nation's origin" (p. 5).

They exchanged letters frequently, with intimacy and delight in their response to each other's eagerly awaited letters. They were so caught up in this correspondence that, in a letter to Adams, Dr. Rush quoted his wife's comment that "you and I corresponded like two young girls about their sweethearts" (Schutz and Adair, 1966, p. 222).

THE DREAMERS

Before turning to the dreams themselves, some background for each of the dreamers is in order. Both men had served effectively in the events of 1774 and 1776 (the Revolution and the decisions embodied in the Declaration of Independence). Both had been members of the first Continental Congress, later representing their states in drafting the Constitution; both had been signatories of the Declaration of Independence, and both had felt the sting of criticism and the failure of society to recognize their contributions adequately or to report them accurately. Each was vitally important to the other, whose understanding of the hurt, omission or commission, became vital in restoring the strength and vigor of these two very unusual men and returned to them their zest in pursuing their ambitions and goals.

BENJAMIN RUSH

The Rushes were early settlers in the colonies, making their home in the area surrounding Philadelphia. Rush was only five when his father died prematurely and his mother necessarily had to provide for her five children. She established a "general merchandise business and managed the household in a spirit of kindness, generosity and attention to the morals and religious principles of her children" (Rush, 1949, p. 26). He was 13 when he enrolled at the College of New Jersey at Princeton and was already interested in medicine. He apprenticed himself to a leading physician and worked in laboratories and hospitals until he departed for further education at Edinburgh, its medical faculty then recognized as the most eminent in the world. Before returning home, he was able to attend medical lectures in London and Paris, meeting distinguished writers and philosophers.

Rush had some difficulty in establishing himself but secured an appointment to the College of Philadelphia, a platform from which he could publicize his various methods and prescriptions. His humanitarian views on temperance and slavery were published and circulated widely. He had more charity patients than those who could pay a fee, and as he wrote in his autobiography, his shop was crowded with the poor in the morning and at mealtimes, and nearly every street and alley was visited by him every day. "There are few old huts now standing in the ancient parts of the city in which I have not attended sick people . . . many hundreds of times have been obliged to rest my weary limbs upon the bedside of the sick [from want of chairs] where I was sure I risqued [sic] not only taking their disease but being infected by vermin" (Schutz and Adair, 1966, p. 12).

Though he was close to the poor, increasingly he grew closer to the politicians as the Revolution enveloped the city. He discovered Tom Paine, encouraged the writing of *Common Sense*, and assisted in its publication. His revolutionary ideas were nourished by Samuel and John Adams among others. Adams, however, feared the leveling influence of *Common Sense* and looked to the establishment of a constitution as a guarantee of liberty. Rush was more deeply committed to the establishment of a republican government.

> Their paths separated when Rush volunteered for the army and he was appointed surgeon general. . . . The overcrowded hospitals and the inefficiency of the director general brought blunt protest from Rush who put the problem before Washington. When Washington refused to take drastic action that Rush advised and Congress backed the general, Rush resigned his commission and criticized all concerned for what he felt was near criminal neglect of the sick and the wounded. Rush returned to Philadelphia, active again in hospital work, lecturing and writing; he enlarged his practice and won friends. But he could not forget the inefficiencies of army medicine and the lack of purity of purpose in republication leadership [Schutz and Adair, 1966, p. 13].

JOHN ADAMS

In contrast to Rush, Adams had grown up in a family of New England farmers, active in their community and civic affairs. He idealized his father, Deacon John, a man of probity, who was public-spirited and self-taught, but widely read. He had never attended college, but when John said he would rather be a farmer, Deacon John took him to cut thatch from early morning to late evening, asking him at the end of the long day if he still wanted to be a farmer. When John replied enthusiastically that he would, his father replied that he, nevertheless, wanted him to go on with his schooling. When John complained that it was not that he did not like books but that he did not like the instructor, his father respected his complaint and chose a mentor whom John admired, setting him on his way to Harvard and a lifelong devotion to books. A telling comment by Adams to his own son was, "One can never be lonely with a poet in your pocket" (McCullough 2001, p. 19). McCullough, in Adams's own words, describes "the unparalleled bliss of roaming the open fields and woodlands of the town, of exploring creeks, hiking the beaches, making and sailing boats, swimming, skating, flying kites, shooting marbles, bat and ball, wrestling, boxing, running about to quiltings and frolics and dances among the boys and girls. . . . The first fifteen years went off like a fairy tale" (McCullough, 2001, p. 31). "This unusually high-spirited lad, open to all sorts of activity, was nevertheless unusually sensitive to criticism [and] quickly responsive to praise" (McCullough, 2001, p. 33).

His parents were intimately attuned to his needs and his interests. He described his mother as a highly principled woman of strong will and exceptional energy. As for his father there were not words enough to express his gratitude for the kindness his father had shown him. His father was his idol. Deacon John's independent spirit and love of country were his son's lifelong inspiration. It was from this New England environment of many generations of continuity that Adams, at 15, went off to Harvard.

McCullough (2001), the author of the most recent biography of John Adams, drew from Adams's diaries to present the young Adams in his early twenties, reading law with an admired mentor.

> Chide himself as he would about time spent to little purpose, his appetite for the pleasures of society was too central to be denied. Further he had a talent for friendship. To many he seemed prickly, intractable . . . but as a friend would write, "Adams had a heart formed for friendship. . . . He needed friends, prized old friendships." In his diary he wrote, "Friendship is one of the distinguishing glorys [sic] of man. . . . From this I expect to find the chief happiness of my future life" [p. 47].

The intensity with which he corresponded and maintained friendship with a variety of individuals reflects the importance for him of selfobjects in strengthening and invigorating the self, in affirming ambitions and goals. To correspondents who related their experience of being misunderstood or going through difficult times, he responded promptly with reassurance, appreciation, and suggestion.

Unlike his father, who had spent his whole life in Braintree, Adams was attracted to Boston but feared its distractions. He looked to Cicero and was inspired and guided by his words: "The first way for a young man to set himself on the road towards glorious reputation is to win renown. . . . Reputation ought to be the perpetual subject of my thoughts and aim of my behavior" (McCullough, 2001, p. 46). But though he valued the law and his mentor highly and thinks law is a fine profession in which one can do much for humanity, his thoughts steal away to tea parties, dancing and other such activities. And when he sleeps, he dreams!

Unfortunately, we do not have a record of these youthful dreams. We read instead his critical review of his behavior: In the presence of women, those he wanted to impress above all, he considered himself too susceptible to the least sign of approval; "good treatment makes me think I am admired, beloved, so I dismiss my guard and grow weak and silly" (McCullough, 2001, p. 48).

Though he felt ill at ease and hopelessly awkward, he enjoyed an evening of "chatter, stories by candle light . . . and gallanting with the girls" (McCullough, 2001, p. 48). By contrast, Jefferson would later describe him as naturally amiable, so amiable that it was impossible not to like him. He was widely read, and he could talk on almost any topic and in any direction. On another occasion, Jefferson would describe him as "vain, irritable, stubborn, endowed with excessive self-love" (McCullough, 2001, p. 489).

Adams was no different from his peers; the difference lay in his ability to write about his feelings. He longed for some brilliant thought that would surprise the world. He scolded himself for his disorderly desk, for his inability to concentrate on just one book, one subject: "Why did imagination so often intervene, why did thoughts of girls keep intruding. . . . Ballast is what I want. . . . I totter with every breeze" (McCullough, 2001, p. 47).

The death of his father, when Adams was 26, came as a difficult blow. He experienced "want of strength and courage" such as he had never known (McCullough, 2001, p. 53). Still he stepped in as head of the family, as was expected, and as time passed, expressions of self-doubt and the fits of despair and self-consciousness that had so characterized the outpourings of his diary grew fewer. His relationship with his father was admiring, idealizing, and instructive. His father took pride in him and offered thoughtful guidance without sternness. Much later in life, Adams undertook with zest the many farming tasks involved in running the farms, noting on completion of a barn that his father, too, many years earlier, had built a barn.

Adams then turned to marriage with Abigail Smith, a union that endured until her death in 1818. Her importance to Adams in maintaining a vigorous cohesive self borders on a merger and cannot be overstated. Describing his mental state without her when they were separated because of her temporary illness, he wrote, "My soul and body have been thrown into disorder by your absence and a month or two more would make me the most insufferable cynic in the world. I see nothing but faults, follies, frailties and defects in anybody lately. People have lost all their good properties or I my judgment. But you who have always softened and warmed my heart, shall restore my benevolence as well as my health and tranquillity of mind" (McCullough, 2001, p. 57).

The letters that passed between them during the long periods of separation when he served as ambassador to England or France reflect their deep attachment and their intimate understanding of the travails through which each was passing. Their long separations were difficult for both; their letters kept them in as close contact as the uncertainties and vagaries of mail necessarily sent by boat permitted. Abigail was left with the care of the children, their home, and the farms, and these she managed with great success. Her own keen interest in the nation's problems matched John's, and her letters reflect her good judgment and skill. But she felt his absence keenly.

On one occasion, she expressed this with great poignancy: "No man even if he is sixty years of age should spend more than three months at a time from his family. . . . Oh that I had a bosom to lean my head upon" (Ellis, 2001, p. 174). His characteristic playfulness is evident in his reply: "But how dare you hint or lisp a word about sixty years of age. . . . If I were near I would soon convince you that I am not above forty!" (Ellis, 2001, p. 174).

At this time, Washington's second term was drawing to a close, and the choice of his successor was being hotly contested. Adams felt it was beneath him to campaign for the office of president. In later times he would regret that he had not hired "puffers" as others had. Character defamation was rampant and few came to his defense. In the publication of a particularly damaging pamphlet, Jefferson, who had ambitions of his own, silently colluded. Adams, struggling with the prospect of defeat when it looked unlikely that he would be elected president, wrote Abigail:

> Fear takes hold of me. . . . I laugh at myself twenty times a day for my meditations and speculations in which I find myself engaged. Vanity suffers. Cold feelings of unpopularity. Humble reflections. Mortifications. Humiliations. . . . I can pronounce Thomas to be chosen president of the U[nited] S[tates] with firmness and good grace . . . that I don't fear. But here alone, abed, by my fireside, nobody to speak to, poring upon my disgrace and future prospects—this is ugly [McCullough, 2001, p. 463].

Adams did, however, become the second president, and as he contemplated his responsibilities, a sense of despair overtook him. His deep need of Abigail and the sense of desperation in her absence are clear in his plea during his first months as President, "I never wanted your advice and assistance more in my life. . . . The times are critical and dangerous and I must have you here to assist me. . . . I can do nothing without you" (Ellis, 2001, p. 185). Again, the impression is almost that of a merger, yet it is Adams's capacity to respond quickly with a restoration of coherent vigorous pursuit of his goals. However, Adams failed to achieve a second term, largely because of the bad press he experienced, both for some courageous and for some ill-advised stands he had taken.

THE DREAMS

The dreams to which we now turn stem from the years of Adams's retirement. Across the span of 200 years, dreams, viewed through the lens of self psychology, readily lend themselves to our contemporary scrutiny and yield greater understanding of the inner life of these two venerable patriots.

When the correspondence between Adams and Rush began, Adams had been out of the presidency for five years. Adams and Rush were exquisitely in tune with each other, affirming their aspirations, recognizing and understanding the pain of slights and criticism from others, free to tweak and tease. An example is Adams's comment to Rush, upon receiving a dream of his, "Whatever it is that inspires your nightly dreams, I would not exchange, if I had it, for the dreams of Socrates. You have more wit and humor and sense in your sleep than other people, I was about to say, than you have when awake" (Schutz and Adair, 1966, p. 143). They refer to their dreams from time to time, familiarly calling them by name as in "the Versailles" dream or, especially in the case of Rush, sharing them with friends in admiration for the creativity and complexity of the dreams.

When the history of events began to be written by others who had participated in the events, both men were offended by the attribution to them of acts they had not committed or failure to describe accurately the important roles they had played. More than history as lived and history as remembered, they could expose to each other the pain of betrayal or defection.

Indeed, in a letter to Rush, seeking empathic response to wounds he had received from inaccuracies published by Tom Paine, Adams wrote:

> Though I was strenuously opposed to the whole system [location and design of the plan for the City, the Capitol, etc.] in every grade of its progress, yet Tom Paine has transmitted me to the world and posterity, as casting my eye over the great City . . . exultingly exclaiming, "Is not this great Babylon that I have builded!" And I never had one friend in the world to contradict the lying rascal, tho' hundreds were able to do it of their own knowledge. It was a great oversight in me not to hire puffers [Schutz and Adair, 1966, p. 252].

After receiving this letter, a night or two later, Rush responded with a dream supporting Adams's plan for a navy. He wrote:

> I fancied in [my] dream that I was elevated upon a bench in our Hospital yard surrounded by between 60 and 70 of my lunatic patients. Deeply impressed by the contents of your letter, I addressed them upon the subject of a Navy. While I was speaking, one man came up to me and said, "I am Solon," a second said he was William Penn, a third said he was Numa Pompilius, and all of them asked me how I dared to instruct them upon the means of defending our country. A 4th spat in my face, a fifth hissed me, a 6th called me a fool, a 7th said I was crazy, an eighth took up a stone and threw it at me. In an effort to avoid it, I awoke, satisfied that such would have been my treatment in the House of Representatives in Washington had I addressed them upon the same subject and had they not been restrained by the habits of civilized life [Schutz and Adair, 1966, p. 252].

The issue involved was the necessity for building a navy to protect American shipping, for which Adams had been forcefully attacked. Rush, responding with a dream of his own in support of a navy, sympathetically joins in experiencing the attack of those who opposed Adams's pressure for the establishment of a navy. Rush had included the gift of his newly published volume, *Medical Inquiries and Observations upon the Diseases of the Mind: The Standard American Guide for Mental Illness*, for which Rush would become famous as the father of American psychiatry (cited in McCullough,

2001, p. 609). Adams was highly appreciative of the book, "which will run mankind still deeper into your debt. You apprehend 'Attacks' I say the more the better. . . . You would not have been so industrious nor so useful if you had not been persecuted. These afflictions are but for the moment, and they work out greater glory" (Schutz and Adair, 1966, p. 254). The letters strikingly illustrate the importance of each to the other as selfobjects.

The comfort Adams offers his friend stimulates his own search for understanding to relieve hurt. At this point Adams offered a

> Dream for a dream. . . . When it was proposed to institute a democracy in France, I dreamed that I was mounted on a lofty scaffolding in the center of a great plain in Versailles, surrounded by an innumerable congregation of five and twenty millions, at least, of the inhabitants of the royal menagerie. Such a multitude is not to be described or enumerated in detail. There were among them the elephant, [the] rhinoceros, the lion, the hyaena, the wolf, the bear, the fox, and the wildcat, the rat, the squirrel as well as the calf, the lamb, and the hare. There were eagles, hawks and owls of all sorts, and storks and cormorants and crows, and ducks, geese, turkeys, partridges, quails, robins, doves and sparrows. There were whales, sharks, dolphins as well as cod, mackerel, herrings and even minims and shiners.
>
> My design was to persuade them to associate under a free, sovereign annimatical [sic] government, upon the unadulterated principles liberty, equality, and fraternity among all living creatures. I had studied a long speech, arranged it in exact method, with a beginning, a middle, and an end, with an exordium and a very pathetic peroration, according to the most orthodox rules of the most approved rhetoricians. Throwing my eyes round and gracefully bowing to my respectable audience, I began:
>
>> "My beloved brothers! We are all children of the same Father who feeds and clothes us all. Why should we not respect each other's rights and live in peace and mutual love!" I had not pronounced all these words before the elephant pouted his proboscis at me in contempt, the lion roared, the wolf howled, the cats and dogs were by the ears, the eagles flew upon the turkeys, the hawks and owls upon the chickens and pigeons. The whale rolled to swallow twenty at a mouthful, and the shark turned on his side to snap the first he could reach with his adamantine teeth. In a word, such a scene of carnage ensued as no eye had ever seen and no pen or pencil ever described. Frightened out of my wits, I leaped from the stage and made my escape—not, however, without having all my clothes torn from my back and my skin lacerated from head to foot. The terror and the scratches awakened me and convinced me forever what a fool I had been" [Schutz and Adair, 1966, p. 255].

There is an illustration here of Kohut's (1977) description of dreams as "covering unnameable processes with nameable visual imagery" (p. 108). Adams describes his flight from the menagerie of animals, birds, and reptiles who tear his clothes from him, leaving his skin lacerated. Adams was exquisitely sensitive to criticism, and the metaphor represented in the dream is well taken.

After validating the pain and affirming the reality of the misunderstanding of events in which each had participated, both men return to the discussion of the current world of national affairs. Occasionally, Adams or Rush will slip in a comment about a dream and dreamer, such as when Rush writes to Adams, "You have so far out-dreamed me in your last letter that I shall be afraid hereafter to let my imagination loose in that mode of exposing folly and vice. My whole family was delighted in contemplating you upon your rostrum in the garden of Versailles and in witnessing the effects of your speech upon your hairy, feathered, and scaly audience" (Schutz and Adair, 1966, pp. 257–258).

Rush thanks Adams for his

> kind reception and favorable opinion of [my] book on diseases of the mind which had been favorably received by many of [my] fellow citizens . . . but not a single physician in our city [one young man excepted] has taken the least notice of it in any interviews with them since its publication. It is a curious but not a singular fact that those of them who owe me most obligations are the most hostile to me [p. 281].

He concludes with another comment about Adams's dream, which he has read to a friend who was delighted with it: "What an imagination the old gentleman possesses" (p. 258).

What is striking is that both men begin their account of their dreams seeking to right a wrong and begin deftly to undertake setting out the facts. Rush addresses a relatively small audience—60 or 70 of his patients—speaking while standing on a bench in the hospital yard. For Adams the venue is magnificent. In his dream, he is mounted on a lofty scaffolding in the center of a great plain in Versailles. Surrounded by an innumerable congregation of "twenty-five million at least of the inhabitants of the royal menagerie." Although such a menagerie is not to be described or enumerated in detail, he proceeds to do just that—furred, feathered, four-footed, two-footed, wild, tame, winged, or not. There is more than a hint here of the role dreams play as selfobjects with these dreamers.

Despite the fact that Adams is long out of the presidency at the time of these dreams, their manifest content is on a grand scale. On one of his long rides home by horse he encounters a man who offers to sell him a horse, and this serves as stimulus to another dream. In a waking state, Adams admires the three-year-old colt:

> Broad, strong, and well-filled in proportion, as tame, gentle and good natured . . . as a lamb . . . thinks I to myself, this noble creature is the exact emblem of my dear country. I will have him and call him my Hobby. He may carry me five and twenty years should I live, but I should shudder if he should ever discover . . . his own power. By one vigorous exertion of his strength, he might shake me to the ground on the right hand or the left, pitch me over his head, or throw me back over his rump [Schutz and Adair, 1966, p. 258].

When Adams comes home "well exercised, in good health and spirits," he goes to bed and dreams of an open theater erected in the center of a vast plain in Virginia, "where were assembled all the inhabitants of the U.S., eight millions of people, to see a new play advertised as the most extraordinary that ever was represented on any stage, excelling [among others, Shakespeare and Moliere]" (p. 283). Against a distant view of the sea, elements of the success of the navy, the ships it has taken as prizes, and the conquering captains are cheered for their activities during the War of 1812.

> Dame Siddons, slowly and gracefully swimming over the stage, pointing to the "glorious spectacle of the Navy," sings out, "America, this, fair creature, is thyself," calling attention in the same spirit to a lock of Samson's hair, the strength of Hercules, and David's prowess with the sling that will overcome monsters. . . . Observing that this overgrown colt of a nation, after all this, not any sense of its glory, any more than my Hobby, I made a motion that the play should be dismissed and the nation resolve itself into a committee of the whole house on the state of the nation, Dr. Rush in the chair [p. 284].

One senses the ironic pleasure as he writes Rush, "Oh, the foresight, and the hindsight, the rightside and the leftside, the northside and the southside, the eastsight and the westsight that appeared in that august assembly . . . the sun now blazed through the windows upon my eyes and woke me" (p. 285). Even the expectation of Rush's reply restores a self-state of vigor and humor.

Rush and Adams continue their playful interchanges, Rush by cautioning Hobby, "Tread gently and safely, highly favored beast, while your master bestrides your back. Shake every blood vessel of his body and gently agitate every portion of his brain. Keep up the circulation of his brain . . . excite aphorisms and anecdotes and dreams for the instruction and amusement of his friends" (p. 286).

For his part, Adams writes a lengthy letter from Hobby to Rush, addressing him as "Honored and Learned Sir," noting that (Adams) is 77 and asking "How many pains and aches, which I cannot shake away, has he to endure? How much low spirits? How many gloomy anxious moments for the dangers, disgraces, disasters, degeneracy . . . follies, ignorance, stupidity, and vanity of his country?" (Schutz and Adair, 1966, p. 262).

The manifest content of the dreams, at least those they report, had to do with sweeping vistas, magnanimous gestures on behalf of their young country struggling to maintain itself. Both recognized their own envy and resentment in their observation of many compatriots who had done little to establish the country but had profiteered and achieved great wealth and were then living in ease with their families and were well provided for. At times, Adams regretted his sacrifices for statesmanship, the dreams offering an opportunity for reflection and recognition that, despite these sacrifices, they were necessary to maintain the values and goals important to him. He strove to bring his compatriots to his views, particularly for example, the importance of building a navy. In a dream, he used the persona of Dame Siddons, a beautiful and talented actress who appears and swims grandly the length of the stage on which the captured ships of the British are being displayed. "She approached near enough to be heard by all, with all the advantages of her face, figure, gestures and intonation" (p. 283).

I do not think it is overreaching to suggest that, in this dream, Adams is seeking to regulate tension and to develop new psychic structure. He uses Dame Siddons, an actress of great beauty, gracefully swimming across the expanse of the stage, pointing to the glorious spectacle of the navy, and calling to America to recognize and claim its strength and courage, its place among nations. But this was only one act of a play, and Adams, in a thrust, or surge, in his need for the development of new psychic structure to be able to persuade the audience, moved that the play should be dismissed and the house meet as a committee of the whole on the state of the nation, Dr. Rush being the chair. He sought to bring a strong majority to adopt plans for a sizable number of ships and supporting manpower. The audience had forgotten their abuse of his efforts to promote the building of a navy, a navy that was now saving America from destruction. Then they cheered and shouted, "Did we not always tell you so?" (Schutz and Adair, 1966, p. 259).

The grand scale of Adams's dreams reflects the reality of his long public service, not only as President, but more particularly as ambassador and as commissioner to England and France. For many years he was involved in strengthening America as a force among nations, serving often at great sacrifice both in deprivation of closeness to Abigail and his children and in compensation. That he gave of himself unstintingly and was supported by Abigail in this imbued in him a strong wish for recognition and acknowledgment.

This is a dimension of his personality that apparently aroused a certain amount of criticism. By some, he was seen as vain. Ellis (2001, p. 195) described him as of an iconoclastic and contrarian temperament that relished alienation. Every effort to redeem his reputation only confirmed what had been claimed in the infamous pamphlet circulated during the presidential campaign of 1800—namely that Adams was an inherently erratic character who often lacked control over his own emotional impulses (see Ellis, 2001, p. 214). In his later correspondence with Rush, "Adams seemed to embrace that very conclusion. . . . There have been many times in my life when I have been so agitated in my own mind as to have no consideration at all of the light in which my words, actions, and even writings would be considered by others" (Ellis, 2001, p. 214). In his diaries, much as he had during his youth, he would criticize himself and strive to correct his behavior. In his Versailles dream, he described the preparation for his oration to the Royal Zoo. He makes an effort to control himself so as to function more persuasively, "I had studied a long speech, arranged it in exact method, with a beginning, a middle, and an end, with an exordium and a very pathetic peroration, according to the most orthodox rules of the most approved rhetoricians . . . gracefully bowing" (Schutz and Adair, 1966, p. 279) and so on.

Fosshage (1988) aptly described the manner in which dreaming mentation not only seeks to maintain organization, but contributes to the development of new organization and the management of affective cognitive experiences. In this dream he renewed his efforts to gain approval for the building of a navy, but even when he succeeded he was deprived of acknowledgment. "Didn't we always say so?" Though his audience exploded, set upon him, and drove him from the meeting place, his verdict that he had been a fool did not turn him from efforts on behalf of his country. His own values and goals were precious to him and necessary to his own self-esteem.

Rush's dreams were cast upon a much smaller screen: 60 or 70 of his lunatic patients on a bench in the hospital yard. Their responses to his speech advocating Adams's efforts for a navy were hostile, irrelevant, or attacking, one to the point of throwing a stone. To avoid this, he awoke, convinced that such would have been his experience in the House of Representatives in Washington if they had not been restrained by the habits of civilized life, yet he is not turned from, but instead, he experiences affirmation from Adams.

CONCLUSION

The main thrust of the dreams of both dreamers is to set the record straight, to clear away misattribution of word or deed, and to restate as clearly as possible what their acts and intentions had been. At the Royal Zoo, a metaphor for the many different individuals who make up the Congress, Adams prepared his speech with the utmost care, according to all the rules of rhetoric, as if to say, "This time I'll get it right."

In the Dame Siddons dream, he borrowed her voice and manner, recognizing within himself that he did not excel in public speaking, only to be greeted by the shouts from the audience to the effect that they had "known it all along"; in fact, "Didn't we tell you so?" Here his capacity for humor helped restore his equanimity as he shared with Rush the "hindsight, . . . eastsight and the westsight," and so on of the people who had opposed the creation of a navy but now took over his plans.

For both men, the failure to evoke warm praise or at least approving response to their efforts—for Adams, his effort on behalf of the emerging independent nation, for Rush, his work on behalf of the health of the nation—was the equivalent of a bodily attack. Each found comfort in intimately sharing their hurts and disappointments, and each experienced restoration of energy and creativity. It is of interest that Schutz and Adair (1966) call their first chapter "The Love of Fame, the Ruling Passion of the Noblest Minds."

It is likely that these two distinguished patriots had been overpraised in childhood or that their appropriate grandiosity had not had an opportunity to become modulated. The ability to experience pleasure in their accomplishments remained at an earlier level. They needed openly expressed approval and praise. In common with all men and women, in the same measure as the energy and time they have expended, they required the response of selfobjects throughout the span of life.

Dreams, as employed in therapy, provide an opportunity for patient and therapist to share associations that can provide the answer to such questions. It offers an opportunity for the patient to heal an injury, to reorganize, regulate, and restore the capacity for strengthening the self, of developing new psychic structure. Lacking their immediate associations, nevertheless, these dreaming patriots do offer us a printout of their self-state and the general circumstances that evoked the dreams. Adams, in particular in his youth, exposed the importance to him of friends. Indeed, as a friend wrote, "Adams had a heart formed for friendship; he needed friends, prized old friendships" (McCullough, 2001, p. 47). And, as he wrote in his diary, "Friendship is one of the distinguishing glorys [sic] of man. From this I expect to find the chief happiness of my future life" (p. 47)—foretelling Kohut's (1971) dictum that we need selfobjects from birth to the end of life.

This is not to say that all friends are selfobjects or that selfobjects may not also be found in music, theater, government, teaching, and all the varieties of life from which we draw sustenance. Indeed, in the case of Adams and Rush, their dreams become selfobjects from which each draws sustenance.

Throughout the 20 years or more of his retirement, Adams corresponded with numerous family, friends, and colleagues. But it is in his correspondence with Rush that we have an opportunity to observe the therapeutic effect of their dreams, of the intimacy with which each empathically responds to his need for validation. Each has provided the other, in timely fashion, with that inner experience of harmony, of being deeply understood, freeing a surge of energy in a strengthened and coherent self. The feeling of having labored in vain for their fellow citizens and their country, of having failed to amass a fortune for their families, subsides. Benjamin Rush's recommendation to his students that dreams should be allowed to sport themselves idly in their brains, for their dreams might provide useful inferences, certainly offered sober reflection to these dreaming patriots. Jointly and individually, they cling to the important principles that have guided their lives and they experience restoration. It is instructive, as one follows their correspondence, to recognize the process by which psychic structure in the form of a strengthened self takes form. The response each drew from the other made it possible for each to face quirks of character or failures in judgment without destroying himself with self-criticism. Supported and understood by one who functioned as an alter ego or twin or an object of idealization, they could express anger, envy, longing, or hurt and move on spurred by the values and ideals that had so strongly guided their lives.

REFERENCES

Ellis, J. (2001), *Founding Brothers: The Revolutionary Generation*. New York: Knopf.

Elson, M. (1986), *Self Psychology in Clinical Social Work*. New York: Norton.

Fosshage, J. (1988), Dream interpretation revisited. In: *Frontiers in Self Psychology: Progress in Self Psychology, Vol. 3,* ed. A. Goldberg. Hillsdale, NJ: The Analytic Press, pp. 161–176.

Freud, S. (1900), The interpretation of dreams. *Standard Edition*, 4 & 5. London: Hogarth Press, 1953.

Kohut, H. (1971), *The Analysis of the Self.* New York: International Universities Press.

——— (1977), *The Restoration of the Self.* New York: International Universities Press.

——— (1984), *How Does Analysis Cure?* ed. A. Goldberg & P. Stepansky. Chicago: University of Chicago Press.

McCullough, D. (2001), *John Adams.* New York: Simon & Schuster.

Ornstein, A. & Ornstein, P. (1996), Speaking in the interpretive mode and feeling understood: Crucial aspects of the therapeutic action in psychotherapy. In: *Understanding Therapeutic Action: Psychodynamic Concepts of Cure,* ed. L. Lifson. Hillsdale, NJ: The Analytic Press, pp. 103–125.

Ornstein, P. (1987), On self state dreams in the analytic process. In: *The Interpretation of Dreams in Clinical Work,* ed. A. Rothstein. Madison, CT: International Universities Press, pp. 87–104.

Rush, B. (1949), *The Autobiography of Benjamin Rush.* London: Oxford University Press.

Schutz, J. & Adair, D. (1966), *The Spur of Fame: Dialogues of John Adams and Benjamin Rush.* San Marino, CA: The Huntington Library.

Tolpin, P. (1983), Self psychology and the interpretation of dreams. In: *The Future of Psychoanalysis,* ed. A. Goldberg. New York: International Universities Press, pp. 255–271.

Chapter 13

Making Contact with the Perception World of a Child: Undetected Disabilities in Sensory Motor Integration and the Effects on the Development of Self-Esteem

Eva Rass

The development of a child is embedded in complex psychosocial conditions. In this chapter the emphasis will be on the importance of the child's undetected neurological deficits, which cause psychological problems in the interaction with the environment. I will discuss the mutual influencing of the child's disposition and his environment and the consequences for the child's emotional development.

Children and adolescents with neurologically caused disabilities in their motor and perceptual skills are a challenge for their caretaking environment, especially for parents and educators. These deficits and

---

I am very thankful to Anna Ornstein for her help and support while revising and preparing this article, especially for her valuable hints, scrutiny, and removing my "Germanisms."

their consequences for development have been given little attention to date.[1]

Up until recently, only people with clear handicaps in motor skills or sensory integration disorders have been receiving adequate treatment. The treatment appears to be dependent on the degree of visibility of these handicaps and/or the alertness of the environment. Children with slight disabilities, whose neurological deficiencies are difficult to detect and are undiagnosed, are considered intact and therefore experience indifference and unempathic surroundings. Empathic surroundings, however, are imperative for the development of a stable and healthy self (A. Ornstein, 1976). Parents lacking insight are ill-equipped to cope with the demands of a neurologically handicapped child, and a security-given bond is so essential for these children.

Neither during my pedagogical studies nor during my training as a psychoanalyst was I helped to recognize subtle neurological deficits as a potential source of later emotional difficulties. Only in 1985, when I began to work with children and adolescent groups from preschool age up to young adults, did I become aware of these problems. As a group psychoanalyst, I observed the manner in which certain children expressed their rivalry among their peers. These were different from what I had previously seen in children with behavioral or mental disorders; these behavior patterns indicated to me the presence of neurocognitive deficits and their consequences as they emerged in group situations.

The theoretical and clinical problems concerning the impact on the child's development remained largely unexplored. Only a few studies in neurophysiology (e.g., Lempp 1970; Milz 1996; Esser 1991; Spekman, Goldberg, and Hermann,[2] 1992; Werner, 1999) disproved the purely emotional causality of many forms of childhood disorders and have been able to demonstrate their neurological origin.

---

[1] The frequency in the normal population alternates between 2% and 20%, depending on the perspective. On June 6, 2001, the *Deutsche Ärzteblatt,* a monthly German journal for medical doctors, published a study of the health ministry of the state of Baden-Württemberg. Six thousand children, six years of age, were examined before starting school: the screening showed that 23% of them had deficits in the area of auditory and visual perception, which in most cases led to enormous school underachievement. Psychomotor and tactile abilities were not included.

[2] Spekman et al. published a long-term study in 1992 that described the educational, employment, and social–emotional status of a group of young adults with learning disabilities who were former patients at the Marianne Frostig Center of Educational Therapy. Their quantitative and qualitative findings showed that learning disabilities must be treated as a lifelong condition.

Knowledge from other disciplines, particularly the neurosciences, must be integrated into in-depth psychology, conceptualizing a theory that integrates the impact of neurological deficits on a child's development and on the shape of the adult's sense of self. Lichtenberg (1983) and especially Stern's work (1985) represented a break with traditional psychoanalytic developmental theories. Stern's method of empirical observation and his proposal of development made it possible to integrate the findings of neuropsychology into a psychoanalytic perspective. Further, Palombo, who had been exploring the association between neurocognitive deficits—so-called learning disabilities—and disorders of the self, presented his findings in numerous papers (e.g., 1995, 1996) and in his recent book (2001), in which he discusses the conceptual problems and specific disorders and provides a framework to apply material to the therapeutic process. He offers a developmental perspective based on self psychology that enables us to understand the impact of learning disorders in child development and their resulting adult personalities; therefore, I can restrict myself to the detailing of the very practical aspects of these issues.

This chapter is divided into three sections: First I describe the impaired child's experience of everyday life. In order to make it comprehensible, I will illustrate, in a rough schema, the three most important perceptual areas that have proven useful and successful in the cooperation with doctors, teachers, parents, and so on. Next, I will present findings from my study and clinical implications, and finally, I will describe the treatment possibilities (Rass, 2002).

THE IMPAIRED CHILD'S EXPERIENCES OF EVERYDAY LIFE

The term *learning disorder* is mainly linked to aspects of learning that are related to academic settings. *Perception,* which comes from the Latin *capio, cepi, captum,* is more in accordance with grasping, catching, and comprehending, which indicates that stimuli from the outside world have reached the neuronal system, which is only as good as its receptors can absorb and process. The three areas of perception I use (the tactile–kinesthetic perceptual area, the auditory deficits, and the visual perception deficits) can be differentiated more extensively by psychologists, which is essential for further special support and training, but not for psychotherapy.

Tactile–Kinesthetic Perceptual Area

From birth on, the tactile-kinesthetic perceptual area is of extreme importance (Ayres, 1979); the development of all future schemata are influenced by this;[3] for example, a mother attempts to sooth her baby by touching him tenderly. With this caressing closeness, she is indicating to him that he is not alone; however, the mother's efforts to promote bonding and attachment in this manner may be rejected by a child who is unable to decode the physical contact and therefore experiences it adversely. When the baby reacts to the mother's efforts with irritation, she loses confidence in her ability to comfort her child. This interaction between mother and infant interferes with their sharing affective states and, therefore, with the proper development of their relationship.

Cognitive schemata can only be developed through secure physical action schemata; the impaired child experiences the world, as it were, with "boxing gloves," that is, vaguely and indistinctly and therefore less lively and joyfully. The child cannot grasp events as exactly as others do. The coordination of movements, the vestibular security, and the security in experiencing the space around him or her are also reduced. If "space" is not experienced with physical security, and this is only possible with a secure body feeling, all spontaneous and joyful freedom of movement suffers: for example, swinging, climbing, jumping into the parent's arms, childlike jostling and shoving, running away, rollicking at the play-ground, cycling, swimming, inline skating, or playing with a ball.

Contact in play among children is mostly physical: if a child is not able to enjoy this rivalry and competition, he is completely bewildered; this disorder distorts the child's eagerness for independence. When children have to cope with these kinds of handicaps, even the best relationship to the parents does not help. A child with a sensorimotor integration disturbance tends to be cautious and sceptical and tries to avoid healthy rivalry. This creates an enormous injury to the child's self-esteem. Since the insult is caused by his own body, the child loses confidence in its capacities.

The next step in this faulty development is the appearance of shame. The child is then labeled as suffering from "anxiety"; however, such a label only stresses the emotional aspect of the problem and the cause

---

[3] Each act of cognitive "comprehension" needs to be preceded by a tactile grasping action; this was studied and described by Piaget. He designated the first two years of life as belonging to the sensorimotor stage of intellectual development. During this stage, learning is based on physical action, the related and increasingly coordinated sensory sensations, the experienced effects of the action, and their final organization into a mental structure—this he called "schema." The infant interprets the world and makes sense of it in accordance with these rudimentary cognitive structures. These capacities set the stage for the next phase of development in which the infant refines the semiotic function and can use symbols. The achievements of the sensorimotor stage of development are the base for all further cognitive growth (Inhelder and Piaget, 1977; Buggle, 1997).

of the anxiety and physical insecurity goes undetected. Caretakers, doctors, and teachers remain unaware of the extent of the problem; however, these difficulties often do not appear in the familiar and trusted environments because the parents are used to them and unconsciously and automatically compensate for them. Such a child prefers to be with adults and with younger or older children; boys like to play with girls because physical rivalry is not so much a part of play among girls. If such a child has siblings, the problems become more evident, even at home. Sometimes the child does not feel he belongs to his family. Encounters outside of the familiar frame with its trusted interactions (e.g., kindergarten) cause massive troubles because prediction, which is a skill necessary for rivalry in the peer group and in an untrusted environment, is not available. Playing, doing puzzles, coloring, or drawing are not joyful. In school reasoning, manipulating numbers, and writing essays require the perception of a mental space that can only be developed if the young child's body had been able to conquer the real space around him with adequate security. Calculating in reverse (i.e., subtraction, division) is only possible if one is able to walk backwards securely. Somebody who cannot coordinate movements has difficulties planning complex actions, for example, clearing up a room, washing, and getting dressed in the morning. An example would be a child who, in the winter, first puts on his gloves, then the jacket with a zipper, and then the shoes; the proper sequence in these actions appears to be lost. The child, rather than being helped, is being scolded or criticized; he is unable to conceptualize a plan and initiate steps to implementing a plan. Procrastination, which makes parents furious, is probably one of the most prominent symptoms. This particular difficulty has consequences for school performance and makes a realistic career choice difficult.

Case Illustration[4]

A six-year-old girl was referred because she had problems when planning complex actions; she was not able to see the sequence in an action. The diagnosis was an intersensory dysfunction. During our talk, the mother understood that her daughter had difficulty organizing many simple everyday actions. After the session, as we entered the area where mother and daughter were about to put on their coats, the girl had her teddy bear in her arm and grasped her jacket; helplessly, she

---

[4] The following short vignette gives an insight into a typical sequence and into the impact of sensory integration difficulties on a mother–child relationship: a simple everyday task → helplessness → insecurity → misunderstanding → misattunement → criticism and shame.

hesitated, and her mother became impatient. I realized that the child needed help and said: "Put the teddy on the chair first," and when she had done this, "Now you can put on your jacket." She put it on, and then, with deep relief, she grasped her teddy. Although this was a calm and clearly structured situation, without unpredictable actions, it was difficult for the child to cope. In this moment, the mother instantly understood more than during the whole session. Meanwhile, the next mother of a patient had entered and witnessed these moments. In my office, she commented: "Now I understand why my son always returns from school with his jacket under his arm—even when it is raining." Obviously in a hurry at the end of school, he first puts his schoolbag on his back, after which, he was not able to reorganize the situation, that is, the sequence of first removing his schoolbag and then putting on his jacket.

Case Illustration

John, a 13-year-old pupil at secondary school, was transferred by a school psychologist because of a lack of self-confidence and self-assertion. He was often attacked by aggressive classmates, and he could not defend himself. He had little contact with the other children during the break and was an outsider. These problems had already become evident in kindergarten. The adults considered him to be a friendly and calm boy who seemed to be self-confident in his contact with adults, and they explained difficulties as being a "late developer" and a little bit introverted. As the class planned a two-week trip, John did not want to participate, because he—rightly—feared that he would become the class scapegoat. It was only through this intense refusal to join groups that attention was given to John's basic difficulties.

The checking of John's motor skills showed a poor body perception and body coordination. John could not ride a bike or a tricycle. As a small child, he was considered "just lazy and clumsy." John always succeeded in avoiding the examination of body coordination by any pediatrician. In kindergarten he always seemed to "forget" his gym suit and ended up watching the others. He did not learn to swim; he never took part in team sports and was called a "coward" by the sport teachers, so that he welcomed even minor injuries and was excused from sport by a doctor.

Through my examination, I could immediately sense the child's deep anxiety, his feeling of shame, and a feeling of inferiority, and I saw his avoidance strategies. The parents had not thought that physical security was so important. Although they compared him with other children, they did not consider the difference between John and the other children as indicating any form of a dysfunction. The pediatrician trusted the description of the dedicated and reliable family; he knew them well and therefore did not examine the child in any depth. In puberty, in order to avoid the feeling of shame because of his bodily clumsiness, John retreated from his peer group. He studied a lot and never caused any difficulties.

In treating John, a multidisciplinary approach was necessary: first, a psychomotor physiotherapy was initiated and, after he gained physical security, this was supplemented by therapeutic horseback riding. At the same time, he took part in a group therapy where he could speak about his feelings with other boys who had the same difficulties. Here he received empathy and understanding of his experiences; he learned to be angry and not to accept everything unconditionally. He even began to protest against the parents. Up until then (because of his insecurity), he was very dependent on them and did not dare to risk independence.

Observational aids in the area of tactile–kinesthetic perception are:

- trying to avoid close physical contact with others
- having to wash dirt off, because of severe feelings of disturbance (e.g., the child does not like to paint with fingerpaints, play in sand and mud, or play with plasticine)
- *difficulties in fine motor control* (e.g., when painting, writing, putting on clothes, etc.)
- *lack of tactile sensitivity;* child being too rough with delicate things
- difficulties when peeling apples, potatoes, and so on
- *lack in the body feeling of left/right dominance* (laterality)
- difficulties when filling a glass from a bottle (i.e., *dysfunction of the deep muscle sense*)
- difficulties with turning movements (e.g., screwing and unscrewing bottle tops and jars, winding a thread round a spool)
- insecurity on a swing and see-saw, in balancing on a tree trunk or on rough, uneven ground
- *unable to localize where he has been physically touched* in the absence of a visual cue
- no joy when running, romping, or rocking; is more concerned with security
- *insecurity in body movement feeling*
- avoids sliding
- insecurity when hopping on one leg or skipping
- *no rhythmic "movement flow"* when hopping on two legs
- insecurity when riding a tricycle or going up or down stairs (can not go one foot on one step)
- anxiety when riding a bicycle, inline skating, or swimming

- problems playing ball, especially catching the ball (i.e., *intersensory or cross-modal dysfunctions*
- problems trying to do handstands or somersaults
- *problems when planning a complex action; not seeing the central line (sequence) in a situation* (in a game, in building, succession of letters in a word)
- *difficulties in coordinating movements* (e.g., brush and dustpan)
- *difficulties in imitating the movement of frogs, horses and so on*
- difficulties in doing jumping jacks
- *insecurity when crossing the vertical axes of the body* (i.e., crossing midline) or painting a laying eight in the air
- difficulties when transferring a visual impression into physical expression
- difficulties when walking backwards or going on all fours (crawling in early childhood)

Auditory Deficits

A child who cannot decode fast enough what others have expressed often has deficits in auditory discrimination (Affolter, 1987; Milz, 1996). The child looks irritated; becomes insecure; does not find his place in the group; becomes, therefore, frustrated, aggressive, or withdrawn; and then plays alone. The uninformed adult then comments: "This child just doesn't listen," "It is like talking to the wall," or "Is the child deaf or something?" Teachers often speak of "concentration difficulties." Auditory deficits are very common, they cause deficiencies in speech comprehension and may result in a reading-writing disorder. I do not have to emphasize how important the auditory channel is for human communication. Sometimes, fortunately, such a child asks "What?" "Huh?" but then the reaction is: "Why don't you just listen? How often do I have to tell you!" Several noises, simultaneously—similar and comparable to a hearing aid that amplifies without differentiation—appear to the child as a big, loud murmur, whose single and important aspects he can not filter and recognize. With a single person in a calm and clear situation, often no problem arises—that's why this problem cannot be recognized in individual therapy—but interactions with more noises, like in school, in kindergarten, in an indoor swimming pool, or on a playground, are dangerous. Often, parents consult a specialist because they presume that their child is not able to hear clearly, but when the diagnosis is: "hearing intact"—as it mostly is—the criticism of the child is likely to increase.

Case Illustration

Manuela, a 15-year-old girl, was referred to me by her lifelong pediatrician because of "selective mutism." She suffered from a strong inferiority complex, and she spoke little, especially in school. Now at the end of the extended primary school (a German type of lower secondary school), the situation seemed critical to everybody, because Manuela had to choose a career. She had twice begun a psychotherapy in preceding years, which was broken off because Manuela could not be brought to speak. She had no clear idea what she wanted to be in life, but she knew that she wanted to continue her school education; however, all her teachers advised against it.

My diagnostic exploration presented a completely different picture: in the test Manuela cooperated eagerly—even though she was unsure—and endeavored to seek contact. She had a healthy will to communicate, but verbal communication caused great efforts and shame because of disabilities in elocution. Therefore, she depended on empathic understanding of the environment to help her to develop means of communication. The test result was slightly above average. The profile of the subtests was balanced; only in the field of auditory perception was she evidently weak.

During the appointment to discuss the test result, the mother gradually began to understand: when Manuela was a little child she suffered continuously from severe otitis media and thus did not hear well, so tubes were inserted. During primary school, her hearing was so bad that doctors considered a hearing aid. During her childhood, therefore, Manuela was an outsider, and her speech development was unsatisfactory; her speech reflected her hearing difficulties, and her speech lacked clarity and was vague and tentative. A symptom-orientated speech therapy was initiated but achieved little. Her classmates jeered at her, and adults criticized her until, out of self-defense, she literally shut her mouth.

Until this time, nobody had seen the problem in relation to the hearing difficulty. The girl shed tears of relief when she felt herself understood. Hope and courage have emerged since then. A speech therapist who works with the elements of occupational therapy has treated her. Now Manuela can cope much better with her disability.

Manuela is in the process of restoring her injured self-confidence in an analytic all-girl group therapy. Her school marks have so improved that she is considering doing her intermediate high school certificate. She has always been a good soccer player and now plays for a first-class ladies soccer team. Her speech has matured, and she likes to chat continuously like most teenagers do, and she now enjoys life.

Observational aids in the area of auditory perception are:

- child often asking for spoken words to be repeated
- *confusion of similar sounds (d, t)*
- doctor visit because the child "just doesn't listen"
- child appearing bored when somebody is reading to him
- no concentration when being read to
- *non- or misunderstanding in a complex noise situation* (kindergarten, school, indoor swimming pool, sports or playing field, etc.)
- compensatory visual orientation to others during play and teamwork
- educators feeling that they are "talking to the wall"
- *child having a distinctly better understanding of conversation in a single situation*
- *child having difficulties with auditory short-term memory*
- "angst" in new, complex, and unpredictable situations
- *insecurity in localization of noises*
- "angst" in sudden and unexpected noise situation (e.g., fireworks, balloon bursting)
- *difficulties in differentiating distance and closeness of a noise* (e.g., a car comes or goes; miscalculation when judging speed)
- *difficulties with rhythm* in verse and nursery rhymes
- difficulties when retelling a story heard or an experienced event
- *difficulties with linguistic terms of special explanations* (besides, under, above, etc.)
- *deficiency in imagining the sequence of a complex action*
- preferring familiar, stereotyped actions
- *speech problems* [sigmatismus interdentalis (lisp), schetismus, indistinct pronunciation, etc.]

Visual Perceptual Deficits

Children with a visual perceptual deficit experience all new and nonfamiliar situations like a film that runs too fast in front of their eyes; they cannot decode and differentiate their visual images quickly and exactly. Children with this particular handicap want to play with others but cannot follow the interplay as the group constellation changes constantly. Since the others do not wait until the child has realized all the important details, play proceeds and the impaired child subjectively experiences that "the others do not like me, do not want me playing with them," "I am an alien among peers." But the child does not know why. All new and unfamiliar situations are dangerous; avoidance strategies will be developed to evade shame because of the disabilities.

Motivation research shows that a child begins to compare himself with other peers from the third year on (Heckhausen, 1971; Oerter, 1995; Rheinberg, 1997). He experiences the expectations of the caregivers (which he internalizes) and his failure because of his insufficiencies: he feels alone and without support. Visual perceptual deficits have their impact on almost every situation in life; "looking through" is necessary in rivalry among peers, in overcoming complex and unpredictable situations, and in all logical processes. These early life experiences of not being successful highly influence the child's self-esteem, so that even the start of school is put under a cloud, which over the years leads to more and more extensive vicious circles.

Case Illustration

In a very urgent case a general practitioner contacted me because a 15-year-old patient of his was clearly in acute crisis. Susanna had lost a great deal of weight and was in danger of becoming severely underweight. In addition, there were daily aggressive eruptions in the family, whereby Susanna verbally abused her parents to an unacceptable extent. The child appeared highly agitated and said that she did not like herself any more. This unhappy condition had developed slowly and unnoticed for over a year. Susanna was in the ninth grade of high school. She was a successful pupil until the end of the sixth grade, but now had to put enormous effort into achieving an average standard. Although she studied for hours, her learning was not as successful as previously; she was deeply depressed by this. Her teachers and parents could not explain the drop in her achievements; the teachers considered it to be related to puberty or to sibling problems. Her elder sister and younger brother had no problems in school, were able and successful in the peer group, did only the required amount in school, and nevertheless, achieved good results.

The adolescent was clearly under pressure; she suffered and so did her environment. She had become very thin and pale, and because she needed extra time for her studies, she retreated from her peer group and other interests. She considered herself to be too fat, and she hoped that, by losing weight, she would regain self-esteem. Without doubt, there were puberty problems and fights with her parents, but this did not explain the seriousness of the deep crisis.

The test end result was average, but in the field of visual perception, there were enormous deficits. This meant that, in day-to-day school life, it was extremely difficult for Susanna to recognize logical and mental structures that she could not have learned before. In previous years she had teachers who had a very functional teaching method and a well-structured approach that was suitable to Susanna's intellectual capacities. The increasing demands on her ability to recognize and transfer logical structures brought her to her intellectual limits. She tried to compensate for the deficits by excessive rote learning, whether in math, Latin, or history. During our therapeutic talks it became clear to the parents that Susanna had always tried to avoid new and complex situations, that every change had been a crisis (e.g., from family to kindergarten, from kindergarten to school, etc.), which, however, was successfully overcome because of good family stress management. The visual disability was very well compensated for in the security of the family.

All members of this family placed high demands on their intelligence, which also marked the self-esteem of Susanna. This was now threatened with the appearance of school difficulties. Failure now led to a permanent hurt of the narcissistic system, which the patient tried to overcome with hateful attacks on her family. This was not very successful because Susanna still loved her parents and was tormented afterwards by a great deal of guilt. After the initial surprise at the test results, the parents could eventually accept them and were relieved that an essential aspect of the crisis had become comprehensible. But Susanna was very disappointed with herself. She began to understand that a visual perception disability marks different aspects of life and makes studying more difficult. The considerations of the parents to take Susanna from a higher to a lower level secondary school were vehemently rejected by her. She could not accept this injury; however, as school became more strenuous, her parents decided to make a move against her will. With much empathy, they overcame six difficult weeks of summer vacation, in which Susanna was full of anxiety because of the new situations. At the same time, she experienced an enormous feeling of personal failure and was envious of the uncomplicated life of her siblings.

In the new school, Susanna repeated the ninth grade, and because of her ability to learn, she soon experienced success. The improvement in her grades improved her self-esteem. In the beginning, she could not show her joy at this development because she would be admitting to her parents that they were right, but puberty could not and would not allow this. Her facial expression became happier and freer, the eating problem disappeared, and again, she found interests in keeping with her age. As her school marks improved, her hope to return to the higher secondary school reappeared. But in the tenth grade, she had to put a lot of effort into learning and realized, with the help of therapy and her growing self-confidence, that her abilities lay in practical areas. Instead of a third-level education, she could now accept a career in the commercial sector, which probably would provide her with more possibilities of success and joy of life. For daily life, Susanna could accept that new and complex situations will always be difficult for her to master. Through her learning ability, she developed strategies to predict and to plan future situations as far as possible. Of course, there is still a certain risk that can lead to failure; however, her self-esteem has become stable enough to reconcile herself to her weak points. It was equally important that the parents could accept this bitter reality and that they supported Susanna's process of finding herself and, through this, her emotional stability. It was very important that the parents loved their daughter so much that they could endure the hate caused by Susanna's disappointment with herself and that they persisted and made necessary parental decisions for this healing process, even against her will.

Often it was difficult for me to cope with the negative transference from Susanna. She hated me and often could not look me in the eye and wanted to break off the therapy because it was I who had obviously violated her juvenile dreams of grandiosity. Success in school was totally overvalued; all her other skills were not as important and did not compensate for the perception disability. But she felt that neither the parents nor I could be destroyed by her narcissistic rage, that we did not break the so needed, security-given emotional bond. She could begin to mourn about her limits and the general realities of life. This course repeated itself several times during the long therapy, and in this healing process of interruption and reparation, mature self-structures could be constructed.

Observational aids in the area of visual perception are:

- *visual motor coordination* (hand-eye coordination) is difficult (e.g., pouring liquids)
- frequent colliding with obstacles (bumping into) because *visual information is not coordinated fast enough with gross motor control*
- *difficulties imitating movement* (e.g., jumping jacks)
- difficulties decoding body language (e.g., are the others really fighting or just playing?)
- child understanding visual information much better in a one-to-one situation
- *visually perceived complete actions cannot be differentiated into structures, order, and sequence*
- structuring of exercises on child's own is difficult (e.g., essays, logic problems, etc.)
- "angst" in new situations that are complex and unpredictable (absence of an overview)

- *deficiency in organizing different visual impressions,* comparing different impressions
- *deficiency in processing speed*
- *spatial orientation difficult*
- difficulties coping with groups
- visual experiences not causing deep impression, having no appeal, and details going unnoticed
- *difficulties with differentiation of figure–background perception* (i.e., perceiving a small part in a complex whole)
- child very subjectively valuating and overestimating single aspects of a situation, which are less important for the "norm," and insisting on his perspective
- *deficiency in spatial memory and discrimination* of objects
- child always touching objects
- deficiency in sensitivity for distance and closeness
- deficiency in discrimination of tiny parts (e.g., p, q, b, d)
- *deficiency in understanding body language;* disability in transferring body movement into thoughts

SUMMARY

Children are born with a wide spectrum of abilities. In the last century, psychological research and in-depth psychology made evident how important all emotional experiences in childhood are for development; therefore, all "disturbances" in the process of raising a child have been considered primarily the result of an unsatisfactory parent–child relationship. There is no doubt that these disturbances exist, but this is not the subject of our concern here. Knowledge about mental disorders caused primarily by psychological factors often leads to the result that the hidden impairments go unnoticed and that these tragic consequences (perhaps a behavior disorder) are seen as the original disorder.

Rarely only one perceptual area is deficient; mostly, there are more. Surely a lot of children have strengths at their disposal; however, these only cover and do not compensate for the deficiency, so that the weakness is felt in a deep layer and makes life insecure. The weakest part in the complex capacity to cognitively process information determines the intersensory integration and the processing speed (Lempp, 1982), comparable with the traffic flow during rush hour in a big city, which begins to break down if only one traffic light malfunctions slightly. The hope that these problems can be outgrown or will resolve themselves is unrealistic.

FINDINGS OF MY OWN STUDY AND CLINICAL IMPLICATIONS

In making diagnoses, in my psychological workup during the last 15 years, I have included the examination of the child's perceptual and motor capacities. This resulted in treatment plans that often differed from those of my colleagues. However, the combination of an in-depth psychological with a neurological workup has proved reliable and patients rarely drop out of treatment.

In order to investigate and fully understand the field, 338 patients were examined and diagnosed using this concept in my practice from September 1997 to November 1998. Usually, the patients were referred to me on the advice of their General Practitioner, teachers, social workers, and so on. Table 1 is a list of problems given by the patients on the registration form as to why they need help.

Nearly every patient was tested with HAWI, which was developed out of the Wechsler Intelligence Scales and which has, meanwhile,

Table 1. Problems that cause patients to seek help

	Frequency of Stated Reasons		
Reason	**Male Pat. (%)**	**Fem. Pat. (%)**	**Total (%)**
Sibling problems	24.7	23.6	24.3
Angst toward all new things	50.0	39.3	45.6
Separation anxiety	22.7	21.4	22.2
Bedwetting	8.6	12.9	10.4
Lack of self-confidence	39.9	35.0	37.9
Provocative behavior	17.1	11.4	12.4
Disobedience	7.5	6.4	7.1
Sleeping problems	8.6	14.3	10.9
Psychosomatic complaints	4.6	7.9	5.9
Restlessness	15.7	27.1	20.4
School performing problems	39.9	30.7	36.1
Peer group problems	8.1	8.6	8.3
Concentration difficulties	15.7	9.3	13.0
Withdrawal tendencies	6.1	4.3	5.3
Aversion to everyday and school demands	5.1	1.4	3.6
High self-expectation	16.7	10.7	14.2
"Just doesn't listen"	7.6	6.4	7.1
Parental difficulties with upbringing	33.8	16.4	28.4

been twice revised. It has been given approximately 5000 times in my practice. More important than the final IQ, which is no more than a number, is the test profile because it can give hints of hidden neurological deficits (Tewes, Rossmann, and Schallberger, 1999).

Only 12.7% of the boys and 8.7% of the girls tested had no under average values in any of the subtests concerning auditory, visual, and psychomotor perception. It seems that there exists a connection between symptoms and functional disability. Because of the treatment plan, a highly differentiated diagnosis is vitally important. The treatment, for example, of a child with low self-esteem caused by the depression of his mother who cannot sufficiently fulfill the selfobject function has to be different from the treatment of a child with a psychomotor disorder that makes life and competition difficult in the peer group. This mother also does not offer adequate selfobject experiences—but for a totally different reason.

Children with slight disabilities, whose neurological difficulties are unknown and undiagnosed, are considered to be intact and therefore experience nonsensitive and unempathic surroundings. Empathic surroundings are, however, as we all know, imperative for the development of a cohesive self-configuration (Kohut 1977, 1984). Because of this lack of knowledge, the parents cannot cope with the demands of the developing child, for whom this security-given bond is so essential. Attachment research has clearly proven (Bowlby, 1975; Ainsworth et al., 1978; Brazelton and Cramer, 1994) how extremely important a secure attachment is in the early years and how grave the consequences are when this secure attachment cannot be created. Only children with clearly evident handicaps in motor skills or sensory integration receive adequate treatment from their social environment. Concerning the patients described here, a lack of self-esteem, recognized by a teacher or doctor, is mostly considered to be the result of an emotional conflict between the child and his caretaker. The possibility that this child is suffering from a deficiency in his vestibular or visual system, which leads to anxiety with every movement, is often neglected. Because of disabilities in tactile, auditory, and visual perception, caretakers and the child's whole living environment are experienced in a different way: the child, perhaps subjectively, values and overestimates single aspects of a situation and obstinately insists on his perspective, or the child experiences the psychosocial events around him imprecisely and unstructured and therefore becomes insecure and anxious. These children cannot use their parents as empathic selfobjects because these parents cannot sufficiently mirror and offer adequate selfobject experiences and, therefore, cannot be used as idealizable selfobjects. They cannot fulfill the needed selfobject functions that they are willing to provide. Under these circumstances, establishing a strong nuclear self is difficult. Such a misunderstood child will always be more unhappy than an intact child who can use the "good enough" parent's capacities as selfobjects and who can confirm them in their parental efforts of being empathic and therefore effective. If this mutual mirroring is disappointing, the relationship dialogue can become derailed by continual misunderstandings. An unfortunate vicious circle may develop and stamp the developing personality. As long as sensitive parents instinctively feel this hidden deficit, it can be compensated for and/or accepted within the family frame so that the child seems to be intact. However, as soon as this trusted framework changes (i.e., playground, unfamiliar visitors in the family, kindergarten, etc.), the insecurity becomes apparent and the child reacts, depending on temperament, with anger, fear, retreat, whining, or aggression. Under these circumstances, beginning with the rebellious toddler years, the process of becoming independent is very difficult. The effects of these deficits become more evident when the child is on the threshold of preschool; the vicious circle of unhappiness continues to turn, and under increasing demands, the development becomes pathological. The child internalizes these demands from the adult world. His or her own expectations, often very high, lead to underachievements, and as a consequence, the child suffers from an enduring feeling of being hurt, of injustice, guilt, shame, and lack of self-esteem. The inner tension state is high; it allows little tolerance for everyday stress, not to mention large twists of fate. In difficult moments, this can lead to narcissistic rage with catastrophic reactions, because the self is fragile and the danger of fragmentation is high. Research on learning disabilities by Mannheim University (Esser, 1991) proved that the group of formerly impaired children, which resulted in extended school and career problems, is highly represented in delinquent, addicted, and mentally ill adults who have failed in life. As children, they were not picked up at the point where they really were in their development. They were always confronted with a false self-perspective: "You could if you really wanted to." An undesirable development and a fragile self was the tragic outcome.

The quality of attachment, beginning with the initial caretaker–infant bond, develops throughout childhood and is in fact a life-span issue. Stern (1985) assumed that there are clinical consequences concerning constitutional differences and emergent relatedness:

> The capacities that permit the infant to yoke his diverse experiences of the social world are to an enormous extent constitutionally—that is, genetically—determined. Either they are present right away or they unfold

> on an innate timetable, given an intact central nervous system and an intact environment. For the immediate future, the study of individual differences of these capacities may prove to be the most fruitful area of clinical research on the development of psychopathology in the very young. Whenever new capacities are identified, especially those needed in social perception and competence, they naturally become the focus of intense scrutiny, speculation, and hope. The hope is that the earliest deviation in social and intellectual functioning will be traceable to abnormalities in these capacities. If so, we would have an understanding of the underlying mechanisms that would help explain the emergence of pervasive developmental disorder, autism, later learning disabilities, attention deficit, character logical difference, and various problems in social conduct and competence. Discrete therapeutic strategies would also be more obvious.
>
> Let us look briefly at some possible clinical ramifications of deficits in these capacities. The capacity to transfer information from one modality to another is so central to integrating perceptual experience that the potential problems resulting from a deficit are almost limitless. One of the first to leap to mind is learning disabilities, since so much learning calls for a transposition of information from one sensory mode to another, especially back und forth between vision and audition. . . . Infants could also be socially and emotionally disabled by such deficits; intermodal fluency greatly facilitates the apprehension of the social behaviour of other persons as well as the integrated actions, sensations, affects, and so on of one's own self. These findings are still too new for one to have any idea, as yet, of the limits of their psychopathological relevance [pp. 188–189].

My own findings confirm these considerations of interaction and emphasize the importance of the quality of relatedness. The caretaker must have empathy at his disposal, as well as a well-functioning perception to decode the affect-motoric phenomena. If he cannot soothe and reduce the inner tensions caused by overwhelming irritations in the child, the child will be inundated by anxieties and negative affects. Especially with disabled children, the caretaker must be able to protect the child from these unbearable tensions. A later psychic disease is not primarily the result of the deficit: rather, the inadequate selfobject reactions, the lack of attunement and responsiveness, and therefore an insecure attachment lead to a weak and fragile self.

TREATMENT POSSIBILITIES

The referring doctors and the patients themselves want a precise diagnosis and a clear treatment plan. Normally, the widespread field of perception deficiencies is more a psychological and psychiatric area than a subject of psychoanalysis. Psychologists and psychiatrists are trained to observe and to deal with "external" behavior and reality.

But as a self psychological oriented psychoanalyst, I have to consider both—the external and especially the inner world of the patient—and to use empathy and introspection as informers. Kohut (1981) emphasized in his last speech: "In other words . . . 'put yourself into the shoes of,' think yourself appropriately into the inner life of another person, then you can use this knowledge for your purposes" (p. 142). The information collecting, psychological examination, data gathering via external observation, and empathy and introspection allow one to differentiate and to understand the roots and the triggers of the suffering. As a child analyst who works with patients who range from young children to parents, the level of empathy has to cope with all the different capacities and ages. A little child perhaps needs the body-close form of empathy, while his parents need the higher form of warm explanations or interpretations.

In the case of a child with neurological deficiencies, the analytic therapist, with a knowledge of neurocognitive problems and her insight in the inner world of the child, has a multidimensional role: sometimes she has to be a "case manager," staying in touch with teachers, occupational therapists, and others, placing herself sometimes between child, teacher, and parents and interpreting and "translating" the psychological and self psychological meaning of obvious difficulties. Sometimes it is not an analysis in the traditional sense, but it is an indepth treatment in the field of applied analytic self psychology (see Eldridge, 1996).

Of the 338 patients I have diagnosed, 43% urgently needed a basic therapy in the form of either an occupational, speech, or psychomotor physiotherapy. The neurocognitive problems had evidently led to related relationship problems that nobody had suspected. Only 30% of the children were treated in a psychoanalytic therapy; a lot of these children were simultaneously supported by occupational, speech, or psychomotor physiotherapy. The remaining families had understood enough through the five diagnostic sessions to be helpful to the child. They had experienced these hours as helpful toward self-help, and with deep relief, they realized the new emotional bridges to the child and his grateful response. They were no longer in the dark about the child's requirements, and they had regained confidence in their parenting. As parents, they could cope more sensitively and could guide the child more empathically. If there was only a slight perceptual deficit, free time activities such as horse riding, dancing, and self-defense sports were recommended because these actions stimulate and enhance body perception and perception organization in general.

In the cases that required therapies, I often chose a child-centered family therapy (Ornstein, 1999) as the adequate treatment form, especially when the child is young.

My task is to try to put the parents in the shoes of the children, which means to teach them to see and experience the world through the eyes of the children with their perceptual disability. I show them how important the empathic bridges are in everyday life and that unavoidable difficult situations can be mastered, so that the child does not feel totally alone and "lost in space" (Eldridge, 1996). In the case of perceptual deficits, it is almost impossible for parents to be "average" and "expectable" (Winnicott, 1962). This has severe consequences for the child's development and therapy. His environment must be intensively involved so that a "therapeutic milieu" can be created. It is necessary to work with the most important members of his environment. Kohut's theory of a self within an empathically responsive selfobject milieu insistently shows the ongoing mutuality and reciprocity between the child and his caretakers throughout his long development (Ornstein and Ornstein, 1985). Instead of continuous accusations, the child experiences attachment security because the caretaker has put himself in his "perception shoe." In other words, indepth psychological knowledge, knowledge of neurocognitive processes and of educational theory, as well as empathy, are necessary to cope adequately with these problems.

I found that, not only individual work, but parents in once a month groups can benefit from therapy. Once the parents are able to create a therapeutic milieu, they, in turn, can inform other caretakers about the proper response to these symptomatic children (e.g., grandparents, who so often play down these problems, teachers, etc.). Mostly, the parents have to work through their own sadness, disappointment, and shame because many hopes and expectations concerning the child's real capacities may not be realized. Similar to their children, they often have problems accepting and integrating the reality of the child's endowment (Palombo and Berenberg, 1996). This disappointment sometimes leads to disturbances in the child–parent relationship, but only the integration leads to psychic reparation.

This kind of psychotherapeutic session is sometimes a combination of teaching, counselling, and interpretations. Using only one aspect of these is bound to fail. Psychoanalysts do not like to be seen as counselors or educators, but in our work with patients who suffer from neurocognitive disabilities, we have to cope with these overlapping areas. Neglecting one of them would mean not fulfilling the therapeutic demands. It is extraordinarily noteworthy that because of early educative and self psychological interventions, vicious circles, which would end in a vulnerable and fragile self, can obviously be broken and the developmental process progressively influenced. In spite of these developmental disturbances, the caretakers acquire capacities to support their children with adequate responsiveness and selfobject experiences, which are necessary to build up a coherent self. In most of the cases, the parents realize that the symptom of the child is a very healthy reaction because, without symptoms, nobody would notice either the developmental or the self psychological need. They understand the symptom's deeper sense, that it is a chance for everybody, and they are happy that, via the symptom, they have received and decoded the alarm signal, not as SOS, but SMS—Save My Self.

REFERENCES

Affolter, F. (1987), *Wahrnehmung, Wirklichkeit und Sprache.* Villingen-Schwenningen, Germany: Neckar.

Ainsworth, M., Blehar, M., Waters, E. & Wall, S. (1978), *Patterns of Attachment.* Hillsdale, NJ: Lawrence Erlbaum Associates.

Ayres, J. (1979), *Sensory Integration and the Child.* Los Angeles: Western Psychological Services.

Bowlby, J. (1975), *Bindung. Eine Analyse der Mutter-Kind-Bindung.* Munich: Kindler.

Brazelton, T. B. & Cramer, B. G. (1994), Die frühe Bindung. Stuttgart: Klett Cotta.

Buggle, F. (1997), *Die Entwicklungspsychologie Jean Piagets.* Stuttgart: Kohlhammer.

Eldridge, A. (1996), Lost in space. Presented at the 19th Annual Conference on the Psychology of the Self, October 19, Washington, DC.

Esser, G. (1991), *Was wird aus Kindern mit Teilleistungsschwächen.* Stuttgart: Enke.

Heckhausen, H. (1971), Förderung der Lernmotivation und der intellektuellen Tüchtigkeiten. In: *Begabung und Lernen,* ed. H. Roth. Stuttgart: Klett, pp. 193–228.

Inhelder, B. & Piaget, I. (1977), *Die Psychologie des Kindes.* Frankfurt: Taschenbuch Verlag.

Kohut, H. (1977), *The Restoration of the Self.* Madison, CT: International Universities Press.

——— (1981), On empathy. In: *The Search for the Self, Vol. 4,* ed. P. Ornstein. Madison, CT: International Universities Press, pp. 525–535.

——— (1984), *How Does Analysis Cure?* ed. A. Goldberg & P. Stepansky. Chicago: University of Chicago Press.

Lempp, R. (1970), *Frühkindliche Hirnschädigung und Neurose.* Bern: Hans Huber.

——— (1982), Wenn das schwache Glied in der Intelligenzkette nicht früh genug erkannt wird. *Musik & Medizin,* 12:26–36.

Lichtenberg, J. (1983), *Psychoanalysis and Infant Research.* Hillsdale, NJ: The Analytic Press.

Milz, I. (1996), *Neuropsychologie für Pädagogen.* Dortmund: Borgman.

Oerter, R. (1995), Motivation und Handlungssteuerung. In: *Entwicklungspsychologie,* ed. R. Oerter & L. Montada. Munich: Beltz, pp. 758–822.

Ornstein, A. (1976), Making contact with the inner world of the child. *Comprehens. Psychiat.* 17:3–36.

——— (1999), Child-Centered Family Treatment: A Conceptual Framework in Child Psychotherapy. Brief course in child psychotherapy, March 6, Zürich.

——— & Ornstein, P. (1985), Parenting as a function of the adult self: A psychoanalytic developmental perspective. In: *Parental Influences in Health and Disease,* ed. E. J. Anthony & G. H. Pollock. Boston, MA: Little Brown, pp. 181–231.

Palombo, J. (1995), Psychodynamic and relational problems of children with nonverbal learning disabilities. In: *The Handbook of Infant and Adolescent Psychotherapy: A Guide of Diagnosis and Treatment,* ed. J. A. Incorvia & B. Mark. Northvale, NJ: Aronson, pp. 147–178.

——— (1996), The diagnosis and treatment of children with nonverbal learning disabilities. Child & Adolesc. Soc. Work J., 13:311–332.

——— (2001), *Learning Disorders and Disorders of the Self in Children and Adolescents.* New York: Norton.

——— & Berenberg, A. (1996), Working with parents of children with nonverbal learning disabilities: A conceptual and intervention model. In: *The Handbook of Learning Differences: A New View of Attention Deficit Disorder, Learning Differences, Issues of Intelligence,* ed. B. Mark, & J. Incorvia. Northvale, NJ: Aronson.

Rass, E. (2002), *Kindliches Erleben bei Wahrnehmungsproblemen. Möglichkeiten einer selbstpsychologisch ausgerichteten Pädagogik und Psychotherapie bei sublimen und unerkannten Schwächen in der sensorischen Integration.* Frankfurt: Lang.

Rheinberg, F. (1997), *Motivation.* Berlin: Kohlhammer.

Spekman, N. J., Goldberg, R. J. & Hermann, K. L. (1992), Learning disabled children grow up: A search for factors related to success in the adult years. *Learning Disabil.—Res. & Pract.,* 7:161–170.

Stern, D. (1985), *The Interpersonal World of the Infant.* New York: Basic Books.

Tewes, U., Rossmann, P. & Schallberger, U., eds. (1999), *HAWIK–III.* Seattle: Hans Huber.

Werner, E. E. (1999), Entwicklung zwischen Risiko und Resilienz. In: *Was Kinder stärkt,* ed. G. Opp, M. Fingerle & A. Freytag. Munich: Reinhardt, pp. 25–36.

Winnicott, D. W. (1962), *The Maturational Processes and the Facilitating Environment.* New York: International Universities Press.

Chapter 14

Tragic Man and Narcissistic Disturbance in the Films of Ingmar Bergman

Gordon A. Schulz

In *The Restoration of the Self,* Kohut (1977) hypothesized that the great artists address the crucial psychological issue of their era in their society. Kohut observed that the great European novelists of the nineteenth and early twentieth centuries dealt with the problems of Guilty Man, who was torn by his drives and internal prohibitions, and with oedipal disorders, which were characterized by neurotic conflict. These oedipal disorders developed out of the emotional overcloseness and rigidity of parent–child relations in the bourgeois family of the 1800s. In contrast, the great Western artists and writers of the twentieth century, such as Picasso, Kafka, and O'Neill, dealt with the problems of Tragic Man, who failed to fulfill his ambitions and ideals, and with narcissistic disorders, which were characterized by tendencies toward empty depression and fragmentation. These narcissistic disorders developed out of the child's emotional deprivation fostered by such social factors as the shrinking size of families and the increasing employment of both parents outside of the home, in response to

Special thanks to my friend and colleague, Catherine E. Wilson, Psy.D. for her helpful feedback on an earlier draft of this chapter.

increasing industrialization, since around the 1890s. Kohut (1977) speculated about modern artists: "The musician of disordered sound, the poet of decomposed language, the painter and sculptor of the fragmented visual and tactile world: they all portray the breakup of the self and, through the reassemblage and rearrangement of the fragments, try to create new structures that possess wholeness, perfection, new meaning" (p. 286).

In his art films, the world-famous Swedish writer-director Ingmar Bergman vividly represented, however intuitively or unconsciously, the problems of Tragic Man and narcissistic disturbance in the era after World War II. He did so partly by evoking a vaguely depressive mood and employing modernist aesthetics and a fragmented narrative style in many of his films. However, Bergman addressed the crucial psychological issue of his era most explicitly through his choice of subject matter. While his primary themes were broadly psychological, interpersonal, existential, and religious ones, an important secondary theme was mental disorder, including narcissism, empty depression, psychosis, and less severe forms of fragmentation. Psychosis alone is prominently featured in such films as *Through a Glass Darkly* (1961), *Persona* (1966), *Hour of the Wolf* (1968), *The Passion of Anna* (1969), and *Face to Face* (1976). Thus, one film scholar dubbed Bergman "The Disintegrated Artist" (Armes, 1976, p. 95). Another declared, "I doubt whether there has been a filmmaker who has done more for insanity, as well as for those lesser forms of neurosis and psychopathy that verge on and sometimes spill over into it, than Ingmar Bergman" (Simon, 1981, pp. 128–129).

The son of a Lutheran pastor, Bergman was born in Uppsala, Sweden, in 1918. Enchanted by a puppet theater and a movie projector as a child, he pursued a career as a director in the Stockholm theater and as a screenwriter for Sweden's principal movie producer, Svensk Filmindustri, as a young man. Beginning in the mid-1940s, he scripted and directed very personal films about youth, love, and marriage, but with limited critical and commercial success. Then, in 1956, he made an international breakthrough when his romantic comedy, *Smiles of a Summer Night* (1955), won a prize at the Cannes Film Festival. In the next few years, his existential allegory, *The Seventh Seal* (1957), helped inspire an almost cultish adulation, "Bergmanomania," in the art houses of the world. In the 1960s, his so-called chamber cinema, consisting of simple, compact dramas with a small cast of characters, cemented his standing as a leading European auteur, on par with Italy's Federico Fellini and Michelangelo Antonioni. In the 1970s, he scored his biggest box-office hits with the dreamlike *Cries and Whispers* (1972) and the realist *Scenes from a Marriage* (1973). In 1982, he announced his retirement from filmmaking and released his penultimate film, the life-affirming family saga, *Fanny and Alexander,* which is widely regarded as the summation of his career. Distinguished by his preoccupation with the dark side of the human condition, as well as by his dazzling artistry, and with over 40 films to his credit, Bergman has been hailed by some critics as the greatest filmmaker ever.

This chapter analyzes self-psychological themes in Bergman's films from his mature, classic period, from 1957 to 1982. In the course of viewing almost all of these films, I discerned four key issues that are related to Tragic Man and narcissistic disturbance. These issues are narcissism, traumatic de-idealization, empty depression, and fragmentation. Narcissism is illustrated most vividly and consistently in *Wild Strawberries* (1957), traumatic de-idealization in *The Seventh Seal* (1957), empty depression in *The Silence* (1963), and fragmentation in *Persona* (1966). Among the most critically acclaimed and renowned of Bergman's oeuvre, these four films will be discussed here, not exhaustively or even in their entirety, but with a focus on those parts that are relevant to the self-psychological themes.[1] First, though, the meaning, significance, and sources of Bergman's art as a whole will be explored.

BERGMAN'S ART

From the late 1950s until at least the late 1980s, no film director was written about more than Ingmar Bergman (Lauder, 1989). Partly accounting for this exceptional attention, Bergman was credited with bringing a new seriousness to the silver screen. "What was 'entertainment' became 'art'; the 'movies' became 'cinema,'" Kakutani (1983) explained, "and he also demonstrated the medium's ability to probe philosophical issues and interior states of mind" (p. 26). Moreover, some critics and fans perceived Bergman to be a modern-day prophet of sorts and his films as offering fundamental truths about the human psyche and the meaning of life (Gado, 1986; Timm, 1995). Simon (1972) singled out his unsurpassed mastery of sights and sounds, of the visual and aural aesthetics of film. Steene (1968) claimed that his main strength as an artist, apart from his technical skill, was his ability to create abstract, archetypal, and therefore broadly appealing

[1] Although *Wild Strawberries* was released after *The Seventh Seal,* it will be discussed first because its theme of narcissism is more basic to self psychology than the theme of *The Seventh Seal,* traumatic de-idealization, and because the latter readily segues into empty depression, which is the theme of the next film, *The Silence.*

characters in visually clear and emotionally intense scenes. However, his very intuitive films also resonated with the *Zeitgeist*. Indeed, Young (1971) observed, "In his own boreal and phobic way, Bergman has engaged that subterranean crisis of the spirit which we have agreed to call modern" (p. 283).

Not all of the attention that Bergman received was positive, of course. Common criticisms of his films were that they are esoteric, pretentious, obsessive, unrelentingly grim, overly subjective, and irresponsibly apolitical. In 1962, a rival Swedish director, Bo Widerberg, likened him to "a souvenir peddler selling Nordic brooding, metaphysical angst, and alienation to the world" (quoted in Cohen, 1993, p. xii). While recognizing Bergman for raising important existential questions, Donner (1964) suggested that his answers rang false because they were romantic and too individualistic. Kael (1968) called him "a tiresome deep thinker of second-rate thoughts" (p. 216) and claimed that his then-recent films "had been organized so subconsciously that they were only partly on the screen—the rest still in his head" (p. 214). Höök (1972) judged Bergman to be indifferent to the characters in his dramas, except insofar as he could manipulate them like marionettes. Although early on he was praised for the emotional depth of his female characters, in the 1970s feminists criticized him for the sexist aspects of his portrayal of women (Mellen, 1973; Steene, 1979). A Marxist interpreted his works as mystifying capitalist class relations by overgeneralizing "the conflicts and moral disintegration of the bourgeoisie" to all of humankind conceived as an abstraction (Bergom-Larsson, 1978, p. 8). Attesting to Bergman's formidable influence, one historian commented that "a large foreign public sees Sweden for better or worse through his eyes" (Derry, 1979, p. 389).

In the effort to determine the sources of Bergman's art, Kohut's (1977) identification of the sources of classical psychoanalysis is instructive. To explain why Freud developed a psychology of drives rather than a psychology of the self, Kohut cited three key factors: the prevalence of certain psychological problems, the style of thinking that dominated late nineteenth-century science, and the influence of Freud's personality. Analogous factors can be extrapolated to Bergman's art. One factor was the prevalence of certain psychological traits and problems in Sweden. Drawing on both quantitative and qualitative research, Daun (1989) found the following traits—all of which are common to Bergman's film characters—to be typical of the Swedes: emotional reserve, communication anxiety, interpersonal distance, pent-up aggression, seriousness, and melancholy. Daun attributed the historical development of these traits to a combination of natural and social forces, including the harshness of the climate, the sparseness of the population, the puritanism of the Lutheran Church, and the early psychological separation of children from their mothers. Cowie (1982) claimed that the social isolation associated with the sparseness of the population encouraged introspection and fatalism in artists like Bergman. Additionally, the industrialization that Sweden began to experience in the second half of the nineteenth century presumably fostered the development of narcissistic disorders in the country, as Kohut (1977) hypothesized about the West generally.

A second factor that informed Bergman's art was a mix of various elements in Swedish culture. The son of a Lutheran pastor, Bergman was steeped in the religious dogma of guilt and expiation through suffering (Steene, 1968; Cowie, 1982). Artistic influences included the dark, romantic nineteenth-century playwright August Strindberg and the early Swedish cinema, with its fantasy, dreams, and supernatural themes (Young, 1971; Cowie, 1982). A literary influence was the *Fyrtiotalists,* the nihilistic, antirationalist writers of the 1940s, who themselves were influenced by the French existentialists and such European giants as Eliot, Kafka, and Joyce (Donner, 1964; Young, 1971). Bergman was also affected by a national spiritual unrest that was fueled by the gradual decline of traditional Christianity, in the wake of advancing secularization and materialism, and by Sweden's "neutrality complex," its sense of guilt for not having fought Nazi Germany in World War II (Donner, 1964). Bergman could more readily devote his films to spiritual and metaphysical matters, to the exclusion of concrete social problems and political issues, because of the rising affluence, material security, and political complacence generated by the country's booming economy and welfare state in the postwar era. Given the spiritual unrest and the general satisfaction of basic human needs, the educated middle class and intelligentsia, if not others, were more inclined to go to movies about abstract, high-level concerns of life.

A third factor that informed Bergman's art, and certainly the most distinguishing one, was the filmmaker's own personality. In his autobiography, Bergman (1988) disclosed horrible childhood experiences, which presumably helped form his personality. Having almost died at birth and having suffered from several illnesses as a young child, he recalled that at the time he could not decide whether he wanted to live at all. He described an ambivalent relationship with his mother, marked by his alternately tender and hostile attachment to her and by her preoccupation, indifference, and rejection of him. He presented his father, the pastor, as a rigid perfectionist and authoritarian disciplinarian, who ritualistically whipped little Ingmar's naked buttocks with a carpet beater and then required him to kiss his father's hand to be absolved of his sins. Other punishments included the silent treatment, being shut in a cupboard, and when he wet himself, being forced to wear a red skirt. Bergman reported an antagonistic relationship with his older brother, who frequently beat him up. He also claimed that on the hospital grounds near where his family lived, he witnessed the corpses of patients in various stages of decay and loads of body organs and amputated limbs being cremated in furnaces. Bergman had commented on this experience previously: "For a child, it was traumatic, and I loved it" (Cowie, 1982, p. 9).

It can reasonably be hypothesized that Bergman developed a narcissistic disorder. When he was four years old, he attempted, unsuccessfully, to strangle his newborn sister, the object of his jealousy (Bergman, 1988). Chronic childhood problems included angry outbursts, faking illness to gain attention, lying, and difficulty distinguishing fantasy from reality. At age seven, he told a classmate that his parents had sold him to the circus; after the classmate exposed this fantasy-lie and thereby got him into deep trouble, Ingmar chased him around the playground with a knife. Bergman (1988) indicated that his tendency toward narcissistic rage continued into young adulthood: "If I felt attacked, I snapped like a frightened dog. I trusted no one, loved no one, missed no one" (p. 146). The actress Liv Ullmann, who was one of his leading ladies and lovers during his middle-aged years, described him as egotistical, controlling, and extremely possessive, with an explosive temper (Ullmann, 1977). He was also plagued by mental and physical hypersensitivities, phobias, obsessive-compulsive symptoms, and possibly even hallucinations (Cohen, 1993). Thus, having been deprived of adequate early mirroring and idealizable selfobject experiences, as well as having been subjected to abuse and humiliation, Bergman became predisposed to the temporary breakup, enfeeblement, and serious distortion of the self.

Psychoanalytic studies of creativity have mainly been based on the concepts of mastery, symptom formation, dreams, and object relatedness (Oremland, 1997). Most scholars have interpreted Bergman's films roughly in terms of the first three concepts, for example, as his means of mastering childhood trauma (Dervin, 1985); of venting aggression, gratifying a narcissistic wish for omnipotent control, and compulsively reworking his past (Cohen, 1993); and as dreams that reveal his inner secrets (Kinder, 1981). Bergman (1981) himself stated that "the practice of art is an exorcism, a ritual act" and that he has produced "dreams, sensory experiences, whims, fits of hysteria, neuroses, religious spasms, and a lot of pure lies" (p. 52). However, the fourth concept, object relatedness—or, modified somewhat, selfobject functions—also applies. Bergman (1960) suggested that filmmaking served an idealizable selfobject function for him when he disclosed that he aspired to be like one of the anonymous artists who participated in the collective effort of building a cathedral for the glory of God in premodern times. When he received Holland's prestigious Erasmus Prize, Bergman (1965) alluded to the mirroring selfobject function of his art:

> Artistic creativity has always manifested itself in me as a sort of hunger. . . . I remember from very early childhood a need to show what I had achieved; progress in drawing, the ability to bounce a ball against the wall, my first strokes in the water. I remember feeling a great need to attract the attention of the grown-ups to these manifestations of my presence in the physical world. I never, it seemed to me, excited enough interest in my fellow human beings. And so, when reality no longer sufficed, I began to make things up, regaling my contemporaries with tremendous stories of my secret exploits. . . . The need to get people to listen, to correspond, to live in the warmth of a fellowship, remained. It became stronger and stronger as the prison walls of loneliness closed around me. It was fairly obvious that the cinema should be my chosen means of expression [pp. 11–12].

NARCISSISM

In his seminal paper on self psychology, "Forms and Transformations of Narcissism," Kohut (1966) postulated the existence of a developmental line of narcissism, which he defined as the libidinal investment in the self, separate from the developmental line of object love conceptualized by Freud. Kohut identified two basic forms of narcissism: the narcissistic self, which is the source of ambitions, and the idealized parental imago, which is the source of ideals. He claimed that as narcissism matures, it is transformed into the qualities of creativity, empathy, acceptance of one's mortality, humor, and wisdom.

Wild Strawberries

Wild Strawberries (1957) is about a 78-year-old man, Dr. Isak Borg (Victor Sjöström), who drives through the Swedish countryside, from Stockholm to Lund, to receive a jubilee degree honoring his 50 years as a professor of medicine. Through revealing memories, dreams, and encounters that he experiences on his journey, Isak gains insight into his narcissism and the limits of its transformation into the mature qualities of empathy, wisdom, and acceptance of one's mortality. Bergman (1990) claimed that he based the character on himself, as he was, at the time, a loner "cut off from all human relations," although successful in his career (p. 20). Recognized as a classic of the cinema, *Wild Strawberries* won more awards than any other of Bergman's films.

The film opens with Isak introducing himself to the viewer. He states that he had an unhappy marriage, that his wife is dead, and that he has a son who is married but childless. Although he is grateful for his life's work, he discloses that he is lonely, as he has "withdrawn from nearly all social intercourse." He adds, "I am an old pedant often rather trying for myself and those around me," including his housekeeper, Agda. His comments hint at the narrow focus on work, neglect of interpersonal relationships, and undue formality characteristic of the obsessive-compulsive personality.

Isak then recounts a nightmare, in which a corpse that bears his likeness tries to pull him into a coffin. Apparently disturbed by this nightmare and the idea of his own mortality, he decides, on a whim, to drive, rather than fly, to Lund for the jubilee ceremony, so that he can stop by landmarks from his past along the way. Agda, who was planning to accompany him on the plane and who will now fly by herself, angrily suggests that he is one of many "selfish, crabby old men" who never think of their faithful longtime servants. His daughter-in-law, Marianne (Ingrid Thulin), joins him instead. Early in their trip, she pointedly, but coolly, confronts him for his lack of empathy and compassion, particularly in response to her recent marital problems: "You're an old egoist, Uncle Isak. You're utterly ruthless and listen to no one but yourself. . . . Beneath your benevolent exterior, you're as hard as nails."

Soon after, Isak and Marianne stop at the summerhouse of his family of origin. While Marianne goes for a swim, Isak, feeling nostalgic, dozes off in a wild strawberry patch and dreams about events from his youth. In his dream, he watches as his older brother, Sigfrid, tries to seduce Isak's sweetheart, Sara (Bibi Andersson). Later in the dream, he eavesdrops on Sara suggesting to her cousin that Isak is stuffy and aloof, whereas Sigfrid is naughty and exciting. Isak is then roused from his sleep by an exuberant young woman also named Sara (also Bibi Andersson). En route to Italy, she and her two boyfriends get a ride with Isak and Marianne. As the three hitchhikers evoke the love triangle from his youth, Isak tells them that he was once in love with a girl named Sara but that she married his brother.

Later in their trip, Isak and Marianne pay a visit to his 96-year old mother, while the hitchhikers wait outside. Isak's mother is a cold and bitter woman, who harshly criticizes her family and contemptuously refers to a photograph of Isak, Sigfrid, and herself as "rubbish." After they leave his mother's, Marianne drives, allowing Isak to sleep and to be "haunted by vivid and humiliating dreams." He dreams that his young sweetheart, Sara, says to him, as he is now, "Have you looked in the mirror, Isak? Then I'll show you what you look like. You're a worried old man who's soon going to die." When she tells him that she will marry his brother, he initially denies his hurt, but then he tearfully acknowledges it. Distinguishing his book learning from wisdom, Sara declares, "As Professor Emeritus, you ought to know why it hurts. But you don't know. You know so much, and you don't know anything."

In another dream, Isak is subjected to a series of bizarre examinations in a medical school setting. He flunks all of them, including one in which he misdiagnoses a patient as dead; the patient opens her eyes and laughs maniacally, mocking his empathic failure to recognize life in others. The examiner's verdict is that Isak is guilty of such offenses as callousness and selfishness—all charges made by his wife. Then the examiner leads him into the woods, where he witnesses, as he did in 1917, his wife having sex with another man, to whom she complains that Isak is as "cold as ice." In the end, the examiner rules that Isak's punishment will be loneliness.

When Isak wakes, the car is parked, and the hitchhikers are stretching their legs a little ways away. He informs Marianne, "I've had the most weird dreams, as if I must tell myself something I won't listen to when I'm awake . . . that I'm dead. Although I'm alive." His revelation prompts her to disclose that she is pregnant and that her husband, Isak's son, wants her to have an abortion because of his existential despair, which is rooted in his having been, in his words, "an unwanted child in a hellish marriage." She asserts that she nonetheless plans to have her baby because she wants to end "the cold and death and loneliness" that began with Isak's mother and continued with Isak and his son. Then, in an amusing, ironic moment, the three hitchhikers present a bouquet of flowers to Isak as a naive, idealizing Sara proclaims, "With these simple flowers, we want to say that we are very impressed that you've been a doctor for 50 years. We know that you must be a very wise old man who knows *everything* about life."

At the jubilee ceremony in Lund, Isak looks sad amidst the pomp and circumstance. Certainly, he experienced the mature transformation of narcissism into creativity, into professional work and achievement, recognized at the ceremony. However, he grieves for his impaired capacities for empathy and connection to others. Isak is a Tragic Man, who has only really just begun to understand and care about others, to gain the wisdom of old age, and to accept his own mortality. He tries to start afresh with his housekeeper by apologizing for his self-centeredness and by proposing that they drop their formalities and address each other by their first names. Although Agda rejects his suggestion out of a concern for appearances, she shows signs of a new openness to him.

Alluding to an idealizing selfobject experience, Isak tells the viewer that "if I have been worried or sad during the day, it often calms me to recall childhood memories." The film ends on a hopeful, poignant note, as he lies in bed and fantasizes about his young sweetheart, Sara, helping him—as he is now, an old man—find the parents of his youth. In the distance, his mother and father are fishing on a bank by a lake, and they wave to him lovingly, in a very picturesque scene. Basking in their mirroring like a young child, Isak, in closeup, looks absolutely serene.

TRAUMATIC DE-IDEALIZATION

In *Analysis of the Self,* Kohut (1971) theorized that the young child attributes perfection to the idealized object, the parental figure with whom it merges to feel strong, content, and whole. Normally, the child's idealization gradually diminishes in the face of optimal frustration and the real limitations of the idealized object. This gradual disillusionment fosters transmuting internalization—the child's development of new psychological structures that assume the functions previously performed by the idealized object. However, if the child's frustrations and disappointments are severe and unmanageable, transmuting internalization will be impaired. If such trauma occurs in the oedipal or early latency periods specifically, the child will develop a deficient superego and will forever search for external idealizable figures with whom to merge.

The Seventh Seal

Set in the fourteenth century, *The Seventh Seal* (1957) is a medieval morality play about an idealistic, but disillusioned, knight, Antonius Block (Max von Sydow), and his instinctual and skeptical squire, Jöns (Gunnar Björnstrand), who have returned to Sweden after 10 years in the Crusades, the Christian military expeditions against the Muslims in the Holy Land. As they journey through their homeland, which is ravaged by the Black Plague, the knight struggles with his belief in God, the meaning of life, and the black-robed figure of Death himself. Bergman (1990) suggested that the film was his means of working out a philosophical quandary, an intrapsychic conflict "between my childhood piety and my newfound harsh rationalism" (p. 236). The most celebrated of Bergman's works, *The Seventh Seal* is widely regarded as a masterpiece.

The film opens with a seahawk hovering in a troubled sky. On the soundtrack, an intensely urgent religious chorus gives way to silence and then to a narrator, who reads from the Book of Revelations: "And when the Lamb had opened the seventh seal, there was silence in heaven about the space of half an hour." Referring to Judgment Day, this ominous biblical passage sets the tone of existential angst that pervades the whole film.

On a rocky shore, the war-weary knight prays, while the squire sleeps. Suddenly and silently, the personification of Death, clad in a long black cloak and cowl, with a painted white face, appears before the knight. In an effort to save his life, the knight challenges Death to a game of chess on the condition that if he wins, he will be spared. Apparently intrigued, Death accepts the challenge. In one of cinema's most famous scenes, the two play chess against the background of a turbulent sky and sea. Their symbolic game spans almost the entire film, as they take breaks and resume play for brief periods at dramatic intervals in the story.

After the first break, the knight and the squire continue their trek home to the knight's castle. At a church, the knight confesses "my indifference to man" to a hooded figure whom he assumes to be a priest. He also discloses that he does not want to die because he is waiting to gain knowledge about God. Traumatically disillusioned by the Crusades, the knight is a Tragic Man tormented by religious doubts. "I want God to put out His hand, show His face, speak to me. But He is silent," he grieves. "I cry to Him in the dark, but there seems to be no one there." The supposed priest replies, "Perhaps there *is* no one there." The anguished knight responds, "Then life is a senseless terror." However, he wards off existential despair by recognizing that the respite that Death has granted him enables him to perform "one significant action" that can give meaning to his life. After getting the knight to disclose his strategy in the chess game, the supposed priest reveals that he is really Death! Seeing that he has been tricked, the knight is shaken at first. Then he recovers his narcissistic equilibrium, admires his own hand, and zestfully exclaims, "The blood is pulsing in my veins. The sun is still at the zenith—and I, Antonius Block, am playing chess with Death!"

Meanwhile, in another quarter of the church, the squire denounces the Crusades to a muralist. Explaining that the Crusaders endured all sorts of suffering "for the glory of God," he asserts, in an implicit attack on the knight, that "our Crusade was so stupid that only an idealist could have thought it up." Traumatically disillusioned like the knight, the squire consciously rejects ideals per se and adopts a defensive semigrandiose stance marked by a light-hearted nihilism. Thus, after he paints his self-portrait, he tells the muralist, "Here's squire Jöns: he grins at Death, chuckles at the Lord, laughs at himself, and smiles at the girls. His world exists only for himself. Absurd to all, even to himself. Meaningless in heaven, indifferent in hell." Despite these words, the squire later exhibits a basic human concern for others, or perhaps an unconscious adherence to chivalrous ideals, as shown when he prevents a rape and stops a mob from humiliating and torturing an actor.

When the knight and the squire exit the church, they come upon a barely conscious young woman locked in stocks. She is being punished for allegedly having had sex with the Devil and thereby inciting God to visit the plague upon the land. Obsessed with his quest for knowledge and indifferent to her suffering, the knight asks this supposed witch if she has seen the Devil, whom he wants to inquire about God; understandably, she does not respond. Later, when she is being burned at the stake, the atheistic squire challenges the Christian knight about her fate after death: "Who will look after that child? The angels? God? Satan? Emptiness? No—emptiness, milord!" The knight replies, "It cannot be." The squire presses, "Look at her eyes. Her poor mind is making a discovery: Emptiness!" Extremely anguished, the knight seems traumatically disillusioned by his own realization that the squire might be right.

At another point, the knight and the squire encounter a roving throng of religious fanatics, infected with disease, who bear crosses and lash themselves and each other. Like traumatized children with deficient superegos, these poor souls have turned to external idealizable figures, religious demagogues, who preach that the plague is God's punishment for their sins and that His forgiveness can be gained through self-flagellation. Commenting on such superstitious beliefs, the squire asks rhetorically, "Do they really expect modern people to take that drivel seriously?" The sad truth is that, yes, masses of traumatized people might take such "drivel" seriously because they desperately need to merge with idealizable figures, however irrational or hysterical, to obtain the selfobject experiences of guidance, support, and soothing.

Although the knight never resolves his religious ambivalence, he is eventually able to perform "one significant action," a noble deed, that fuses his ambitions and ideals and gives meaning to his life. He decides to save a loving family, whose warmth and hospitality had temporarily alleviated his existential angst, the reason for his self-admitted "indifference to man." While playing chess with Death, the knight knocks the pieces off the board, as if by accident. Consequently, Death is distracted, enabling the family, whose members were marked to die, to escape his reach. However, after Death reassembles the pieces, he checkmates the knight in his next move.

The film ends as Death claims the knight, the squire, and the knight's whole entourage at his castle. In another famous scene, Death, wielding a scythe, leads this group of people, all holding hands, in a macabre dance, silhouetted atop a hill against the skyline.

EMPTY DEPRESSION

In *The Restoration of the Self,* Kohut (1977) theorized that some parents fail to mirror their children and to offer themselves as targets for idealization because of their own narcissism.[2] This narcissistic unresponsiveness produces a tendency toward empty depression—the depletion of self-esteem and vitality—in the child. Empty depression can lead the child to develop an excessive sexual interest to fill an emotional void, especially if the parent is seductive. Similarly, in adulthood, the person may seek sexual stimulation and may even develop a sexual perversion to defend against underlying empty depression.

The Silence

The Silence (1963) is a chamber drama about the distant, strained relations between two adult sisters, the possessive, terminally ill Ester (Ingrid Thulin) and the sensual, rebellious Anna (Gunnel Lindblom), and Anna's emotionally neglected preadolescent son, Johan (Jörgen Linström), during their stay in a hotel in an unnamed European country. Following *Through a Glass Darkly* (1961) and *Winter Light* (1963), the film is the third and final installment of Bergman's bleak religious trilogy, even though it contains almost no explicit references to religion at all. Alluding to the decline of traditional Christianity, Bergman explained that *The Silence* represents the silence of an absent God and "the collapse of an ideology and a way of life" (Björkman, Manns, and Sima, 1970, p. 181). The film is most noted for its austere visual style, minimal plot and dialogue, and bold, controversial portrayal of masturbation, sexual intercourse, and homosexual incestuous desire. At the time of its release, conservatives objected to its sexual explicitness per se, whereas feminists have since criticized the film for reinforcing traditional prejudices against female sexuality in general and lesbianism in particular.

---

[2] For a compelling portrait of parental narcissism related to creative genius (Kohut, 1977), see Bergman's *Autumn Sonata* (1978), about a woman (Liv Ullmann) who confronts her mother (Ingrid Bergman) for having neglected her as a child to pursue her career as a concert pianist.

The film opens with Ester, Anna, and Johan riding in a train. The sisters' body language indicates their emotional distance from each other, while Johan seems lethargic. When Ester coughs up blood in her handkerchief, Anna tends to her, but she is clearly repelled. Because of Ester's condition, they get off at the next stop, in a mysterious foreign city, where they do not know the language and where signs of the military loom ominously.

In their hotel room, Anna is somewhat seductive with her son. She has him scrub her back while she takes a bath, and he rests his head on her back, revealing a deep, quiet yearning. They take a nap together, with Johan in his underwear and Anna in the nude. In the adjoining room, Ester smokes, drinks liquor, and listens to music. Hungry for emotional and physical contact, she lightly touches her sister's hair and her nephew's arm while they sleep. Back in her own room, her restlessness and need to soothe herself lead her to masturbate. She later gazes lustfully at her topless sister as she washes herself; perhaps her incestuous desire flows from a sexual perversion that defends against underlying empty depression. After Anna informs her that she is going out, apparently on the town, Ester fragments somewhat and has a brief, agonizing spasm. Downing more liquor to kill the mental and physical pain, she begs God to let her die at home. Then, regaining her composure, she says to herself, "I must try and eat something. I feel empty."

An unattended Johan wanders aimlessly through the dark, shadowy corridors of the cavernous, baroque-style hotel, where few guests appear to be staying. These corridors can be interpreted as an externalization of empty depression—"the world of unmirrored ambitions, the world devoid of ideals" (Kohut, 1977, p. 243). Lonely and bored, Johan, at various points, studies a painting of a naked woman, makes a monster shadow on the wall, urinates on the floor, whistles, kicks a piece of garbage, slides down the bannister, and plays a solitary game of walking on patterns in the carpet. Occasionally, he encounters strangers, including a janitor, a porter, and a troupe of entertainers. In contrast to his usual flat affect, Johan smiles and laughs when the kind, but presumptuous, strangers interact with him.

In their hotel room, Ester informs Johan that he will spend the summer and winter at his grandmother's home. When he asks if he will see his parents, his aunt assures him that he will see his mother and that his father will probably visit him "if he has time." Expressing the sadness and anger that he feels in response to his mother's current absence, he draws a picture of a face with a frown and fangs. After his mother goes out for a second time, Johan plays with his hand puppets and has Punch beat down Judy, explaining that Punch is angry. Overwhelmed by his feelings of empty depression caused by maternal neglect, he wipes the tears from his eyes and runs to Ester for a soothing embrace. Later, he asks, "Why doesn't Mummy want to be with us?"

Meanwhile, at a café, a waiter shows sexual interest in Anna, but she does not respond. Then she goes to a cabaret, where she witnesses a mostly clothed couple in the dark engaging in sexual intercourse—an illicit spectacle that both shocks and arouses her. She subsequently returns to the café and now signals a reciprocal interest in the waiter. She is next shown returning to the hotel, where Johan enthusiastically greets her. As Anna freshens up, Ester examines the dress that her sister just took off, notices that it is soiled, and drops it on the floor in disgust. Anna angrily tells her to mind her own business and to stop spying on her.

After Anna announces that she is going out again, Ester interrogates her about where she went before. Anna reveals that she had sex with a man in a church, a sacrilegious act that surely reflects the decline of religious ideals in contemporary society. Expressing sexual jealousy, Ester asks her sister not to meet the man again, nuzzles and kisses her cheek, and tells her that she feels humiliated by her tryst. However, Anna does meet the waiter again, in another room in the hotel. Having noticed his mother kiss the man and enter the room with him, Johan listens briefly at their door before once again wandering aimlessly in the corridor. After they finish having sex, Anna says, "How nice—how nice that we don't understand each other." Her statement refers to the language barrier and to her consequent ability to alleviate her empty depression, if only temporarily, through sexual activity uncomplicated by verbal communication and emotional involvement. Then she declares, "I wish Ester were dead."

After Johan informs his aunt of the whereabouts of his mother and the man, Ester goes to the couple's room to talk to her sister. Out of spite, Anna allows Ester to walk in on her and her lover, half-naked in bed. Then, in an angry, explosive tirade, Anna attacks her sister for her "principles" and her "self-importance" and for being "full of hate." Anna continues, "When Father died, you said, 'I don't want to go on living.' Then why *are* you living?" Critics have interpreted this first-ever reference to the death of the sisters' father as signifying Bergman's theme of the death of God, or the decline of religion. After Ester exits, the waiter and Anna engage in anal intercourse, a sexual act prohibited by Christianity that Bergman probably included to indicate the characters' "moral decadence."

On her deathbed, Ester confesses to the porter her aversion to sex with men and her consequent loneliness, but he does not understand

Swedish. The film ends on a cold, vindictive, and implicitly homophobic note, as Anna and Johan take a train home, leaving Ester to die in the hotel.

FRAGMENTATION

In *The Restoration of the Self,* Kohut (1977) theorized that parental unresponsiveness produces a tendency toward fragmentation, or regression from a state of cohesion to one of disorganization, as well as the tendency toward empty depression, in the child. The most extreme form of fragmentation is psychosis.[3]

Persona

Persona (1966) is a chamber drama about a needy and insecure young nurse, Alma (Bibi Andersson), who is assigned to work with a psychiatric patient, the famous actress Elisabeth Vogler (Liv Ullmann), who had suddenly become catatonic—psychotically withdrawn, immobile, and mute. In the course of their professional relationship, Alma apparently experiences an incipient psychotic process herself, in which she partially loses herself to, and merges with, Elisabeth. Bergman reported that his inspiration for the film was the resemblance between the actresses Bibi Andersson and Liv Ullmann (Björkman et al., 1970). The film was probably also informed by Bergman's own tendency toward fragmentation. Considered by many critics to be his finest work, *Persona* is widely regarded as a modernist masterpiece, with its experimental break from conventional form, particularly its mixing of fantasy with reality.

The film opens with a perplexing and disturbing montage of brief, disjointed images and dissonant sounds. They include the inner

---

[3] For an obsessive treatment of fragmentation and aggression, see Bergman's *The Passion of Anna* (1969), which features an animal-killing "madman," a vengeful mob that brutalizes an innocent man, and a romantic idealist (Liv Ullmann) who suddenly, inexplicably tries to strangle her lover (Max von Sydow), who, in turn, later tries to strike her with an axe, in an angry outburst that is only minimally motivated. The overall impression that the film gives is that human beings are naturally, inevitably, and incomprehensibly violent. As such, it exemplifies Bergman's main strength and weakness from a psychological realist view. His strength was his ability to portray the distilled expression of certain psychopathological experiences (e.g., extreme fragmentation and aggression). His weakness was that his obsession with these experiences led him to project them onto an excessive number of characters, who are not portrayed as adequately motivated to have them, making the characters seem more like abstract personifications of the experiences, rather than real, concrete, living people, and making the experiences seem more prevalent, independent of context, and mysterious than what they really are.

workings of a movie projector being turned on, an upside-down cartoon, a crawling tarantula, blood draining from a shorn lamb, a nail driven into a palm, snowy wooded grounds, corpses in a morgue, water dripping, and a phone ringing—all preceding the opening credits. Simon (1972) interpreted this prologue as Bergman's representation of his subjective experiences of Ménière's disease, an affliction of the inner ear that causes vertigo, and of his consequent hospitalization, during which time he conceived *Persona*. Whatever its sources, this montage sets the film's tone of confusion and dread.

Dressed in her nurse's uniform, Alma introduces herself to her new patient, Elisabeth, in the psychiatric hospital. Alma immediately starts talking about herself, perhaps in a conscious effort to engage her catatonic patient or perhaps out of an inadvertent looseness of professional boundaries. Foreboding the film's central dynamic, Alma informs the attending psychiatrist of her doubt in her own ability to work effectively with Elisabeth: "If she won't speak or move because she decides not to, which it must be if she isn't [physically] ill, then it shows that she is mentally very strong. I might not be equal to it." Indeed, the extreme nature of the challenge that Elisabeth poses is stunningly revealed when she calmly rips a photo of her young son in two.

In a therapy session with Elisabeth, the psychiatrist makes an interpretation of her catatonia that is informed by both Jung's concept of *persona,* the conscious role that an individual plays for others, and the theatrical concept of *persona,* the mask that an actor dons for a dramatic role. In a cold, smug manner, she explains that Elisabeth's immobility and mutism allow her to abandon the role-playing of her life: "At least you don't have to lie then. You can shut yourself in and stop playing games, show any faces or make wrong gestures." She asserts that Elisabeth's pathological negativism is also a role, which she encourages her to play until she loses interest. Reflecting Bergman's imagination and lay knowledge, the psychiatrist's interpretation is doubtful, or at least incomplete, because it does not relate the patient's psychosis to a traumatic stressor or injury. However, the anxious and angry body language that Elisabeth exhibits in response to the interpretation suggests that it captures the painful truth.

Subsequently, Alma and Elisabeth stay at the psychiatrist's secluded summerhouse by the sea as part of Elisabeth's treatment. As Elisabeth becomes less withdrawn and immobile, the professional boundaries between the socially isolated nurse and patient become loosened, initially shown by Alma's replacing her uniform with casual clothes similar to Elisabeth's. Then, in five back-to-back scenes, their roles are reversed as the still mute Elisabeth listens attentively to a needy and relaxed Alma, who talks incessantly—about her laziness, her nursing vocation, her affair with a married man, her group sexual encounter, and her subsequent pregnancy and abortion—and eventually breaks down and cries. As Elisabeth massages Alma's shoulders, Alma alludes to her unmet mirroring needs when she discloses that no one ever listened to her before as Elisabeth does now. Slightly tipsy, Alma rests her head on Elisabeth's shoulder and talks intimately to her as if they were lovers. Caressing Elisabeth's cheek, Alma reveals a fantasy fueled by idealizing, alterego (twinship), and merger needs:

> I've been talking all the time. How boring for you. You can't possibly be interested in my life. I ought to be like you. Do you know what I thought after I saw your film? When I came home, I looked in the mirror and thought that we are alike. You are much prettier, but somehow we are alike. I think I could change myself to be you. I mean inside me. You could change yourself to be me, like this [snapping her finger]. You would have too big a soul. It would break out.

Later that night, while Alma is in bed, Elisabeth appears, ghostlike, in a nightgown, in Alma's room. In a famous scene, the two embrace and caress each other's hair, and Elisabeth, standing behind Alma, leans down to gently kiss the nape of her neck. The next day, when Alma asks Elisabeth if she came into her room the night before, Elisabeth shakes her head no. Since nothing in the film suggests that Elisabeth is not telling the truth, it can tentatively be assumed that the erotic encounter between the two was Alma's dream—or psychotic fantasy.

Later that day, Alma presumptuously reads a letter that Elisabeth wrote to her psychiatrist. In the letter, Elisabeth states that Alma "is quite fond of me, even a tiny bit in love in a charming way. Besides, it's really funny studying her. Sometimes she cries over past sins—an orgy with strangers and later the abortion." Alma is shocked and humiliated by her patient's penetrating insight, superior attitude, and casual disclosure of the private, intimate details of her life, which she had shared with her in a spirit of confidence. Alma fragments and expresses narcissistic rage by setting it up for a barefoot Elisabeth to step on a shard of glass. At this point, the physical film itself appears to fragment, as if the heat generated by Alma's rage were melting it, burning a hole through it—a modernist touch that Bergman employed to illustrate the correspondence between artistic form and content. Then the conflict between the two women escalates into a physical fight, with Alma barely restraining herself from scalding Elisabeth with a pot of boiling water. Later, Alma begs Elisabeth for forgiveness, but Elisabeth ignores her.

The next part of the film features bizarre, surreal scenes. In the first scene, Elisabeth's husband acts as if Alma is Elisabeth. Alma initially resists his apparent delusion or charade, but then she enthusiastically joins in, even having sex with him. In the second scene, Alma delivers a monologue in which she explains how Elisabeth came to hate her son. The scene climaxes in a closeup in which the right side of Alma's face is grafted onto the left side of Elisabeth's face, which suggests a psychological merger of the two women. In the third scene, Alma, back in her nurse's uniform, adamantly insists to Elisabeth that she will never be like her. Then Alma cuts her own arm with her nails and allows Elisabeth to suck her blood, vampirelike, before Alma strikes her repeatedly. In the fourth scene, Alma coaxes Elisabeth to say her first word since the onset of her mutism: "Nothing." While the meaning of these scenes is highly ambiguous, they can be tentatively interpreted as Alma's fantasies or as metaphorical representations of the women's experiences. Wood (1969) speculated on their dramatic function:

> It seems to me clear that none of these incidents is to be thought of as literally "happening." . . . The doubt is as to the precise level of reality or unreality on which they are to be thought of as operating. Subjective fantasy? If so, whose? Bergman does not, I think, for reasons both thematic and formal, intend us to be able to answer such questions. By this point in the film the idea of the interchangeability of experience, of the identification of Alma with Elisabeth and of both with the spectator, has been carried about as far as it can go through an objective presentation of "real" actions. Bergman needs a means of finding a dramatic approximation for inner states of breakdown, disintegration and merging—at once the loss of identity and a kind of universal extention of identity [p. 152].

The film ends with Elisabeth returning to her work in the motion picture industry, apparently no longer withdrawn and mute, but for reasons that are not clear. Just before Alma, in uniform, leaves the summerhouse, she looks in the mirror and imagines Elisabeth sensually pulling Alma's hair off her forehead, as she had done in the bedroom fantasy; however, her vision of Elisabeth quickly dissolves. Alma smiles faintly, puts on her hat, locks up, and then catches a bus. Perhaps she can now begin to shore up her fragmented self.

SUMMARY

Distinguished by his preoccupation with the dark side of the human condition, the Swedish writer-director Ingmar Bergman was a leading auteur of the European cinema from the late 1950s through the early 1980s. His art was informed by the prevalence of certain psychological traits and problems in Sweden, a mix of various elements in Swedish culture, and his own personality, including a presumed narcissistic disorder. Many of Bergman's films vividly depict self-psychological issues that are related to Tragic Man, who fails to fulfill his ambitions and ideals, and narcissistic disturbance, which is characterized by tendencies toward empty depression and fragmentation. In *Wild Strawberries* (1957), Dr. Isak Borg represents a Tragic Man who gains insight into his narcissism and the limits of its transformation into the mature qualities of empathy, wisdom, and acceptance of one's mortality. In *The Seventh Seal* (1957), the knight embodies a Tragic Man suffering from traumatic de-idealization after his unsuccessful search for God in the Crusades. In *The Silence* (1963), Ester, Anna, and Johan, each in his or her own way, defend against underlying empty depression. In *Persona* (1966), fragmentation is exemplified by Elisabeth's catatonia and Alma's partially losing herself to, and merging with, Elisabeth. These intuitive portraits of Tragic Man and narcissistic disturbance illustrate Kohut's (1977) hypothesis that the great artists address the crucial psychological issue of their era.

REFERENCES

Armes, R. (1976), *The Ambiguous Image: Narrative Style in Modern European Cinema*. Bloomington, IN: Indiana University Press.

Autumn Sonata (1978), Produced by Persona Film and directed by Ingmar Bergman. Chicago: Home Vision Entertainment. Videocassette [with English subtitles].

Bergman, I. (1960), *Four Screenplays of Ingmar Bergman*, trans. L. Malmstrom & D. Kushner. New York: Simon & Schuster.

——— (1965), The snakeskin. In: *Persona and Shame: The Screenplays of Ingmar Bergman*, trans. K. Bradfield. New York: Grossman, pp. 9–15, 1972.

——— (1981), On dreams, the subconscious and filmmaking. In: *Film and Dreams: An Approach to Bergman*, ed. V. Petric. South Salem, NY: Redgrave, pp. 51–56.

——— (1988), *The Magic Lantern: An Autobiography*, trans. J. Tate. New York: Penguin Books.

——— (1990), *Images: My Life in Film*, trans. M. Ruuth. New York: Arcade.

Bergom-Larsson, M. (1978), *Ingmar Bergman and Society*, trans. B. Selman. London: Tantivy Press.

Björkman, S., Manns, T. & Sima, J. (1970), *Bergman on Bergman: Interviews with Ingmar Bergman*, trans. P. B. Austin. New York: Simon & Schuster, 1973.

Cohen, H. I. (1993), *Ingmar Bergman: The Art of Confession*. New York: Twayne.

Cowie, P. (1982), *Ingmar Bergman: A Critical Biography*. New York: Scribner's, 1998.

Cries and Whispers (1972), Produced by Cinematograph and directed by Ingmar Bergman. Chicago: Home Vision Entertainment. Videocassette [with English subtitles].

Daun, A. (1989), *Swedish Mentality*, trans. J. Teeland. University Park: Pennsylvania State University Press, 1996.

Derry, T. K. (1979), *A History of Scandinavia: Norway, Sweden, Denmark, Finland, and Iceland*. Minneapolis: University of Minnesota Press, 1995.

Dervin, D. (1985), *Through a Freudian Lens Deeply: A Psychoanalysis of Cinema.* Hillsdale, NJ: The Analytic Press.
Donner, J. (1964), *The Films of Ingmar Bergman: From* Torment *to* All These Women, trans. H. Lundbergh. New York: Dover, 1972.
Face to Face (1976), Produced by Cinematograph and directed by Ingmar Bergman. Not available on videocassette.
Fanny and Alexander (1982), Produced by Cinematograph and directed by Ingmar Bergman. Santa Monica, CA: MGM Home Entertainment. Videocassette [with English subtitles].
Gado, F. (1986), *The Passion of Ingmar Bergman.* Durham, NC: Duke University Press.
Höök, M. (1972), Ingmar Bergman: Craftsman and visionary. In: *Focus on* The Seventh Seal, ed. B. Steene. Englewood Cliffs, NJ: Prentice-Hall, pp. 16–24.
Hour of the Wolf (1968), Produced by Svensk Filmindustri and directed by Ingmar Bergman. Culver City, CA: MGM/UA Home Video. Videocassette [with English subtitles].
Kael, P. (1968), *Going Steady.* Boston: Little, Brown, 1970.
Kakutani, M. (1983), Ingmar Bergman: Summing up a life in film. *New York Times Magazine*, June 26, pp. 24–37.
Kinder, M. (1981), The penetrating dream style of Ingmar Bergman. In: *Film and Dreams: An Approach to Bergman*, ed. V. Petric. South Salem, NY: Redgrave, pp. 57–73.
Kohut, H. (1966), Forms and transformations of narcissism. In: *The Search for the Self, Vol. 1,* ed. P. Ornstein. New York: International Universities Press, 1978, pp. 427–460.
——— (1971), *Analysis of the Self.* New York: International Universities Press.
——— (1977), *The Restoration of the Self.* New York: International Universities Press.
Lauder, R. E. (1989), *God, Death, Art, and Love: The Philosophical Vision of Ingmar Bergman.* Mahwah, NJ: Paulist Press.
Mellen, J. (1973), *Women and Their Sexuality in the New Film.* New York: Horizon Press.
Oremland, J. D. (1997), *The Origins and Psychodynamics of Creativity: A Psychoanalytic Perspective.* Madison, CT: International Universities Press.
Passion of Anna, The (1969), Produced by Svensk Filmindustri-Cinematograph and directed by Ingmar Bergman. Culver City, CA: MGM/UA Home Video. Videocassette [with English subtitles].
Persona (1966), Produced by Svensk Filmindustri and directed by Ingmar Bergman. Culver City, CA: MGM/UA Home Video. Videocassette [with English subtitles].
Scenes from a Marriage (1973), Produced by Cinematograph and directed by Ingmar Bergman. Chicago: Home Vision Entertainment. Videocassette [with English subtitles].
Seventh Seal, The (1957), Produced by Svensk Filmindustri and directed by Ingmar Bergman. Chicago: Home Vision Entertainment. Videocassette [with English subtitles].
Silence, The (1963), Produced by Svensk Filmindustri and directed by Ingmar Bergman. Chicago: Home Vision Entertainment. Videocassette [with English subtitles].
Simon, J. (1972), *Ingmar Bergman Directs.* New York: Harcourt Brace Jovanovich.

——— (1981), Ingmar Bergman and insanity. In: *Film and Dreams: An Approach to Bergman*, ed. V. Petric. South Salem, NY: Redgrave, pp. 127–138.

Smiles of a Summer Night (1955), Produced by Svensk Filmindustri and directed by Ingmar Bergman. Chicago: Home Vision Entertainment. Videocassette [with English subtitles].

Steene, B. (1968), *Ingmar Bergman*. New York: Twayne.

——— (1979), Bergman's portrait of women: Sexism or suggestive metaphor? In: *Sexual Stratagems: The World of Women in Film*, ed. P. Erens. New York: Horizon Press, pp. 91–107.

Through a Glass Darkly (1961), Produced by Svensk Filmindustri and directed by Ingmar Bergman. Chicago: Home Vision Entertainment. Videocassestte [with English subtitles].

Timm, M. (1995), A filmmaker in the borderland: Bergman and cultural traditions. In: *Ingmar Bergman: An Artist's Journey on Stage, on Screen, in Print*, ed. R. W. Oliver. New York: Arcade, pp. 88–98.

Ullmann, L. (1977), *Changing*. New York: Knopf.

Wild Strawberries (1957), Produced by Svensk Filmindustri and directed by Ingmar Bergman. Chicago: Home Vision Entertainment. Videocassette [with English subtitles].

Winter Light (1963), Produced by Svensk Filmindustri and directed by Ingmar Bergman. Chicago: Home Vision Entertainment. Videocassette [with English subtitles].

Wood, R. (1969), *Ingmar Bergman*. New York: Praeger.

Young, V. (1971), *Cinema Borealis: Ingmar Bergman and the Swedish Ethos*. New York: David Lewis.

Chapter 15

The Applicability of Self Psychology to Psychotherapy with the Elderly: With Emphasis on Twinship Selfobject Needs and Empathy as a Mode of Observation

Hideki Wada

Although, in his last book, Heinz Kohut wrote, "Much remains to be done; we need investigations of the special selfobject needs of the elderly" (Kohut, 1984, p. 194), very few works have been published addressing the applicability of self psychology to the elderly. A noteworthy contribution to this small literature is Muslin's (1992) *The Psychotherapy of the Elderly Self.*

The relative lack of attention to the relationship between self psychology and the elderly is surprising because the needs of the elderly are a good fit with the approach of self psychology. Kohut (1987) asserted: "In old age, as one's powers narrow down, one naturally has

The author wishes to express sincere appreciation to Wolfgang E. Milch, M.D. for his thoughtful comments and suggestions that contributed to this chapter.

to husband one's forces and look after oneself. One is naturally more narcissistic, and therefore such narcissism is more adaptive" (pp. 8–9). Consequently, the selfobject needs of the elderly are heightened. Furthermore, the very nature of self psychology is its focus on both acceptance of interdependence and respect for the patient's subjective world. In my clinical experience, accepting elderly patients' dependency needs and validating their subjective experience are both essential for successful psychotherapy.

In addition, during the same period of time that Kohut's theory has developed and gained in acceptance, we have seen a growth in the population of elderly. And there is a great need for psychotherapy for this population. There are 10%–20% of community-dwelling elderly that express sadness or feel ill at ease (dysphoric mood), and close to 5% have a clinically diagnosable depression (Gurland and Cross, 1982). The percentages are higher for those in institutions providing long-term care: 12% are diagnosed with major depression, and 31% have significant depressive symptomatology (Allen and Blazer, 1991). Because antidepressant medication is often not tolerated by the elderly because of side effects (Gallagher and Thompson, 1982), effective psychotherapy is especially necessary for elderly patients.

I, as a geriatric psychiatrist, direct attention to the applicability of Kohut's self psychology for the psychotherapeutic treatment of the elderly. In this chapter, through the use of two case vignettes, I illustrate how I applied Kohut's self psychology concepts to the elderly, and I discuss how it is useful for psychotherapy with the elderly, especially in terms of twinship selfobject needs and empathy as a mode of observation.

CASE REPORT

The case that follows illustrates the importance of the twinship selfobject transference in the establishment of a self–selfobject bond in the treatment of a 71-year-old nursing home resident.

Mrs. U saw me twice a week for psychotherapy. She had a gait disturbance of unknown origin. Neurological findings, including an MRI, showed no abnormality. Believing the problem was of psychological origin, a neurologist had referred Mrs. U to me.

Mrs. U had had an illustrious past as a dancer and had married a very rich businessman. But his business had gone bankrupt, and after his death, she was left heavily in debt. When forced by her circumstances to work as a janitor, she fell down a flight of stairs and could no longer work. The welfare office referred her to the nursing home connected to the hospital in which I work.

At first, I focused on Mrs. U's assets and her wonderful past, and I tried to mirror her in those areas. She looked younger than her age, and she still had good posture. I praised her for these assets. But she didn't respond in a positive way to these interventions. Rather, she complained that I could not understand her pain.

In addition, unlike many elderly patients, she never idealized me. Instead, she blamed me for not curing her because I was inadequate. She had had every relevant medical test. Internists regarded her symptoms as psychogenic, and they didn't see her as a patient for their department. Yet she wanted to see an internist, not a psychiatrist; she didn't regard me as a doctor. She often told me that she wasn't a human being anymore, and she wanted to die from ordinary diseases, not from her present diseases.

After about six months of therapy, I was at a loss and felt sad for myself. At this point, I responded to her complaint about my inability to feel her pain or to cure her by saying that a doctor who cannot cure the patient also feels pain. She smiled for the first time in the course of the psychotherapy. After that, she showed her feelings more explicitly and talked more actively about her illustrious past. I then understood that after my comment about my pain, she experienced me as a human being essentially like her; that is, she experienced me as a twinship selfobject.

After her longing for a twinship selfobject was met within the transference, I came to understand the meaning of her earlier statement: "I am not a human being any more. I want to die from ordinary diseases." She was no longer beautiful and rich. She was no longer healthy and active. She had no friends among the residents in the nursing home, and the staff was far younger and healthier than she. Feeling so different from what she had been and so different from those around made her feel that she had lost her position as a human being among other human beings. Her sense of being outside of the normal human experience was exacerbated by being told by her doctor that her symptoms were not from an "ordinary" physical disease. I believe that she came to experience doctors, including me, as a totally different kind of people who never experience sadness like her. Once I expressed my feelings of sadness, she could feel that there was another human being who had feelings like hers.

When a patient experiences a twinship selfobject longing, he or she seeks an experience in which another human being serves the selfobject function of making him- or herself available for the reassuring experience of essential alikeness. This selfobject longing takes place when the patient feels estranged or singular. If such a patient can find the yearned-for soulmate who is essentially like him or her, this feeling of alikeness can alleviate feelings of painful singularity (Stolorow, 1994; November 1, 1996, personal communication). In this situation, the therapist serves the function of being a person toward whom the patient can feel, "I am like you," thereby providing the patient with the confirmation of having the status of a human being like the therapist.

Elderly patients often view themselves as very different from their therapists, especially when the therapists are far younger and healthier than they are. In such situations, some patients idealize their therapist. But in other cases, the patients feel that they could never be understood by the therapist because the therapist is so different. At yet other times, the patients feel envy for the therapist. In such situations, which can set the stage for therapeutic impasses, the establishment of a twinship tie can be a very powerful therapeutic agent. For example, if the therapist can communicate, "If I were in such a tough situation, I would feel the way you feel," this might provide the patient with the "confirmation of the feeling that one is a human being among other human beings" (Kohut, 1984, p. 200). In other cases, providing timely and proper interpretations might give the patient the feeling of being understood and, thereby, promote the twinship tie between the patient and the therapist (Stolorow, 1994). Sometimes appropriate self-disclosure by the therapist can lead the patient to experience the therapist as another human being like him- or herself (Wada, 1998).

In the treatment of Mrs. U, I had actually at times self-disclosed prior to the time I told her that a doctor who cannot cure the patient also feels sad. For example, I sometimes showed personal interest in her glorious past and its loss. I revealed that my grandfather had been a sculptor and had been reduced to poverty after the Second World War, communicating linkages between her experiences and my family. But she repeated, "You are a different kind of people from me. I am not normal. I want to die from an ordinary disease." These self-disclosures were probably not effective because my love for my grandfather who had been in a similar situation to hers did not resonate with her affective state. Rather, they just made her feel I was different from her, causing her to envy me and want to just extinguish me. My saying, "a doctor who cannot cure the patient also feels pain" was an effective self-disclosure because there was affective resonance, shared affect. Her twinship longing was met when I expressed a *feeling* that matched hers.

Not only did I not exist as a human being for her before she experienced me as a twinship selfobject, but I also could not experience her as a human being. When I saw this patient, I felt as if there was only one person in the consulting room. There was no patient. She was just forced to be there. I felt very little sense of psychological involvement with her. In Stern's (1985) sense, there was nonattunement, no intersubjective relatedness between this patient and me; there was no sharing of subjective experience between us. I felt not only sad, but also alone. I wanted to end the aloneness and be with her as a living person in my subjective world. Therefore, I had a twinship longing that I wanted to be a human being with her in the consulting room. I was at a loss how to find a moment of meeting with the patient (Stern, 1985).

Why does this kind of unshareability of subjective experience often happen in treatment with the elderly? I think narcissistic loss plays an important role in making such nonattunement with the therapist. Narcissistic loss is pervasive for the elderly. There is loss of mirroring from the environment caused by loss of respect because of retirement and so forth. There is loss of figures to idealize because of the death of parents or mentors and so forth. But, from my clinical experience with the elderly, the most serious narcissistic loss for the elderly is the loss of "confirmation of the feeling that one is a human being among other human beings" (Kohut, 1984, p. 200). The elderly often feel they are not who they were or are so enfeebled and aged that they are no longer human beings. Many elderly individuals struggle with feelings of differentness from others, especially when they are severely ill or when their physical functions are damaged.

For elderly patients who struggle with severe feelings of differentness, the twinship selfobject function is a very strong therapeutic agent (Wada, 1998). According to Robert Stolorow (November 1, 1996, personal communication), the affect states pertinent to the twinship selfobject function are those related to feelings of estrangement or singularity. These affect states can be transformed and then integrated as a feeling of being like others if they are responded to in a way that is attuned to the needs of patients for reassurance that they are like other human beings. This approach to psychotherapy with the elderly is a very important key for the establishment of selfobject ties with elderly patients. It is interesting to note that Kohut, himself, recognized the importance of the twinship selfobject function toward the end of his life.

The case of Mrs. U illustrates that when the patient experiences the therapist as a totally different sort of human being, the twinship selfobject function is a strong tool to break the therapeutic impasse.

In the next case, I will illustrate how another essential concept of Kohut's self psychology, empathy, plays an important role in psychotherapy with the elderly.

CASE REPORT

Mrs. M, an 84-year-old nursing home resident, was referred to me because of her delusion that her roommate, Mrs. W, a newcomer, occasionally stole expensive items (such as a Japanese kimono or rings) from her. Mrs. M was very intelligent, having graduated from college (which was very rare in Japan, especially for a woman, when she was young), and she had grown up in a wealthy family. She was proud of her intellectual gifts and the high social status of her family of origin, and she was known to be kind to other residents. Because of her fine reputation, some residents believed her claim that Mrs. W had stolen from her. But when the staff checked Mrs. W's personal belongings, none of Mrs. M's possessions were found. As a result, Mrs. M's accusations against Mrs. W were regarded as delusions. After that, Mrs. M believed the nursing home staff was conspiring with Mrs. W, and she complained directly to the president of the home.

When I first met Mrs. M, she talked a lot about her past, how high ranking her family was and how intelligent she had been. I listened and listened. After two months or so, she began to talk about Mrs. W having stolen from her. She told me that she had a relative who is a public prosecutor, so it would be easy to have Mrs. W arrested. But she refrained from doing that because it would cause trouble for the nursing home. I only said it was wise of her to refrain from taking legal action.

After that, I gathered information from the nursing home staff. I found out that Mrs. M was really from a noble family in Hiroshima. But her family's numerous real estate holdings had been destroyed, and her father had been killed by the A-bomb. After that, her husband left her. She had to go to work, and she reared her children in poverty. But she did so with dignity, intelligence, and pride. She was kind to everyone. After entering the nursing home, she had a good relationship with her previous roommates. One of them had a gait disturbance, and Mrs. M took care of her with much devotion. But when this roommate's legs got worse, she was moved to a special care nursing home, and Mrs. W moved in. Feeling guilty about his mother being in a nursing home, her son visited her very often and brought gifts or special food each time. With this information, I came to understand that prior to Mrs. W's arrival, Mrs. M could feel that she was queen of the room, a status that was threatened by Mrs. W's arrival because Mrs. W had advantages Mrs. M did not.

It was in this context that Mrs. M's delusion that Mrs. W was stealing from her developed. If only Mrs. W had stolen from her, it would devalue Mrs. W both because it meant that Mrs. W envies Mrs. M's beautiful and expensive belongings and because it makes Mrs. W a thief. Therefore, Mrs. W stealing from Mrs. M proves that Mrs. M is superior to Mrs. W, both financially and characterologically. By holding to this delusion, Mrs. M could subjectively maintain her status as queen of the room. But the public exposure of Mrs. M's delusion led her to feel that she was being regarded as a liar, which was greatly shaming for her.

With this understanding, I listened to what Mrs. M said, putting myself in her situation. From this perspective, I could understand that at this point what agonized her the most was the shame at being viewed as a liar. This situation subjectively necessitated the perpetuation of the delusion. As long as Mrs. M clung to the belief that Mrs. W stole from her, Mrs. M was not a liar. I said, "I can understand your pain that you are now regarded as a liar."

"Yes," she replied in a clear voice. "I don't care if Mrs. W stole some property from me. She is such a kind woman, I know. Rather, I now feel sorry for her. But I can't bear that I am called a liar. There is no one in my family who has ever done such a disgraceful thing! My family has been around for more than 300 years!" I did not gratify her complaint that Mrs. W had stolen her property, but I respected her subjective world and showed her that I understood how painful it was for her that her subjective world was rejected and she was regarded as a liar. After this session, she talked to me about her glorious childhood and how hard she had worked. Although the delusion persisted, it weakened to the degree that she never again complained directly to the president of the home or talked much about it to other residents.

Historically, psychotherapy is not considered very effective in the treatment of delusional disorders. Kohut (1977) himself asserted that the paranoid personalities are, in principle, not analyzable. It is true that, even if the patient idealizes the therapist, that is, even if the therapist functions as an idealizing selfobject, the therapist cannot necessarily cure the patient's delusions.

However, Kohut's (1959, 1971, 1982) concept of empathy as a mode or tool of observation is very relevant to the treatment of delusions. Stolorow (1994) has described this conceptualization of empathy as follows: "an attitude that consistently seeks to comprehend the meaning of a patient's expression from a perspective within, rather than outside, the patient's own subjective frame of reference" (p. 44).

In the case of Mrs. M, after I employed this mode of empathic investigation, I could understand why she needed to hold on to her delusion. Stolorow, Brandchaft, and Atwood (1987) asserted that "essential to the psychoanalytic treatment of psychotic patients is that the therapist strive to comprehend the core of subjective truth symbolically encoded in the patient's delusional ideas" (p. 134). In this process, the patient's "belief in his own personal reality can become more firmly consolidated. Concomitantly, we have found, the delusional concretizations become less necessary, recede, and eventually even disappear" (pp. 134–135).

After I could understand that what agonized Mrs. M the most was the shame at being viewed as a liar and that her subjective reality was rejected and I communicated this understanding, her delusion became less necessary.

The importance of adopting an empathic attitude of seeking the meaning of what the patient is saying "from the patient's subjective frame of reference" extends beyond the treatment of delusional patients to the world of the elderly as a whole. This applies because the subjective frame of reference of the elderly is often different from that of their surroundings, which is often dominated by younger people. In this way, empathy is an important tool for investigating and understanding the elderly patient's subjective world.

In the case of Mrs. M, how are we to understand the self–selfobject relationship? To explain this case, we need the concept of another kind of selfobject transference beyond those defined by Kohut. In fact, as self-psychological theory has developed, additional selfobject transferences have been offered. For example, Stolorow, Atwood, and Brandchaft (1992) proposed the concept of the "self-delineating selfobject transference," in which the patient experiences the therapist as a validator of his or her subjective experience. Stolorow (1994) specifically applies this type of transference to patients with a particular kind of early experience, stating that this type of patient is

> prone to fragmented, disorganized or psychosomatic states, for whom broad areas of early experience failed to evoke validating attunement from caregivers and, consequently, whose perceptions remain ill-defined and precariously held, easily usurped by the judgments of others, and whose affects tend to be felt as diffuse bodily states rather than symbolically elaborated feelings [p. 51].

Yet these states are very applicable to elderly patients, who often fail to receive validation from their current environment of their subjective experience. Rather, they are often regarded as help-rejecting complainers or as having psychosomatic or other kinds of delusions.

It was the self-delineating selfobject transference that helped Mrs. M to let go of her delusion. Yet after her delusion receded, I continued to validate her experience in other areas. For instance, Mrs. M sometimes complained of psychosomatic symptoms, such as low back pain, gait disturbance, or dizziness. When she complained about such symptoms, I never labeled such symptoms as "psychological ones" but listened attentively to her complaint and validated her subjective pains. After some time, her symptoms usually dissipated.

If the therapist is experienced by the patient as providing the missing and longed-for validation of his or her psychic reality, this often alleviates the patient's symptoms. In order to facilitate the emergence of such a self–selfobject tie, the therapist needs to articulate the patient's subjective experience, always from the patient's perspective. In my clinical experience, especially in the early phase of psychotherapy, this kind of self-delineating selfobject function is needed. In order to establish this type of transference, the therapist should listen empathically to the patient without making any suggestions from his or her own judgment.

DISCUSSION

After presenting two cases that illustrate relevant aspects of self psychology to the psychotherapy of the elderly, I will discuss the differences between self psychology and traditional psychoanalytic theory in terms of their advantages in providing psychotherapy for the elderly. Within this discussion, I will address some connections between self psychology and Japanese culture.

Kohut's most revolutionary revision of psychoanalytic theory is acceptance of human dependency needs. Kohut not only accepted dependence as a universal form of human relationship but also regarded it as necessary for human psychological survival. This is conveyed in his famous quote: "A move from dependence (symbiosis) to independence (autonomy) in the psychological sphere is no more possible, let alone desirable, than a corresponding move from a life dependent on oxygen to a life independent of it in the biological sphere" (Kohut, 1984, p. 47).

Kohut understood well the adaptive aspect of narcissism for the elderly. According to this view, one can utilize others for narcissistic purposes, one can depend on others, and "the best dying man's helper is the kind of person who continues to give narcissistic supplies to the dying person" (Kohut, 1987, p. 63).

Old persons experience a lot of narcissistic loss. Narcissistic loss is "the loss of anything that has been relied upon to sustain one's sense of self-cohesion, self-continuity, or self-esteem. For example, loss of selfobject ties, loss of capacities, loss of status, or loss of sources of admiration" (Stolorow, February 12, 1997, personal communication). It is clear from this list that old age is associated with these types of losses, and providing narcissistic support, not only by accepting the dependency needs of the elderly but by maintaining an attitude of respect toward the elderly, should alleviate the torment of the elderly.

In contrast, in classical ego psychology, the strength and autonomy of the ego are emphasized, including for the elderly. For example, in Erikson's (1982) epigenesis model, the developmental task for the elderly is achieving "integrity," acquiring wisdom, a difficult task for the elderly patient with an enfeebled body, deflated self-esteem, and decreased brain function.

Some traditional psychoanalysts have reported successful psychoanalyses in old age: Sandler (1984) emphasized structural change; Limentani (1995) stressed the creativity of the elderly; King (1980) asserted the possibility of ego growth in the elderly along with the life cycle; and Simburg (1985) highlighted adaptation to the developmental task. However, the cases presented by these authors are of patients in their 60s, who are therefore younger than the patients whose cases have been used to illustrate the points in this chapter. Settlage (1996), a Mahlerian ego psychologist, reported the psychoanalysis of a very old patient, which began when the patient was 94 and concluded with her death at the age of 104. Although he emphasized the acquisition of wisdom, in his conclusion, the list of the patient's achievements in the analysis began with "acceptance of necessary dependency" (p. 561). Thus, even when a traditional psychoanalytic approach is used for the very old ideas that are central to self psychology, human dependency needs emerge in a report of a successful psychotherapy. How to depend on others, how to utilize others for narcissistic purposes, is a crucial theme of old age, and self psychology provides a conceptual understanding of the process.

In Japanese culture, interdependency has traditionally been widely accepted (Johnson, 1993). *Amae* is "the ability and prerogative of an individual to presume or depend upon the benevolence of another" (p. 63). The environment should meet one's dependency needs to be cherished and have security, and at the same time, one should wait for recognition of one's expectation without requesting it overtly by verbal expression. This form of dependency is allowed to remain manifest throughout the lifespan, including old age. As part of this, in Japanese culture, the elderly can expect others to satisfy their dependency needs more than in western culture.

In addition, in Japan, under the influence of Confucianism, elderly people have received a high level of respect. Therefore, the elderly in Japan can expect others to meet their needs for mirroring. Under these circumstances, Japanese elderly can lead easier lives than the western elderly. The longevity of the Japanese, especially their healthy longevity, might result from these circumstances.

The westernization of Japanese culture has, however, led to an emphasis on autonomy and individualism and a diminishment of respect for the elderly. Under these circumstances, Kohut's ideas of supporting narcissism are increasingly relevant to psychotherapy for the elderly in Japan.

Beyond the recognition of interdependency needs function, another feature of Kohut's self psychology relevant to the elderly is the focus on the patient's subjective experience. Classical psychoanalysis tends to regard patients' subjective worlds as distorted by their unconscious, id, or superego, and it stresses that this distorted experience should be corrected by proper interpretation. Kohut challenged this view, declaring in his last book (Kohut, 1984):

> If there is one lesson that I have learned during my life as an analyst, it is the lesson that what my patients tell me is likely to be true—that many times when I believed that I was right and my patients were wrong, it turned out, though often after a prolonged search, that my rightness was superficial whereas their rightness was profound [pp. 93–94].

This view is especially applicable for psychotherapy with the elderly. For these patients, because of their retreat from social activity and loss of intimate surroundings, there are fewer resources for validating their subjective experience. A common countertransference issue for therapists working with the elderly is the imposition of the therapist's judgment on the patient (Malamud, 1996), which interferes with the therapist's ability to understand what the patient is really experiencing. For example, not all of what the elderly are experiencing is pain. They can also enjoy their lives and feel pleasure in what they are experiencing. Therefore, to avoid such countertransferential judgment, it is crucial that therapists adopt an attitude of empathic observation, that is, strive to see patients' experiences from their perspective and to respect their subjective experiences.

CONCLUSION

Self-psychological theory is very relevant to and promising for the psychotherapeutic treatment of elderly patients for two reasons. First, acceptance of patients' dependency needs is a core tenet of self psychology. By serving selfobject functions for elderly patients, therapists can compensate for these patients' narcissistic losses and help these patients develop their subjective world, which leads to a richer psychological life.

Second, respecting the patients' subjective reality is intrinsic to self psychology. Empathic investigation of the elderly will provide us with greater understanding of the mind of the elderly. This will help to validate the subjective realities of our patients, which will help them to enhance their sense of self-cohesion or self-continuity and lead to growth in the body of knowledge about the elderly to help a broader range of the elderly. With this approach, even very old patients with an enfeebled body and decreased brain function can benefit from psychotherapy.

With the development of clinical practice and theory within self psychology, I believe that this branch of psychoanalysis will become increasingly applicable to the elderly.

REFERENCES

Allen, A. & Blazer, D. G. (1991), Mood disorders. In: *Comprehensive Review of Geriatric Psychiatry,* ed. J. Sadavoy, L. W. Lazarus & L. F. Jarvik. Washington, DC: American Psychiatric Press, pp. 337–351.

Erikson, E. H. (1982), *The Life Cycle Completed.* New York: Norton.

Gallagher, D. & Thompson, L. W. (1982), Differential effectiveness of psychotherapies for treatment of major depressive disorder in older adult patients. *Psychotherapy,* 19:482–490.

Gurland, B. J. & Cross, P. S. (1982), Epidemiology of psychopathology in old age: Some implications for clinical services. *Psychiat. Clinics N. Amer.,* 5:11–26.

Johnson, F. A. (1993), *Dependency and Japanese Socialization: Psychoanalytic and Anthropological Investigations into* Amae. New York: New York University Press.

King, P. (1980), The life cycle as indicated by the nature of the transference in the psychoanalysis of the middle-aged and elderly. *Internat. J. Psycho-Anal.,* 61: 153–160.

Kohut, H. (1959), Introspection, empathy and psychoanalysis. *J. Amer. Psychoanal. Assn.,* 7:459–483.

——— (1971), *The Analysis of the Self: A Systematic Approach to Psychoanalytic Treatment of Narcissistic Personality Disorders.* New York: International Universities Press.

——— (1977), *The Restoration of the Self.* New York: International Universities Press.

——— (1982), Introspection, empathy and the semicircle of mental health. *Internat. J. Psycho-Anal.,* 63:395–407.

——— (1984), *How Does Analysis Cure?* ed. A. Goldberg & P. Stepansky. Chicago: University of Chicago Press.

——— (1987), *The Kohut Seminars: On Self Psychology and Psychotherapy with Adolescents and Young Adults,* ed. M. Elson. New York: Norton.

Limentani, A. (1995), Creativity and the third age. *Internat. J. Psychoanal.,* 76: 825–833.

Malamud, W. I. (1996), Countertransference issues with elderly patients. *J. Geriatric Psychiat.,* 29:33–41.

Muslin, H. L. (1992), *The Psychotherapy of the Elderly Self.* New York: Brunner/ Mazel.

Sandler, A. M.(1984), Problems of development and adaptation in an elderly patient. *The Psychoanalytic Study of the Child,* 39:471–489. New York: International Universities Press.

Settlage, C. F. (1996), Transcending old age: Creativity, development and psychoanalysis in the life of a centenarian. *Internat. J. Psychoanal.,* 77:549–564.

Simburg, E. J. (1985), Psychoanalysis of the older patient. *J. Amer. Psychoanal. Assn.*, 33:117–132.

Stern, D. N. (1985), *The Interpersonal World of the Infant*. New York: Basic Books.

Stolorow, R. D. (1994), The nature and therapeutic action of psychoanalytic interpretation. In: *The Intersubjective Perspective*, ed. R. D. Stolorow, G. E. Atwood & B. Brandchaft. Northvale, NJ: Aronson, pp. 43–55.

——— Atwood, G. E. & Brandchaft, B. (1992), Three realms of the unconscious and their therapeutic transformation. *Psychoanal. Rev.*, 79:25–38.

——— Brandchaft, B. & Atwood, G. E. (1987), *Psychoanalytic Treatment: An Intersubjective Approach*. Hillsdale, NJ: The Analytic Press.

Wada, H. (1998), The loss and restoration of the sense of self in an alien culture: An application of the concept of the twinship selfobject function. In: *The World of Self Psychology: Progress in Self Psychology, Vol. 14*, ed. A. Goldberg. Hillsdale, NJ: The Analytic Press, pp. 107–123.

IV

A Personal Memoir

Chapter 16

A Personal and Professional Reminiscence of Heinz Kohut

Constance Goldberg

I am writing this chapter as a bit of a dinosaur or perhaps a relic of a former era. Once upon a time, in the 1960s and 1970s, I knew Heinz Kohut as an accidental friend and colleague. That description may strike some as self-deprecating, devaluing, and all those other frowned-upon descriptions of one's self-state. Instead, I am deeply grateful that some of the choices that I made early in my personal and professional life resulted in my being included in a small group of friends of Heinz Kohut. My life has been the richer for it in ways that I can only begin to express.

Let me tell you something of the tale itself—with a bow to narrative theory. In the fall of 1968, with more apprehension than you can imagine, I began what would become a 10-year stint as a social worker in the clinic of the Institute for Psychoanalysis of Chicago. The first few months were spent in a haze of unbridled transferences toward every analyst whose path I crossed at 180 North Michigan, including that of Heinz Kohut, whose office was right down the hall from mine and whom I barely knew at all until the following spring. In May of 1969, the spring meetings of the American Psychoanalytic Association were held in Miami Beach, Florida; one of the perks of being a social worker at the Institute was the opportunity to attend these meetings, and although I was low person on the totem pole, as it were, it was decided that I was the one to go.

As I was preparing to leave, Dr. Fred Robbins, the medical director of the clinic, suggested to me that I might be interested in hearing the presentation that Dr. Kohut was going to make at the meetings to a small group of his colleagues. Fred said something about Heinz having been busy at work on some new ideas that he would be presenting to some of the more senior people in the American. Fred said that all I needed to do was ask his permission. So, on the morning of the workshop, I rather hesitantly approached Kohut as he was having breakfast by the pool of the hotel and, in effect, said that Fred had sent me. Although we had exchanged nods in the halls of 180, I don't believe that we had been introduced, but he greeted me very warmly and said that of course I would be welcome at the workshop.

At 4 P.M., I went to the appointed room. As I walked through the door, a very officious analytic gatekeeper came forward, looked at my nametag, and then announced that only analysts would be permitted in this session. Bear in mind that I was 28 years old and felt about 14. As I was attempting, without much conviction, to explain that I had been invited, Heinz looked over toward the door, jumped up from his chair, and proceeded to deliver a heated dressing down to the astonished analyst. He then ushered me to a seat and went around the end of the table to take his own chair.

There then took place one of the most amazing experiences of my professional life, an experience that might be described as an epiphany. For three hours, without interruption, Kohut laid out the major ideas in what would eventually become *The Analysis of the Self* (1971). He spoke at length about the role of empathy in his unfolding theory, about its crucial importance in defining the perimeters of a depth-psychological approach to the understanding of another human being. He explained that empathy, defined by him as vicarious introspection, is indeed the only way that we have of knowing about the psychological depths of another person. Remember that this was 1969—years before his terse and yet emphatic reexamination of the concept of empathy that would see the light of day at his final public appearance in Berkeley in 1981 and then again in the posthumously published paper, "Introspection, Empathy, and the Semi-Circle of Mental Health" (1982).

In this riveting presentation in 1969, Kohut spoke with great energy and conviction about his understanding of the need to consider the self of the person as being the primary focus of our attention. The cohesion of the self as well as its propensity for fragmentation, were discussed as were, of course, the two major constituent poles of the self—mirroring and idealization. It was not until later that the twinship function joined the first two as a full partner in understanding the needs and functions of the self.

Kohut spoke firmly of his belief that the phenomenon of the drives had no basis in the actual physical make-up of the person and that when evidence of these "drives" was seen in the clinical situation, it was an indication that the self was in a state of fragmentation. He explained that he believed that Freud had developed the concept of the drives and then held onto them over the years because he had been, first and foremost, a physician whose findings needed to be firmly placed within the physical realm in order for them to be heard with any modicum of receptivity by his physician colleagues. In this presentation, Kohut was foreshadowing a position that was to be expanded upon much more fully in the years ahead, namely, that he believed that his ideas were a way of positioning psychoanalytic theory definitively within the psychological realm and removing it from the world of physical explanations where he felt it did not belong. This debate is now being held between those who essentially agree with the limits of psychology as outlined by Kohut and expanded upon by his intellectual descendants and those who feel that the increasing knowledge of the physical make-up of the brain will eventually supplant psychological explanations.

Back for a moment to Miami Beach. Why was this intense late afternoon meeting such a revelation to me? There is a long and a short answer to this question, and so I will settle on an intermediate one. Let me begin with the internal reasons first by saying that I felt strongly that this energetic, intense, creative, and, yes, empathic man would in his consulting room make absolutely every effort to understand me if I were to be in that situation. His focus on the centrality of the self as opposed to the more isolated or fragmentary interest in the drives resonated strongly with me and would remain central throughout my association with him and beyond. That I was so taken with the novelty of his approach could, of course, be seen as having personal antecedents in my own history. Furthermore, at the time of this meeting in Miami Beach, I was in analysis with a very competent analyst who, of course, was not a self psychologist since none then existed, but who was conducting my analysis in a manner that seemed at considerable variance from what I had read about analytic theory and heard from the experience of others; although I didn't understand it, I was just relieved that this was the case. It was only considerably later that both he and I came to understand, to paraphrase the famous gentleman in Molière's *Le Bourgeois Gentilhomme,* that we had been speaking self psychology all along! My questions to him were often answered, silences were present but not endlessly endured, and in many ways there was the presence of what Kohut (1971) would have called sufficient psychological oxygen. I would not have done well as a patient with the degree of abstinence that, in the mid-1960s, was still the order of the day in many analyses.

Accompanying my personal responses to the meaning of Kohut's presentation was a parallel professional response. I had received my social work education in the early 1960s from Columbia University and was eternally grateful for the stimulating academic environment and fieldwork assignments that were part of a very carefully crafted clinical curriculum. To have Florence Hollis as a teacher while she was writing the second edition of her book on casework (1964) was a rare treat, and there were others; however, for those of you much younger than I, it may be hard to envision the nature of the psychoanalytic theory that was earnestly taught to us. I think of it as hard-core Freud, with a bow here and there to ego psychology. What I did—and I really don't think I was the only one!—was to learn what I could, pass the tests, and then go to my fieldwork assignment. My first was in the Department of Welfare in the Bronx where my down-to-earth and smart fieldwork instructor helped me to be of some help to those under my care. And Freud's presence was barely felt.

Remember, I'm only speaking for myself, but what happened for me in school and then continued in my first job at the Institute for Juvenile Research in Chicago was that I simply split off most theoretical constructs from my clinical experience, while retaining the capacity to write up cases that included the most commonly used formulations and seemed to pass muster with the powers that be. It wasn't that these formulations were wrong, but more discouragingly, they seemed irrelevant. Bear in mind that all of this was not something that was causing me great anguish at the time; I just thought that this was the way it was for everyone.

It was with all of this as background that I heard and responded to Heinz Kohut as I did. It slowly began to dawn on me during that memorable afternoon that he was suggesting something entirely radical or, at the very least, at variance with my heretofore experienced way of thinking about theory. Theory did not have to be, in his words, experience distant, but instead, experience near (1984). Theory could be a true organizer of the clinical situation, as I regarded the experience of both the patient and myself. I felt some intimation that the days were numbered for my having to go through the motions in a formulaic exercise to try to make links between theory and my clinical practice; vaguely, I began to sense that this theory could enliven my understanding of my patients and of my interactions with them. It was a sense of my professional world opening up, and I will never forget it.

So why, you might ask, did *you* respond this way and not every colleague who heard Kohut speak or read what he wrote? First, let me just say that to hear Heinz speak was an amazing experience. He was charismatic in a manner for which there is absolutely no clue in his written words. The cumbersome Germanic sentence structure was there as he spoke, but it was infused with the vibrant enthusiasm of a master storyteller. I remember many times being in the audience when, in response to a question, Heinz would weave such a complex answer, go off on so many tangents, that no one thought he would ever return to the question at hand, yet return he would, and it was stunning.

The question about why some responded so positively to Heinz and the psychology of the self and others so negatively or indifferently is basically an unanswerable question and one that perplexed Heinz no end. I remember sitting in Jerome's Restaurant in Chicago one snowy February evening with my husband and the Kohuts and listening to Heinz present his puzzlement about just this matter. He described an analytic colleague who had gone to great pains to read everything Heinz had written and yet clearly did not get it. Nothing enraged him more than criticism from those who clearly did not bother to read what he had written and yet were not thereby constrained by this fact from having all kinds of negative opinions. But toward the colleague under discussion at Jerome's, Heinz had a certain respect because of the effort he had expended in an attempt to understand these new ideas. The only conclusion he came to was that there has to be some kind of resonance between a theory and the person attempting to make use of it if the theory is going to exist as more than just an intellectual exercise. For whatever reason, such resonance was lacking with this colleague.

Many have read Charles Strozier's biography, *Heinz Kohut: The Making of a Psychoanalyst* (2001), which so beautifully tells the tale of Kohut's early years in Vienna, his schooling there, his traumatic departure from the city that he so loved, and his professional and personal life first at the University of Chicago and then at the Institute for Psychoanalysis. This book is filled with a psychohistorian's fine eye for detail and, even more important, with well-buttressed theories about why Kohut developed a theory of the self that he eventually came to believe was the overarching explanation of human experience as understood psychologically.

At one point, Strozier states that it is his belief that Kohut had to rework analytic theory until he could find a place for himself within it. The beauty of that statement, of course, is that it was true of Freud and applies to all other revolutionary theorists as well. David Terman is quoted in the book as saying that to know Heinz Kohut was to know self psychology. I think it is fair to say that to know Kohut was to struggle with the glaring contradictions in his personality—the phenomenal demonstrations of thoughtfulness on the one hand, and the casual disregard for the feelings of others on the other hand. I was never at the receiving end of his most painful dismissal of others, but I did witness it. He was unfailingly gracious to me, even when he firmly corrected me for holding my white wine glass by the bowl rather than by the stem; I was unwittingly heating up the wine! And it was Heinz who, after seeing our daughter Sarah while at a meeting at our house, later in the afternoon sent a beautiful bouquet of red roses celebrating her 6-month birthday!

Although Heinz experienced what seemed to be a very urgent need to have his theories accepted by the analytic world, there were exceptions that he seemed to make regarding the worthiness of the person making the attempt. It was toward some of his colleagues who actually had tried to understand his new ideas that he could be harshly dismissive if he did not feel that they somehow mattered; needless to say, this attitude cost him a great deal in terms of solidifying his own base in Chicago. He made enemies where he did not need to.

Then there was the fascinating issue of Kohut's relationship to the professions of social work and pastoral psychotherapy, both of which I have ties to—the former by training and daily work and the latter by my association with the Center for Religion and Psychotherapy as board member, teacher, and supervisor. Very early in the unfolding of Kohut's ideas about the centrality of the self, it became apparent to several professionals in both fields that self psychology fit nicely with the basic underlying values and ideals of both social work and pastoral psychotherapy. Kohut's emphasis on the importance of the selfobject surround of the developing child helped to bridge the internal and external realities of childhood in a way that felt highly compatible with the historic interest of social workers in the interpersonal and physical environment of their clients. Kohut presented an addendum to or expansion of psychoanalytic theory that seemed to place the person in a more inclusive field than had the more traditional analytic theories; no longer was the developing child just a bundle of drives seeking expression with others, but was generally independent of their influence. Via the concept of the selfobject and the introduction of the three major poles of development (idealization, mirroring, and twinship), the importance of the responsive milieu was stressed.

Within the field of pastoral psychotherapy, there was also a sense that this was an analytic theory within which concerns about the whole person could comfortably fit, and even more importantly, many pastoral psychotherapists sensed that the concepts of idealization, mirroring, and twinship could be very directly used as ways of understanding their patients' spiritual and religious experiences. Rector (2000) has written, for instance, on the twinship pole of development and its usefulness in conceptualizing religious and spiritual phenomena.

Accompanying Kohut's understanding of the sense of compatibility between self psychology and these two professions, there was, on his part, what I experienced as a very real ambivalence about this state of affairs. On the one hand, he worked tirelessly to have those analytic colleagues whom he valued achieve both an understanding and an acceptance of his ideas; nothing mattered to him more, and in a general sense, he was enthusiastic about the positive responses that his ideas evoked; however, I always sensed some hesitation within him about the enthusiasm that his ideas generated in nonanalytic circles. He seemed to fear that a ready acceptance in the nonanalytic world would mean some disparagement of self psychology within psychoanalysis itself. To some degree, I could understand that fear, knowing how concerned analysts were, particularly when Kohut was writing, about the essential uniqueness of analysis and its explanatory theories.

Underlying this concern was the issue of the unconscious and its role in theory and practice. Kohut felt that self psychology was truly an extension of analytic theory, and he worried that it would be diluted by other disciplines, many of which had more interpersonal leanings and were less concerned with the dynamic unconscious. To the extent that these were his concerns, he was probably correct; many contemporary writings in self psychology do reflect a drift away from this central focus on the unconscious, and it is probably fair to say that one of the contributors to this is the enthusiastic embracing of self psychology by professions for whom the concept of the dynamic unconscious seems to have less explanatory valence.

I had one direct experience with Heinz that involved my being a social worker. He called one evening, and he said he had received a letter from a social worker from a small Midwestern town. This social worker wanted to write a column on self psychology for the local newspaper, and he had included a list of questions that he wanted Heinz to answer. Heinz told me that he thought I would be just the person to respond to these questions and that, if I agreed, he would let the writer of the letter know that he was passing his inquiries on to a knowledgeable colleague—or some such phrase.

No amount of flattery at that point could conceal the central issue, namely, that Heinz was besieged by all manner of requests from all over the globe, and this one was not going to be attended to by him. I was amused, felt vaguely coerced, and agreed to do it. Heinz asked that I send him my responses just so he could look them over before I sent them out. As anxious as he was not to do this particular assignment, he also would never allow any thing with which he was associated to go out without his imprimatur, and so I sent it off to him, wondering what would be his response. He called immediately upon receiving it to say that I had done a fine job and that he had one or two suggestions. I no longer remember exactly what they were, except that they were not matters of substance, but rather of style, and I, of course, acquiesced.

Kohut was a person who had a very intense need for other people, and to be at the other end of this need was to experience firsthand some of what he meant by the concept "selfobject." Did one experience oneself when in relationship to Heinz as "an independent center of initiative," the way he described the other in the selfobject matrix? Often not. The sense that he had a pressing need for some experience while in connection with another person was often palpable, and the self of the other was at times barely allowed to register. This need, of course, does not separate Kohut from the rest of the human race; however, the frequency of the sense of being experienced as a selfobject when relating to Heinz was marked.

For many years, Kohut was an almost nightly caller to my husband, Arnold Goldberg, as well as to several others who were in the circle of colleagues with whom Kohut discussed all of his theoretical advances and whose support was so vital to him. The pleasantries of friendship were exchanged without fail and often with a good deal of mutual enthusiasm, but the conversation would quickly turn to the concern of the moment; these concerns varied widely. Could a letter be written to a particular journal further explicating the finer points of one of his ideas? It would not be appropriate for him to pursue the matter further himself.

Could an appearance be made at a conference, with the same goal? He had neither the time nor the fortitude to be present whenever he was asked. What about a particular choice of words for an article he was writing? The recipient of the call usually knew Kohut's preference and recognized that he was calling for reassurance and/or congratulations for having made such a felicitous choice. The calls were frequent but not of great length; there was something to be negotiated, and when the business was accomplished, the call was cordially concluded with warm best wishes for all family members currently in residence. These calls were very much a regular ritual in our household, as well as in several others, and of course, there were times when it was an intrusion. On the whole, however, the ritual was met on our part by varying degrees of humor and, more importantly, with the recognition that our lives were being enriched by a most fascinating and gifted man.

Let me say something about the importance of language for Kohut. Although the final texts of most of his writings still had an almost impenetrable Germanic essence, Kohut labored extensively to find the words that best gave expression to the new territory that he was exploring. The best example of this for me was his initial use of the word *self-object* and his eventual decision to remove the hyphen so that the word read *selfobject*. During a dinner party where his circle of close colleagues and spouses were gathered, Heinz rose from his chair with smiling determination and almost theatrical timing and said that he had an important announcement. We were all a bit surprised as he said with a flourish that he had made the decision that the hyphen in *self-object* needed to be removed and, from that point forward in his writing, the word would appear as *selfobject*. He gave a brief explanation, and we all understood that no matter how playfully he may have presented this change, it was of great moment to him; it was not his wont to take up theoretical matters at dinner parties.

I cannot write a reminiscence such as this without some mention of the issue of Kohut and Judaism—and right off the bat, even the phrasing of the topic is awkward. Is "Kohut and his Jewish identity" more to the point? Or "Kohut's lack of acknowledgment of being Jewish?" So, from the start it is difficult. Strozier (2001) has discussed this topic in great detail in his book and, I think, strikes all the right chords about it; what I have to say is on a personal level and comes from my experience with Heinz and my own resonance with the problem. I use the word *problem* advisedly and for a reason I will mention in a moment.

First of all, I cannot say that I was surprised to learn of Kohut's Jewish background, although the extent of it was more all-encompassing than I had thought. Growing up in Hyde Park in the midst of the University of Chicago, I had many close friends whose ancestry was, to a greater or lesser degree, Jewish. I vaguely remember hearing that one of Heinz's grandparents was Jewish, and although I knew that he was an enthusiastic participant in Christmas festivities, I always chalked that up to its being a part of his wife's tradition. This mixing of traditions was common among the families of many of my Jewish friends.

It is really only in retrospect that I understood a very definitive difference between the Kohut household and that of several childhood friends; in the Kohut household, not only was there no personal identification with Judaism, but there was also on Heinz's part an ostensible complete lack of *knowledge* of Judaism, its practices and customs. Again, in retrospect I can see how odd this was. Indeed, his seeming lack of familiarity with Jewish practices had an exaggerated quality to it. How could a sophisticated intellectual of his era be as in the dark as he was about Judaism? And then there is the Unitarian Church in Hyde Park which he attended with some degree of enthusiasm. My own experience of that church somewhat dulled my critical faculties in thinking about Heinz's Jewishness. I knew several members of that congregation whose heritage was Jewish; it seemed to be a place where such congregants felt reasonably comfortable, but again, and importantly, not a place where one shed completely one's sense of one's Jewish heritage. Therefore, when I heard that the Kohuts had attended services there, it made perfect sense to me that it would be a place where Heinz's heritage and Betty's could come together without denying either one. In the interest of full disclosure, I should add that my knowledge of this church came from my direct involvement; I grew up one block north of the church, and for a year or so, my parents, in an ongoing struggle to find a Sunday school that didn't drive either them or their three offspring berserk, sent us there. It proved to be benign (flower communion instead of the real thing), but its lack of theological rigor annoyed even the three of us teenagers, and at some point we left in yet another revolt. My parents could only agree.

Although, as I said before, I was not surprised by what I eventually heard about Heinz's Jewishness, I *was* surprised by the extent of it and therefore by the extraordinary degree of denial of it on his part. I was bewildered, and the central focus of my bewilderment had to do with the strong emphasis that Heinz placed on the crucial importance of continuity in one's life narrative (1971). He wrote and spoke often about the price that is paid when one is not in touch with all parts of one's experience, from the most painful to the most joyful. Over and over, he stressed that it is the sense of oneself in continuity over time that is vital to a cohesive sense of self. So, my first reaction was to think, "How could he have denied so completely that part of himself that was so crucial in his early years and, in fact, was the reason for his being forced to leave his beloved Vienna and eventually come to the United States?"

You probably have read or heard the multitude of explanations for his remarkable denial of his heritage, and those speculations really lie beyond the scope of these reminiscences. Let me just suggest one idea about why Heinz took the stand that he did about the importance of a sense of continuity in one's life. I believe that Heinz did not live out the continuity that he so ardently stressed to others because, for reasons best known only to him, he could not do so. To remain the Jew that he had been in childhood and young adulthood would have been too painful, and so he literally remade himself as a Gentile. However, and this is where his emphasis on continuity enters, I think that he understood at some level the price he had paid for his denial. I think he knew that this was not the way a full, cohesive life should be led. In other words, I think that, in this instance, as in many other aspects of his theories, he knew what constituted health, *not* by the way in which he had lived his life, but by what he had learned from making the choices he had made; the price that he paid was the recognition of the psychic cost of these discontinuities.

As I move toward concluding these remarks, I would like to mention Betty Kohut more explicitly. Betty was, for many years, a valued social worker on the staff of the Student Mental Health Service at the University of Chicago. Her quiet, thoughtful manner contributed to her effectiveness as a therapist and to her steady, devoted presence as a wife to Heinz and a mother to Tom. She was the embodiment of the supportive spouse, preparing lovely dinners for friends and always appearing at conferences and lectures when Heinz was presenting. She was very quiet around Heinz, which was true of many others as well; he needed to be at the center of the stage most of the time. I don't think Betty was always comfortable being so eclipsed, and there are indications in the Strozier book that she would take Heinz to task for the way in which he monopolized any gathering. I could sense that tension within her, but I never saw it openly displayed.

The warmest memory I have of her is of a visit that she made alone to me not long after our daughter was born. She was an accomplished knitter and she had made a beautiful sweater for Sarah. We sat and talked about babies, about our homes and families, and all the other things that women chat about, and I felt that we had had a more open, relaxed visit than ever before—or after.

One can gather from the range of my experiences with Kohut that he was a very complex man with whom to be in a relationship, but at any given point, it was the excitement engendered within me about his ideas that always served to center me. Yes, he was exasperating, self-centered, and more, but the contributions he made that had captured my attention in Miami Beach continue to do so to this day. Kohut was fascinated by narcissism and, equally important, by the transformations of narcissism, which, I believe, he understood so well because of the trajectory of his own life. He wrote about creativity, the capacity for empathy, the capacity to contemplate one's own impermanence, the capacity for humor and wisdom as being the major transformations of narcissism. It is a hopeful framing of human possibilities; attributes that once might have seemed unruly are transformed via the selfobject milieu in combination with basic endowment (1966). This list represents qualities that I believe Heinz saw as possibilities in himself, possibilities that were realized with varying degrees of success. His creativity was probably his crowning achievement, as was his capacity for empathy under many circumstances. Heinz thought he had a good sense of humor, but, interestingly, he rarely found anyone else to be funny. He had a certain wisdom that does come from experience in living, but probably the most striking transformation to me was his capacity to contemplate his own impermanence. Kohut's end-of-life struggle with his diminishing strength and his urgent desire to work productively to the very end—and then let go—was enormously moving to witness. After his last public appearance in Berkeley in the fall of 1981, just a few days before his death, he knew that he was dying, and he spoke to his family and close friends openly about it. He regretted that his life was coming to an end much earlier that he had expected, but he made his peace with this fact; he had completed the work he had set out to do, and the rest was up to others to carry on. While this resolution would not work for everyone, it did for Heinz, and this was part of his genius. He knew that there were many ways for a fulfilling life to be led, and it was his life's work to understand the origin and development of these multiple pathways. It was my privilege to know him during these exciting years.

REFERENCES

Hollis, F. (1972), *Casework: A Psychosocial Therapy.* New York: Random House.

Kohut, H. (1966), Forms and transformations of narcissism. *J. Amer. Psychoanal. Assn.,* 14:243–272.

——— (1971), *The Analysis of the Self.* New York: International Universities Press.

——— (1982), Introspection, empathy, and the semi-circle of menthal health. *Internat. J. Psychoanal.,* 63:395–407.

——— (1984), *How Does Analysis Cure?* ed. A. Goldberg & P. Stepansky. Chicago: University of Chicago Press.

Rector, L. (2000), Developmental aspects of the twinship selfobject need and religious experience. *How Responsive Should We Be? Progress in Self Psychology, Vol. 16,* ed. A. Goldberg. Hillsdale, NJ: The Analytic Press, pp. 257–275.

Strozier, C. (2001), *Heinz Kohut: The Making of a Psychoanalyst.* New York: Farrar, Straus & Giroux.

Author Index

Subject Index